THE

Vedas

FOR EVERYONE

NĀRADA KUSH

Published in India by:
Embassy Book Distributors
120, Great Western Building, Maharashtra Chamber of Commerce
Lane, Fort, Mumbai 400 023, India
Tel: (+9122) -30967415, 22819546
Email: info@embassybooks.in
www.embassybooks.in

First Dutch edition 2006
Second Dutch edition 2008
Third Dutch edition 2010
Fourth Dutch edition 2013
Fifth Dutch edition 2014
Sixth Dutch edition 2016

This book also has been published in the Hungarian and Russian languages.

ISBN: 978-93-89995-19-0

Cover Design by Sonal Churi

Layout and typesetting by Sonal Churi &
Gangaram Dhuri (Brand Soul Creations)

English Translation: Imola D. Hollo

Pictures: Rozalia Hummel, Wikipedia a.o.

Printed & Bound in India by Repro India Ltd., Navi Mumbai

*By meeting together, talking together and apprehending your minds
alike, in the same manner as the ancient gods accepted their portion of the
sacrifice, I will offer you a common oblation. By acquiring for a common
goal, a common purpose and by common wishes in your heart, there may be
thorough Union created among you all.*
– Rigveda, X.12.40

For all those who desire inner happiness
and peace in the world.

CONTENTS

HYMN TO SHRI GANESHA SON OF LORD SHIVA AND MOTHER PARVATI

Gajananam bhuta ganadi sevitam
Kapittha jambu phalasara bhakshitam
Umasutam shoka vinasha karanam
Namami vighneshvara pada pankajam

Oh Lord with the elephant head, Ganesha, Thou, who art waited upon by nature spirits; Thou art eating sweet apples and black berries from the forest; Thou art the son of Uma, I bow down to Thy Lotus-feet, Oh, Remover of all obstacles.

FOREWORD

We are delighted to see this Vedic publication from Shri Narada Kush and feel honoured to write a foreword. Our first meeting with Shri Narada Kush was many years ago when he came frequently to India for participating in the Ramayana conferences.

We noticed that he shared a deep love for the ancient Vedic wisdom, Ayurvedic healing arts, and spiritual practices of India. After meeting him, he expressed the desire to stay in our Ashram for some time and participate in its programs. This led to subsequent visits to our Ashram in Udaipur, to share his wisdom and to spend time in spiritual practice.

We have experienced that Shri Narada Kush has a deep, natural understanding of the Vedic teachings and practices of India. He has a passion for Vedic Astrology and Ayurveda and a deep love for the teachings of Ramayana and Bhagavad Gita. This is evident in the joy he expresses in his role as a teacher and the great respect and admiration of his students from around the world. His wisdom comes from the depth of his own spiritual practices, and his passion for learning has led to his great creativity in teaching. He makes concepts simple and motivates the reader to engage in the practices.

The subject of this book, "The Vedas for Everyone" is a very relevant one in today's world, including India. Nowadays, the human being is mainly considered as a physical being and the idea of holistic being is yet to become mainstream. This is why many of our systems are challenged. We need the ancient Vedic wisdom that has been with us for thousands of years, teaching us the holistic way of life. Therein lays the secret that can help us to deal effectively with the challenges of today.

Instead of focusing only on the cure of diseases, we should be giving more attention to its prevention. Our bodies have been designed with a powerful self-healing system. We need to tap into the wisdom and practices that are focused on this support system. In this book it is beautifully explained how we can benefit from the ancient Vedic wisdom of life in all its aspects.

This book goes into detail on the ideal Vedic lifestyle for wisdom, happiness and fulfilment. It explores the natural rhythms of life and how to live in harmony with them. It gives insights into every important area of human life and activity that will equip us for life's journey and challenges.

"We want to thank Shri Narada Kush for the efforts he put into making this book now available in English language to all seekers of true wisdom, health, and happiness. This book needs to be in the hands of every reader, seeking to know more than what we are traditionally taught today. We offer our best wishes for the publication and distribution of this book in India and elsewhere".

Dr. Dinesh Khatri **Dr. Saroj Sharma**

Founders and Directors of
Kala Ashram Foundation & Ayurveda Health Centre,
Udaipur (Rajasthan) INDIA, January 2021

THE VEDAS FOR EVERYONE

PART I

THE MEANING OF THE VEDA

CHAPTER I

INTRODUCTION

In the Beginning there was God, the source of light,
He was the Only Lord of all created beings.
He supports this earth and heavens,
it is to Him that we direct our prayers.

- Rigveda X.121

It seems an impossible task to write a commentary on something that is infinite and beyond human comprehension. The author of this book therefore asks in all humility the blessings of *Shri Ganesha*, the god of wisdom and remover of obstacles. He asks Shri Ganesha to support him and to accompany him in his quest to explain the meaning of the Vedas in a simple way to those who are still ignorant of them. He asks in all humility to make use of the wisdom of the enlightened souls on this planet who were or are able to fathom the deeper meanings of the Vedas. There are probably very few souls on earth who can claim this knowledge, but in the past there have been great seers who have cognized the Vedas in their universal consciousness and shed their light upon them. Among them were Vasishtha, Vyasadeva, Adi Shankara, who commented upon important parts of the Vedas and put them in the right perspective. And of course, the divine incarnations like Lord Krishna, Shri Rama and Buddha who lived in the different *yugas* and who practiced the wisdom of the Vedas, not only in their words but in their lives as well.

I.1. VEDA AS DIVINE REVELATION

In most of the modern comments, the Vedas are characterized as *hymns of praise to the gods*, in other words they are considered to be a kind of primitive, though holy scriptures, that once served (and maybe still serve) as books of prayer with no or very little connection to our present time. From these limited viewpoints they seem to be sacred monuments of an ancient and mystical past, comparable to the British Stonehenge or the pyramids of Egypt. Apparently, the rituals described in the Vedas do not fit any longer in our fast-modern lifestyle. Even in India, the birthplace of Vedic wisdom, people do not allow themselves to spend much time on it. This all has to do with the fact that the original divine meaning of the Vedas has been lost throughout the ages.

The Vedas are not just some ordinary holy scriptures, on the contrary, they contain all practical knowledge needed for mankind to lead him back to his divine origin. The word Veda comes from the root *vid* and simply means knowledge, to know. Words for instance in the English language like wisdom, vision, video, and in the German language *wissen* and *Weisheit* are derived from it. The Veda is the knowledge about life comprising everything and is expounded in perfect sequential steps. In the present work all care has been taken to maintain their original set-up, structure and divisions and it is very fortunate that we still have important parts of the original texts at our disposal.

We have to go far back in time when the immortal Vedic mantras were still actively enlivened by the people and were considered to be indispensable. This was in the time of the saints and sages, in the time of yore. Throughout the ages it has been the task of the Brahmin priests to preserve the texts of the Vedas. By reciting daily, the mantras or hymns were transmitted in their purest form to the next generation. After the Vedas have been entrusted to paper several thousand years ago, others could benefit as well from the knowledge and usually interpret them in an intellectual way. Apart from the Brahmins having been sometimes authoritative or displaying other type of undesired behaviour, this did not serve the purity of the interpretation of Vedic wisdom well. Since those times they faded away from human consciousness and the real deeper meaning sank completely to the background.

Although the Vedas contain more wisdom than all modern science taken together, it is very rare that a scientist takes interest in their real content. This is because the Veda does not fit easily into a modern scientist's frame of reference. Its language and word usage are inaccessible to outsiders and its way of investigation is holistic, meaning that it is complete in itself. Moreover, all its different parts are also complete in themselves. In this it distinguishes itself from modern research approaches. In modern science the intellect is supreme. It is called the objective approach of gaining knowledge, but how objective is our intellect? Modern science, furthermore, deals only with researching phenomena concerning the outside world and is therefore by definition fragmentary. Fragmentary means that they want to place in the front-light a small piece of a big puzzle without considering the whole puzzle. Nobody considers the meaning of the pieces in the context of the totality of knowledge. A student will hardly be satisfied by studying merely the infinite number of isolated branches of modern science. They do not offer him or her any insight into the totality of existence, its connection with the different disciplines, nor its connection with the researcher himself.

The Veda is not a part of any branch of the tree of sciences, it is the tree itself. It forms the source, course and fulfilment of all branches of knowledge. It is not even enough to describe the Veda as a tree. It is much more than a tree, it is the silence of the forest, the essence of the planet, the spirit of the universe, and the Word of God. It was Lord Krishna Himself who handed over the Veda to Brahma, the creator of the material world. That's why this wisdom includes the whole creation – creation, maintenance and dissolution – a process that repeats itself countless times. Rigveda, the oldest records of human life, says:

***

*'First there is Brahman, Lord of all, together with the Word,
and verily the word is Brahman.'*

***

The Word is Veda and Veda is the Word. The complete knowledge of existence is contained in the sounds, structure and sequence of the Vedic hymns. It becomes visible by the perfect sequence in which these sounds are arranged and in the way the Vedic hymns are placed in verses, paragraphs, and chapters. This structure of the Veda is indestructible and made it possible that its essence has been preserved throughout time, generation after generation.

The range of the Veda, as a divinely inspired revelation, is infinite, its lifespan is immortal, and its structure invincible. While the modern scientist preferably engages himself in the different areas of fragmented knowledge, the Veda oversees the whole and there is nothing that exists or can exist outside its range. Everything that places a scientist before unsolvable enigmas and anything that he might want to research more has already been explained in the Veda thousands of years before. But only for those who understand the language of the Veda, it will open up and deliver its uncountable secrets. In other words: the deeper meaning of the Veda will become alive only for those who are able to function on the consciousness level of the Veda.

There are many ways to scrutinize the Veda. We can view it as an old relic from an age where religion was characterized by polytheism. Or we can try to explain the meaning of the words, though these are only individual parts of a holistic approach. Most commentators have limited themselves to this approach, but the Vedas are much more than just the meaning of the words. They form the vision, the process, and the structure of all knowledge. They contain the hardware and software of life. They contain all possible knowledge a human soul can comprehend. They are the goal of all modern branches of science together. They explain existence from within the *source* of existence, the same source that is being sought by all modern physicists. That source lies within ourselves, but our modern scientists have not yet come to that discovery. The Vedas comprise the totality of knowledge: the knower, the process of knowing and the known. They provide a complete and holistic explanation of consciousness (the cognitive faculty), energy (transformation) and matter (the material world). They deliver all possible practical applications and the perfect wisdom to lead ourselves back again to God. They give all the knowledge of who we are, where we come from, and where we are going.

It has been the ancient seers or *Rishis*, who possessed the knowledge to directly cognize from within how creation works and how it is connected to their own lives. On a higher level of consciousness, they were connected to the divine spheres and could directly communicate with them. They used their wisdom to maintain and protect the eternal law of life without the slightest self-glorification. Together they are known as the ancient Vedic Tradition of Masters and their universal insights are systematically noted down in the Vedic scriptures.

I.2. HISTORICAL PERSPECTIVE

Indian wisdom of life does not assign great importance to the chronological sequence of historical events. For an elaborate description of the four great eras of mankind – called *yugas* - I am referring to my book 'Hinduism, back to the source' published earlier. More than 5000 years ago Lord Krishna announced the age of Kali-yuga, at the end of the great battle of Kurukshetra. In those days the wise people already foresaw that the wisdom of life was destined to gradually deteriorate with time, and they searched for solutions to preserve the Vedas in their original form. For this reason, the Vedas were put on paper and in due time *commentaries* were written on the Vedas, from which the Upanishads, Itihasa, Puranas and other parts of Vedic literature emerged. Right now, we are living in Kali-yuga, the iron age, the age of ignorance. When we look around in the world (and in ourselves) we can easily ascertain that degeneration has taken place in all fields of life. However, this period of ignorance is also the age that precedes Sat-yuga, the Golden Age. Within these long periods of human existence the waves of wisdom continuously emerge and submerge. As we can observe these days, the ups and downs of knowledge in human consciousness go together with corresponding climatological and planetary changes. In other words: it seems that human civilisation and Mother Earth are much more intimately connected than what we have ever been aware of before.

Scheme 1.1
Emergence and decline of wisdom

100% WISDOM	75-50% WISDOM	50-25% WISDOM	25-5% WISDOM
SAT YUGA	TRETA YUGA	DVAPARA YUGA	KALI YUGA

Scheme 1.1 There are four great ages of mankind – called yugas – i.e. Sat-yuga, Treta-yuga, Dvapara-yuga and Kali-yuga. These ages are also called subsequently the Golden, Silver, Copper and Iron Age. The whole cycle of these four eras is called Maha-yuga.

These yugas last for different periods in time. The period of Treta-yuga is equal to three quarters of Sat-yuga. The period of Dvapara-yuga is equal to two quarters of Sat-yuga and Kali-yuga equals one quarter of Sat-yuga. During Sat-yuga, the Golden Age, the Veda, or pure knowledge is fully lived in perfect health accompanied by ideal behaviour. But after Sat-yuga there inevitably comes a time in which the purity of knowledge starts to get lost and humanity falls more and more into decay. In the remaining three periods the quality of life deteriorates by one quarter. In Kali-yuga, the present time, this decline is visible in all areas of society: political, economic, religious, administrative, social, et cetera. In terms of wisdom, humanity has arrived at its lowest point. Yet it is inevitable that one day a period emerges in which its spiritual nature will fully blossom again.

The course of war on the battlefield of Kurukshetra, which introduced *Kali-yuga*, is elaborately discussed in the epic Mahabharata, of which Bhagavad Gita is a very important part. Bhagavad Gita is about the dialogue between Lord Krishna, representing the Divine, and his devoted disciple and friend Arjuna. Arjuna was known to be the best archer of his time. Long before the war of Kurukshetra broke out, the northern part of India had already formed the centre of a blooming culture possessing a high political, scientific, and social order. The land was fertile, rains came in time and harvests were abundant. The inhabitants of this area were endowed with wisdom that reached far beyond mere daily existence, and could somehow be comparable to the highlighted days of Mesopotamia and ancient Egypt. In the areas of astronomy & astrology, mathematics, urban architecture, music, art, administration and martial arts the society was far ahead of its time. Remarkably, this Vedic culture kept close relations with the higher intelligentsia of the universe. The Vedic priests invoked their powers and regarded them as the cosmic administrators of their existence.

The divine forces they worshipped were called demigods or *Devas*, impulses of universal intelligence, who remained in higher spheres. These demigods were communicating continuously with men and with each other as well. Kings were considered to be the representatives of the Supreme God and administered their kingdom in His Name. Many Devas were adored by means of invocations and sacrifices. Vedic Sanskrit, the original form of Sanskrit, was the language that was recited and chanted.

Throughout this period the Veda was highly esteemed. It was generally considered as the revelation of the Divine (shruti) and its sounds, melodies and rhythms constituted the cosmic instruments that were used to communicate with higher dimensions. From times immemorial Vedic hymns were transmitted orally from father to son in Brahmin families (Vedic priests). The Devas they worshipped were known under the names of Mitra, Varuna, Indra, Aryaman, Bhaga, Yama, Soma and others. After the invasion of the Aryan people in the north of India Indra, the god of thunder, became first among the demigods. Usually also Agni, the god of fire, took an important position in this pantheon of gods and demigods. Simultaneously, there was an ancestor worship, too, and the corresponding rituals formed a strong basis of the Vedic culture and of the close family ties that were a part of it.

Throughout ages the Vedic wisdom has been delivered from teacher to his students

Also, in this period an animal cult gained ground – in particular cows, bulls and snakes – but this had mainly a symbolic value. The concept that all existence was part of the cycle of creation, maintenance and destruction formed a key element in their philosophy. The Vedic priests, who guided the religious services, were considered to be the authorities who guard and perform the sacrifices. Because they kept the Vedic wisdom secret, preserving and transmitting it only within their own circle, they gained a special status within the Vedic community. Since times immemorial, the society was naturally divided into four social categories, the *Brahmins* (priests), the *Kshatriyas* (rulers and warriors), the *Vaishyas* (farmers and merchants) and the *Shudras* (servants).

Ancient cities like Harappa and Mohenjo-Daro, located at the river Indus, still remind us of the power and influence of a highly developed civilization. The building of these cities reveals a striking system and architecture of houses, water wells and pipes, based on the ancient science of Vastu Shastra or Vedic architecture. In later times, several objects were found all over India that have been associated with the ancient Vedic culture. Some of these objects appeared to be more than 40,000 years old. On one of these objects of a later date, a person is depicted in lotus position, with a snake standing on its tails on both sides. The object is estimated to originate from about 4,000 BC. The snakes possibly symbolize the awakening of *kundalini energy* in the yogi as a result of an ascetic way of life (see Chapter XVI). On other objects we find pictures of the god Rudra, who is an early representative of Lord Shiva. Lord Shiva is one of the mightiest gods in Indian culture, who is responsible for the dissolution of the universe. He, who also represents the Absolute, the unchanging and eternal aspect of existence, is worshipped in the form of the *lingam.* This worship is performed by pouring milk, honey or oil over the lingam and putting flowers on it. The worship of an erect pillar like the lingam we can observe in many cultures (see Chapter XII).

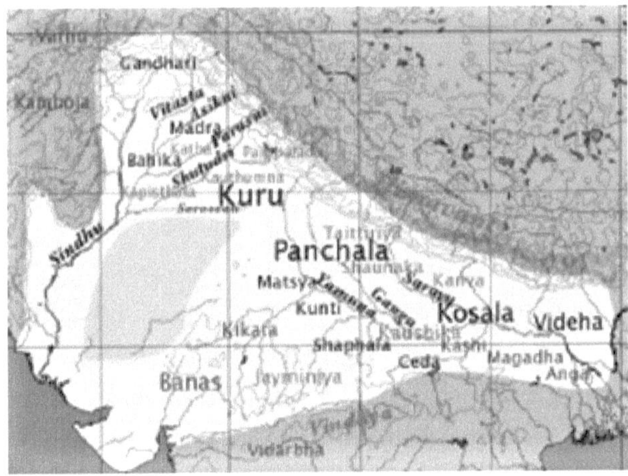

Map of Ancient India (source: Wikipedia)

There are also indications that in the pre-Aryan period commercial relationships were held with Mesopotamia, the present Iran. The remains of this advanced civilization were still present between 1000-800 BC, at the time when the Aryan people, originating from Central Asia, invaded the subcontinent and settled in the north of India. A theory exists that the Aryans had left India at an earlier point in time. In Iran they would have kept their ancient Vedic culture alive. Their most important scriptures were gathered in the *Avesta*, of which little is preserved, but which shows a striking resemblance to some Vedic scriptures. After different attacks and conquests of Persia, the Aryan people fled back to India for religious reasons. This would explain that both cultures, the Aryan and the original inhabitants of the Indus valley, had mixed with each other, though this would not have always occurred without any (religious) strife. After the invasion many original inhabitants of the Indus valley migrated to the south bringing their own cultural and religious heritage. The dominant Aryans had the tendency to put their own demigods, like the god Indra, in the limelight. After some time, balance gradually restored itself within the Indus culture or whatever was left of it. It is certain that very long ago, before the Aryan invasions, Vedic culture was abundantly blossoming. Furthermore, there is no doubt that both cultures worshipped gods and demigods by means of prayer, recitation and sacrifice. It was the great and divine soul *Shrila Vyasadeva* who recorded the Vedas and divided them into four parts in order to preserve them for later generations.

I.3 SCIENCE AND RELIGION

In Hinduism, generally considered as a religious application of the Vedas, Vedic features and ancient rituals are still in use among hundreds of millions of believers all over the world. In my book *Hinduism, back to the source* (see literature list in the back), I elaborately deal with the priceless value of Hinduism as a world religion and model for an ideal way of life. The unique feature of Hinduism is that it emerged directly from the Vedas, not based on the experience of one founder or a group of persons. It emerged from the timeless Veda itself, which has been revealed to humanity through the intuition and extraordinary abilities of the ancient seers. Because of its unifying power, its all-embracing nature and its universal approach towards violence (*ahimsa*), Hinduism is like a bright shining Sun in the family of world religions. In essence, it embraces all convictions and all forms of spiritual and religious experience.

Often, Western scholars and philosophers have recognized the greatness of Hinduism and described it in an inspiring way, emphasizing its complexity as well as its simplicity. Also, they found that the religious values blend into the life of every Hindu from the moment of conception until the last transition to another world. In this context it does not matter much whether we speak of a sincere believer, a scholar or an illiterate Hindu. In Hinduism belief or dogma is not a priority, the main object is true devotion to the Divine, correct behaviour and a way of life appropriate to one's destiny. True devotees of Hinduism think that all religions are just different approaches to worship the same Supreme

Being. There is no religion that can claim a monopoly on spiritual wisdom, but Hinduism, based on the Vedas as divine revelations, is the firstborn child among religions.

After all, there is an important difference between religion and science. In a religion one *believes* in supernormal things that cannot be comprehended by the mind alone. A science is characterized by *knowing* about what one has been investigating. The study of the Vedas is a science by which it is possible to become acquainted with every part of creation, including everything about ourselves. Vedic science is the science of the *totality of knowledge*. Some authorized scriptures are sufficient to display its essence and a few others to explain and preserve it for the next generations. We call this the Vedic literature which, next to the four main Vedas, consists of different commentaries or explanations. This relatively small number is only possible because every word in a Vedic hymn fulfils, from a scientific viewpoint, an extremely important function. Every word is essential in its own context, but also in the totality of the whole. Moreover, all facets of a word are very functional, for example the sound value, the meaning, the grammar, the subdivision in parts, the placement in the sentence, the time value, and the possible action it implies.

The scientific value of the Veda for the well-being of mankind can easily be tested. In the first place we possess a treasure of information from the ancient seers recorded in the Vedic scriptures. Secondly, every part of the Veda can be put to the test by the findings in modern sciences and, thirdly, it can be verified by *direct experience* on the level of human perception. The Veda is not limited, like modern science, to the research of the objective world, it extends into man himself (the subject of investigation) and to the relationship between subject and object. It is this all-encompassing range of Vedic approach that makes it so completely and absolutely unique.

I.4 TOWARDS A NEW AGE

Another important element is that the Veda does not lend itself to abuse or falsification, as has happened among others with the texts of the Bible. The reason for this lies in the fact that by virtue of its invincible sound structure Vedic Sanskrit cannot be tampered with. Sound and form of the Vedic recitations of many ages ago are in essence exactly the same as the ones that are being used at this very moment in the Brahmin families in India. Sanskrit is called the language of the gods, it is the language of the cosmic computer, which can withstand any human virus. It is therefore beyond the human power to change or annihilate it. Essentially all languages are directly or indirectly derived from Sanskrit. It is no coincidence that Sanskrit is the most suitable language in computer technology. As we will discuss later, Sanskrit is intimately connected to the sounds or vibrations from which the whole creation, including our own spirit and body, have been created.

Originally, the Veda is the embodiment of divine wisdom revealed by the Supreme God Himself to humanity. For a very long time, it made life on earth orderly and understandable. There is a strikingly great difference between the Vedic civilization and our time which seems to be overcome by complexity, chaos and administrative inability. Whatever area of life we look at – political, economic, social, educational or religious – it is likely that developments are going in a downward spiral. And though we get exhausted from everything that comes our way, we are apparently unable to give it up, even if our painful journey on this globe leads us only further away from Heaven on earth. In other words: by its own strength and efforts mankind cannot make a real turnaround in his spiritual evolution. This would imply that an intervention and support from other spheres is indispensable. And thus it has always been, since the first humans were cast out from Paradise.

On the other side it is satisfying to see that millions of people today are preparing for a New Age, in which the wisdom of life forms an integrated part of society and in which all applications of this wisdom can be practiced. Many belief systems in the world have discovered the *direct experience* of the unchanging energy field from which the whole creation emerges. Humanity is preparing itself for a time in which it will be supported and guided by a higher dimension of consciousness. This book has been written for anyone who cherishes life based on this vision and innate trust. In particular, it wants to offer a new perspective to the present-day youth, who yearn to live in a world that is not totally aimless, empty and seemingly lacking any higher goal. Especially the youth seems to be engulfed by emptiness and seeking their satisfaction in drugs and other distractions. It would be very sad if this tendency continued, especially because the essence of the Veda is unsurpassed in purity, scope and potentialities. It is able to lead us back to the source of our existence, by devoted souls, in a relatively short time.

Indian civilization could only survive through thousands of years of its existence because its tradition is firmly rooted in the indestructible wisdom of the Vedas. In order to gain a correct understanding and insight into Indian culture and its philosophical implications, knowledge of the Vedas is indispensable. All subsequent Vedic literature is based on their authority. Because they are an expression of the Life principle, the divine breath, they represent the highest authority in the area of religion, science, philosophy and morality. India is the holy land where the age-old traditions of *Yoga* and *Yajna* have developed. Yoga is the search for contact with the Supreme Divine by turning within, and this approach has not only influenced India but the whole world. *Yajnas* are procedures or rituals that have an evolutionary character and are performed by very experienced Brahmin priests. The Vedas lay great emphasis on the performance of yajnas in order to strengthen the harmony between man and his immediate environment. In the ancient hymns gods and demigods (Devatas) are invoked, who represent the impulses of creative intelligence of the universe. However, while studying the Vedas we should never forget that these qualities or forces can also be found *within ourselves*. The Vedas, therefore, describe in the first place the origin of our own selves, our consciousness, the effects of our actions and our personal growth, and the way we can bring all this into harmony with the divine world.

CHAPTER II

VEDIC COGNITION

The Vedas contain the knowledge of all areas of life.

- Manu Smriti II.7

Veda in the sense of divine revelation is called shruti. This literally means: that what is heard. The Vedic hymns have been cognized or *heard* by the ancient *Rishis* or seers in the fathomless depths of their mystical experiences. The mantras were performed in a certain rhythm (sound and form) and were then orally transmitted to later generations. This went in the following way. A teacher taught the mantras to his students. By daily repetition, they learned the texts by heart and transmitted these in their turn to their own students. By making use of the human memory, the Vedic wisdom of existence was transmitted age after age. In those days there was no need to put anything in writing. The systematizing and writing down of the Vedas happened only a few thousand years ago – a relatively short period. One feared that through a possible decline in the quality of human existence certain parts would be lost. Based on a few astronomical indications in the text some cognitions from Rigveda are at least 8000 years old. But the wisdom of the Veda, which has been developed from the beginning of time, can never really get lost, because it is forever stored in the container of human consciousness. One could compare it to the electron, which is as old as the material world, but the existence of it was only scientifically established at a certain moment in the evolution of man.

Shruti and Smriti

There are four Vedas: Rigveda, Samaveda, Yajurveda and Atharvaveda. They are accompanied by scriptures called Brahmanas, Aranyakas and Upanishads which usually are attributed to the *shruti*, the divine revelation. All other parts of Vedic literature are called *smriti*. *Smriti* means: that what is remembered. Just like our own consciousness, Vedic knowledge is not static and not connected to a certain place or person. The seer or yogi is a medium who allows the eternal wisdom of existence and consciousness to flow through him. This wisdom can, at any moment in time, undergo new impulses and be developed or extended further. The commentaries and practical applications of the Veda, the smriti, are not divine revelations in the literal sense of the word. The shruti is *nitya* (eternal) and *apaurusheya* (divine) while the smriti is of human origin. If these two are in conflict shruti prevails (Karma Mimamsa I.3.3). Nevertheless, very prominent scriptures belong to the smriti, like for instance the Vedanta, the Yoga-sutras and the Ayurveda; books that are famous all over the world for their illustrious content. Their role is to explain the elevated wisdom of the shruti, elaborate on it and illustrate it with the help of practical examples taken from daily life and countless metaphors.

II.1 PURUSHA AND PRAKRITI

In Rigveda *Purusha* (lit. Supersoul) is spoken of as the name for the Ultimate Reality, that contains everything in its own nature, but stands alone in itself. The nature of Purusha is *Prakriti* (lit. nature). We can consider Prakriti as the seeds that are stored in the infinite field of Purusha, ready to sprout. Purusha and Prakriti together form the male and female aspect of nature. In the doctrine of Kundalini Yoga it is known as *Shiva-Shakti*, and in the Chinese tradition of knowledge as *Yin-Yang*. Prakriti, the dynamic nature of Purusha, manifests herself in her totality as an infinite cosmic desire to complete fulfilment of life. On a human scale the same actually happens. As above so below.

Prakriti exists by virtue of the interplay of the three gunas – *sattva, rajas,* and *tamas* – which form her threefold nature. *Sattva* is the pure and orderly force in nature, *rajas* is the active force and *tamas* is the inert and decaying force. All three forces are necessary to keep the evolution going. They are always and simultaneously active in every stage of evolution, but in different proportions. It is quite easy to determine which guna is predominant in ourselves. When we are wise and loving and live a pure life, the element of sattva dominates. When we are mainly focussed on work and material gain, the rajasic quality dominates our mind. When we are lazy and bored and have difficulty in getting out of bed in the morning, tamas guna dominates.

At the basis of creation we locate Purusha, the one undivided principle of Universal Intelligence that knows no second: the Supreme Being. Within man the cosmic being manifests itself as the inner Self, *a field of experience* that lies beyond our thoughts. We call this the field of pure consciousness. The experience of pure consciousness occurs when our thoughts have settled down completely and our mind has transcended even the most refined thinking activity. In this state the limited mind dissolves into the unlimited state of Being: consciousness is not any more conscious *of something*, it is only *conscious-ness*. In other words: the subject and object of perception melt together in one state of consciousness, a state wherein consciousness only refers to itself and nothing else. Because this state rises beyond all mental activity, it is also called *transcendental consciousness.* This spiritual experience is not reserved for yogis only, but can be developed and experienced by ourselves through yoga, meditation or devotion. Moreover, by reciting Vedic mantras or even just listening to them, or to their explanations, we can develop and deepen our spiritual experience.

II.2 VEDA AND SCIENCE

The ancient seers were able to cognize the *ultimate reality of existence* at the most refined level of their consciousness and were also able to give expression to it. The worldview – the knowledge one has about life – for every human being depends in fact on the ability of its awareness to perceive. That is why everyone experiences a different reality. It is therefore no wonder that we often disagree and quarrel with each other and feel hurt. But then, what is true and what is not? According to the ancient seers, there is only one ultimate reality, namely the one where the human mind is established in the state where it is in complete harmony with the universal laws. In that state the laws of nature – the mechanics of creation – can express themselves for 100% in the Rishi, by virtue of the purity of his nervous system. In the time of the highly developed Vedic culture many people were able to live in a state of purity and wisdom. They were *living* the Veda. In later periods of human existence, the quality of human perception gradually declined. In our time we are mainly overshadowed by sensory perception. This is the age of *Kali-yuga*, the iron age, a time where mankind has almost arrived at point zero of inner wisdom.

The whole structure of creation is based on the functioning of the laws of nature. These laws are always the same, only the knowledge and experience of them in the human mind differs according to the cycle of inner development and decline. Whenever spiritual decline takes place, science, religion and philosophy emerge as separate aspects of life. They become methods dominated by intellectual knowledge, overshadowing the ocean of happiness and well-being that can be found within. However, the power of nature is invincible. Therefore, we may assume that there always comes a moment when the pendulum swings back to the other side. The Vedic scriptures confirm this, and give the precise duration of a single cycle of emergence and disappearance of knowledge, namely 4,320,000 human years. A full cycle of creation lasts 1000 times longer.

For many ages the real meaning of the Veda has been kept *secret* by the Brahmin priests and it has only happened a short time before that the Vedas have been written down and humanity can consult them. Even in our time, though, the Vedas are almost exclusively recited by Vedic priests, common people hardly read or understand them. This is because of their very abstract and often mystical character. Only the Upanishads and Bhagavad Gita may rejoice themselves in an enormous popularity. Next to those, an extensive range of Vedic literature has gradually developed which includes, among others, the Vedangas, the Upangas, the Upavedas, Itihasa (Ramayana and Mahabharata) and Puranas. They play an important role in explaining the Vedic codes and it is hard to deny that behind this elevated wisdom there must have been a highly developed civilization. Where in the world is so profoundly spoken about the relationship between macro- and microcosm than e.g. in the *Samkhya* and *Vaisheshika*? And is it not the sign of an unusual and superior class that Vedic scholars sought the origin of the universe mainly within themselves? Long before modern science emerged, they already spoke of consciousness, mind and nerve channels in the brain and their relation to the outer world. By making direct connections between earth and body, water and seed, sun and eye, moon and wind, wind and breath, fire and speech, they made clear that they were far ahead of their time. Vedic wisdom originates in the first place from the *container* of all knowledge, which is without any doubt human consciousness. It makes use of the age-old adage *Know Thyself.* By fully knowing ourselves, we can know anything.

Of course, no doubt, that modern science & technology have brought mankind innumerable achievements, practical tools and contributed immensely to the wellbeing of society and eventually led us to nowadays globalization. Nothing in the last few hundred years had more impact on human civilization than the progress in modern science. Nowadays hundreds of thousands of scientific experts all over the world are passionately continuing to develop their discoveries and practical applications and the results are amazing. But so far modern science has not been able to integrate its research with the field of consciousness. Actually, it is very afraid to do so, and does not want to see the relationship between science and the subjective field of existence. The result is that some of the applications of modern science & technology have been misused to unacceptable proportions and have almost ruined our civilization. This is where we can locate the missing link in the field of modern science; the integration of research done in the fields of matter and energy with our own consciousness. It is the ancient wisdom of the Veda which can fill in most wonderfully this missing link in the field of science.

So, we can say that modern science occupies itself mainly with the external world; *the known*. By investigating that which lies in the outer world, one tries to understand and penetrate into the origin of existence. However, someday we will accept that the essence and potency of all existence and evolution of humanity lies within the universal quality of the *wholeness of consciousness*. The Rishis fully understood that real knowledge of the universe is impossible until man gets the full knowledge of who he is himself. In order to enter this important and necessary development the Vedic scriptures offer myriad suggestions and applications to help us find ourselves back and put a halt to uncontrolled lust, anger, power and greed that are so prevalent in our world today. These are the destructive forces that ring the bell for the decay of human civilization and are ultimately leading it to its downfall. The whole science of yogis is nothing else but a positive, perfectly formulated and urgent call to return to harmony and tolerance in the community of nations. The principle is: by transforming ourselves we will be able to transform the world. And this can only happen when human consciousness gains the status of *the wholeness of knower, process of knowing and knowledge.* Herein lies the totality of knowledge contained, and that is Veda.

Scheme 2.1
Wholeness of Knower, Process of Knowing and the Known

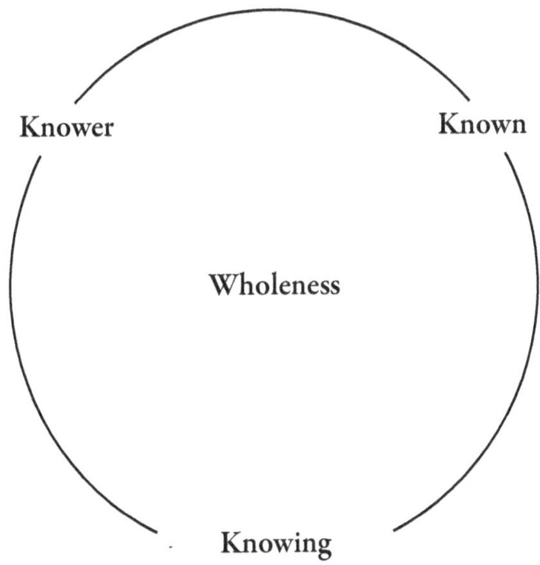

Scheme 2.1 In each process of creation and in every activity that we perform as human beings, we can distinguish 3 aspects:

- the knower   (the one who perceives)
- knowing   (the process of perception)
- the known   (that which is perceived)

In a higher state of consciousness, it is possible that one perceives the wholeness of these three components in one integrated state of consciousness. The goal of the Veda is to establish this state of wholeness in every human being and society.

Wholeness of consciousness in daily practical life refers back to the memory that we are spiritual beings, living in a physical environment. Our original nature is pure awareness, silent consciousness, that lies beyond the subtlest emotions and thoughts. We are connected with an infinite field of intelligence – the field of the silent witness within. At this level consciousness knows itself as conscious Being. When we have become established in this field of pure existence, we experience everything through cosmic lenses. Although we stand in the world with both our legs, there is something in us that *stands apart*, the independent, inner observer who has an enormous potency of peace, power and happiness. If we can just *observe* this way, witnessing ourselves innocently, our ego, intellect and feelings will operate in a totally different way. This is what we call *wholeness of awareness*. Later we will come back to this.

Lords Vishnu visits the Rishis (source: Wikipedia)

II.3 INTERPRETATION OF THE HYMNS

When we look at the literal meaning of the hymns, it strikes us that they mainly deal with cows, horses and other things, seemingly without any logical interconnection. How can these verses be considered as the eternal and true knowledge of existence? Did we overlook something? The only explanation is that these Vedic texts have a hidden meaning. Rigveda gives indications about this in several places of its text. We therefore may accept that what is written there has presumably another, deeper meaning. We know that by virtue of the unique system of oral transmission the mantras have not changed over time. Furthermore, we know that every word in Sanskrit can have different meanings and can be explained in different ways. Every translator or commentator was free to make his choice and that is exactly what happened. For instance, the word *go* that normally means cow has been interpreted in many different ways. The word *ahi*, meaning snake, has often been translated as cloud. Vedic gods like Mitra, Varuna, Savita, Aditya and Indra were all associated with the Sun god. That is why the hymns were overloaded with different meanings, resulting in interpretations that do not resemble each other at all.

If the Vedas really contain all knowledge of existence, we may assume that the ancient seers did not tamper with the original texts. To preserve the wisdom, it was not even allowed to change one word or even one letter of it. In fact, every word was carefully selected and very precisely placed at a certain position in the text. Why is it, that the apparent meanings of the words are not the correct ones? The reason why the commentators started doubting, springs from the fact that they did not understand the original meaning of the hymns and presumably had a hard time making sense of them. This resulted in a vast number of interpretations, of which probably not a single one is correct, or fully correct. In his remarkable book, *Vedic Physics, scientific origin of Hinduism,* the author *Raja Ram Mohan Roy, Ph.D.* simply decides to return (1) completely to the original meaning of the words and from there (2) to start an investigation into the possible scientific meaning of those words. This leads him to very surprising results, of which we will talk more about this in Chapter IX.

From an objective viewpoint, the Veda explains how the universe was born, expands and finally contracts. And this process repeats itself eternally in small as well as big cycles. Seen from a subjective viewpoint, a similar process takes place which we can describe as human evolution. The unique feature of human consciousness is that– in its pure form – it is able to register the complete range of its own evolution and translate it into sequential sounds. The Veda is a living example of this. It is set up in a way to fully comment on itself in its search for existence, creation and evolution. In reality the Vedic hymns have a profound, though for the outsider hidden, meaning. Every mandala (lit. circle) or chapter is the description of a certain cycle of evolution and all mandalas together are, in the form of a spiral, intimately connected to each other. Every sentence, every word, every letter fulfils an essential role in the hymn as well as in its relationship to the paragraphs (suktas) and chapters (mandalas). Moreover, the gaps between the words play an essential role, too. For example, the tenth mandala of Rigveda contains - according to the scientist and spiritual master Maharishi Mahesh Yogi - the commentary on the gaps between the words of the first mandala.

Furthermore, in his Vedic Science Maharishi explains that every *sukta* (paragraph) consists of a number of hymns or *richas*. A hymn is the result of the refined perception or cognition of a *Rishi* (lit: he who sees). Human consciousness in its pure form has an infinite scope. In this state of *unlimited awareness*, the Rishi is able to cognize the mechanisms of the processes of creation and can express them in sequential sounds on the manifested level of existence. The sequential sounds of the Vedic hymns represent the creative process perfectly *in the field of consciousness*. Three elements are essential in the process of cognition, namely the seer, the deity who is invoked, and the metre used. In Sanskrit we express this respectively as *Rishi, Devata* and *Chhandas.* Together they form the wholeness of knower, process of knowing and the known, in which the whole is more than just the sum of the parts. Every Vedic hymn, without exception, is accompanied by these three components. Let us take the first hymn of the ninth mandala as an example:

***

Rishi is Madhucchandas, son of Vishvamitra;
Devata is Pavamana Soma;
Chhandas is Gayatri.

Purify thyself with the most exhilarating stream,
Oh Soma, pressed for Indra to drink.
– Rigveda, Mandala IX, Anuvāka 1, Sukta 1.

***

Madhucchandas is the seer of this hymn. The deity (law of nature) he enlivens in his awareness is Pavamana Soma, who is the devata of the whole ninth mandala of Rigveda. The deity, or law of nature is the impulse of creative intelligence responsible for a specific part of the process of creation. In this first sukta of the ninth mandala the metre is *Gayatri,* the metre that occurs most frequently in the Veda. The metre indicates the structure of the investigation of the seer and is related to the specific quality of his nervous system. In the following chapters we will explore all the above-mentioned concepts further, including the deeper meaning of the hymn itself.

Again, according to Maharishi, the mantras of Rigveda, Samaveda, Yajurveda and Atharvaveda are *apaurusheya,* which means that they are not composed by the seers, not even by the most enlightened yogis;

they are divine revelations of the process of creation. The Vedic hymns therefore, are not bound to time, place, people or cultures. However, just as there have been many revelations in the past, present and future, other revelations can still take place. We should not envision the Vedas as a fixed structure that will be the same for every generation to come, but as something that is continuously on the move, growing and evolving, but still keeps the same core. In addition, new cognitions therefore are always possible. If they are true revelations, they will always stand the test of time easily. Moreover, in other ancient cultures similar processes have taken place. The performance of initiation rites, the age-old oral transmission of the wisdom of life and the very detailed descriptions of the land we can also find with the Australian Aboriginals. Their transmission of he knowledge of life and their finely detailed descriptions of their land still takes place today together with the so-called song-lines; the transmission of their traditional and cultural achievements through songs. Like in Vedic civilization, this kind of knowledge transmission of the Aboriginals has always been the responsibility of men. The Vedic seer therefore is not the inventor of the eternal laws and cycles of existence, just as Newton is not the inventor of gravity. He only is a medium who experiences in himself the impulses of existence, creation and evolution from the level of wholeness. This is what the seer means by *Vedoham* – I am the Veda. It seems that he, in his unbelievable purity, stands far above us, and to a certain extent this may indeed be the case. But ultimately every human being has the ability to experience the subtle waves that vibrate within the field of pure consciousness. This is the ultimate experience of wholeness of consciousness, the very basis of our existence and of all existence. And the Vedas give the direction and the practical applications of how to reach that goal.

The relationship between the field of pure consciousness (wholeness) and our mind as its instrument is one of the main themes of the Vedas, and it is from here that existence and creation, intelligence and evolution are being investigated. In modern quantum physics one has discovered that the researcher influences the result of the research. Some physicists therefore came to the assumption that the prime mover of the creative process must be creative intelligence or consciousness. This is in full contrast with classical science, which has always presumed that consciousness arises from the complex functioning of the brain. However, this has never been proven and, by the way, it is impossible to prove. In the Vedic hymns the cognition of the process of creation is administered by the specific consciousness of the Rishi or seer. In the field of pure consciousness, he cognizes the seeds of the laws of nature (the deities) who are responsible for the process of creation. The seer translates these dynamics (the seeds in the field) into sounds and brings them to the surface of existence. The hymns consist of the perpetually ongoing, dynamic activities within the unified field of consciousness, independent from any human contribution whatsoever. How this process emerges, takes place and where it leads, *that* constitutes the theme of the Vedas.

II.4 THE BRAHMIN FAMILIES

During the times of the far advanced Vedic civilization the Rishis were highly esteemed. They often were married and led a detached, withdrawn and strictly vegetarian life. They possessed enormous spiritual abilities for which they were surrounded with great respect. Maitreya, Bharadvaja, Atri, Markandeya, Gritsamada, Vishvamitra and Vasishtha were such great seers.

Throughout time, many myths and legends gathered around these seers. Their spiritual centre (ashram), located deep within the forest, often grew into a famous place of knowledge and education. The seers recited the Vedic hymns, performed their daily rituals or *yajnas*, and guided the cultivation of the soil and the tending of the cattle. Being members of the Brahmin caste, they were seen as the protectors and guards of the holy tradition of wisdom. They were asked to give (astrological) counsel, played a role in the institution and maintenance of law, and were specialists in natural health care. Their whole life was based on discovering the reason for existence and relationship with the Divine. Their names have always been connected to the Brahmin families who for ages passed on the Vedic hymns to later generations through an oral tradition of recitation.

The great saint Vāsishtha, one of the seven rishis, with his wife Arundhati and Kamadhenu, the wish fulfilling cow (picture: Wikipedia)

The transfer and maintenance of the Vedic tradition of knowledge has always been reserved to male Brahmins. By birth they belong to a certain branch (*Shakha*) that takes care of a certain part of the recitations. The Brahmin boys already went at an early age to the *gurukula*, the school of the spiritual teacher, where they underwent an initiation ritual. This ceremony is a so-called second birth that transforms the young Brahmin into a *dvija*, or twice-born. Next to the recitation of Vedic hymns, the students had to abide by certain rules of behaviour, with respect to celibacy, clothing and the use of food. A twice-born student wears a chord around his shoulders as a token of his special status. This Upanaya ritual was also accessible to boys from the *Kshatriya* (warriors, administrators) caste and the *Vaishya* (farmers and merchants) caste. The latter were expected to learn the hymns and recite them but were never entrusted with the teaching and transmission of the Veda. For them the learning and reciting was important in order to secure their position in worldly life. It is by the way not only the memory that plays a role in recitation, but also other parts of the physiology. For instance, certain recitations are accompanied by particular hand and/or head gestures, depending on the melody and rhythm of the given Vedic text and the tradition of teaching.

The question may arise now why the recitation and transfer of the hymns is not also done by women. This is related to the structure of the chromosomes that are different in men and women. The presence of the Y-chromosome in the male cells seems to be most fit for long and unchanging transfer. Nevertheless, there names of female Rishis are also known, like Lopamudra, Apala, Surya, Juhu, Yami and Ghosha, but they form an exception.

The recitations of Vedic hymns were used of yore in the performance of holy sacrifices or *yajnas*, that were executed with extremely precise procedures and performances which created certain effects. The Brahmin priests knew various kinds of recitations that differ per ritual and these rituals were sometimes very extended, costly and complex. Some yajnas could last a year or longer, but in our time these are rarely performed. Nowadays in India the main emphasis lies on domestic rituals like those performed for conception, birth and death, which are much simpler to set up and less costly. The Yajurveda and in its track the Brahmanas (see Chapter IV) are par excellence the scriptures in which the rituals and their correct ways of performing are described. Some sound combinations or *mantras* supporting a yajna are so strong that they can move mountains. However, it requires a high quality of awareness to achieve the desired effect and unfortunately the real deeper meaning of the Veda got lost through the long lapse of time. Atharvaveda is the only one of the four Vedas that is not concerned with the ritual aspect, but contains numerous directions about daily affairs related to well-being of persons, families and society.

CHAPTER III

CONSCIOUSNESS, ENERGY AND MATTER

Veda is the source of all Dharma.

- Manu Smriti II.6

The word Dharma is one of the core principles of Vedic wisdom and implies the totality of existence and men's destiny. Dharma is that which supports life in all areas – on both cosmic and individual level. Sanatana Dharma means: the eternal law of existence, the eternal religion. After Satyuga, the golden age, Dharma degenerates more and more, and the human faculty of thinking gradually becomes weaker. Time after time great world teachers came to rescue and remind mankind of the purity of knowledge, as expressed in the Veda. Their whole life was dedicated to the revelation of Truth. Among them we find Shri Aurobindo, Ramakrishna, Paramahamsa Yogananda, Ramana Maharshi, Baba Nityananda, Maharishi Mahesh Yogi, and others. They still have followers all over the world.

It has been in particular Swami Dayananda Saraswati (1824-1883), the founder of the Arya Samaj, who desired to revive the deeper core of the Veda in Indian society. He stated that the Vedas constituted the only revelation of Truth, wherewith he took a stance against the strongly exaggerated devotion to statues and emphasis on the performance of rituals. Swami Dayananda's aim was to return to the pure origin of the Sanatana Dharma, to the One Absolute Truth. The Arya Samaj society founded many schools and gurukulas that are, to this day still actively carrying out the Vedic knowledge, as taught by Swami Dayananda.

But even now, amongst us, there are enlightened teachers who want to shed light on the Vedas and make their practical applications fit for sadhana or spiritual discipline. Maharishi Mahesh Yogi, who passed away in 2006, was a teacher of our time who interpreted the Vedic scriptures in a very special way. Maharishi's teacher was Swami Brahmananda Saraswati (1868-1953), Shankaracharya of Jyotirmath, Himalayas, who was a direct representative of the holy Adi Shankara (5th age BC). Maharishi made the universal knowledge of the integration of life accessible in a new way.

Also, the great saint Shri Sathya Sai Baba contributed in a unique way to the promotion of Vedic knowledge. He emphasized that in the first place it is all a matter of applying the wisdom, that he expressed in words, into daily life. And more teachers all over the world add their part to it and play an essential role in explaining the Vedas in terms of consciousness, energy and matter (See scheme 3.1). We presumably live in a time of great spiritual transformation. When we take an overall look at everything, it seems to be only a matter of time before the world opens up to a much greater extent to Vedic wisdom and accepts Vedic scriptures as the practical manuals of life.

Each Veda is subdivided into different branches, called *shakhas*. And each shakha consists of three parts that are connected to the triple division of consciousness, energy and matter.

Scheme 3.1
Consciousness, Energy and Matter

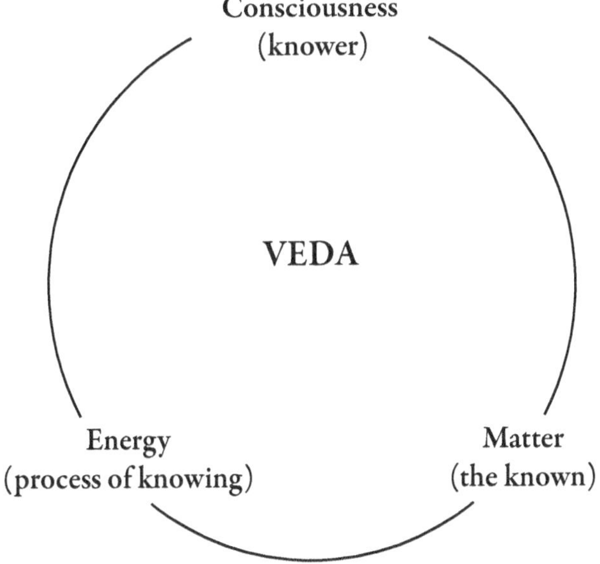

Scheme 3.1 As soon as we start realising that the Vedas contain all knowledge about consciousness, energy and matter, it becomes clear that this ancient science got lost through the long lapse of time. From this the conclusion also follows, that modern science is not the only way of bringing to light the ultimate reality of existence.

In this regard we speak of body, mind and soul, where by soul we mean our common source, the Self. In Chapter VII we will unfold the concept of shakhas and the threefold division. In this chapter we focus on the concepts of consciousness, energy and matter, and on how these concepts are interpreted and explained by our contemporary teachers.

III.1. CONSCIOUSNESS

Veda is the wholeness of knower, process of knowing, and the known.

It is the structure of pure knowledge which reflects very systematically the course of the process of creation. This course leads from the eternal, non-manifest Being throughout all possible relative manifestations, to its ultimate fulfilment in Being again. We can compare this to a thought. A thought arises out of nothingness, develops into something concrete, and disappears after a short moment back into nothingness. A thought is therefore an impulse of energy and intelligence that manifests itself for a split second only to disappear again into nothingness, as if it had never existed. Thoughts are like waves arising from the ocean and submerging again into it. What is and remains is the ocean. This phenomenon is an expression of the cosmic law of creation, maintenance and destruction, to which the whole universe is subject. A body cell, a human life, a universe, a galaxy, in short, any kind of creative manifestation, follows the same universal course (see scheme 3.2).

Scheme 3.2

Birth, Maintenance and Dissolution

UNIFIED FIELD OF ALL THE LAWS OF NATURE

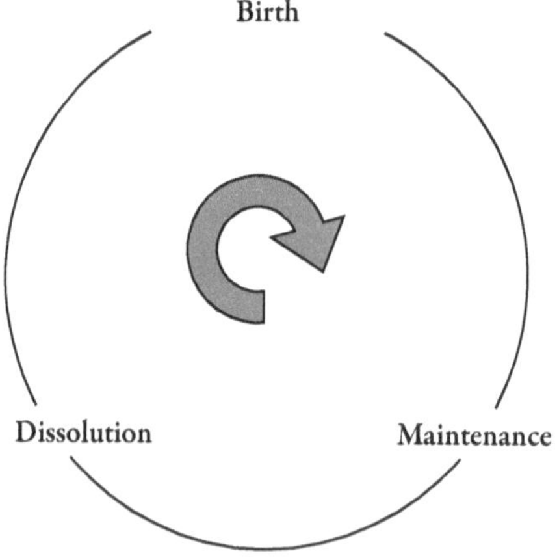

Scheme 3.2 Everything in the universe is subject to the cycle of creation,

maintenance and dissolution. Everything emerges from the unified field of all possibilities, where all laws of nature are gathered in wholeness, and everything again returns there after a certain period of relative existence. Not only men but even the demigods are submitted to this principle.

The only thing we can describe as being really existent is the non-manifest field from which everything emerges, the field of Pure Being. All creative impulses that emerge from there and also submerge into it are extremely ephemeral and are often described in Vedic literature as an illusion (*maya*). They both are real and unreal. Seen from the material world they are real, but from the viewpoint of Being they are not more than virtual vibrations within the field of Being. The manifested expressions of Being – the impulses of creative intelligence in the universe –throughout all consequent manifestations adhere to their quality of Being. This is the perfect vision and reality behind the universe. Our own vision on reality is limited by the material veil that obscures our sensory organs. Our intellect, which we usually are so proud of, gives a distorted image of reality. Our mind lives in a dream world, which is hardly different from the dream state we experience during the night. Our consciousness is only developed to a limited extent. Although we are spiritual beings, we identify ourselves with the physical world. We think that we mainly consist of a mind, intellect and a body, and that forms our insight into who and what we are, therefore we limit our real status and possibilities. The reality is that we are at all levels (physical, mental, causal) based on the quality of Being, our real essence. We are spiritual beings in a material world. We are the wholeness of knower, process of knowing, and the known, of which Being is the perpetual, silent witness. The knowledge of the Veda is the knowledge of how the whole universe unfolds systematically; from a seed growing into a tree and then again creating new seeds. Relative life progresses from seed to seed, from ocean to ocean, from birth to birth. As soon as we realize this, we are able to understand the phenomenon of death and we can put it into perspective.

The notion of our immortality is an observation or experience of consciousness. Only in the laboratory of our own consciousness we can experience life as it appears to us. *Knowledge is structured in consciousness*, Maharishi used to say. Our knowledge of the world depends on the quality of our consciousness and not so much on our mental abilities. Professors can be very ignorant and there are very wise gardeners. Shortly after birth our consciousness may still be open and receptive, but very soon it closes up and we can only use it to a certain extent. The whole reservoir stays always at our command, but it gets overshadowed by conditioning, stress, and intellectual distortion of reality. The quality and experiences of past lives plays an important role herein. Also, the intrauteral experiences, when we are in the mother's womb, and those of early childhood have an immense impact on our later life and behaviour. In general, we are the result of what we have ever built up of (excessive) experiences and growth of consciousness. Every human being is submitted to the law of *karma*, the law of action and reaction. But there is little or no use in looking back. Our present perspective is to grow in awareness, in fact this is our only earthly aim; to feel completely at peace with who we really are. The next step is to surrender to the Divine in a humble way. The knowledge gained by developing our awareness is no book knowledge, it is a process of remembering our spiritual origin and essence. The experiences we gain and the insights that emerge in us, can be verified in the Vedic scriptures, the ancient records of that process.

III.2 THE ENERGY FIELD

Modern quantum physics has been searching for some time for the ultimate basis of existence. One of the most recent conclusions it had come to is that the basis of creation is not simply a vacuum state, as was held for a long time, but a *zero-point field*, a field that is fully packed with energy and connects everything with everything else. An infinite silent field that is at the same time very dynamic and strikingly similar to the ancient Vedic principles of Shiva-Shakti! Shiva and his consort Parvati, the absolute and relative aspect of existence, are inseparable. In physics one has determined that when an atom goes back into the field it came from, it is charged again. We also get new energy when we connect during meditation to our silent field of consciousness within. Another remarkable conclusion is that we are able to connect at any time to everybody else at this level of existence. Therefore, it will definitely have effect if we send feelings of love to a sick friend or to poor third world children. And if we do this with a number of people it has an even greater effect.

Well known is the story of the hundred monkeys. In the Great Ocean there was an island with a huge monkey colony. Several thousands of monkeys ate the whole day countless ripe fruits hanging in the trees. But because the fruits were often dusty and dirty, one of the monkeys got the idea to wash it first in the water of the ocean before eating it. In the beginning only a few monkeys followed his example, but after some time about hundred monkeys did the same, then suddenly all monkeys of the island started to wash their fruits. It got even more interesting when, after a short time, the monkeys on an island 200 miles further away also 'decided' to eat their fruits after washing them nicely.

Similarly, during recent years experiments with groups of meditation practitioners have been done. One of the discoveries was that if more than 1% of the population of a city meditated regularly, the rest of the population also experienced and radiated more harmony. The scientists involved measured this effect with the help of crime rate numbers, traffic accidents and hospital admissions. The behaviour of the monkey colony and the 1%-effect are very natural phenomena. In physics we call this a *phase transition*. An example that we all know is the sudden change of water at zero degrees Celsius into ice, a substance with a much more orderly structure. In the ancient tradition of the Vedas it was already known that matter, life and existence are extensions of each other. There always exists an infinite energy field around us of which we still know insufficiently little on how to use and apply it in our daily life. One day everyone in the world can have free access to it. It is like a fish who is extremely surprised when one day discovers that it is surrounded by water, without which it couldn't even live for one minute. Applied to ourselves, consciousness appears to be a field in which we live and move, and it also seems to be a field of all possibilities. Some will describe it as an infinite field of creative intelligence, others just call it the Kingdom of God. The reality is that we all feel something within or without us that we cannot describe, and which transcends our everyday intellect. Only the enlightened Soul, the spiritual preceptor, the saint, the yogi knows what he or she is saying, and wants to point us the way and lead us to the final destination. Those who have realised the Self, feel nourished always and everywhere by that one source, but also some top athletes, yoga practitioners, scholars, spiritual counsellors, and charismatic persons are tapping consciously from it. A top athlete experiences the source energy as *being in the zone*, the spiritual seeker as an inner Light shining on the path of his or her life. The enlightened soul always walks in the Light, his body works as a receiver, actually he *is* the Light. The subtle energy centres in his body are always connecting to the cosmic energy field and reflect its qualities. The bhakti-yogi, the true devotee is detached from the material world and surrenders completely to the Divine. Also, a spiritual master, who is in permanent connection with the *zero-point field* has the ability to scan the level of Being of his students. He or she guides them professionally and transforms them to higher energy levels. However, the number of this kind of spiritual teachers or *sadgurus* in the world is very limited.

The qualities of the field

The universal energy field has three basic qualities which in Vedic literature are called: *sat-chit-ananda*.

Sat   = truth, pure eternal existence

Chit   = intelligence, consciousness
Ananda   = bliss

The sat-quality indicates that the cosmic field exists always and everywhere, it is indestructible and goes beyond the relative concepts of life and death, good and bad, dark and light. It is indicated in the Vedas by the famous aphorism: *Tat tvam asi – Thou Art That.* It is intelligent and aware of itself (chit) and abides in a state of bliss (ananda). It is always there, it is our true essence, but we ourselves have to open the door in order to become acquainted with it. Within ourselves we can experience it as the silent loving witness. This observing quality does not participate actively in relative existence, nevertheless it forms the basis of it, and remains present throughout all its layers from subtlest to gross. In other words, it is *transcendent* (beyond relative existence) as well as *immanent* (present in everything). In meditation, when knower, process of knowing, and the known merge completely together we experience it as bliss.

How can we recognize this inner experience of the source?

Here follow a few keywords:

***

Clarity
Quiet breathing
Streams of love – being in love
Feeling connected to everything and everyone
Coming home to ourselves
Peace, joy, silence
Being in the moment
Wholeness

***

One can undergo such an experience of Being at any moment, on the beach, during a forest walk, while sporting, while making music or listening to it, in the church or temple, during fishing, on an ocean steamer, or wherever and whenever. But most of the time we experience it unexpectedly or in an innocent moment. Boundaries shift into the direction of the boundless – the experience of a different reality. Once experienced, we would always like to be in that state. We wish to have that wonderful outburst again as soon as possible; we try very hard, but this is not exactly how it works. Nature cannot be forced.

The field of consciousness does not need anything else than itself; it is complete in itself, and the experience of itself makes us a fully satisfied and happy person. On the level of pure consciousness awareness only knows itself. To experience that is the most elevated form of *inner knowing* (= Veda). Consciousness that knows itself within itself and that can only be known through itself. The wholeness of knower, known and process of knowing which is more than the sum of the parts: the experience of *awakening*. And it is this experience of the silent field of existence which makes a human being very humble and devoted.

III.3 THE BRIDGE BETWEEN TWO WORLDS

In life we have to deal with two worlds, the inner and the external world. Or: the spiritual and the material world. The quality of the external world depends on our inner state. Nevertheless, we have to survive on this earth, in the external world. Be in the world, not of the world, will be a good guideline. Someone who wants to be successful in life and has a higher goal than mere suburban bliss, starts with seeking God within. This is the essential starting point according to all holy scriptures, including the Bible.

***

'But seek ye first the kingdom of God, that is within you,
and all else will be given unto you....'
- Jesus in the New Testament

***

By spiritual discipline we can systematically foster and stabilize the experience of the source. Once we have got a taste of it, we can have a continuous longing after that one moment of submergence into bliss. It is the quest for the Holy Grail; we move on the road without rest, working on ourselves, longing for further development of our inner growth. Or we search for a spiritual teacher, a *Sadguru*, who is permanently immersed in Pure Being and can lead us on the journey. In the higher spheres the demigods and even the demons have a Guru. The wise kings of the highly civilized Vedic culture did not wage wars nor settled for peace without the counsel of their spiritual teacher, which advice was never neglected. In the West we often make use of the services of physicians, priests, psychiatrists, psychologists, and all kind of therapists, but then we preferably follow on our own course. Besides satisfying results it can sometimes also bring much frustration, doubt and suffering.

In the spiritual relationship between teacher and disciple it is all about the experience of the source, about our *inner* development. The Master himself is an instrument, an important guide, who comes to help discover and experience the qualities of our own, *inner guru*. It is important to understand what happens if we are in his physical presence or attune ourselves to him (or her). It is a process of inner transformation, where he knows who you are and what you need. We often try to do it ourselves, but we cannot do it alone. The higher intelligences are there to guide and support us, the Guru is a messenger of the Divine. Through Him the Divine Grace flows. He is the bridge between the internal and external world, between the spiritual and the material world. Whoever discards or neglects him loses a lot. Only the enlightened one can perceive the perfection in every human being and approach them with unconditional love. A true realised soul is by nature deeply engaged with the good and bad of humanity. The spiritual teacher is full of compassion for his fellow men, and though always remaining in the bliss of the Self, he plays his earthly role with enthusiasm.

Narada Muni with his disciples (picture: Wikipedia)

Because the Guru phenomenon plays such a crucial role in the understanding and experiencing the Veda, we will come back to it extensively in Part II of this book.

III.4 THE MATERIAL WORLD

The material world consists of the elements of ether, fire, air, water and earth. When we consider the physical world as a tree, then the five elements are the subtle elements making up the tree. However, a tree is a living organism, an expression of cosmic intelligence. The cosmic intelligence is the seed from which the elements, one after the other, have developed. That is why the material world is nothing else, but the expression of the universal source of intelligence, which is indivisible, unchanging and eternal. The five elements, from which the material world is built, move continuously together with that field of universal intelligence. They derive their reality from the substratum that is cosmic intelligence, the only area that is *real*. The five elements therefore do not create themselves, but are a manifestation of an intelligent power/energy that underlies them. You could compare it with thoughts we have in our dream state. In the state of the consciousness of the dreamer they are very real, but in reality they are not more than fluctuations of an underlying field of consciousness. Energy and power fields in the universe derive their fluctuations ultimately from the cosmic Spirit, the Supreme Being or Divine, who is the cause of all causes.

Scheme 3.3
The Five Elements

ELEMENT	SANSKRIT	MEANING	SENSE
Ether	Akasha	Space	Hearing
Air	Vayu	Movement	Touch
Fire	Agni	Energy	Sight
Water	Jala	Humidity	Taste
Earth	Prithivi	Solidity	Smell

Scheme 3.3 All levels of the material world, from subtlest to gross, spring forth from ether or akasha. From ether comes air, from ether and air comes fire, from ether, air and fire comes water and from ether, air, fire and water originates earth. Research has for instance shown that we first perceive movement (air) and only then colour (fire). This scheme shows how the senses are connected to the elements.

What exactly is ether? According to modern science, ether is the most refined matter that fills up all space in the universe. The space between the stars and solar systems, but also between the worlds of atoms, molecules, electrons and even smaller particles. Ether is subtler than gas or air and cannot be touched, seen or smelled. Modern science accepts its existence, because otherwise the transmission, for instance, of light and heat could not be explained. In the Veda ether is called *akasha*, which is the Sanskrit term for the first manifestation of intelligence developing into matter. According to the Vedas it permeates everything in the world, it is everywhere, that is, omnipresent.

This would mean that we might even be able to *hear* the ether and that indeed is the case. Ether generates a cosmic *hum* that vibrates throughout the universe and that can be perceived at a very subtle level. This vibration, again, consists of seven subsequent shades, from which the ether is built up. At a gross physical level, they are the musical scale in music, the sevenfold cosmic colour palette, and the seven energy centres (*chakras*) in our body. Our hearing, therefore, is the subtlest sense we have and is intimately connected to the cosmic intelligence. This is the reason why the ancient seers did *hear* the Vedic mantras in the silence of their consciousness and thereafter expressed them in sequential sounds. It is for this reason that speech (*vach*) plays such a fundamental and central role in the Vedas. It is important to know that there are many levels of spirit and matter in the universe which cannot be perceived on a sensory level. For instance, angels are spiritual entities whose forms consist of pure ether. Only the highest forms of intelligence, that use the very refined essence of akasha as their vehicle, can move on this subtle level. They are intimately connected to the cosmic spirit and can hardly be distinguished from it. At the beginning of every cycle of creation only akashic beings exist at the most refined level of matter. Propelled by the life breath of *Prana* of the cosmic spirit they develop themselves into the lower levels of air (movement) and fire (energy). Prana, the cosmic principle of life, permeates the whole universe, and through our own breath we can refine it so that we can feed and enrich our subtle bodies with it. This is the purpose of *pranayama*, the science of regulating the breathing process, making it ready for the admission of Prana (see Chapter XVI).

III.5 DETACHMENT

The unbelievable reality is that the Divine, the Supreme Being, is always around and *within* us, as Paramatma. We, as human beings, are little particles of Him. In the Vedic Scriptures he is called Lord Krishna, who lives in the heart of every being. He is always in a transcendental form, even when he descends to the material world. He is closer to us than a mother to her child, than our own heart, our own blood. The Divine is always here and there. As little particles, we are all connected to the Divine. Although we come into this world alone, we are never alone. Feelings of loneliness mean that we are separated from the higher Self, from our Divine. But as soon as we search for It or Him, and re-establish the connection, loneliness disappears like a snowflake in the sun. And this is the universal reality for every human being, high or low, old or young, poor or rich. The only difference among us is in the level of *recognition* of the higher Self, or in the surrender to the Divine that reveals to us that the world of the non-Self is extremely relative.

Herein lies the secret of creation. Our attachment to the world – and the forced holding on to all kinds of material objects – has to do with our presumption that the material world is the *only reality*. We are looking in a mirror and assume that what the mirror reflects is reality and act upon it. The Vedas call this limited way of perception *maya*, or the world of illusion. We people are bound to matter, like mystics always have said. And throughout the ages it has become apparent that it is quite difficult to really become detached from the material world. One person might be a little step further than the other, which may depend on how far we have advanced on the spiritual path. Although, this is a concept we have to use with care, after all it is not that easy to estimate someone's *level of evolution.* On the day of judgement many last ones will be the firsts. As long as we still make a difference between 'me' and 'you', like TV news shows us every day, we may assume that spiritual liberation is still far away.

Life on earth is meant for discovering that we are as important to God as He is for us, and that we are a part of His cosmic plan. It is important to open ourselves up to divine love and wisdom and be ready to grow and become detached. Vedic hymns apply to the smaller than the minutest and to the greater than the greatest. The same laws of nature that administer the whole universe, regulate the smallest atom, too. The more research we do on the Veda and the more we open up to its field of Being, the more we will experience the Ultimate Truth. And this Truth is nothing else than pure, infinite Love and the capacity to devote all our thinking and actions to the service of the Divine.

CHAPTER IV

THE VEDIC SCRIPTURES

Mantra brahmanayor-veda nama dheyam
Mantra and Brahmana together form the Veda

- Apastamba Shrautasutram, XXIV.1.31

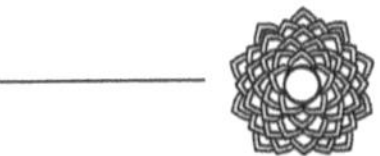

The four Vedas express the *Samhita* value, or the *integrated wholeness* of life. Integrated wholeness means: the wholeness of *Rishi, Devata* and *Chhandas* or, in other words: knower, process of knowing and known. The knower has the ability to perceive an object of knowledge (the known). The ability to perceive through the cognitive senses forms the process that connects knower and known. Vedic knowledge therefore comprises the totality of all knowledge and is therefore a complete science of life and of all aspects of existence (see scheme 4.1).

In the context of this book it is not necessary to go into all kinds of historical details of the Vedas, enumerate how they have developed in time, or how exactly they were composed. In this book we are primarily focussed on the hidden meaning of the Vedic hymns, and how to apply this wisdom in our daily lives.

Scheme 4.1
Veda declares Totality of Existence

VEDA	SAMHITA	WHOLENESS	INDIVIDUAL	UNIVERSAL
RIK	Rishi, Devata and Chanddas	Knower, Process of Knowing and Known	Self, Mind and Body	Consciousness, Energy and Matter
SAMA	Rishi	Knower	Self	Consciousness
YAJUR	Devata	Process of Knowing	Mind	Energy
ATHARVA	Chanddas	Known	Body	Matter

Scheme 4.1 The Vedas are, all four, complete in themselves. The only difference is that they each have their own, special viewpoint from where they function in the domain of consciousness. (Source: Maharishi Vedic Science)

Originally, though, there were three Vedas – Rik, Sama and Yajur – called the threefold wisdom (Trayi Vidya) dealing with knowledge, devotion and activity. Rigveda declares the integrated knowledge of life, Samaveda expresses devotion in poetic terms and melodious sound structures and in Yajurveda activity is the theme. They are also known as the 'eternal three Vedas' (*trayam brahma sanatana*). They are composed of mantras, that are called respectively *rik, yajus* and *saman*. It was the great saint Vedavyasa, also known as Krishna Dvaipayana, who gathered the pieces of wisdom and put them in a system. The fourth Veda, the Atharvaveda, seems to be of a younger date, and is even now usually not mentioned in this line. Because the three Vedas express principally the same knowledge, but from a different point of view, many verses are similar to each other, if not the same. These similarities are less present in Atharvaveda, although in this Veda a number of verses occur that are also found in Rigveda. We will come back to this in chapter VIII.

IV.1 MANTRAS AND BRAHMANAS

Each of the four Vedas consists of two values: *Mantras* and *Brahmanas*. Mantras express the eternal, unchanging knowledge of life (Purusha) in sequential sounds, verses, paragraphs and chapters. The Brahmanas explain the eternal, dynamic activity (*Prakriti*) that lies locked up within the immutable nature of Purusha. Moreover, they explain the infinite organizing power that can be located, remarkably enough, in the *gaps* between the words. In their turn, the Brahmanas consist of three parts, namely the *Brahmanas*, the *Aranyakas* and the *Upanishads*. Maharishi Mahesh Yogi distinguishes them according to their function as follows:

(1) The *Brahmanas* comment on the Samhita in terms of the relative. They indicate that certain rituals, called *yajnas*, if performed in the correct way and under the proper conditions, can generate any possible, imaginable effect on the material plane (!). This is based on the principle that in the yajna procedure, there is complete identity between sound and form. Veda is sound and sound transforms itself into form. The sequential structures of the sounds used during the yajna are so natural that they automatically produce the corresponding forms or phenomena (situations, circumstances). Here we hit upon a strong feat that man can accomplish in his most developed, divine form.

***

'Verily I say to you,
if you have faith like the size of a mustard seed,
you will be able to move mountains.
– Jesus in the New Testament

***

(2) Aranyaka means: scripture of the forest, so called because they were developed in the early days by ascetics dwelling deep within the forest.

The Aranyakas explain the organizing power of the *gaps* between the Vedic hymns. The gap represents non-manifest silence between two Vedic sounds. These gaps are important as a transcendent porch from which every following word is pre-programmed in the wholeness of consciousness. There is really something going on in these spaces in between! Every space has a different content and a specific organizing power that is enlivening the sounds in the most perfect way. This aspect shows a great similarity with the statement that Wolfgang Amadeus Mozart once made when he said that the essence of his music was mainly hidden in the pauses between the notes.

(3) *Upanishad* means: sitting near. Probably this has to do with the devotional sitting posture of the disciple at the feet of the Master. The Upanishads are a commentary on the Samhita of the Veda seen from the perspective of the Absolute. Among the Brahmanas, the Upanishads have been without doubt the most frequently studied and commented upon throughout the ages and can easily compete in popularity and authority with the four Vedas, even with Bhagavad Gita. As is true for all Vedic study, for the deeper meaning and scope of the Upanishads, an explanation of a spiritual teacher is needed. The teacher needs to have the status of Self-realisation and should be familiar with the other *shastras* (holy scriptures), too.

IV.2 THE UPANISHADS

The Upanishads deal with the deepest vital questions of humanity, and are in turn closely connected to *Vedanta*, which forms the crown of Vedic wisdom. They also have a close relationship with the Vedas and throw an indestructible bridge between the Vedas and the Bhagavad Gita. Just as in the case of the Brahmanas and Aranyakas, each of the four Vedas is connected to their own Upanishads. Not only in India, but all over the world, the universal philosophy of existence, as expressed in the Upanishads, has been recognised and highly praised. Unparalleled in their depth and overflowing with spiritual wisdom, they touch the heart and mind of everyone who recalls longingly their primordial state.

The immortal dialogues between the enlightened seers and the devoted seekers of truth contain all the great questions of existence. What is the source of the universe; what is the sense and goal of human existence; what is the essence of the immortal flame in each of us; what lies behind the cycle of life and death; what is our relationship like with the Divine and how can we gain unity – *Yoga* – with it during this life? These are some vital questions wherewith the Upanishads are dealing, and this is done with so much modest love and compassion, that nobody can slip aside from their considerations and observations, without forcing oneself to do so.

Although 108 Upanishads have been developed throughout the ages, only ten (some say eleven, others eighteen) belong to the real core. These ten Upanishads have been selected and provided with an authoritative commentary by the wise *Adi Shankara* himself. They are known as the classical or most important Upanishads. We can see how they are related to the Vedas in scheme 4.2.

Scheme 4.2
The Ten Classical Upanishads

No.	UPANISHAD	CORRESPONDING VEDA	PERIOD OF ORIGININ
1.	Aitareya	Rigveda	800 BC
2.	Brihadaranyaka	Yajurveda	800 BC
3.	Chhandogya	Samaveda	800 BC
4.	Isha	Yajurveda	Unknown
5.	Katha	Yajurveda	Unknown
6.	Kena	Samaveda	Unknown
7.	Mandukya	Atharvaveda	200 BC

8.	Mundaka	Atharvaveda	600 BC
9.	Prashna	Atharvaveda	200 BC
10.	Taittiriya	Yajurveda	800 BC

Scheme 4.2 Of the ten main Upanishads belongs to Rigveda, four to Yajurveda, two to Samaveda, and three to Atharvaveda. These Upanishads are not only commented upon by great Indian scholars, like Shri Aurobindo, but also by many outstanding Western scholars, like Schopenhauer and Max Müller.
(Source: Ten Upanishads of Four Vedas)

Other than the Vedas, which can only be known and entered on the level of pure consciousness, the Upanishads appeal to the human mind and intelligence. They excel in making precise observations, investigations and findings. They make use of observations of the external world, but also of the internal world, which is the source of all perception. The three relative states of consciousness (sleeping, dreaming and waking) are used to unravel the mysteries of existence and creation. What is their basis? What is their common source? In the Mandukya Upanishad, which consists of only 12 verses, an explanation is given to the phenomenon of the fourth state of consciousness, called *Turiya*.

***

'This indeed is the Atman, the Self, peaceful, silent, the One without a second, that can be established, known and realised.'
- **Mandukya Upanishad, verse 7**

***

The Upanishads make it clear that this fourth state of consciousness is the basis of all we can perceive and experience. Within us this is the observer, the independent perceiver, the silent witness of all activity. In one of the Upanishads, a story is told of two birds sitting on a tree. One bird is busy all the time (our mind, the ego), the other one is undisturbed and keeps looking around quietly (the Self). In the same way, the primordial sound OM or AUM, the universal symbol of the Absolute, is the immutable Self, as well as all its relative expressions. In the String-Theory of modern physics, extremely small vibrating strings, that have both a wave and particle aspect, are considered to be the ultimate building blocks of the physical world. Are not the Vedic mantras vibrating strings in an ocean of Wholeness? Modern science has approached the solution of the riddle of the universe very closely. But to completely solve it, it needs the wisdom of the Upanishads, which continuously indicates that everything – matter, life and spirit – finds its origin in the underlying field of pure consciousness.

In the next chapters, the above mentioned most important Upanishads will be discussed separately in the context of their corresponding Veda.

IV.3 DISCUSSION ON SHRUTI

Throughout the ages there has been a difference of opinion among scholars, whether the Brahmanas, Aranyakas and Upanishads may be counted to the *shruti* (divine revelation) or if they should be more considered as (human) commentaries on the Veda. Some scholars think that this part, like all the Samhita, has sprouted spontaneously from Brahman, without the intervention of the human intellect. Others are of the opinion that only the Veda Samhita belongs to the shruti and are convinced that the rest is not divine revelation but mere commentary or interpretation thereof. Their argument is that the Brahmanas are usually named after their composers and therefore are person-bound and cannot be attributed in a strict sense to the Veda. *Swami Dayananda Saraswati*, founder of the Arya Samaj, was strongly supporting this last theory. He thought it unacceptable that a great number of Hindus have been regarding the adoration of the many (demi)gods more valuable, than the reflection on the ancient Vedic texts themselves. /Or: ...have been attaching more value to the adoration of the many (demi)gods, than to the reflection on the ancient Vedic text themselves. Undeniably, this development had sometimes led to great misunderstandings. Swami Dayananda wanted to lead the Hindus back to the core of their belief, which was, according to his opinion, solely anchored in the four Vedas. He designed a declaration of faith: *'I believe in one God and the Vedas are the books of true knowledge.'* Ever since, the Arya Samaj has grown into a large international organisation, that is not limited to the devotion of statues and the performance of rituals only, but lays great emphasis on the advancement of the general well-being of the world.

The Brahmanas and Upanishads are of a more recent date than the Veda Samhita. There are even Upanishads that are only a few hundred years old. On the other hand, the Vedic hymns – the Mantras – and their dynamic aspect, as expounded in the Brahmanas, form without doubt a unity and can hardly be seen as separate from each other. Both parts are homogeneous and form a harmonious relationship. The intimate bond between the Vedas and Brahmanas is mentioned explicitly in the Apastamba Shrautasutram, which forms a part of *Kalpa*.

From all commentaries on the Vedas it can be said that they have developed at a certain moment in time, some earlier and some later. But the historical sequence of composition and development is in fact less important and was never regarded specifically valuable in the context of the Vedic wisdom. Without the presence of the Brahmanas it would be much more difficult to unravel the secrets of the Vedic hymns. Their sublime added value lies in the fact that the Brahmanas and Aranyakas interpret and provide commentaries on the holy texts of the Vedas, while the Upanishads (and also the Vedangas) expound their hidden philosophy. In that sense they have a divine status. One can remember in this context that the seers have perceived the Vedas in their own silent awareness. This implies that God should not be found so much outside ourself, but that He is seated in the deepest level of our settled awareness. In that common source of all the laws of nature, we cannot only locate the all-encompassing knowledge of existence, but we can also find all the seeds that form the basis of God's creation. We all take part in that. God is within us, and we are and move within God! *Aham Brahmasmi.*

The knowledge of the shruti is beyond any discussion, its authority is untouchable. It represents the divine wisdom that is of all times, all places and all cultures. The rest of the Vedic literature, the smriti (that which is remembered), derives its authority from the Vedas. Its task is to explain the Vedas and especially, to make it practical for daily life. Yet its authority is essentially not less than that of the main scriptures. The different parts have been developed and systematized by prominent enlightened sages who harboured a profound insight into the real hidden meaning of the Vedas. Just as the Vedas are divided into Mantras and Brahmanas, a number of parts of the smriti are built up of *sutras* (aphorisms). These sutras are very concise principles – summarised in a short statement – with a profound meaning. This method was especially practical for Vedic students, who had to learn all this knowledge by heart and recite it. Traditionally it was the Guru, the spiritual teacher, who taught his disciples the deeper meaning of the sutras.

IV.4 VEDIC LITERATURE

Vedic literature consists of a collection of scriptures that can be subdivided into different disciplines. Every part deals with a specific aspect of the universal knowledge. If we talk about *Veda* in this book, we mean the totality of all knowledge, of which Rigveda is the most important exponent. When we speak of the Vedas, we usually mean Rig-, Sama- Yajur- and Atharvaveda including the Brahmanas (Brahmanas, Aranyakas and Upanishads). When we talk about all scriptures together, we speak of the Vedic literature.

The four Vedas together form the central heart of Vedic literature. The other parts of Vedic literature – the Vedangas, Upangas, Itihasas, Puranas, Smritis and Upavedas – give commentary on the Vedas or make them applicable for daily life.

We can make a distinction between the path of the Veda and the study of the Veda. The path of the discovery of the Veda entails that we first gain insight into what the Vedas really have to offer to human life. Furthermore, the path offers a carefully selected package of practices and guidelines of living, in order to enliven Veda in the awareness. The target is not: 'I know everything about the Veda' but 'I am the Veda' – *Vedoham*. Simultaneously, or thereafter, there are many possibilities of profound studies that the Veda yields.

The Veda gives the structure of all knowledge. Throughout the whole Vedic literature, the concept of knower, process of knowing and known is clearly visible. Moreover, all the parts are logically interconnected with each other and form one wholeness. Furthermore, the scriptures are arranged in such a sequence that every part joins in smoothly to the next level of knowledge. In a similar way, all the chapters and paragraphs within a certain part, systematically join each other. Within a certain subdivision, all chapters and paragraphs systematically merge with each other in a similar way. Finally, every aspect of Vedic literature represents, in a certain context, one of the values of Rishi, Devata and Chhandas. This is what Maharishi Mahesh Yogi has brought to light in his *Apaurusheya Bhasya*. The Apaurusheya Bhasya is a cognition received by Maharishi in the eighties of the previous century about the logical, sequential structure of the Vedas and their parts. It is this cognition that can, once penetrated enough into the collective human consciousness, form the basis of a new Vedic civilization in the world!

As it has been shown in the previous chapter, Maharishi, together with his team of scientists, made the unique discovery that there is a very intimate connection between the worlds of consciousness and of matter. For instance, there seems to be a perfect correspondence of the number of parts of Vedic literature and their division into chapters and paragraphs with the formation and structure of the human body! Our body, including the layout and composition of the brain, seems to be the physical reflection and exact copy of the Veda.

IV.5 RELATION WITH OUR BODY

The human body is a product or expression of nature. It is composed of the enormous diversity of the laws of nature, which we can find in the universe. Our body is subject to the universal laws of gravity, electromagnetism, strong and weak interaction and so forth. The whole universe is based on the process of creation, maintenance and destruction, and the human body undergoes exactly the same destiny. It is in fact, therefore, nothing else than a *replica* of the universe. Everything we come across in our body and that expresses itself in it, including its structure and function, speech and action, is a display and expression of the universal laws of nature. When we claim that the Veda reflects the structure and dynamics of the universal laws of nature, there must necessarily be a very close connection between the Veda and the human body. The same laws of nature, that are responsible for the dynamic order in the universe, are active on all levels of existence. The whole animate and inanimate creation is based upon these laws and the way they arise sequentially from the field of Purusha. This is exactly what the Vedic hymns reflect in their sequential sound values and expressions. The hymns are the laws of nature that let themselves be known to themselves, through the mediation of the seer. They are universal in character and infinite in their diversity. In the same way, our physiology consists of millions of tasks and functions to maintain order and balance, in order to evolve and experience higher levels of success and fulfilment. Maharishi's research has shown that the human DNA has the same holistic structure and function as the hymns of the Rigveda. All components, organs and functions of our nervous system correspond to the different disciplines of Vedic literature, with respect to their tasks as well as functions. Furthermore, it appears that the body cells correspond to the Mantra-aspect of the Veda while the gaps between the cells correspond to the Brahmanas. Maharishi's discovery, which supersedes in its implications Einstein's theory of relativity, leads to the conclusion that man himself is the expression of the Veda, therefore possesses the potency to manifest in himself that same universal level of pure wisdom and bliss.

The well-known adage from the ancient mystery schools of '*As above, so below*' that has been given scientific proof by Maharishi and his scientists in an unparalleled way, is infinite in its practical applications. Vedic science is rightly called the wisdom of nature itself, which explains all about the source, course and goal of life. It is the wisdom that, through a sequential structure of sounds, directs the course of the laws of nature and therewith the whole process of creation.

The laws of nature emerge from the non-manifest field of cosmic intelligence and are responsible for the creation of the whole material world – from the more subtle to the grosser levels. Now that the meaning and basis of the Veda is known, the practical application of it at every scale of existence seems to be only a matter of time.

IV.6 SPECIFIC PARTS

Here follows a short overview of the different parts of the Vedic literature, that will be dealt with more elaborately further on in this book. In sequence of manifestation, after the Vedas and Brahmanas, Aranyakas and Upanishads, the Vedangas emerge first from the non-manifest field. Then the Upangas, Itihasas, Puranas, Smritis and Upavedas follow.

Vedangas

The Vedangas are the six organs or limbs (angas) of the Vedas. From different angles, they give a clarification on the mechanics and structure of the Vedic hymns. Out of which parts do the hymns consist, how are they built up, and how can we understand them in the light of their total value? Only very enlightened spirits were able to bring this knowledge to light, which enabled later generations to unravel the hidden secrets of the Veda and apply it in every area of their life. One can compare the knowledge of the Vedangas with the indication and explanation of the first ripples on the ocean of wholeness, on that level where the untouched surface of the non-manifest creation becomes aware of itself. According to Maharishi, they express the sequential transformations of the Rishi, Devata and Chhandas values, at the moment when they emerge from the Samhita -field. The Vedangas are, like the Upangas, composed of sutras.

Upangas

The Upangas are the six systems meant to investigate and explain the wisdom of the wholeness of life through an intellectual approach. Together they give a complete picture of the meaning of the Vedas and of the principles underlying them. You could call them the limbs of the Vedangas. In their relation to the Vedangas they explain the mechanics of transformation of the wholeness of existence. They contain the totality of all knowledge about the objective and subjective world and about what connects these worlds with each another. This makes the Upangas a very complete science of existence. They are also known as the six Darshanas – *that what has been seen.* The six Upangas are: Nyaya, Vaisheshika, Samkhya, Yoga, Karma Mimamsa and Vedanta and are composed by six different sages (see scheme 4.3)

The Upangas mainly deal with the path and goal of the Veda. In chapter X we will further pursue the profound and practical knowledge that is brought forth by the Upangas.

The Itihasas, Puranas and Smritis are further elaborations of the Vedas, Vedangas and Upangas. The common recurring theme in the Itihasas, Puranas and Smritis is the nature of correct and incorrect action, including the consequences springing therefrom.

Scheme 4.3

The Upangas

UPANGAS	AUTHOR	INSIGHT
NYAYA	Gautama	Gaining complete knowledge
VAISHESHIKA	Kanada	Properties of objective world
SAMKHYA	Kapila	The knower / the subject
YOGA	Patanjali	Experience of the Self
KARMA-MIMAMSA	Jaimini	Field of action
VEDANTA	Vyasadeva	Unity of all existence

Scheme 4.3 The Upangas sprang forth from the human intellect, but through their direct relation with the Vedas and Vedangas, they are also universal in their scope and approach. They are a philosophy as well as a religion and a science, based on the totality of knowledge already structured deep within the awareness of every human being.

Itihasa

The epics Mahabharata and Ramayana, that together make up the Itihasa, are mighty metaphors depicting the complete Vedic knowledge in the form of stories. The practical thought behind this was to acquaint the unlettered part of the population with the ancient wisdom. It creates a similar effect as when you read an exciting story from a book to a child. In all parts of India and abroad, dramas, puppetry, dances and musical shows are performed on holy celebrations, in which Shri Rama, Shri Krishna, or Vedic heroes like the Pandava's or Hanuman play the principal roles. From the highest value of wisdom, Itihasa expresses the holistic aspect of the Veda through living examples familiar for everyone. Next to the highest moral virtues and integrity many pitfalls in the area of human behaviour are dealt with in greater depth.

Impression of the epic Ramayana (Painting: Rozalia Hummel)

In Ramayana, the principal character is Shri Rama, the expression of the full value of the Veda, the Self. His behaviour is without blemish and fully in accord with *dharma*, his allotted duty in this life. Even today, he stands as a divine example for millions of devotees. His great opponent is the demon king Ravana, expressing the ego.

Mahabharata, in contrast with Ramayana, has many heroes who, taken together, represent the total value of the Veda. An important role in this great and very elaborate epic is reserved for the *blind* king Dhritarastra, in whom attachment, pride and lack of surrender initiate his downfall.

Bhagavad Gita

Bhagavad Gita, the most famous part of Mahabharata, can be considered to be the pocket edition of the Veda and a holy textbook of divine wisdom. Its practical goal is to restore the fundamental principles of life in order to be applied anew to everyone's life. It occupies a very special place in the totality of Vedic literature. In fact, it is a summary of all Vedic knowledge in the form of a metaphor. The whole treatise consists only of 700 verses that have been extensively commented upon by countless scholars and sages. After the Bible, it is probably the most read and translated book in the world. It captures the dialogue between Lord Krishna, the incarnation of the Supreme Being, and his disciple Arjuna, on the battlefield of life. Family, friends, and teachers are standing opposite each other, in order to engage in a battle of life and death, with the rights of the succession of the kingdom at stake. Arjuna is the most famous archer of his time. Before the battle starts, Arjuna asks Lord Krishna, his charioteer and friend, to place their chariot in the midst of the two armies to oversee the situation. And he asks the Lord: What is the purpose of this battle? It all seems completely senseless to Arjuna. And even if he and his allies would win the battle, he still would grieve the disastrous consequences a war would bring about. After a desperate Arjuna has given vent to his resistance, a sublime treaty follows about the deepest human questions concerning life and death, duty and devotion, knowledge and experience, love and hate, ignorance and enlightenment. Smilingly and full of compassion, Lord Krishna offers universal wisdom and practical solutions, that till this day retain their full value. Self-discipline, selfless devotion and service unto the highest Intelligence are, in this most refined dialogue, the key to inner growth and fulfilment in life.

Puranas

The *Puranas* contain many mythological stories about higher beings, that are still popular, but happened sometime in long forgone periods of time. There are eighteen Puranas that are the most important, or the most elaborate, and eighteen Upapuranas of smaller size and of less importance. Some of the Mahapuranas are very extensive, like the Shrimad Bhagavata Purana, which describes the life, play and activities of Lord Krishna and consists of eighteen thousand *sloka's* (verses).

The Puranas generally treat five subjects:
1. Sarga — the creation of the universe
2. Pratisarga — the destruction of the universe
3. Vamsha — lineage
4. Manvantara — heroic stories
5. Vamshanucharita — history

Sometimes it happens that the same story, for instance the story of creation, is described differently in different places. We can compare this to a number of stories from the New Testament, that have been noted down differently by the evangelists. Maybe something else plays a role here. The historical context is less important than the deeper meaning that lies hidden in all these stories. The intent of the Puranas is primarily to indicate the processes through which life moves, so that people gain insight into the consequences of their actions. It is most likely that we can scout the subtle questions of life through mythological stories and utilise their teachings for the well-being of men and society. Some of these stories lie millions of years behind us and are situated on other planets than earth.

Shrimad Bhagavatam occupies a very special place within the collection of Puranas. It contains the transcendental qualities, plays and activities of Lord Krishna, the Supreme Being and cause of all causes. It was recorded by the holy saint Vyasadeva and consists of twelve Cantos (volumes). The study of Shrimad Bhagavatam can lift up the reader or listener to a high level of devotion and service to the Divine.

Smritis

Smriti means memory, or 'that which is remembered'. The most well-known of the eighteen Smritis is the Manu Smriti. Manu, a son of Brahma the creator, is considered to be the first law-giver of the world.

The Smritis are therefore a kind of law-books, in which an enumeration of the codes and rules of conduct is given. This conduct can pertain to one person, but also to a community, a society, or a whole country. In the Manu Smritis rules of conduct are given for the student, the householder, the ascetic, the king, and so forth. The deeper value of the Smritis does not lie in the strict following of the rules and injunctions, they are rather meant as a *mirror* for the quality of our consciousness. They are definitely unique in their universal value, and can even prove useful in this present Kali-yuga, as a tool for the growth towards enlightenment.

Upavedas

In the totality of the Vedic literature the Upavedas play a separate, but very important role. They contain the practical applications of the Vedas for daily life. The four Upavedas are *Ayurveda, Gandharvaveda, Dhanurveda* and *Sthapatyaveda*. Literally, they are the sub Vedas of the Vedas, meaning that they are their practical applications (see scheme 4.4) Because of their intimate relationship to the Vedas, the four Upavedas are discussed at the end of the next four chapters.

Scheme 4.4

The Upavedas

UPAVEDA	SUB-VEDA OF	VIEWPOINT	SUBJECT
Ayurveda	Rigveda	Wholeness	Health
Gandharvaveda	Samaveda	Consciousness	Sound and Music
Dhanurveda	Yajurveda	Energy	Activity, Rituals
Sthapatyaveda	Atharvaveda	Matter	Vedic architecture

Scheme 4.4 As the scheme shows, every Veda has its own Upaveda. While the four Vedas move in the field of consciousness, the Upavedas take this line and follow it through to an area of daily life. The Upavedas are the switch between consciousness and matter, between the Self on one side and the areas of spirit, body, activity and environment on the other side.

Till here we have given a short overview of the Vedic literature. Although it is of great importance, real wisdom of life cannot be found in a book. Best we can do is to consider the Vedic scriptures as a kind of blueprints of Absolute Reality. The real Veda can only be localized in the simplest form of our awareness, the container of pure knowledge.

Nevertheless, the Vedic scriptures derive their great value from the fact that they are the scientific and plain proof of the intimate relationship that exists between consciousness, energy and matter. At the same time, they give profound insight into the differences between the material and the spiritual world. This holistic approach of knowledge makes their content a complete science of all existence, that deserves to be discovered and applied by all human beings.

CHAPTER V

RIG VEDA: WHOLENESS IN BEING

Richo akshare parame vyoman
yasmin deva adhivishve nisheduh.
The verses of the Veda are structured
in the immutable transcendental field
of pure consciousness, where all Devatas reside.

- Rigveda I.164.39

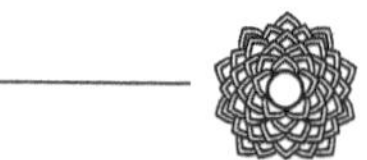

Astronomical indications in the text of Rigveda show that the hymns were already known more than eight-thousand years ago. But the Vedic wisdom itself is as old as the world, because it is connected to everything that exists, including human consciousness. The same is true for the Sanskrit sounds that correspond to the subtle energy centres in the human nervous system. The wisdom of the Vedas cannot simply get lost, because it is the expression of the universe and is inherent in it. Although humanly speaking it can be forgotten and that is what happened during the last few thousand years. The human being got more and more overshadowed by the material values of life. Our 'collective' consciousness is on a very low level in the Kali Age and our perception of the world and ourselves is therefore very limited. It is well known that even some animals perceive usually more than humans. They cannot make use of such a dominant intellect as we can, but trust their intuition much more and are therefore closer to nature. A highly developed human civilization, apart from its intellectual qualities, is characterized by a highly developed intuition, and inner values like happiness, contentment, purity and well-being of the society. Where can we still find these qualities nowadays?

Vedic wisdom aims to re-establish balance and harmony between spirit and matter, individual and society, and amongst countries. The Vedas pronounce it in numerous expressions: '*Ahimsa parmodharmah*' – Non-violence is the highest human duty. '*Sarve bhavantu sukhinah*' – May every man be happy in this world. '*Mitrasya chakshusha samikshamahe*' – May every human being treat his fellow men with friendliness. Furthermore, the Veda says: '*Ano bhadra kratavo yantu vishvatah*' – May noble thoughts emerge from all sides.'

These are not just some loose expressions in the hope for something better. After a period of spiritual decline, there inevitably comes a period of flourishing of spiritual values. At a certain dramatic moment, the divine Intelligence intervenes in order to enliven its evolutionary power in human consciousness.

V.1 THE FIELD OF CONSCIOUSNESS

Rigveda is strongly connected to the field of *pure consciousness*, that has anchored all knowledge of life in its universal structure. According to it, all Devatas (gods and demigods), impulses of creative intelligence, reside on this level of existence (RV. I.164.39). In other words, Rigveda explains the basis of all existence and all expressions thereof, within its own structure of wholeness; wholeness on the level of Being. God is One, without a second.

There is a famous verse from Rigveda:

***

God is One, but sages call Him by different names.
They call Him Indra, Mitra, Varuna, Agni,
Divya Garutmat, the universal celestial bird.
They speak of Yama and Matarishvan.
– Rigveda I.164.46

***

When we become acquainted for the first time with the recitations of the Vedic mantras, that are still sung every day by Indian *pundits* (priests), we might get disappointed or even shocked. What is this all about? The nasal sounds that the pundits produce do not make us assume immediately that we are dealing with the highest wisdom here, meant to bring man back to his divine origin. Nevertheless, the authority of the Veda is beyond doubt, because it offers us a complete insight into the basic universal laws of nature that act outside as well as inside us. In this way it is the goal and fulfilment of the modern branches of science. Take for instance quantum physics, still passionately searching for the ultimate secrets of our existence. It is important to realise that the Vedas are dealing with ourselves, with the functioning of our inner Being and its modes of expression on the relative plane of existence. It is the greatest treasure, the Holy Grail, for which humanity has always been searching and which it ultimately can find in the innermost core of its own consciousness.

Consciousness in its pure form is the essence of our existence. Even when we are not thinking, feeling or remembering, this field of consciousness is present. It is the pure observer deep within us, the silent witness of everything, a *field* of existence, not participating in the process of perception. Its qualities are *sat-chit-ananda*, or eternally present (*sat*), intelligent or aware (*chit*) and always in a blissful state (*ananda*). It is an infinite field of consciousness from where all our thoughts, feelings and memories arise. This field has the ability to store and remember everything. To expand the quality of our consciousness, it is necessary to make contact with this underlying field. In other words, unlike animals, we people are able to expand the quality of our ability to perceive! The Vedas call this our ability to hear, our power to grow. In the Bible, Jesus says: 'Whoever has ears he should hear'. this is clearly a reference to a different and more refined level of perception. Whenever we are able to stay in contact with the Self, the unlimited source inside of us, it becomes the natural motivating force for all our actions.

Rig Veda says:

***

Brahma bhavati sarathih
For those established in the Self,
the infinite organising power of this level of existence
becomes the charioteer of all actions.
- Rigveda I.158.6

***

The essence of the goal of Vedic knowledge lies hidden within the meaning of this verse. But until the connection with the underlying field of consciousness has not been established, man keeps getting lost in superficial levels of thinking, feeling and acting (he does not hear). He therefore lives a life characterized by attachment to the material world, limitations and mistakes. The result from this is suffering.

V.2 ACCESSIBILITY OF THE VEDA

Essential is the ability of the seer to perceive. Albert Einstein could never have done his remarkable findings, if he had not been a brilliant mind himself, intimately connected to the deeper layers of consciousness. Einstein, like many other Western scholars, has studied Bhagavad Gita, the encyclopaedia of Vedic wisdom, and said:

***

'Whenever I read it (the Gita), the only question that remains is how God created the universe. Whatever more one can think of, is in fact redundant.'

***

The Vedas give a very clear answer to Einstein's question. God did not create the universe; the universe creates Itself from Itself. But God, being the cause of creation, plays of course a very important role in this process. The creative process of the material world is based upon the same principle as the emergence of a human thought and its disappearance again into nothingness. Of course, this implies somebody or something administering the thought, namely the human mind. The same is true for the whole universe, the great Administrator of the universe who we call God or cosmic Intelligence, is the universal Administrator of all that exists.

The deeper wisdom of the Veda is only accessible to just a few *directly*, namely to those who are permanently established in their inner source, the enlightened yogis and saints among us.

***

'Those who know and experience this level of reality are established in equanimity, in the fullness of life. What can these verses mean for him who does not know this level?
- Rigveda, I.64.39

***

It is for this reason that the great teachers step into the limelight from time to time in order to explain the Vedic texts to their followers, and restore their dignity. In our modern time of science and technology Maharishi Mahesh Yogi went even further. He has, in many of his lectures and in a great quantity of study materials developed by him, drawn parallels between the Veda, as an area of pure knowledge, and the *'Unified Field of all the Laws of Nature'*, as studied by modern science. Quantum physics has developed the unified field theory with the goal to explain how all phenomena and matter in the universe emerge from an unchanging source of pure energy. According to Maharishi's Vedic Science we can compare this basic level of objective creation with the level of our own consciousness, namely that level on which consciousness has no other content than itself. This is, like we have described before, Being or *Brahman*, an area of pure silence and of completely settled mental activity. At the same time, paradoxically enough, the area of emptiness is also an area of fullness, otherwise complete creations would not be generated out of it. It appears to be a field *of all possibilities*, from which we can draw continuously.

V.3 MEANING OF THE DEVATAS

The collection of mantras of Rigveda, that is called *Rk*, is definitely the oldest. This Veda is the first and most important among the Vedas. The one who completely fathoms the hidden wisdom of the Veda possesses undoubtedly all knowledge of existence. The other three Vedas and the whole Vedic literature are based upon Rigveda, which consists completely of verses (not prose). The Devatas or gods that are invoked in the Vedas represent the impulses of creative intelligence in creation, but also in ourselves. Devata literally means: the one who shines. The hymns in Rigveda are devoted to thirty-three different Devatas, of which more than half are dedicated to Indra and Agni. Other important Devatas, that occur in Rigveda are Soma, Mitra, Varuna, Aryaman, Surya, the Ashwins,

Brihaspati, Pushan, the Maruts and Vishnu. They all are manifestations of Brahman and all have their cosmological, as well as their individual meaning in the field of consciousness (see scheme 5.1)

Scheme 5.1
The Cosmological and Individual Meanings of the Devatas

DEVATAS	COSMOLOGICAL	INDIVIDUAL
INDRA	Wholeness of existence	Wholeness of consciousness
AGNI	Creative intelligence	Digestion
MITRA	The Day	Inhalation
VARUNA	The Night	Exhalation
ARYAMAN	The Sun	Eyes
SURYA of PUSHAN	The Sun	The Self
THE ASHWINS	Guardians of Wellbeing	Health
BRIHASPATI	Teacher of the gods	Wisdom, Speech
SOMA	The Moon	Mind
THE MARUTS	The Wind	Organs of Perception
VISHNU	Principle of Maintenance	Feet

Scheme 5.1 The Vedas consider a human being as a miniature universe.
The Devatas represent different aspects of the cosmos and are invoked
to strengthen their corresponding qualities in man.
(Source: Ten Upanishads of Four Vedas)

The cosmic energy expresses itself in countless ways, but it can be divided into three main groups. The Devatas or demigods, as mentioned in the above scheme, belong to the intermediate energy of Purusha or the Supreme Lord (see also below). The living beings, including humans, are also products of the intermediate energy of the Supreme Lord. The material world is a creation of the external energy of the Lord, and the spiritual world, the Kingdom of God, is the revelation of His internal energy.

V.4 SETUP AND CONTENT

The complete Rigveda (lit. totality of wisdom) consists of about 10,472 richas, spread over ten mandalas or books and one *Valakhilya*. The last is a supplement with eleven hymns that probably has been added later. The ten mandalas are further subdivided into *anuvakas* and *suktas*. The first mandala of Rigveda knows, for instance, 24 anuvakas and 191 suktas. In total the whole Rigveda counts, including the Valakhilya, 1,028 hymns. According to the *Shatapatha Brahmana* all hymns in total would consist of 432,000 syllables, but after a recounting this number seems to be not completely correct.

Every hymn is set in a certain metre, called Chhandas. It knows one or more *Rishis* (seers) and *Devatas* (gods), who give it, together with the specific metre, form, meaning and effect. The seer is the one who cognizes the specific part of the process of creation. The deity represents the natural law or impulse of creative intelligence, who processes the relationship between the knower and the known.

The sequence of the mandalas happens according to a very conscious system, but it is remarkable that only the mandalas II – VII are connected to a certain Rishi and his progeny. These families are:

Mandala II   Gritsamada (of the family of Angiras)
Mandala III   Vishvamitra
Mandala IV   Vamadeva
Mandala V   Atri
Mandala VI   Bharadvaja
Mandala VII   Vasishtha

According to Maharishi, the first and tenth mandala of Rigveda should even have, instead of 191, 192 suktas, but the last of each should be invisible or transcendental. The first mandala of Rigveda deals with the

Samhita (totality) of the whole creation (Purusha and Prakriti), while the tenth mandala explains the Samhita of the non-manifest existence. According to Maharishi, this knowledge of the transcendental existence (Purusha) can be found in the gaps between the words, verses and hymns. The wholeness explained in the tenth mandala is then more than the sum of its parts. The latter can be compared to the totality of a house or body that is more than the sum of the materials or parts out of which it is made up of. The mandalas II-IX represent the eight Prakritis: earth, water, fire, air, space, mind, intellect and ego. The ninth mandala (ego) is the famous Soma mandala, which is completely dedicated to the deity Pavamana Soma. Concerning its meaning, it is a warm plea to purify the mind (soma) from the limited ego. The whole mandala contains verses like this:

***

Flow on, Soma, seeking the gods, hastening on in your purifying course;
enter Indra, O Indu, the showerer.
- Rigveda IX.2.1

***

The moral of this verse is that as the ego is purified, the mind will be able to enjoy more and more the Devas, the impulses of creative intelligence. It is followed by the prayer that Indu (the mind) may strongly be united with Indra (the wholeness of consciousness).

In the Vedas the Soma sacrifice occupies a central place. The god Pavamana Soma, who is invoked, stands for the universal mind, which is represented by the Moon in our solar system. Soma is the most subtle substance of the universe. Materially speaking it is a very refined glue at the junction point of consciousness and matter, that connects everything in the universe with each other. It is considered to be the nectar of the gods. In the Soma ritual in ancient days, a rare plant was used, the soma plant, that grew only in the Himalayas. There has always been a lot of discussion about the origin and meaning of this mysterious plant, that was pressed and drunk during the sacrifice. In later times the sap of the Soma plant, that might have been a hallucinogenic mushroom, was replaced by a symbolic substance.

Indicated by the specific set-up and poetic style of the hymns, it seems obvious that a special branch of the Brahmin families was responsible for Rigveda. The biggest part is dedicated to the yajnas or sacrifices. In ancient times, the process of creation was considered to be one big sacrifice and that may be the reason why the yajnas have begun to play such an overwhelming role. Apart from a funeral hymn, a hymn to the *pitris* (ancestors) and a hymn dedicated to the Vishvadevas, we come across some beautiful, dramatic dialogues in Rigveda between Yama and Yami, and between Pururava and Urvashi.

According to Maharishi, the core of the wisdom of existence lies already hidden in the first lines of Rigveda. The first hymn goes as follows:

***

Agnimile purohitam
yajnasya devam ritvijam
hotaram ratna dhatamam

We adore Agni, the fire god,
He who always does the best for others,
the abundant giver of riches,
worthy of praise is the Lord of the sacrifice.
– Rigveda I.1.1

***

The literal meaning of Agni is: he who goes first. Agni is the most important deity after Indra in Rigveda. All mandalas in Rigveda, except the ninth, start with a hymn dedicated to Agni. Agni became *Ignis* in Latin and it can also be found in other cultures. Agni stands for the creative intelligence in creation. Maharishi explains that already the first word of Rigveda *Agnim* contains all knowledge in seed-form and that the rest of the text, including the other Vedas, is nothing else but a further elaboration and commentary on it. All knowledge of existence springs forth from the first letter A, which represents the Absolute. 'A' is the first letter of Rigveda, of our own alphabet, and also of the Sanskrit alphabet. It is not a coincidence that the A-sound occurs in all languages of the world and always plays a dominant role. It is striking how much the letter A occurs in Sanskrit texts. It expresses the transcendent, the total expression of sound, that contains all knowledge in seed-form. The Sanskrit alphabet, being the primordial mother of all languages, is unsurpassed in its perfection, set-up, pronunciation and in its relation between sound and meaning. From A automatically all other Sanskrit vowels, I, U, R, L, AI, AU roll forth and thereafter all fifty consonants follow in a fascinatingly perfect sequence.

Once somebody asked an Indian sage how world peace could be achieved. The wise man became silent for a moment and then answered: 'As soon as people in the world start learning Sanskrit'. Research has shown that the study of Sanskrit has a special, cohesive effect on our brain functioning. This shows beautifully the great importance of Sanskrit language for the well-being of mankind.

V.5 PURUSHA SUKTA

The universe, that consists of infinite forms and phenomena, originates from the formless, pure consciousness or Brahman. But Brahman is the objective field of the Supreme Being, who in the Vedic scriptures is referred to as Lord Krishna. Both, namely Lord Krishna and the material world which He created, are inseparable. While the universe is the embodiment and expression of consciousness on the macro level, so is the human being on the micro level. In Rigveda this is expressed in the word Purusha, which means the Supreme Being, and which on a micro scale we can locate in the heart of every living being (Paramatma).

The famous Purusha sukta, consisting of eighteen verses, reveals the essence of the Veda. The fact that this sukta occurs in all four Vedas, emphasizes its outstanding value. On one side, we can state that Purusha is the field of pure consciousness, the silent witness, which is mentioned in a different context as *Brahman*. But, at the same time, Purusha is a living Being, it is God Himself. This sukta gives a metaphoric explanation of the process of creation and says among others:

***

Purusha, with a thousand heads, is in all that is, in both the visible and invisible worlds. Purusha already existed before creation and from Him the three Vedas emerged: Rik, Sama and Yajur. From the primordial vibrations of the Vedas originated thereafter the animate and inanimate worlds, made of gods, men, animals, plants and minerals.
- Rigveda X.7.6

***

It is clear that this sukta deals with the personal aspect of the Supreme Lord, about which we will speak more later. It describes in a profound way the relationship between the Supreme God, the human soul and the universe. As a myth of creation, it occurs in different varieties in other Vedic scriptures, too. It is recited daily by countless Hindus and is cherished as a means to connect to the Divine. So, there is no contradiction between the coexistence of an impersonal primordial state (Brahman) and a personal God (Ishvara), who can be praised and worshipped. The Absolute

Truth and the personal God are One. He appears as a transcendental Intelligence, who has a specific form and reveals Himself to man in the form of the highest Wisdom, Love and Goodness.

Prakriti, the nature of Purusha, manifests itself as a great cosmic desire for fulfilment of life. In man, the primordial vibration of Purusha or Brahman manifests itself in the Self or Atman. When, through the realisation of the Atman, we merge into the infinite bliss (ananda) of Brahman, then we attain Self-realisation. We achieve this by laying emphasis on harmony, tolerance and spiritual merit in our life. All Vedic arts, literature and music are based on the Veda, but also the many coloured rituals and festivals lasting many days, have only one goal, the growth of harmony among the people and attention for the connection of the individual with the Supreme Lord.

The most striking and at the same time most moving fragment in this connection is the last verse of the tenth mandala of Rigveda, in which humanity is urged to join in one spirit, one thought, one heart and one soul.

*****

Samanam astu vo mano yatha vah susahasati
May you experience unity in your heart, may your thoughts be harmonious so that you may live in togetherness and happiness.
– Rigveda X.191.4

*****

V.6 RELATIONSHIP WITH BHAGAVAD GITA
In chapter X.33 of Bhagavad Gita, Lord Krishna says that from all letters He is the letter A. *Akara*, the first letter of the Sanskrit alphabet, is also, as we have seen, the first letter of Rigveda and therefore the first letter of all Vedic literature. Without the letter A in Sanskrit, nothing can be

pronounced and therefore it is considered as the primordial source of all sounds. It represents the wholeness, the Absolute without beginning or end, from where all sounds emerge.

As the Purusha sukta makes it clear, the process of creation takes place within the nature of Purusha. It inspires everything to appear and withdraws everything again into itself, as if nothing has ever existed. This is what is meant in the Bhagavad Gita when Lord Krishna says:

***

'Prakritim svam avashtabhya vishrijami punah punah'
Curving back unto My own nature, I create again and again.
- Bhagavad Gita 9.8

***

This verse also shows that Lord Krishna and Purusha are one and the same. Purusha is transcendental, full of bliss, ever existing and already present before creation. Regarding the proof for the difference between paramatma and atma, Supreme Soul and our soul, we should turn to the *shruti*, the Vedic revelations, because there is no other source to establish the existence of the soul.

Finally, in chapter III.15 it is indicated that all human activities find their basis in the Vedas, because they contain divine directions, that are pure and efficient. In other words, the Vedas are the guidelines for our actions. Moreover, this will protect us from the karma resulting from action. The Vedic instructions for living and action point out the most comfortable way leading home, back to the Kingdom of God.

V.7 UPANISHAD OF RIGVEDA
Millions of people all over the world are deeply touched by the poetical

texts of the Upanishads, that are closely connected to the four Vedas. The Vedas and Upanishads contain the essence of the wholeness of Being. They reveal the underlying unity in the outer diversity of man, nature and cosmos. They can only originate from enlightened souls, who were inspired by God Himself. There are ten Upanishads that are considered to be the most original and they all belong to one of the four Vedas.

The *Aitareya Upanishad*, consisting of only three short sections, belongs to Rigveda. Its theme is the same, namely the emergence of all universal forces and phenomena, from the One Universal Being, which is formless and transcendental, and that, when animated, is called Purusha (or Atman).

***

In the beginning there was only the Absolute, the Self or Atman. There was nothing else than that. Then the desire arose: 'Let me create the worlds'.
- Aitareya Upanishad I.1.1

***

Purusha was there before creation. Out of a cosmic desire He created the material world *and entered it*. This indicates that Purusha, the Supreme Lord, is present in everything and supports everything – animate and inanimate, gross and subtle, object and phenomenon, macrocosm and microcosm. Man is a mini-cosmos and everything out of which we exist, such as our sensory instruments and our mind, has its cosmic counterpart.

In a next verse the Aitareya Upanishad speaks of four worlds (*lokas*) that are created in order to let the universe function. It is clear that tiny seeds have formed themselves, within the cosmic intelligence, that correspond with the four elements air, fire, water and earth. Then there is a need to administer these worlds. From Purusha, the Cosmic Soul, several souls originate that we call Devatas or demigods. Next the cosmic egg bursts asunder, in the same way as an embryo appears from an egg, or a foetus from the womb of the mother. And again, there is nothing new under the sun, microcosm or macrocosm follow exactly the same steps in their creative processes.

The cosmic intelligentsia, the Devatas, are also subject to the world of diversity and change and to the cycle of birth and death (*samsara*), although their lifespan can be extremely long. The story goes that they got hungry and thirsty after being created, meaning they got desires that needed to be fulfilled. The Devatas asked for a residence where they could stay and fulfil their desires. The Creator first offered a cow as a residence, then a horse and in the end a human being for them to reside in. The gods accepted man as the crown of creation, they entered him, and fulfilled all sensory tasks needed for him to function properly. The Aitareya Upanishad gives eight examples of cosmic forces that reside in man in order to strengthen his organs of perception and action (see scheme 5.2)

Scheme 5.2

The Connection between Microcosm and Cosmic Forces

ORGAN	FUNCTION	DEITY
Mouth	Speech	Fire
Nose (Nostrils)	Smell	Air
Eyes	Sight	Sun (Aditya)
Ears	Hearing	Space
Skin	Touch (hair)	Herbs and trees
Heart	Mind	Moon
Navel	Expiration (apana)	Death
Generative organ	Seed (procreation)	Water

*Scheme 5.2 This scheme shows how the human bodily functions
are intimately connected to the forces of nature.
(Source: Ten Upanishads of Four Vedas)*

The third step after (1) the creation of the universe and man, and (2) of how they could function through the forces of nature, was the responsibility for the desire for food. For this no separate sense organ was created, but this task was assigned to the expiration (apana), which is connected to the digestive system. The function of *apana* in the body is that the food gets processed, and transformed into energy through digestion and that it is transported to the different body parts. Purusha himself, the Cosmic Soul, entered the human being as *Atman*. Atman is the common field in which the different states of consciousness (waking, dreaming and sleeping) move. After Atman had entered the human body, he looked around curiously, and saw that he was endowed with the same cosmic qualities as Purusha Himself, the Cosmic Soul.

In summary: Rigveda Samhita already existed before the creation of the universe and was given by the Supreme Lord to Lord Brahma, the creator of the material world. Thereafter this wisdom was cognized by the rishis and passed on through the succession of Vedic masters. It is indestructible in nature, ever existing, and it is the source of all creation. The Vedic hymns are an expression of the cosmic principles, that are eternally unchanging, and carry out their work, creation after creation. Because the Veda is immutable and eternal and also gives insight into the creative process, as well into the evolution of man, it is throughout time as an anchor for the ship of life. It is the essence of all life.

V.8 UPAVEDA OF RIGVEDA

Ayurveda, the science of health and longevity, is the Upaveda (subordinate Veda) of Rigveda. As Rigveda offers all knowledge on consciousness and how consciousness expresses itself at all levels of creation, Ayurveda teaches that everything in our body is also an expression of intelligence or consciousness. This intelligence is not only seated in our mind, but is present in the whole central nervous system, in all cells and in all tissues. We are completely pervaded by the same intelligence that is omnipresent in nature. Ayurveda lays a bridge to the human physiology and makes Vedic wisdom practical for daily life. From the holistic vision that all disease processes originate in the mind, stemming from the wrong use of this intelligence, it has developed fundamental approaches that reach much further than just the treatment of the symptoms only.

Shri Dhanvantari, who is a manifestation (avatara) of Lord Vishnu, is considered as the primordial God of Ayurveda (picture: Wikipedia)

Typical for Ayurveda is that in all phases of diagnosis and treatment – prevention, tracing of diseases and the methods of restoring health, the totality of body and mind is taken into consideration. Every man consists of a hierarchy of systems, ranging from atoms, molecules, cells, tissues and organs to the human organism as a whole. This whole again forms a part of the family, society, and even of planet earth, which we can also consider to be a living organism. But in all systems, we find the same principles of intelligence and natural processes over and over again. It is from this universal viewpoint, that Ayurveda unfolds a richness of methods and techniques for cultivating and developing further the health of man and of all aspects of nature. The goal of Ayurveda is, therefore, to create a dynamic balance in the human physiology whereby our system becomes optimally service oriented in the context of all evolving systems.

The origin of Ayurveda
Unfortunately, the practice of Ayurveda got into a decline long ago, after repeated invasions of India by foreign powers. Also, during the colonial time of India, many ancient texts disappeared or were destroyed. In the Charaka Samhita, an Ayurvedic encyclopaedia of the scholar Charaka (8th century B.C.), it is described how, according to stories, the original Ayurveda was developed.

***

'Once upon a time, very long ago, when diseases appeared and formed a hindrance for the happiness of people, the most virtuous wise people sat together in a blessed valley of the Himalayas and discussed, full of compassion for all creatures, this holy topic:
"Sound health lies at the root of virtuous action, the acquisition of riches, the fulfilment of desires and ultimately the attaining of enlightenment. Diseases are the destroyers of health, well-being and a happy life. They form a great hindrance for human life. What could be the remedy?" With this problem in their mind, they went into meditation.'

***

Then Charaka describes that during this meditation, the wise men felt in the wholeness of their consciousness that their question would be answered. It was Bharadvaja, the greatest seer of his time, who cognized the complete knowledge of Ayurveda in his consciousness.

In no time Bharadvaja understood the whole science of life and transferred it to the wise. These men acted according to the rules of this science and gained for themselves and others a high level of well-being and a long and happy life.

Ayurvedic knowledge and methods

As soon as we start studying the Ayurvedic scriptures, it becomes clear that a number of methods and medicines of our time were already known and applied in this tradition. The knowledge of anatomy, physiology and organs we can find back in the time of Ayurveda. Already in the 8th century B.C., there were descriptions of connective tissue layers, the lymph vessel system, nerve plexuses, fat tissues, mucous membranes, synovial membranes and the muscular system. The Ayurvedic physicians in those days, called *vaidyas* (lit.: he who knows), had a very profound understanding of the digestion process, the different functions of the gastric juices, the menstrual cycle, and the development of the foetus. The famous physician Sushruta (5th century BC) reported in his Sushruta Samhita extensively about surgery, obstetrics, nutrition, the use of baths, herbs, child nutrition, hygiene, and medical care. He described the treatment of cataract, groin hernia, caesarean cut, and operations like amputation, skin transplantation, the setting of bone fractures and the removal of bladder stones. He also applied plastic surgery and probably he was the precursor of the contemporary general surgery as well as of otolaryngology and ophthalmology.

The dosha concept

Ayurveda is directly derived from the wisdom of Rigveda, which assumes that the material universe, including the human body, consists of five basic elements. In Sanskrit these elements are called *mahabhutas*. The fact that man and the universe are made up of exactly the same components, implies that all laws of growth, maintenance and destruction are applicable to both. The five mahabhutas correspond, subjectively spoken, to our sensory organs of hearing, touch, sight, taste and smell. Based on the five elements, Ayurveda indicates three dynamical principles, called doshas, through which all functioning of all organisms can be explained (see scheme 5.3).

Scheme 5.3
Basic Elements and Doshas

5 BASIC ELEMENTS	5 SENSORY ORGANS	SENSE OF	3 DOSHAS
SPACE	Ears	Sound	VATA
AIR	Skin	Touch	
FIRE	Eyes	Sight	PITTA
WATER	Tongue	Taste	KAPHA
EARTH	Nose	Smell	

Scheme 5.3 We can find the five basic elements or mahabhutas in every atom of the universe. They also form the building elements of our body, i.e. body cells, tissues, and organs. The three doshas are generated from the five elements: from space and air originates vata (movement), from fire pitta (transformation), from water and earth kapha (structure).

In Ayurveda the three dosha concept is a very important instrument for diagnosis and prevention or treatment of diseases. We can only speak of good health when the three doshas – vata, pitta and kapha – are present in the right proportion (this is different for everyone) and in harmony with each other in our body. Our health is suffering if, through bad eating and living habits or other causes, a disturbance or imbalance of the three doshas takes place. In that case disease, physical or mental, is unavoidable. Ayurveda has at its disposal the simple but very profound means of pulse-diagnosis to diagnose which doshas are out of balance in a living being. In chapter XVIII we will discuss the practical implications of being and staying healthy.

V.9 RELATIONSHIP WITH OUR BODY

As Rigveda represents the Samhita of knower, process of knowing, and known, so Ayurveda gives insight into the Samadosha of vata, pitta and kapha. Like Rigveda, Ayurveda is Brahma Vidya – knowledge of the totality. Therefore, all the principles treated in Rigveda return in the applied areas of Ayurveda. Considered practically, this means that it is possible to learn and know how to integrate in our daily life the fundamental wisdom of the Veda.

Concerning the link with the human body, as expounded in 'Human Physiology, Expression of Veda and the Vedic Literature', written by Dr. Tony Nader, Rigveda corresponds to all Samhita-values of the central nervous system. The universal quality of Ayurveda in relationship to the human physiology lies in our remembering the Self again on all levels of the human nervous system. The three doshas correspond to all rishi, devata, and chhandas values in the physiology. Each dosha has five subdoshas, 15 in total, corresponding to the 15 physiological and anatomical structures, organs and organ systems. The six Ayurvedic Samhita scriptures (Charaka-Samhita, Sushruta- Samhita, et cetera) comprise all aspects of physiology on the basic level of cell tissues and organs.

CHAPTER VI

SAMAVEDA: WHOLENESS IN PERCEPTION

- Samaveda

Rigveda expresses the wholeness of existence. But within this wholeness arises the desire for diversity. The question arises: Who or what is this wholeness? Is wholeness able to experience itself? Can it see, feel, taste, and smell itself? The wholeness starts like this, inspired by desire, to experience itself, step by step, as wholeness in diversity. That which experiences we call the knower, the seer, the observer. All forms are manifestations of Brahman and are a part of the same integrated vision of non-duality. These manifestations appear and emerge sequentially on different levels of existence, from the very subtle to the grossest matter.

Even the demigods, who are frequently referred to in the Vedas, have appeared or been born, just like other mortals, at a certain moment in time. Most of them are considered to be the offspring of Aditi, the Sun, or source of creation. As other Vedic scriptures explain, the Sun itself has been created by Lord Brahma, who was instructed by the Supreme Being to be the first creator of the material world. It is possible for the demigods to descend into gross matter, while earthly souls can sometimes rise up to great heights in the experience of their divine qualities. As a result of their intense self-discipline and humble devotion to the Supreme One, they can awaken the Divine in themselves and express this through sound. The possibility of direct communication between demigods and men lies in the form of sound and vibration. You do not have to be a Vedic seer in order to make use of certain sounds or mantras to ask for the blessings and protection of the demigods. This, too, is a direct consequence of the universal character of the Vedas.

VI.1 DIVISION AND CHARACTER

Creation in its non-manifest primordial form is vibration or sound. Samaveda corresponds to the area of the cosmic hum-m-m, the primordial sound AUM, from which the first vibrations of creation arise. At this basic level of creation there is still complete harmony between name and form, sound and meaning. In Samaveda this is expressed from the angle of the observer, the seer. The seer recognizes himself in the Samhita of the three-in-one structure of existence. In the *Samadhi* state of consciousness, he cognizes the way in which the different vibrations of the laws of nature emerge from their united, non-manifest source. Depending on his specific nervous system he is a *Rishi*, a seer of Rigveda or of one of the other Vedas. The difference between Samaveda and the remaining Vedas is that with the hymns of Samaveda the emphasis lies on the melody and sound and they are meant to be sung. In fact, all music in the world finds its roots in Samaveda.

These days there are only two Shakhas or branches known of Samaveda, while originally there certainly must have been twelve. The verses of the still remaining Samaveda cover about half of the verses of Rigveda. They form the songbook of the Udgatri priest, who performed as of old the soma-sacrifice. They consist of two parts: (1) the 'Purvarchika' and (2) the 'Uttrarchika.' Archika means 'a collection of verses'.

The Purvarchika consists of five Kandas (chapters), namely Agneya Kanda, Ayendra Kanda, Pavamana Kanda, Aranyka Kanda, and Mahanamnya Kanda. Also, the Uttrarchika is divided into different chapters. The hymns or *stotras* in the Purvarchika are of older composition than the ones of the Uttrarchika. But in both, great emphasis is laid upon musical notation, sound and metre. The Vedic recitations reach hereby a high standard of perfection, whereby traditionally a musical octave is being used that is divided into twenty-two quarter tones. Listening to the hymns of Samaveda is like listening to the language of nature, expressed in sound, melody and rhythm and has a specific influence on the health of mind, body and environment.

The Sanskrit word *Saman* means: song or melody. Samaveda is rich in beautiful compositions of sacrificial hymns that express different qualities of creative intelligence. Apart from that, they contain precise instructions of how the verses have to be sung. Famous are the so-called Udgitha verses in the second chapter of Samaveda, which have a very melodious character. Although a number of hymns are the same as in Rigveda, the point is that in Samaveda they are expressed in such a way that the Rishi-aspect becomes apparent. The Rishi and the Devata of the hymn may be the same, but the context and performance of it are different, therefore the meaning or impact is different, too. Just as in Rigveda, in Samaveda the emphasis lies also on the *sound value* of the mantras. In the recitation this is clearly obvious because of the many insertions and deformations of the words and the strikingly melodious metre with which the Sama-hymns are expressed. It is the sound value, the rhythm, the mode of recitation that lies at the basis of the specific characteristics of these hymns. The goal is to express wholeness in the area of perception and this is accompanied by complete surrender to the Divine. It is therefore not relevant to say that many hymns are similar to the hymns of the Rigveda, or are derived from other sources, since the specific angle used by Samaveda is simply a different one.

VI.2 DEVOTION

The hymns of Samaveda are mainly directed to Indra (wholeness of consciousness), Soma (mind) and Agni (creative intelligence). The inner hearing of the ancient seers was attuned to these most refined impulses of nature, through which they could perceive the hymns and transform them into sound. In its spiritual context, devotion to the Self could be considered as the most important quality of the observer and that is what it is all about in Samaveda. True devotion and surrender to God transform every performance into a selfless action (*nishkama karmayoga*).

Worship, the performance of rituals, piety, righteous action and compassion for all creatures, are the external characteristics of the sincere and selfless love of God. One can also add meditation and prayer to this, because they liberate the mind of impurities and attachment. All these expressions of devotion deepen our feelings, strengthen the mind, and purify the ego. The love for a personal God and the spiritual teacher is sincere when it goes hand in hand with the realizing of the higher Self. In this process the identification with the small 'I' is gradually taken away and the ego melts into the Self. The one, to whom this is a permanent experience, sees everything in the Light of the Self. Actually, he becomes the Light.

***

Verily, the sun does not rise nor set for the one who knows the hidden teaching of the Vedas, for him daylight shines uninterrupted.
- **Chhandogya Upanishad III.11.3**

***

Often, the discussion flares up about which path for the seeker of truth is easier and better to walk on, the one of knowledge or the one of devotion. In general, one cannot make a statement about this, because every human being is different and both paths can lead to Self-realisation. But it is clear that the path of surrender forms for many people a crown jewel that is cherished and praised. Samaveda shows this path and guides the aspirant step by step towards deeper experiences of the Self. The rituals, worship and sacrifices take initially place on a grosser level, but gradually become more subtle and symbolic. After some time, duality melts away and full surrender to the Divine is achieved. How long this process lasts, it is difficult to say. People are different in their mental set-up, quality of consciousness and duration of the spiritual process.

Rituals, celebrations and ceremonies are a part of life. We look strange if they come from an ancient tradition, but in the Western culture they happen probably as much. In the latter case, we don't even think about it, it is just as it is. But the real ceremony or celebration is meant to help connect ourselves with and surrender to the Divine. Prayers, sacrifices, retreats and festivals reflect the desire of our soul, who is searching for something that transcends daily reality. All our religious practices and meditations have no other meaning than to fathom and experience the ultimate Reality.

VI.3 VEDIC SANSKRIT

In Vedic Sanskrit, name and form are identical to each other. This implies that in the sounds of Sanskrit the quality and perfection of the totality of existence is reflected. Sanskrit is the language of nature, the language of the Devas, the impulses of creative intelligence. Its script, therefore, is called *Devanagari*, which means *dwelling place of the gods*. That is why all Vedic hymns or mantras are expressed in the language of Sanskrit. Vedic Sanskrit has a logical, mathematical structure and is anchored, like the Veda itself, in the very structure of our consciousness. At the level of silent, pure consciousness sound, grammar, and meaning form a complete unity. There is no language in the world in which the sound harmonies are so exactly and consistently applicable on the language as a whole. The way in which the words develop themselves out of their seed form, goes beyond the conception of any language. A root is always a single syllable, that contains one of the four (!) basic vowels *a, i, u, ri*. Based on a transforming principle, it is the root which creates the word in order to let it resound optimally. The building up of words works with a mathematical precision throughout the whole of the language and gives an extraordinary power to sentence structure.

It is for this reason that by means of letter symbols much attention is given to the correct pronunciation (*svara*) of the sounds or words. In the Vedic hymns, every word and sequence of words has been chosen with the utmost care and nothing has been left to chance. In this flowing stream of sounds, every sound refers to itself and comments on itself as well as on the previous sounds, Maharishi explains. Word and sound of the hymn form one wholeness: every Sanskrit word in Samaveda is naturally provided with a certain tone. This tone is for that word always the same and the melody emerges spontaneously when the different words are set in a certain row. To put it differently: the tones belong to the form of the word itself and the use of another tone for the same word can lead to a completely different meaning.

VI.4 LINK WITH BHAGAVAD GITA

Among the four Vedas Samaveda is highly praised. Lord Krishna says in Bhagavad Gita:

***

'Among the Vedas, I am Samaveda'
– Bhagavad Gita X.22

***

Of all Vedic mantras the mantra AUM – the *Pranava* – is the primordial mantra, and this is Krishna. AUM is very prominently present in Samaveda and maybe for that reason Lord Krishna identifies Himself with Samaveda. A few verses later He adds:

***

'Of the hymns in Samaveda I am the Brihat-Sama and of all poetry I am the Gayatri.'
- Bhagavad Gita X.35

***

A well-known hymn from Samaveda is the Brihat, which has a particularly refined melody structure and which traditionally is recited around midnight.

In Sanskrit, there are fixed rules for rhythm and metre. It is likely that the above verse refers to the Gayatri metre which is frequently used in Samaveda and is highly esteemed in the Chhandogya Upanishad. Because one says that this metre represents *Brahman*, the Absolute, in Vedic tradition it is considered by many as the most important metre. It seems that Brahma, the creator of the material world, used and repeated this metre first, after which it was passed on through the holy tradition of the successive line of divine teachers.

VI.5 UPANISHADS OF SAMAVEDA

The Upanishads that belong to Samaveda are: (1) *Chhandogya Upanishad* and (2) *Kena Upanishad*. The Chhandogya Upanishad calls Samaveda the blossom of the Vedic tree of knowledge. Already from the beginning of this Upanishad, Samaveda is highly praised, especially in combination with Rigveda.

***

'AUM. One should meditate on this syllable as the Udgitha song,
because every chant starts with AUM'

***

'The essence of all creatures is the earth, the essence of the earth is water, the
essence of water are the plants, the essence of the plants is man, the essence
of man is speech, the essence of speech is Rigveda, the essence of Rigveda is
Samaveda, and the essence of Samaveda is the Udgitha chant.'
'Speech is Rigveda, Prana (life breath) is Samaveda, the syllable
AUM is Udgitha. Now, these two form a unity. Speech with Prana,
and Rigveda with Samaveda.
Their unity is anchored in AUM, it is in this sound that they are unified.
Whenever they come together and unite they are each other's fulfilment.'
'The one who knows this and meditates upon this syllable as being the
Udgitha chant, will experience fulfilment himself.'
\- **Chhandogya Upanishad I.1.1-7**

***

It is known that the Udgitha chant is recited traditionally during the

Soma-sacrifice. Moreover, this masterly beginning of the Chhandogya Upanishad is for an ordinary mortal too beautiful and profound to give a commentary on it, and this is actually true for every Upanishad.

Shri Aurobindo (1872-1950) was a well-known Indian philosopher,
yogi and the Founder of Integral Yoga (source: Wikipedia)

The second Upanishad of Samaveda, the *Kena Upanishad*, starts with the question what the original motivating force of the mind, the life breath and the organs like speech, sight and hearing is. And it immediately adds that it is That, which cannot be perceived by one of the physical senses and it cannot be imagined by our mind or be contained in words. It is something else than what we are acquainted with and it goes beyond that with which we are not familiar. It is *Brahman*, the One without a second, that can only be praised and meditated upon, for instance by using the mantra AUM. The question arises then: what is meditation? In the ordinary use of language, we mean the time we spend in silence and isolation, in the morning and the evening. The Chhandogya Upanishad claims that we can be in meditation throughout the whole day. This means, that in the midst of daily activity it is possible for us to be aware of that which is immutable, the innocent perception of the silent witness within us.

The Kena Upanishad has only four short sections. The saint *Shri Aurobindo* has written a very valuable commentary on this Upanishad. He states that matter, life and mind indicate successive levels of evolution in the cosmos, but they are not the higher Self. They are expressions or instruments of that Self. And the ultimate experience of the Self is that towards which everything is evolving. Our evolution, therefore, is not yet complete. Our mind is the cognitive aspect of *Brahman consciousness.* Modern science has established the exchange between matter and energy. The origin of our mind lies in the area of cosmic energy, which is pure creative intelligence. Being a very high form of evolution, the mind itself has the ability to grow towards a state of super-spiritual experience. In this process *Prana* or subtle life breath plays a significant role. Prana is the *cosmic principle* that supports all fundamental laws of nature, gravity, electromagnetism, strong and weak interaction. It also supports our mind. That is why it is possible to learn to allow the mind to transcend its activity and experience a higher spiritual state. But when are we ready for this, and how do we know it?

The first three verses of the Kena Upanishad seem, in this connection and certainly on the first sight, very confusing.

***

'Teacher: When you think you know it (Brahman), be aware then that you know it only a little bit. If it has to do with you or it is something of the gods, also that you have to investigate.

'Disciple: 'I think I know it (Brahman).

'I think I don't know it (Brahman) well enough, but I also do not think that I do not know it. The one of us who summarizes it as both ' *not-knowing' and 'knowing' truly understands.*

'Teacher: 'The one who knows that he doesn't know, knows. The one who thinks to know it, does not know. It is not known by those who think that they understand it. It can only be known by those who do not understand it.
- Kena Upanishad, section 2, 1-3

***

In section three of the Kena Upanishad the famous parable then follows about the three gods *Agni*, *Vayu* and *Indra*. These gods were proud of their achievements, which they attained with the help of Brahman. One day, to teach them a lesson, Brahman appeared to them, but because he was in disguise, the gods did not recognize him. First Agni (fire) was asked to find out who the stranger was. But instead of getting to know about the stranger, the latter challenged him to burn a blade of grass. The fire god though, was unable to burn the blade of grass and disillusioned he returned to his friends. The same happened to Vayu (air) who with all his divine powers was not able to blow away the blade of grass. When Indra tried to get to know more about the stranger, the latter simply disappeared. In the place of the stranger a beautiful lady appeared. Her name was *Uma*. Uma is a different name for Parvati, the consort of Shiva, and Shiva in this context symbolises Brahman. She said that the stranger was none other than Brahman himself.

Shri Aurobindo gives the following explanation to this story. The gods (matter, life and mind) look at their merits as something of themselves and are eager to show off their qualities. Agni symbolises the matter-energy principle (particles-waves) from physics. Vayu symbolises Prana, the cosmic principle. Without the blessings of Brahman or the Supreme

Being, the Absolute, they are not able to do anything, not even to destroy a simple blade of grass. Indra represents the strength of the mind. The mind can only contain something which exists in the relative plane of life. So, when he wants to investigate the Absolute, That just disappears. But the mind does not give up and suddenly catches sight of the beautiful lady named Uma. Uma is *Prakriti*, mother nature or the consort of Brahman, and only through her mediation can the mind ultimately realise Brahman. Is this not supreme knowledge?

In summary: the hymns of Rigveda are called *Rk* and the verses of Samaveda are called *Saman*. Saman is supported by Rk, by wholeness. Saman is the observer, the rishi, who merges with Rk and then experiences fulfilment of life. That is why they are inseparable. They also represent the sound AUM and the life breath (*Prana*) and both of them are expressed in the Udgitha chant. Saman sets the creation in motion. Within the primordial sound AUM several vibrations originate, through which music enters creation.

VI.6 UPAVEDA OF SAMAVEDA

The Upaveda (subordinate Veda) of Samaveda is *Gandharvaveda*. From *Rk* springs Saman and from there creation emerges. The subtle organ of hearing registers very refined vibrations and declares the fabulous beauty of creation. These are the Saman hymns. It starts from the primordial sound AUM followed by the vibrations from which AUM is composed. It is a very differentiated palette of light, colours and vibrations. It is Udgitha.

It is also Gandharva. Gandharvas are angels. Samaveda and Gandharvaveda are to each other what God is to His army of angels. In the Vedic scriptures, the Gandharvas are the celestial musicians playing for the demigods and preparing the nectar of immortality. The word Gandharva derives from the Sanskrit roots *Gai* (to sing, praise) and *Dha* (to drink). The Gandharvas drink from the nectar while making music and deliver in their play pure, celestial sounds. The singing of angels really exists, it seems, and there are people who can perceive it, in the same way as the universal sound AUM can be heard.

The traditional Gandharva music is a logical extension of the Saman recitations and is based on the same fundamental principles. The essence is the conjunction of sound, melody and rhythm in harmony with the natural frequencies with emphasis on the effect thereof. As we often see in the context of Vedic wisdom, the point in Gandharvaveda music is not whether we like it or not, but the effects it has on mind, body and surroundings. The music is completely meant to serve our personal purification, growth and the enlivening of a harmonious environment. Some people play this music all day long softly in the background in their house or practice room. Without doubt they understand the beneficial effects of this music and enjoy its benefit this way.

Well known is the story of *Mian Tansen*, one of the greatest musicians from the ancient Gandharvaveda-tradition. One day the king asked Mian Tansen if there was anyone on earth who could sing even more beautifully than himself. Mian Tansen answered immediately that his own master could sing infinitely more beautiful than him. But because his teacher was a hermit, he never performed in public. The king became very curious and decided to pay a visit to Tansen's teacher. Together with Tansen he went to the forest where the hermit lived. When they arrived to his dwelling place, the king went into hiding and asked Tansen to make sure that his teacher would start singing. Tansen, by starting to sing himself and making some mistakes, got the teacher annoyed who then let him hear how it should have been sung correctly. The king did not know what he was hearing, so pure sounded the song of the hermit. He was greatly moved and deeply impressed by these heavenly sounds. How was this possible? Afterwards he asked Tansen why it was that he himself could not sing that beautifully. Mian Tansen answered that the difference was that he himself only sang for the king, while his master sang solely for the glory of the creation.

To be complete, we repeat here some interesting characteristics of Gandharvaveda music, as was described earlier in *Hinduism*, back to the source (Saraswati Art, 1999, fourth edition). The Gandharvaveda music is traditionally handed down from teacher to disciple in all its refinements. The oldest known work, the *Natya Shastra*, comes from the hand of the ancient seer *Bharata* and is the holy scripture of music and dance. Both music and dance are expressions of the *movement* element. The *Sangita*, the totality of all instruments of song and dance, is subdivided in three categories: *gitam* (song), *vadyam* (instruments) and *nrittam* (dance and theatre art). The art of singing is the most ancient form of making music. Also, the beautiful art of dancing occupies, since time immemorial, an important place in ancient Indian culture. For instruments, mostly wind, string and percussion instruments were used. Of the wind instruments, the *bansuri*, the bamboo flute is very popular, while of the string instruments, the sitar has won great popularity all over the world.

Ragas and their influences

As always, Gandharvaveda music is performed within the musical framework of a *raga*, in which the musician improvises. In each raga specific tone scales and rules are being used. Usually the rhythm is indicated by the *tabla* (two small drums). Sung or played, the ragas generate a certain feeling or mood in the listener.

The basic tone of a raga is the *Sa* (the 'Do' in Western music). This one is continuously in rest and represents the source from which everything emerges and returns again. It all deals with the relationship of every single note to this basic note (rest and activity) and both together produce the desired effect. Every *mela* or music scale, of which there are ten, consists of seven *svaras* or notes *Sa, Re, Ga, Ma, Pa, Dha* and *Ni*.

The structure of each raga is fixed from the beginning. Within this structure the musician can improvise to his heart's content, according to the time of the day and circumstances. Therefore, a raga performance will never be the same. One could easily draw a parallel with the Vedic hymns, where the framework (the text of the hymn) is often the same but the performance given by the rishi is different in each of the four Vedas. When playing a raga, the time and circumstances are very important. For instance, there are ragas for different times of the day (morning, afternoon or evening) and ragas that are played or sung only in certain seasons. One of the anecdotes of Mia Tansen was that his king requested him in the middle of the day to sing a midnight raga. Tansen protested, because this was against the rules, but the king insisted that he sings the raga. Mian Tansen then sang the raga with the result that suddenly in the middle of the day it became pitch-dark.

How far this story is true is not known, but it is definitely true that ragas influence the different times of the day, the weather, and the seasons. Well known is the rain-making raga, which helps to let it rain in times of draught. No doubt, here lies a connection with the (Red) Indian dances that had similar purposes. Depending on the position of the Sun in every moment of the day and in each season, certain laws of nature are livelier. When the ragas are performed, these laws of nature are nourished at their source. The rhythms and melodies of nature start vibrating as it were through the music in our mind and body and in the environment, and this is where the original purpose of making music lies. A process of purification is set in motion by which we start to live more in harmony with the laws of nature. By playing or listening to Gandharvaveda music, our health and the harmony between man and environment is promoted.

Satsangs

Nowadays everywhere in the world *satsangs* are held, of which phenomenon more is written in chapter XVII. During these meetings, *bhajans* (spiritual songs) and mantras are chanted with the same goal of inner purification and personal growth. It will come as little surprise that the bhajans and mantras are predominantly sung or recited in Sanskrit. They are an extension of Gandharvaveda-music and sometimes surpass it in popularity. A striking phenomenon is, that the bhajan or mantra, often consisting of one or more names of God, is repeated several times. Moreover, the repetition effect (kirtana) leads to a certain spiritual freedom or ecstasy. In the Vedic scriptures it is written that in order to gain spiritual liberation in the age of *Treta-yuga* the performance of rituals is the most important merit, while in the age of *Kali-yuga*, the present age, the chanting of the name of God is the greatest virtue. So, as far as this is concerned, we are on the right track.

VI.7 RELATIONSHIP WITH OUR BODY

As in Samaveda, so in Gandharvaveda, the emphasis lies on the Rishi-aspect in the field of pure consciousness. The aimed result in every area of life depends on the quality of the observer. According to the beautiful book of Dr. Tony Nader, one of Maharishi's brilliant scientists, Samaveda represents the totality of all systems and channels in the body that is associated with our perception. In total, there would be 1000 of these perception channels that correspond exactly to the 1000 *Shakhas* or branches of which Samaveda consisted originally. According to Dr. Nader, Gandharvaveda in the human body is represented by all the cycles and rhythms of the physiology, among which it is the metabolism, which keeps the mind and the body in harmony with the rhythms of nature. The seven tones of the Indian music scale SA, RE, GA, MA, et cetera. can also be localised in the body.

YAJURVEDA: WHOLENESS IN SURRENDER

'May you become enlightened by the mighty rays of knowledge and kill not one cow, the Aditi.'

- Yajurveda 13.43

The third Veda, Yajurveda, which expresses and enlivens the process of pure consciousness, is indispensable in the whole of Vedic literature. What process is it dealing with? It deals with the process or relationship between subject (the observer) and object (the observed). It represents the *devata-quality* of the wholeness of consciousness. No wonder, that it describes many rituals called *yajnas* (holy sacrifices). The performance of yajnas and the recitation of Vedic hymns play a special role in Indian culture. *Yaj* means: to offer, to adore. When a *yajna* (pronounced: yadsjna) is performed according to the prescribed rules and is accompanied by the sequence of sounds, as is precisely described in Samaveda, then its effect will be evolutionary and support the path of Yoga. The subtle difference between Rigveda and Yajurveda is, that Rigveda is concerned with *pure*

knowledge, while the emphasis in Yajurveda lies on the *process*. There are yajnas for spiritual growth, but there are also many others that aim for a good material result, like the acquisition of excellent progeny, a rich harvest, rain, or prosperity for the country and peace for the world.

VII.1 WHAT ARE YAJNAS?

Seen cosmically, the phenomenon of *yajna* is called the navel of the universe, which indicates that Purusha, the Supreme Being, has sacrificed Himself in order to create the universe and enter into it. In the famous Purusha sukta this is described as follows:

***

'When the gods performed the yajna by sacrificing Purusha, spring was its butter, summer its fuel and winter its sacrifice.

That Purusha, who was first born, was sprinkled with the sacrificial grass. The gods, the Sadhyas and the wise begun the yajna with Purusha.'
- Rigveda X.90.6-7

***

In the most universal sense yajna refers to the creation of matter, energy and space. This would be in contradiction with the *Big Bang theory*. The explanation of the Veda seems to go in the direction that creation is not caused by a Big Bang, but originates from *emptiness* (the void) and by God's desire to bring forth a creation. In the next chapter we will elaborate more on this topic. Next, Rigveda says:

***

'When, through this yajna all richas (verses) were offered, the Samans were born from there. From the Samans the metres (Chhandas) were born,

from these metres the Yaju was born.'
- Rigveda X.90.9

***

This verse indicates that the Vedas originate directly from God. Because Atharvaveda represents the Chhandas-aspect, it may be assumed that indirectly it is also pointing to this Veda. It often happens, that Yajurveda is mentioned as the fourth and last Veda, but in the Samhita structure of knower, known and process of knowing this seems less logical.

When we describe the yajna at the human level, it is a performance meant to make connection with the spiritual world. It is an act that promotes human evolution, a means to spiritual liberation. In this context, it deals with the *purification* of processes that occur each moment in the relationship between subject and object. Because we are busy all day, thereby we keep using all our senses, everything we do is creating certain effects. Now, usually there is a lot of disturbance in our minds, which obstructs optimal results of our actions. In other words, our actions bring forth fewer desirable effects and what we create is what we are, or become. This is the universal law of *karma* that every human has to face.

***

'As one acts, so one becomes. Someone becomes virtuous by performing virtuous acts and bad by bad actions.'
- Yajurveda, Br. Upanishad 4.4.5

***

Yajurveda therefore is considered to be *karmakanda*, which means that its purpose is to positively influence someone's karma or, for instance, the karma of the world through rituals. As long as we, through our actions and desires, are bound to the law of karma, we remain part of the ever-repeating cycle of life and death. But by the performance of life-supporting actions we can create certain counter effects, or neutralize certain already caused effects on our journey to end the cycle of reincarnation. The same is true for the performance of rituals, because actions that are done in this context are first of all offered to the Supreme God, serve a higher purpose, and thereby create a favourable effect. This indicates the enormous value of the performance of yajnas. Its foremost concern is the well-being of the soul of the yajna-performer, or the one for which the yajna is performed. It sets in motion a process of purification from the undesired effects we have ever caused and bestows auspicious results for the future.

* * *

Svargakamo yajeta
Let he, who desires heaven, perform a yajna.
– Yajurveda

***

For the performance of a yajna it is prescribed that the leading pundit, who represents Brahman, sits at the north side of the altar, opposite him sits the *udgatri*, on his left the *hotri* and on his right the adhvaryu. The pundit recites the mantras of Atharvaveda, the hotri of Rigveda, the udgatri of Samaveda and the adhvaryu recites the mantras of Yajurveda. The four priests represent speech, sight, life breath and mind on the individual level, and Fire, Sun, Air and Moon on the universal level. In some yajnas, a great number of Brahmin priests take part, in the complete Soma sacrifice sometimes seventeen. A yajna can last an hour, a day, a week, a month or even longer.

The sacrificial place, that is first sanctified by the pundit(s), represents an oasis of purity. The altar itself represents earth and water, the basic elements. During the sacrificial ceremony gifts are offered to the deity and burned in the fire. One asks for the blessing of the goddess of wisdom for more insight, the goddess of fertility for a child, and the god of fire for protection. The Devatas represent qualities of creative intelligence. All Devatas together form the total creative intelligence of the universe. In the Vedic tradition they are known under names like Shiva, Vishnu, Ganesha, Indra, etc. If a certain quality of creative intelligence needs enlivenment one can, as desired, perform or let a priest perform a Shiva-yajna, Ganesha-yajna, or any other yajna. In Treta-yuga, the Copper Age of humanity, the performance of rituals was the main virtue. In Kali-yuga, the *sankirtana-yajna*, chanting the name of God, is especially recommended. It is nice to see that all over the world this is actually happening, and is often accompanied by the necessary ceremonials.

VII.2 THE SHAKHAS

In a broader perspective a yajna is an action meant to develop cosmic consciousness (*moksha*). This results from the subdivision of the Vedas into different branches, called Shakhas. Every Shakha has its own Upanishad which refers to Brahman, the ultimate reality. Every Shakha consists of three parts, which from gross to more subtle, namely are the:

- Karma Kanda (the area of action)
- Upasana Kanda (the area of devotion)
- Jnana Kanda (the area of knowledge)

Karma Kanda treats the gross, physical aspect of yajna and deals with the duties of different groups of people, so that they do not act against the laws of nature. Birth (descent), the age in which one is living, the circumstances of one's life, are criteria that play a role in this.

Upasana Kanda is a more subtle form of yajna, wherewith one tries to gain the blessings of the Devatas through *correct* performance of the holy rituals. Here the point is to spiritually establish contact between man and the higher cosmic order, and finally surrender to the Supreme Being, the cause of all causes.

Jnana Kanda deals with the wisdom of the Absolute, and it will not be surprising that the Upanishads belong to it. Jnana Kanda gives insight (physical, mental and spiritual) into how we can transcend the imprisonment of the earthly, material existence, surrender to the Supreme God and become part of His eternal Kingdom.

In the context of Karma Kanda, it cannot be denied that in the past – and still maybe at certain places – animal sacrifices have been made. With these sacrifices one tries to please especially the goddess Kali, but ultimately the yajnas serve a higher and more refined purpose. The word *yajna* literally means *ahimsa* – non-violence – which makes clear that the ritual slaughtering of animals, let alone the eating of meat, should not be the case. In those places where 'the sacrificial animal' or the eating of meat is mentioned, something completely different could be meant (see chapter IX). Yajurveda emphasises in different places that the killing of animals (and also of people) is sinful and does not serve any evolutionary purpose. Interesting in this context is this verse from the Purusha sukta:

***

'Seven were his enclosures (paridhi), thrice seven were made for the wooden fire (samidha). In the yajna that was performed by the gods, they offered Purusha as the victim.'
- **Rigveda X.90.15**

***

This verse has nothing to do with the offering of animals. On the contrary, it has a very profound, universal content and refers to the holy numbers three and seven. The number three refers to the three worlds, earth (*prithivi*), interspace (*antariksha*) and heaven (*dyau*). In their turn, these lokas each consist of seven layers or levels, making up a total of twenty-one. And what is meant by Purusha being the victim in this context? How can God offer Himself? Mohan Roy's explanation in his book *Vedic Physics* (see chapter IX) is that God, in the process of creation, transforms Himself from His eternal non-manifest, transcendental form into a manifest form (the universe). In this context, because the Supreme Being never loses his transcendental form, I would rather say that He sacrifices Himself to the gods, whose sacrifice creates all life-forms, including human beings. In other words, the Supreme Being is the sacrificer and the sacrificed at the same time, without losing His transcendental nature.

VII.3 CHARACTER AND DIVISION

Yajurveda contains 1976 hymns and consists partly of prose, which especially deals with the actual performance of the rites. The texts that are provided with measure and rhythm are called Yajus, which established the name of this Veda. The Yajus are accompanied by certain, exactly prescribed performances that are described in the Brahmanas. One finds many hymns of Rigveda in Yajurveda, but they have a different division and texts are added to them on how to carry out the yajnas. The formulas and invocations in the texts are specifically Yajurvedic.

Yajurveda contains many famous yajnas like the *Soma yajna* and the *Ashvamedha yajna*, the great horse sacrifice. This last yajna was also performed by Yudhisthira, the eldest of the Pandavas, after he was crowned a king. It consists partly of the free roaming of a horse, a stallion, under the guidance of royal servants. All countries that are visited by the horse, automatically fall under the protection of the king who ordained the yajna. The king of the country concerned could, of course, refuse this protection, but that meant war. In those days, there were hardly any kings who dared to defy the mighty King Yudhisthira, who was widely praised for his righteousness. By the performance of this yajna, he gained control over the then known world. Furthermore, Yajurveda prescribes different yajnas to salute the full moon, new moon, the seasons, and contains other extensive prayers and invocations. It also contains many instructions on how to build a yajna altar and how the place of yajna has to be purified.

Brahmin priest performs homa, Vedic ritual. (picture: Wikipedia)

The sacrifices devoted to heavenly beings were further extended in the course of time and accompanied by hymns and prayers. The beverage of the gods, that plays an important role in the rituals, is called *soma*.

Soma is the most refined substance in the universe at the junction point of consciousness and matter. On a cosmic scale it is represented by the Moon, that is placed between the Sun and the Earth, and subjectively represents our mind. In the yajna, Soma is derived from the sap of a rare plant only found in the Himalayas. The sap is pressed out of this plant during the sacrifice. When applied to the human mind, after being pressed on the sacrificial table, he is purified of all ignorance and limitations.

Yajurveda consists of two parts. The first part (even till today) is formed by the *Taittiriya Samhita*, also called the Krishna or 'black' Yajurveda. This part contains 32 suktas. The second part consists of the *Vajasaneyi Samhita*, also known as the Shukla or 'white' Yajurveda. As has been discussed earlier, the Vedas consist of two values, namely the Mantras and Brahmanas. The Mantra-aspect represents the pure knowledge, while the Brahmana-aspect represents the dynamic activity within the structure of pure knowledge. Together they form a state of integrated balance between complete silence and infinite dynamism. In the first part of Yajurveda, the difference between Mantra and Brahmana is hard to find, therefore this part is called *black*. The second part, the *white* Yajurveda, consists only of mantras while the Brahmana-part is separately housed in the so-called *Shatapatha Brahmana*. In both parts the sequence of the sacrifices is the same.

***

'To Thou, oh Lord, we ask for help, for food and strength. May Savitri, god of creation, bliss and knowledge, inspire us to do the most noble deeds. May the cows never be killed, be healthy and strong, laden with calves, and be free of disease. May never a thief and evil person be born among us, who are rich in progeny and free from pain and disease. May the Lord of the land and cattle be always connected to You. May God guard our progeny, cattle, and riches of the sacrificial priest!'
- Yajurveda

***

Only a Brahmin or seer in unified consciousness, who is knowledgeable about the holy texts, can interpret such a text in all its purity. But in general the cows are symbolic for our senses. The Lord of the land and cattle is our mind, including the intellect, who is free and unattached when permanently connected to the divine Savitri, the Self. This clearly indicates that the Vedas are concerned in the first place with human evolution through our own spiritual growth.

VII.4 THE NECESSITY OF YAJNAS

Yajnas are an effective instrument to generate more positivity in ourselves and in world consciousness. In fact, they are a tool in the battle against ignorance. If we look around carefully, we see that chaos rules the world and we cannot separate ourselves from it. We have caused this chaos ourselves and it is reflected in nature, as well. When mankind continuously violates the laws of nature on all fronts; seasons get disrupted, floods take place and heavy storms occur. Besides this rainfall, forest fires or enormous tsunamis can happen and the earth and oceans are battered by catastrophic earthquakes. Political and economic power blocks stand powerless in the face of this. Only through a spiritual approach, like the performance of the right yajnas, can such disasters be prevented. Of course, this is also true for terrorist attacks, which are nothing else than a symptom of the decline of our society.

In order to reach a desired balanced state, a firm wish (*sankalpa*) is spoken out in the beginning of the yajna. Then the yajna is performed by one pundit, or by a group of pundits, to create the desired effect. When a yajna is performed for a certain person, it has mostly to do with the improvement of health, relationships or business purposes. In this case the pundit will make use of the Vedic birthchart (kundali) of the person in order to establish the sankalpa. But here again, to reach the right effect it is necessary that the pundit performs the yajna from the silent level of his own awareness. Only from the transcendental level of nature it is possible to reach a certain result in time and space.

In case a yajna is done for a village, city or for the whole world, it is also preceded by a sankalpa. Something similar happened just before the end of the Second World War. Under the inspiration of Maharishi's teacher, *Swami Brahmananda Saraswati* (Guru Dev) a big, collective yajna was performed for world peace. It seems that the yajna has had a very positive influence on the ending of the Second World War. In our time, Maharishi himself gathered groups of pundits in India to guard the world against even more disasters.

Maharishi's Master His Divinity Swami Brahmananda Saraswati (Guru Dev, 1868-1953), Shankaracharya of Jyotir Math, Himalayas (Painting: Christopher Kufner)

In the past, these massive yajnas were performed under the supervision of kings. Everywhere in Vedic literature the ruler is considered to be a representative of God. King Yudhisthira, Parikshit and Shri Rama are considered as most righteous rulers, who administered their country in the name of God and were honoured by their people as divine instruments. The same happened to the Pharaohs in Egypt and to the kings of the Babylonian Empire. In the present era, Kali-yuga, the religious moral of humanity has declined, governments and religions maintain a separate existence. However, nobody can deny that the responsibility for peace, harmony and the prevention of natural catastrophes lies also with the government of a country. Therefore, every government, just like in the times of Vedic civilization, should devote a part of its tax income to the performance of yajnas. This way it is possible to be one step ahead of negative tendencies in the country and possible natural disasters. A utopia? Certainly not. In recent times some countries made use of Vedic rituals, as they are described in Yajurveda and the way Maharishi offered to them. Yajnas are a great gift for a society who chooses to acquire the best for its people, leaving chaos and suffering behind.

VII.5 THE STORY OF DAKSHA

Yajnas have to be performed with the greatest possible precision, otherwise they have no effect or even create an opposite effect. Once upon a time *Daksha*, one of the ten sons of Brahma the creator, wanted to perform a big world yajna. He invited all the demigods and saints to attend the sacrifice. But, because he disliked Shiva, he did not invite him. Shiva, however, was married, also against Daksha's will, to his youngest and beautiful daughter Sati. Although Shiva warned Satī about possible problems, she decided to go to the yajna, because she had not visited her parents for a long time. On arriving home, she noticed that all the demigods were honoured during the yajna, except Shiva. She became terribly angry and decided to jump into the sacrificial fire. When Shiva came to hear of Sati's death, his army, consisting mostly of trolls and other demonic creatures, invaded Daksha's palace and destroyed the yajna. Demigods and saints fled in all directions to avoid Shiva's anger and amidst all the turmoil Daksha's head was cut off. To console his desperate mother-in-law, Shiva decided to give him another head and Daksha got the head of a goat. The desired effect of the yajna, however, was completely annihilated.

This story from the Vedic scriptures shows how important it is to perform the correct rituals, choose the right mantras, and invoke the right Devatas, to get the desired effect of the yajna. Moreover, considerable demands are made on pundits who are responsible for the performance of the yajna, concerning the purity of lifestyle and the quality of consciousness.

VII.6 THE LAST SUKTA OF YAJURVEDA

A special characteristic of the Yajurveda Samhita is that its last paragraph has the character and form of an Upanishad. This construction only occurs in Yajurveda in such an explicit way. Yajurveda mainly contains invocations and rituals, but ending with an Upanishad gives a separate dimension to it. It has been stated earlier that normally the philosophically oriented Upanishads form a part of the Brahmanas. They contain the holy teachings and wisdom of the Absolute (of the Self) as the basis of all existence. The fact that an Upanishad suddenly appears in the Mantra-part of the Yajurveda, refers to the intimate connection between *karma* (action) and *jnana* (knowledge), as explained above. This Upanishad that only consists of seventeen verses, is a jewel in its philosophical way of thinking and profound wisdom.

A number of its verses go as follows:

***

'This whole world, everything that lives and moves on earth, has been produced by the Supreme God. Find joy in letting go of the ephemeral. Do not desire the riches of someone else.'

Only for him who does not focus on the result of his actions, it is good to desire to live a hundred years. It is the only way not to be overshadowed by your actions.

Immovable, the One is faster than the mind. Even the gods are unable to keep up with its speed. Standing still, he overcomes those who run. Life-supporting actions join him for a very long time.

He moves, and still he moves not; he is far and he is near. He is in all this and simultaneously outside all this.

The one who sees all living beings as his own Self, and the Self in all beings, has transcended doubt.

God is brilliant, all pervading, immaterial, invincible, invulnerable, pure and untouchable by evil. He is a wise Being, a seer, omnipresent, self-existent, and has specified in everything how it proceeds till the end of times.

The one who has all knowledge about knowledge and at the same time all knowledge about ignorance, will conquer death by knowledge and reach immortality.

The ones who adhere to ignorance (avidya) fall into blinding darkness, into an even deeper darkness fall those who are proud of the knowledge they possess.

Oh God, lead us on the straight path to riches and prosperity; oh God you know all our deeds. Take away our sins that are leading us astray. We will honour you abundantly and with all devotion.

Truth is hidden from view by a golden goblet. The Self is far away like the Sun, but It is also here. It is myself! AUM!

***

Like everyone can notice, this Upanishad contains beautiful universal truths in a nutshell. It is like a golden crown, wherewith Yajurveda throws a bridge to Atharvaveda, which has, at first sight, an earthlier character.

Yajurveda indicates the synthesis existing between the necessity of action and the fulfilment of someone's duty based on selfless desire. Therewith it states that the performance of yajnas for the well-being of man and the whole world is an evolutionary action supported by nature.

One could also say that the positive effect of a yajna is reaped by the one who deserves it, from the viewpoint of divine Grace. Somebody's actions, just like someone's thoughts, have an infinite reach, influencing all levels of life. By performing positive, life-supporting actions, the impulses of creative intelligence in the universe are favourably influenced and a reciprocal harmony with the powers of nature is created. In this state, every activity is offered as a sacrifice to God, a state in which every action becomes a yajna and through which one can become *free* of all limiting influences of relative life.

VII.7 RELATIONSHIP WITH BHAGAVAD GITA

Chapter III of Bhagavad Gita deals with *Karma-Yoga*, the performance of action and its results. In chapter III, 9-15 Lord Krishna explains the concept of yajna where He says:

* * *

'Except for actions performed for the purpose of yajna, this world is caught in the web of action. For the sake of yajna, you should perform actions devoid of attachment.' (verse 9)

'Through yajna you support the gods, and those gods will support you. By supporting each other, you will reach the highest goal.' (verse 11)

'From food, creatures are born, from rain, food is created; from yajna, rain is produced and yajna is born from action.' (verse 14)

'Know that action is born from Brahman (the Veda). Brahman originates in the Imperishable. Therefore, the all-pervading Brahman is ever established in yajna.' (verse 15)

* * *

Here Lord Krishna considers yajna not only a ceremonial act, but any way of life or activity that fosters evolution. The yajna or action should be seen as a means to come into contact with the higher planes of existence by propitiating the forces of nature. By offering all our actions to a higher purpose (to serve the Divine), we will automatically enter into harmony with the flow of evolution. At a certain moment, a situation will develop, in which every action is a yajna. Because every action is followed by a similar reaction, we naturally gain the blessings of the forces of nature or Devatas. In this way, we grow towards a state of higher consciousness, in which we are totally free of any limitation and in which we abstain from any damaging actions. Only when more people start experiencing a higher consciousness, it is possible that nature starts reacting in a harmonious manner, like it used to be in the times of the Vedic Civilization; the sun shines in time, rains fall in time, harvest occurs at the right moment and seasons come in time. The whole process can be reinforced by the performance of Vedic rituals, because also through this way the favour of the natural forces can be gained and an influence of harmony and peace can be generated. We can find all knowledge in the Vedas about action, cause and effect, as well as the source of all action: the Supreme Being or Brahman.

VII.8 UPANISHADS OF YAJURVEDA

There are four important Upanishads belonging to Yajurveda: the

Brihadaranyaka Upanishad, the Isha Upanishad, the Katha Upanishad and the Taittiriya Upanishad.

The Brihadaranyaka Upanishad

The Brihadaranyaka Upanishad consists of six chapters, that contain many famous and profound passages. In the first two sections of chapter I, different manifestations and phenomena of the universe are compared to different parts and behaviour of a horse. The famous *Ashvamedha yajna* (yajna of the horse) features here as well, but more as an illustration of the process of creation. In section three, the demigods ask the sense organs of speech, smell, sight, hearing and mind to recite the *Udgitha* (see chapter VI) and one after the other they did. However, the demons (*Asuras*) intervened continuously, with the result that the reciting was spoiled. The lesson from this is that even when we try to do our best, we always violate, for one reason or the other, all kinds of natural laws. Next, the gods ask Prana – life energy – to recite the Udgitha and again the demons try to disturb. This time, however, they are destroyed completely. This indicates that Prana, the life force at the basis of the senses, cannot be impaired by any evil. That is why Prana is needed to enliven the senses in order for them to function harmoniously. By reciting the Udgitha, Prana nourishes itself and is simultaneously able to bring the senses to a higher plane of functioning, and even beyond that.

The last verse of section three contains the famous mantra that is recited at the beginning of a yajna, but today often at the start of a satsang, too, by the 'offerers'.

***

AUM asato ma Sad gamaya
tamaso ma Jyotir gamaya
mrityor ma Amritam gamaya

> *(Oh Lord,)*
> *From untruth lead me to Truth*
> *From darkness lead me to Light*
> *From death lead me to Immortality*

***

The theme of chapter one, section four, of this Upanishad is: I am Brahman, *Aham Brahmasmi*. This is one of the four great sayings – Mahavakyas – of the Upanishads. Also, a version of the process of creation is given: in the beginning there was only the Self, called *Viraj*, a cosmic Being none other than Purusha, the cosmic Soul. The word *'I'* emerged the moment the Self became conscious of himself. Purusha, who was alone, created out of Himself the male and female principle. The desire to procreate became thereby a universal characteristic of all living beings. Because Purusha entered his own universe, everything actually is Purusha. Like the food we eat every day and the energy withdrawn from it, which is keeping us alive.

***

> *Soma is the food, and fire is the eater of the food.*
> - **Brihadaranyaka Upanishad I.4.6**

***

Soma is the most subtle substance of the universe at the junction point of spirit and matter, and fire (agni) is the digestive process that transforms the food into a very refined quality called *ojas*. Ojas is the basic substance for the male seed, that is used for new life. The word food has a universal meaning in the Upanishads, namely all input needed to continue life on an individual, as well as on a cosmic level. Even if we are not able to perceive that all in the universe is pervaded by Purusha, our own Self is

Purusha, also. This is what is meant by *Aham Brahmasmi*, I am part of the Totality, of the Supreme Being. The one who undergoes this reality in his consciousness experiences the whole universe on the level of his own self. In order to make effort to end the cycle of birth and death, through spiritual discipline we can realise the permanent experience of the Self in this life (I.4.10).

The number three is holy in the Vedas. There are three worlds, speech is the lower world (Earth); mind is the middle world (space in between); and life breath is the higher world (heaven). Speech is Rigveda, mind is Yajurveda, and breath is Samaveda (I.5.4-5). Both our organs of perception (*jnana indriyas*) and our organs of action (*karma indriyas*) are, concerning their function, all dependent on Prana, the life breath. Prana is fundamental for all levels and lies even at the basis of mind and energy. It is unchangeable, eternal, and although invisible, it supports all bodily functions (I.5.21-23).

In the context of this book it is impossible to discuss the whole Brihadaranyaka Upanishad in its entirety, but its content is of an unimaginable beauty and profundity. Famous, for instance, is the story of king *Janaka* of Videha who ordered the performance of a sacrificial ritual, which was attended by all sages and saints from those days. Janaka, who was a very wise king, wanted to know who, of all Brahmins present, would be the most learned in the ancient scriptures and he offered a thousand cows for the winner.

Janaka told the Brahmins: 'Let the wisest of you take these cows.' Nobody of the assembled sages dared to demand the cows for himself, until the wise *Yajnavalkya* asked one of his students to lead the cows away.

The other Brahmins became furious and asked: 'How can he proclaim himself to be the wisest among us?'

The sages decided to question *Yajnavalkya* about his wisdom and one after the other fired penetrating questions unto him.

After he had answered several questions correctly, the sage *Vidagdha Shakalya* asked him: '*How many gods are there, Yajnavalkya?*' Yajnavalkya answered that there are 303 and 3003 gods, of which 33 are the most important. But ultimately, he declared, there is only one Supreme God.

The 33 gods are the eight *Vasus* (like fire, earth, space, Sun, heaven, Moon and stars), the eleven *Rudras* (the ten senses and the mind), and the twelve *Adityas* (the twelve months of the year) together with Indra (wholeness) and Prajapati (the Creator). The cosmic life principle, Prana, is the breath of God. Prana is Brahman. The dialogue between Shakalya and Yajnavalkya teaches us that the Vedic sages had only one God in mind, but saw all forces in the universe as divine manifestations of the One. Finally, the sages had to admit that nobody among them had been able to answer all the questions as correctly as Yajnavalkya, so he was allowed to keep the thousand cows.

Chapter six of the Brihadaranyaka Upanishad gives an explanation of the universal value of the sacrificial rites. The essence of section two of this chapter is that the whole creation can be compared to a sacrifice (yajna). For a sacrifice, fire is needed to illuminate it and a gift or offering to be sacrificed into the fire. Every action we perform is like a sacrifice. It creates a subtle vibration, which after some time transforms into a material form, just like the effect of a yajna. Moreover, everything in the universe is connected to each other. This is also true for sacrifices, in which materials like fire, firewood and sacrificial offerings together bring forth the result. Furthermore, the universe is created in such a way that the fruits of a sacrifice give rise to the offering of a next sacrifice and the same is true for our own actions. When at the start of creation the first cosmic phenomena are offered into the fire, Soma is produced.

From Soma, rain is produced, from rain, food is produced, from food, seed is generated, and from seed, a new human child is born. All these sequential steps in the process are like offerings that are deposited into the fire, and transformed by the fire. Like this, the procreative act can be seen as a spiritual performance with the purpose of creating good offspring.

When a man dies, the last sacrifice is the offering of the dead body into the fire of cremation (VI.2.14). Depending on his deeds in this world, the subtle body can follow two paths after death – *devayana* or *pitriyana*. *Devayana* is the northern path of the light, leading to the Sun and from there to the abode of Brahma (Brahma loka). This is symbolic for the state of spiritual liberation after death. *Pitriyana* is the southern path of smoke and darkness. It symbolises ignorance. This path does not continue further than the Moon, the abode of the ancestors (Pitri loka) and from there, returns back to Earth to be born again (VI.2.15-16).

The Isha Upanishad
The Isha Upanishad, also connected to Yajurveda, consists of only 18 verses, which have yet great practical value. This Upanishad emphasizes the unity of God with the universe; the universe is permeated by Brahman. This is what the invocation at the start of this and several other Upanishads wants to emphasize:

***

AUM Purnamadah purnamidam
Purnat purnamudachyate
purnasya purnamadaya
purnamevavashishyate

AUM, That is Perfect, This is Perfect.
From the Perfect springs the Perfect.

If the Perfect is taken from the Perfect,
The Perfect remains.

***

Adah is That: the ultimate reality, the Absolute, universal consciousness, Brahman. Idam is this: the universe, the material world, the expression of Brahman. Purna is perfect: complete, accomplished, all, everything that exists. Generally speaking, when from a seed a tree appears, the seed disappears. This is not so in the case of Brahman. Even when the whole universe springs from Him, Brahman remains unchanged. Brahman minus the whole universe is still Brahman. Brahman pervades the universe as *Viraj Purusha*, the cosmic Soul. In men, He manifests as *Jivatman*, the individual Self. When we become aware that everything, including ourselves, is pervaded by the Divine, our perspective on life will broaden from self-interest to service to God. This is what is meant by yajna. In these days all emphasis is put on work in society, as if it was the most important yajna, but the Isha Upanishad makes it clear to us that work and the development of wisdom are both valuable for life. Work leads to restlessness, while wisdom, which grows through meditation, leads to inner peace. In life we have to try to keep these two in balance and restrain ourselves of too much activity.

Shri Aurobindo says about this: The material vision on life is that the world consists of infinite self-sufficient beings, all trying to get the best for themselves. The spiritual vision is that the world consists of an infinite amount of beings supporting each other and feeling nourished and enriched by service to the Supreme Being.

The last three verses of the Isha Upanishad are a dramatic ode and appeal to the light of life (the Self), the Life principle (Vayu) and the fire of Life (Agni), to gain spiritual freedom.

***

*Oh Pushan, the Sun, the Nourisher, the only Seer, oh guardian of all,
Surya, son of Prajapati! Spread your rays and gather your radiant light,
so that I may see your brilliant form. Whoever is this Being (Purusha),
I am that also.*

*May this life unite with the all-pervading Life principle, may this body
burn to ashes. Oh Spirit, remember, remember Your deeds, remember,
remember Your deeds.*

*Oh Agni, (Fire)! Lead us to riches along a virtuous path.
Oh God, You know all our deeds. Remove all our sins and illusions.
For Thee we bow down in reverence, to the Self in all.*
- **Isha Upanishad, vs. 16-18**

***

Surya, the Sun, represents the Self, the divine light of consciousness. Agni represents the divine power or energy of consciousness and, according to Shri Aurobindo, this is our willpower. The invocation of Agni makes the invocation of Surya complete. Light and Will spring forth from the Life principle (Vayu). Vayu symbolises here the universal Prana or life force. The qualities of the Vedic demigods are analogous with our own instruments of life, body, actions and will power. Our body, however, is of an ephemeral nature. It is an instrument for growth in consciousness and the one who walks the spiritual path should not identify with it.

The Katha Upanishad
Katha means: story. The Katha Upanishad is the story of Nachiketa, a thirteen-year-old boy, who questions his father in a respectful manner about the use of traditional rituals and so-called charity.

His father, Vajashrava, reacts very irritated and shouts: 'I will give you away to Yama.' Nachiketa takes these words literally, and departs to the other world to encounter the god of death. Nachiketa is full of love and sees his visit to the hereafter as an event with a deeper meaning. Because he undergoes everything in such a loving, wise and patient manner, he may ask Yama three questions. First Nachiketa asks forgiveness for his father and that he will not be angry with him, when he returns to the world of the living. Next, he asks to know everything about the meaning of a certain ritual, a fire sacrifice, which helps people go to the heavens. Yama rejoices in fulfilling these desires. But as a third favour, Nachiketa wants to know exactly what happens after death. Where do the people go and what do they have to do for it? Yama is very reluctant to answer these questions and finds all kinds of excuses to evade the answer. But Nachiketa persists and wants to know the truth. Impressed by the power and wisdom of the teenager, Yama delivers in a beautiful dialogue the secrets of death.

***

'The man who has a discriminating intellect has the charioteer as his driver, a disciplined mind as the reins, he will reach the end of the voyage, the supreme abode of That which pervades everything.'
- Katha Upanishad I.3.9

***

The Katha Upanishad consists of two chapters and is a jewel of wisdom of the highest order. Western commentators have described it as a perfect mix of myth, wisdom and poetry of ancient India.

Vajashravas means: he who performs charity by distributing food. Nachiketa means: he who does not know, but is searching to know.

Nachiketa's father was an old-fashioned man. He carried out traditional sacrifices hoping to get to heaven. He relinquished all his possessions for it. The young, but wise Nachiketa realised the absurdity of his father's intentions.

He told his father: 'It is completely absurd to give away your cows. With this you cannot go to heaven. If you have sworn to give away everything, you have to give me away as well.' The fact that Nachiketa's father became angry so quickly, indicates that he had not possessed the proper intention while performing the sacrifice. During a sacrifice one should always be calm and cheerful and free from ego.

At the end of chapter two, it is described when and how one, when going over to the other world, does not reincarnate again. This has to do with the way the soul leaves the body. The soul is of the size of a thumb and is located in the hollowness of the heart. If the soul, at the moment of death, travels through the *sushumna* (the central channel through which the kundalini flows) and then leaves the body through the crown chakra, one reaches immortality and does not return to Earth. If the soul leaves the body in a different way, one does return.

***

> *'The heart has hundred and one nerve channels. One of them (the sushumna) leads to the crown of the head. When the soul goes upward through this nerve channel, one reaches immortality. If the soul departs through one of the other channels, it leads to one of the other worlds.'*
> **- Katha Upanishad II.3.6**

***

This is clearly reminiscent of the pharaohs in Egypt and other old civilizations, where everything was done in order to let the soul depart through the crown chakra. But anyhow, surely when the moment has arrived to depart to the other world, knowledge of the Katha Upanishad serves as food for the soul. It is therefore that this Upanishad is often read to people who are in their transition phase.

The Taittiriya Upanishad

How to know yourself is the central theme of the Taittiriya Upanishad, which consists of three chapters and is connected to Yajurveda, as well. The Self can only be known if we live a virtuous and disciplined life. Therefore, this Upanishad delves deeply into the essence and principles of a good way of life (see also chapter XVIII).

Meditation practice is important to purify the mind. Successful meditation leads to a happy family life, material well-being and spiritual wisdom. When we meditate on the primordial sound AUM, the symbol of Brahman, we gain an increase of intelligence, wisdom, energy, soft speech, good hearing and strong memory. The ultimate goal is to achieve the state of immortality (spiritual liberation). The role of the teacher thereby is important, that is why the teacher pronounces the wish:

***

'May students from far away flock to me
from different directions. Svaha.
May they come in great numbers. Svaha.
May they be disciplined and peaceful. Svaha.'

***

The teacher ends with the words: 'May many disciplined students come to me from all directions, like water streams downward and months go by and together form a year.' The word *Svaha* is used during the ahuti (offering in the fire) and means hail or in a more elaborate sense *this is with the most sincerity and truth from the heart* We can compare it to our word Amen (or in the Koran with: Amin), that itself is related to AUM.

In section five of chapter one, four mystical words are mentioned and explained, namely Bhur, Bhuvah, Suvah and Maha. They each have a number of meanings on different levels of existence and consciousness (see scheme 7.1).

Scheme 7.1
The Four Vyahrtis (mystical words) and their Meanings

VYAHRTI	VEDA	COSMOS	ELEMENT	BREATH
BHUR	Rig	Material	Fire	Prana
BHUVAH	Sama	Space in between	Air	Apana
SUVAH	Yajur	Higher spheres	Sun	Vyana
MAHA(N)	Atharva	Brahman	Moon	Food

(Source: Ten Upanishads of Four Vedas)
Scheme 7.1 Usually the four vyahrtis are associated with the earth
(the material world), the air (ether), the sky (higher spheres) and
Brahman. They are used in several yajnas and are also known to us from
the Gayatri mantra. Mahan is Brahman, or from the subjective angle the
Supreme Being, that which supports everything. Concerning the breath,
we know that all vital aspects of the breath are supported by food.

When we meditate on these key words at the moment of departing this world, our soul will leave the body via the sushumna. We then gain mastery over our sight, hearing, speech and mind. Thereafter we will enter the field of the divine Being, of immortality. Knowledge about and insight into Brahman is only one step on the path to Self-realisation. Self-realisation means that we rise beyond the duality of subject and object; then we are in a higher state of consciousness. In that state we become as Brahman – immortal, indestructible and immutable.

A beloved theme in the Upanishads is that the knower of Brahman attains the highest. But what does the knower of Brahman exactly achieve? And how can a man identify himself with Brahman? These are important themes in the rest of the Taittiriya Upanishad. It indicates that insight in and experience of Brahman is a step by step process and that it is a path that we have to travel alone. A good guide, however, can support us thereby.

There is a nice story of a young student, Bhrigu, and his wise father Varuna on this. When Bhrigu asks his father to reveal to him the secret of Brahman, his father says:

* Meditate on the first three levels of your personality – physical, vital and mental – which are doorways to the knowledge about Brahman;

* Meditate on Brahman (God) as the source of all creation, maintenance and destruction.

Bhrigu starts his investigation and meditates upon the five levels of human existence. These are:

Physical   - *Annamaya*
Vital   - *Pranamaya*
Mental   - *Manomaya*
Spiritual   - *Vigyanamaya*
Being   - *Anandamaya*

Each of these levels of the personality is permeated by the previous level. Furthermore, every level is more subtle than the previous one, whereby the physical body is the grossest level. The body is totally permeated by Being, that can express itself in different ways in our body, for instance as love, joy or happiness. The more we can release our attachment to sense objects, the more our general feeling of happiness will increase. The first three levels (Annamaya, Pranamaya and Manomaya) we can consider as instruments of observation, while Vigyanamaya and Anandamaya together form the individual soul, as the knower and observer. Every time Bhrigu meditated on one of these levels, his father sent him back, until Bhrigu experienced that Brahman is pure Bliss (Anandamaya). Only then he did not return to his father, because at that moment all doubt in him got resolved. Bhrigu became later one of the most famous Rishis who have ever lived.

Brahman is present in everything – in all organs of the body, in our consciousness as Atman and in the rest of the universe. In chapter III.10.2-3, it is said that we become that, on which we meditate. We become that, of which we think intensely, or on which we concentrate deeply. When we meditate with great passion on Brahman, we will become Brahman. He who experiences that, lives in the material world, but is not of this world. He is the knower of Brahman who sings this Sama song:

***

'So beautiful! So beautiful!
I am food, I am food.
I am the eater, I am the eater, I am the eater.
I unite, I unite, I unite.
I am the first born of this cosmic order.
I existed already before the gods did.
I am the centre of immortality.
He alone bestows on me liberation.
I, being food myself, eat the eater of food.
I have conquered the whole world.
I am radiant like the Sun.'
– Taittiriya Upanishad III.10.5

***

135

In summary: This song gives the essence of the philosophy of the Upanishads about the range of human existence. It expresses that the enlightened soul has become one with everything. He is the food, the eater of the food and the principle that unites both. He goes beyond the world of limitations and ascends the quality of the Divine. He experiences this as serving God in all his Fullness. In this way the enlightened spirit, filled with bliss and full of divine Light, gains mastery over existence.

VII.9 UPAVEDA OF YAJURVEDA

The Upaveda of the Yajurveda is the *Dhanurveda*. Dhanur means bow. When we study the Dhanurveda texts, it seems to deal especially with warfare. It contains strict rules for the waging of wars and even for the use of very modern weapons, like missiles. But all these means were allowed exclusively for the destruction of evil and the protection of the weak in society, like saints, alms begging monks, women and children. In that context, Dhanurveda could be in fact quite relevant. Just like Yajurveda, Dhanurveda, too, is all about the process, the devata-aspect of consciousness. The goal of Dhanurveda is to maintain and restore purity in the whole field of activity. This means that first all stress and imbalances in the mind and body should be resolved. Metaphorically speaking, it is all about how one deals with things in all kind of different situations. The art of archery aims to conquer evil in men. Thus, balance can be restored in the field of action. When we are going to battle in life, we will meet all kind of dilemmas, often without the hope to end them. How do we handle things? How do we learn to have respect for our spouse, our fellow people, the earth and the animal and plant kingdoms? Are we aware of our fears? Can we see our enemies as friends? What does it mean to be unprejudiced?

These are very timely themes, which are of the greatest importance in our practical, daily life. Like every part of the Vedas, the Upanishads are also complete in themselves, and offer all knowledge within their specific scope. The aim of Dhanurveda is to promote the health and well-being of every 'warrior' and to create a state of complete harmony of mind, body, behaviour and environment.

VII.10 RELATIONSHIP WITH OUR BODY

One will not be surprised to hear that Yajurveda, in relation to the human body, represents the totality of transformations and transforming processes in the body. This pertains to the connection between the inner processes and the external world. Earlier we saw that Yajurveda is divided into two categories: *Shukla* (white) and *Krishna* (black). According to the author of *Human Physiology /Expression of Veda and the Vedic Literature*, the Shukla Yajurveda is connected to the human nervous system and the Krishna Yajurveda to the autonomic nerve plexuses, lying next to the vertebral column. The difference between the white and black Yajurveda, physiologically speaking, would be on the one side connected to processes in the body that we can consciously guide (white), and on the other side, to autonomic processes that we cannot consciously influence (black).

The area in the body corresponding to Yajurveda, concerns all aspects of the metabolism, not only the digestion of food, but the area of human experience as well. This is a matter of how we perceive and experience things. Hearing and seeing, for instance, can be considered as processes, whereby sound and light are transformed into a specific experience. They are like the *ghee* (clarified butter) that is poured into the sacrificial fire. The fire digests the object sacrificed and transforms it into a certain result. Every sensory experience can be considered to be a sacrifice which is transformed within the body into a certain experience. We can state that the quality and effect of a yajna is directly related to the *intention* of the sacrificer. Although the quality of the ghee offered into the fire could be the same, every yajna has a specific intention (*Sankalpa*) that leads to a certain result. In the same way, according to Dr. Tony Nader, the same impressions from outside can cause different reactions, depending on someone's judgement and purpose. For instance, when two people look at the same rose, one could intensely enjoy the colour, while the other is enormously irritated by the thorns. For some people, their boss is a friend, for others the same boss is an enemy. So, people (and also belief systems or nations) can have totally different reactions to the same situation or, in the terms of Yajurveda, can result in different effects of the sacrifice.

Dhanurveda, representing the quality of *invincibility* in our body, is connected to everything that maintains the continuity in the area of change and evolution. This principle can be found in the DNA, the biochemical and enzyme reactions, the immune system and the skeleton. The word *dhanur*, meaning bow, corresponds to the vertebral column, which somehow has the form of a bow, according to Dr. Nader.

CHAPTER VIII

ATHARVAVEDA: WHOLENESS IN DIVERSITY

*'The noble souls who practice meditation and
treat all beings with care, they protect all animals
and also take care of our spiritual growth.
They always take care that our behaviour
does not harm any animal.'*

- Atharvaveda XIX.28.5

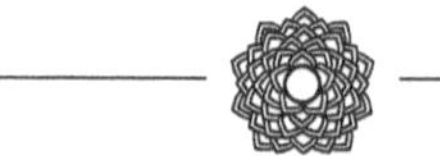

In Sat-yuga, the (unwritten) Rigveda Samhita was the foundation of
life. After the wholeness of life got gradually lost, the other Vedas arose
as light beacons of wisdom. Atharvaveda represents the Chhandas
aspect of the Veda. *Chhandas* means: structure, result, the outer world.
Atharvaveda therefore, at first sight, deals with more material things like
daily duties, the use of medicines, and lots of directions to lead humanity
back towards its divine origin. Furthermore, Atharvaveda is concerned
with the environment, like the quality of the earth, the behaviour of the
people and the non-killing of animals. The above quotation shows that

the taking care and feeding of animals is being described as a spiritual act.

VIII.1 ORIGIN AND CONTENT

It is said that originally there were only three Vedas. Atharvaveda would have been added in a later period. Maybe every *Yuga* knows its own predominating Veda. Anyway, some hymns of Atharvaveda are already very old and date from ancient times. It could very well be that just a number of hymns have become part of Atharvaveda at a much later time, for a significant part is based on the hymns of Rigveda. This viewpoint certainly fits into the concept of the wholeness of knower, process of knowing and known, of which Atharvaveda represents the last element – the known. We can compare this to Brahma, the creator, who has four heads, and of which only three are visible. The fourth head is hidden, probably because it represents Maya – the world of illusion. Reviews on the Vedas often speak first about the *Trayi-Vidya* (threefold wisdom) and only thereafter is Atharvaveda mentioned, or even just negated. This is no evil intent, but fits into the structure of the Samhita. Furthermore, there is no conflict or contradiction whatsoever between the first three Vedas and the Atharvaveda Samhita. They represent different aspects of the same universal knowledge. While the three Vedas are primarily concerned with the higher world of the Devatas and the evolution of mankind, the texts of Atharvaveda are more directed towards daily life and functioning in this world. They deal with the day-to-day problems of people, how to protect against enemies or diseases, political matters and general well-being.

Next to religious tolerance, Atharvaveda pleads for the maintenance of and care for the natural environment. In Eastern countries, there is often a much deeper bond with nature. Rivers, animals, trees, crops and the earth itself are often considered holy. The Veda says: '*Svasti gobhyo jagate purushebhyah*' – 'May all men, animals and birds be blessed with harmony and happiness'. The modern vision on ecology is completely in harmony with these Vedic values. Universal principles and directions about architecture, urban development, and lay-out of the natural environment are worked out practically in *Sthapatyaveda* (see hereafter), the Upaveda of Atharvaveda.

Other parts of the Vedic literature, like the Brahmanas (laws of nature), Jyotish (astrology), Samkhya (investigation of the objective world), Smritis (behaviour) and Vedanta (integrated wholeness), are very much connected to and inspired by the knowledge of Atharvaveda.

VIII.2 PARASHIVA, PARASHAKTI AND PARAMESHVARA

Because of the many philosophical hymns that, whether implicitly or explicitly, deal with the Absolute, or *Brahman*, Atharvaveda is also called *Brahmaveda*. Also, hereby, Atharvaveda rises above the discussion of everyday human problems and contains many indications for achieving a high standard of living. The knowers of Brahman experience that they are spiritual souls, dwelling temporarily in a physical body. Death does not exist anymore to them, because relative existence has risen to an absolute reality. They know that the Absolute, or the Self is omniscient, content, self-referral, timeless, immortal and free of desire and they experience these qualities in themselves.

***

Self-perpetuating, formless, without source and pure,
that all-embracing Being is within us as well as without us.

It even goes beyond the transcendence, the non-manifest,
causal state of the universe.

– Atharvaveda, Mundaka Upanishad 2.1.2

***

Although the Absolute is one and indivisible, for a better understanding, we can split it up into three aspects: Parashiva, Parashakti and Parameshvara.

Parashiva is the aspect of absolute reality, that is timeless and formless. The symbol of this aspect is the Shiva lingam, a phallus-like object that is worshipped in whole India as the expression of the Absolute; eternal and indivisible. One honours the lingam by giving it a ritual bath. While mantras are recited, milk, honey or some other pleasant-smelling liquid is poured over the lingam. When the devotee does this with great devotion, he will surely receive the favour and blessing of God.

The second expression of the Absolute is *Parashakti*, the aspect of omnipresence, that can be traced back at every point or every phenomenon of the universe. When we speak of Parashakti, we mean the divine energy by which the whole universe exists. Consciousness becomes energy and energy precipitates as matter. But even in its physical form, it remains the omnipresent, universal energy. In ourselves, this universal energy manifests itself as *Kundalini Shakti*, which we can awaken with the help of the *Sadguru*.

The third characteristic of the Absolute is *Parameshvara*, the Primordial Soul, the Supreme Lord and Administrator of all three worlds, who is transcendental by nature. Parameshvara is the personal aspect of God, to whom we can pray and surrender. In many Vedic scriptures He is addressed as Lord Krishna.

The performance of a yajna or puja, the chanting of bhajans, prayer, or the practice of yoga and meditation are the means to honour and enliven these three aspects of the Absolute. One characteristic of Parameshvara is, that it makes personal communication with the Supreme Divine possible through complete devotion and service (bhakti-yoga). We are also free to choose our own Ishta Devata, the divine aspect of creative intelligence that appeals to us the most. Like this, all throughout the ages there have been worshippers of Lord Krishna, Shri Rama, Lord Shiva, Devi Mata, Hanuman and Ganesha in Hinduism. This shows the flexibility of Hinduism. It expresses that we can be devoted to our Ishta Devata completely and without restrictions, because the Absolute can be found in every impulse of creative intelligence.

VIII.3 CHARACTER AND DIVISION

About one seventh part of Atharvaveda is inspired by or taken from Rigveda. It contains a mixture of prose and poetry. The metre in Atharvaveda is irregular and deviates from the mantras that are taken from Rigveda. The first thirteen chapters or books (*khandas*) contain mainly poetic hymns characteristic of Atharvaveda, while chapters fifteen and sixteen, probably added later, consist of mainly prose. Chapters thirteen – eighteen each deal with a specific subject. The deliberations about the Absolute belong to the last chapters of Atharvaveda. The texts of this part are mainly inspired by the *Atharvans*, a class of exceptionally learned Vedic priests, who were probably the firsts to introduce the *Fire sacrifice* and the *Soma sacrifice*. The wise *Atharva* was the son of *Maharishi Bhrigu* and Bhrigu was the son of Brahma himself, the creator of the material world. Atharva had twenty sons, and it is said that for this reason is the Atharvaveda divided into twenty chapters or khandas, containing in total about six thousand hymns. The last chapter is probably added later and consists mainly of hymns that we also find back in Rigveda. The connection with the yajnas is missing in Atharvaveda.

The Atharvans, also called the Angiras, have been the producers of the Atharvaveda Samhita. They were known as fire worshippers and were the earliest pioneers of the later Vedanta teaching. There is a remarkable correspondence with the Avesta, the religious scripture of the ancient Persians, who also knew the Atharvans and were also known to be fire worshippers. Apart from being priests, the Atharvans dealtwith magic, comparable, more or less, to the practices of the North Asian shamans and Native American medicine men. One is not amazed, therefore, that Atharvaveda is connected to the Tantra philosophy. Closely connected to this are the passages that deal with the use of magic means, incantations, spells, amulets and herbs, to dissolve diseases and expel evil spirits. Furthermore, we find passages on the anointing of kings, political matters and the protocols around marriages and funerals. The compositions of some of the magic songs are of an exceptionally high level. It is not exaggerating to state that Atharvaveda contains a rich heritage of worldly, spiritual, philosophical and intellectual aspects of a very ancient culture. It offers insight into the highest measure of morality, virtue and attention to the (arrangement of the) environment. It holds a warm plea for the everlasting peace among the family of nations. But in the Vedas, no efforts are made to convince others to adopt the same religious traditions and insights. The original Vedic thought is *sarva dharma samabhava* – equal respect for all religions. Hinduism, Buddhism, Jainism and Sikhism originated directly from the ancient Vedic tradition and are equally respected. This, among others, is shown by the remarkable fact that Buddha, the founder of Buddhism, is considered by Hinduism as the eight incarnation of Lord Vishnu, the maintainer of the universe.

With all this, we should not lose sight of the fact that the four Vedas represent in essence the laws of nature (or subjectively speaking, the laws of consciousness) in a logical sequence and each from its own viewpoint. We should, therefore, not only go by the meaning value of the texts, but also take into account all the facets that have played a role in their creation and development. Atharvaveda represents *the known*, the relative existence. It applies for Atharvaveda also, that its hymns are not the product of the human intellect, but are the revelations of the Divine and, in extension thereof, the evolution of man. With the help of the refined faculty of perception of the ancient seers, the hymns are cognized on the level of pure consciousness, within the structure of the Self. It is therefore valid to say that the hymns of Atharvaveda reflect the *structure* of the Self. The manifested universe, the planet Earth, the human body and the human cell are familiar structures to us for the expression of creative intelligence. As no one else, the great sage *Maharishi Mahesh Yogi* has shown, together with his scientists, that the Veda is fully expressed in all the above-mentioned structures. The theme of Atharvaveda is, that it is very detailed, but at the same time also infinite in its range, moreover, that both extremes fit together perfectly. In summary: as above, so below; macrocosm is microcosm; bigger than the biggest and smaller than the smallest.

VIII.4 VEDANTA

Concerning the relationship with Vedanta, Atharvaveda investigates the concept of the Absolute deeper than any of the other Vedas. Only for this reason it already deserves our full respect. The word Vedanta means: *end of the Veda*. Vedanta is the fulfilment of everything and its teachings are directly inspired by the wisdom of Atharvaveda. It is a very elevated philosophy, the crowning glory of the wisdom of the Vedas. Its subject is the ultimate experience of wholeness within all diversity. The one who is able to integrate, on the level of his own experience, this philosophy which, at the same time, is a science, is a privileged human soul.

***

Vedanta vakyeshu sada ramanta khalu bhagyavanta

The one who is permanently immersed in
Vedanta is an extraordinarily fortunate man.

***

The Vedanta sutras are of the same divine quality as the Vedic hymns. They state that the whole manifest and non-manifest creation is *Brahman*, absolute, infinite and without origin. This is the only ultimate truth. In essence, the goal and doctrine of Vedanta is the complete eradication of all pain and suffering and the permanent acquisition of bliss. The root of all pain is ignorance, when we are separated from the Self. Self-inquiry is, therefore, a first prerequisite to undertake the spiritual journey from ignorance to liberation. We can ask ourselves: who am I; what is the reason and goal of my existence; who has created this universe; wherein lies the cause of material existence? If we only study the world outside us, we are put on the wrong track. The ultimate answers to all these questions we can only find in ourselves. In reality, the existence of the world is an inner experience on the level of our consciousness. Every experience of the external world takes place in our inner world.

Well-known is the story of the snake and the string. We think we see a snake lying on the floor and are very afraid, but after due investigation, it appears to be only a piece of rope. The snake appeared in our mind and seemed to be real but, after looking more closely, we realise there was no snake at all. It was an optical illusion, an illusion on the side of the observer. In the same way, we see ghosts everywhere on our life path, which in reality are not there at all. Nevertheless, they give us a lot of sorrow and pain. This is what is called ignorance. In reality only Brahman exists, that has the qualities of *sat-chit-ananda* – existence (truth), consciousness and bliss.

***

Sarvam khalvidam Brahma

Everything is Brahman (Vedanta)

***

All pain, disappointment, jealousy, dissatisfaction and enmity spring from ignorance, and can only be eliminated by the acquisition of pure knowledge and correct insight. The teaching of Vedanta implies that retrospectively it will seem as if in fact all pain and suffering had never existed. The piece of rope appeared to be a snake. Ignorance only existed in our imagination, we did mistakenly create it, it is not the ultimate reality of existence. The Absolute, or within ourselves, the higher Self, is not something we have to acquire, it is always there and it has always been there. Certainly, a snake has never existed in the piece of the rope. Nevertheless, we have been very afraid of something that was not there at all! It is a matter of viewpoint. We only have to change our point of view, through our insight into the nature of existence. That process takes place through *inner* transformation from ignorance to wisdom, from darkness to light.

Brahman is in everything, and everything is an expression of consciousness, pure awareness. Just as a piece of cloth is woven from thread, water consists of liquid, and gold always remains gold in every ornament made out of it, in the same way the whole universe is permeated with Brahman. In the manifest world Brahman appears as the mind, the senses, the *gunas* and other phenomena, but all these expressions of the manifest world are *not* Brahman. Brahman itself is formless and infinite. How can the Infinite become finite? It is an illusion.

How can we rise above the experience of this illusion? Atharvaveda says: 'A strong desire is already enough to experience the bliss of Brahman'. Step by step, we are also going to perceive Brahman in the world around us. When we start to see It in all beings and experience It in all parts of the manifest creation, we will be fully liberated, fully detached, fully wise, fully enlightened. Nothing will be able to lead us astray. Everything is perfect. *Purnamadah Purnamidam.* This is the most elevated state of human experience. This is the golden crown on perennial existence, the *end* of our study of the Veda.

VIII.5 RELATIONSHIP WITH BHAGAVAD GITA

Atharvaveda is the Samhita of the *Chhandas-aspect* of consciousness. Chhandas means: structure, metre, relative, the known, the field of action, the objective world. In Bhagavad-gita, Lord Krishna takes his disciple Arjuna by the hand and teaches him how to act in this world. In relative existence, we develop all kinds of relations with different levels of life: the world of the demigods, the planets, nature, men, animals, plants and minerals. They all are expressions of the One, the indivisible. In the world of man everyone plays his or her role of grandparent, uncle or aunt, son or daughter, et cetera. But in reality, they are all different expressions of the higher Self. The Vedas are the scriptures that indicate how we should deal with all these relations and our own role therein. In Part II, we will also discuss this matter.

The Vedas are the life books in the understanding of who and what we are and especially offer a meaningful perspective for the future of mankind. As soon as the need comes up to understand and experience all this, we will become naturally an integrated part of that cosmic whole. Like this, we deliver our own contribution to the evolution of this world. We gain the insight that the Absolute – Brahman –in its impersonal as well as in its personal form as Lord Krishna, is the origin of all that exists. In Atharvaveda it is said:

***

'Yo brahmanam vidadhati purvam
yo vai vedamsh ca gapayati sma krishnah'

It was Lord Krishna, who in the beginning instructed
Brahma in Vedic knowledge, and who spread the
Vedic knowledge in the past.

***

This verse makes clear that Lord Krishna is the ultimate Divine Personality, who taught all knowledge of existence to Arjuna, His friend and devotee. Next to the understanding of, and insight into the Vedic wisdom, He emphasized the importance of devotion and service to the Lord. This is called *bhakti-yoga*. By the spiritual discipline of bhakti-yoga we are able to develop and maintain a state of *equanimity* in the field of action. Equanimity implies that we will not be easily confused anymore and will spontaneously perform those actions that are natural and useful for our evolution. The key concept of action in Bhagavad Gita is explained by Lord Krishna in three words:

***

'Yogastah kuru karmani'
Established in Yoga, perform action
- Bhagavad Gita II.48

***

Lord Krishna teaches the wisdom of life to Arjuna
(source: Wikipedia)

There are two worlds wherewith we have to deal in life: the world of unity (yoga) and the world of diversity (karma). The only way to integrate the two is to let them melt together into a harmonious whole. In the material world itself this is possible through the practice of *karma-yoga* to achieve fulfilment in life. Karma-yoga implies that we can be active in the world, while our mind remains established in Yoga. This is what Lord Krishna means when he explains to Arjuna to be *without the three gunas* (Bhagavad Gita II.45). The three gunas are: *sattva* (purity), *rajas* (passion), and *tamas* (inertia); they are the prime movers of *Prakriti* (nature).

Usually our actions are completely influenced by their activity, even if we think most of the time that we all do it by ourselves. It is our ego, that blinds our mind. In fact, we are not the ones who act, but it is nature which acts through us, by means of the three gunas. Whenever we are able to perform all our actions from the higher Self, we rise above the binding influence of the three gunas and live in complete freedom. In this state, we offer all our actions spontaneously to the Divine (*Thy will be done*) and perform exactly those activities that belong to us. This we call our natural duty and allotted role, the personal *dharma*.

VIII.6 UPANISHADS OF ATHARVAVEDA

There are three important Upanishads belonging to the Atharvaveda: the Mandukya Upanishad, the Mundaka Upanishad and the Prashna Upanishad.

The Mandukya Upanishad

The Mandukya Upanishad consists of only twelve verses, in which it delves deeply into the three aspects of mind, meditation and consciousness. It states that the mind and senses are instruments of the Self (*Atman*) in order to experience the world. The daily rhythm of this experience consists of three states of consciousness: sleeping, dreaming and waking. In these three states the mind, senses and body undergo totally different experiences.

The underlying, common ground of those states of consciousness is the immutable Being (*Turiya*). In the state of deep sleep, the mind merges almost completely into Being. In chapter X, this subject will be elaborated further.

The primordial mantra OM or AUM represents the three relative states of consciousness as well as the underlying field of Atman (see scheme 8.1)

Scheme 8.1

The relationship of AUM with the states of consciousness

AUM Sounds	States of consciousness	Aspects of Atman	Aspects of Brahman	Characteristics of perception
A	Waking	Gross matter	Without desire	Extrovert
U	Dreaming	Subtle	Knowledge	Introvert
M	Sleeping	Causal	Potential	No desire
AUM	Transcendent (Turiya)	Pure consciousness (Atman)	Pure Being (Brahman)	Bliss (Ananda)

Scheme 8.1 When we meditate on the mantra AUM, a symbol of Brahman, we grow in the experience of Brahman. We will start experiencing that (a) the physical universe is an expression of a more subtle layer and (b) that this refined layer is an expression of a causal level. It is possible to transcend one layer after the other until we transcend the mantra itself and only experience silence and inner peace. (Source: Ten Upanishads of Four Vedas)

The theme of the Mandukya Upanishad is short and firm. Without many words, it refers to the deeper layers of human existence, relates how to know and ultimately transcend them. The result is the experience of the ocean of wholeness in which all rivers of physical existence come together in Unity.

The Mundaka Upanishad

In this Upanishad, Angirasa is the teacher and Shaunaka, a famous householder is the student. Shaunaka asks his teacher: 'What is that knowledge from which all other knowledge originates?' Angirasa makes a distinction between the world of the Absolute (unchangeable) and the relative world (changeable). The Absolute cannot be described, it is invisible, eternal, all-permeating and the source of all. It is not easy to understand how the universe sprang forth from the Absolute – Brahman. Angirasa illustrates this with the help of some analogies: the spider making a web from out of itself and then entering the web; the little seed that grows without effort into a plant; and the fact that hair can only grow on a living being. The universal principles underlying these three analogies are (1) self-regulation, (2) effortlessness and (3) intelligence.

Next, Angirasa describes the steps that take place in the process of creation. The first step is the practice of *tapasya* (lit. penance), which means unceasing meditation on the Supreme Being. From here, the desire to create arises. Energy is transformed into matter, intelligence into consciousness. From there the five elements, life, mind, states of consciousness, and the field of action originate. On the basis of the law of cause and effect, man is given freedom in the field of action. When he, after many wanderings on earth, starts to follow the path of *Brahma Vidya* (higher knowledge), he finally becomes a humble student of life, guided by a competent, Self-realised teacher in full surrender to the Supreme God.

***

> *In Him (Brahman or the Supreme Being) heaven, earth and the*
> *intermediate space, stand central, together with mind and life.*
> *Know Him in yourself as Atman, the Self*
> *or the One without a second.*
> *Discard any other explanation.*
> *This (knowledge) is the road to Immortality.'*
> **- Mundaka Upanishad II.2.5**

***

In chapter II.2 of this Upanishad, the following famous metaphor is used: realising the Absolute is like hitting the target with an arrow of a bow while simultaneously becoming one with that target. The bow represents the knowledge of the Absolute and is symbolised by the universal mantra AUM. The arrow is the higher Self, sharpened by meditation. The Absolute is the target to be realised. The lesson is that the mind focuses on the goal and becomes one with it. Finally, there is no other goal in life than reaching the spiritual world and becoming immortal.

The famous allegory of two birds sitting on the same tree is about the Self and the ego (chapter III.1). One bird eats from the fruits, while the other is just looking on. The tree is the body. The ego experiences the joys and sorrows of life, while the Self is witnessing it. If everything goes well in our life, we are not much concerned with God, but as soon as life challenges us painfully, we want to learn to know God and ask for help. It is often in difficult circumstances that the ego and the Self approach each other, until the moment the ego realises that he is none other than the Self. From that moment on, we deal differently with our worries and life itself.

How can we promote this? Sticking to the truth, contemplation (meditation), wisdom and self-discipline are the four important conditions for realising the Self. These conditions purify the mind and deepen the spiritual experience. *Satyameva jayate* – Truth alone triumphs – are the famous words of the national motto of India (Chapter III.1.6-7). The Upanishads rejoice in the path of Truth as a divine path, leading to the fulfilment of all desires and ultimately to the dwelling place of Truth. That dwelling place is the Absolute, Brahman, which we can localise in our own heart, and furthermore, in every thinkable point in time and space.

The Prashna Upanishad
The Prashna Upanishad gives an overview of the content of all Upanishads.

Prashna means question. This Upanishad is moulded in the form of six questions. Once there lived six boys coming from very respected families. Although they all believed in the existence of God, they wanted to know more about the underlying principles of the Ultimate Reality, the Supreme, the Absolute. They approached a famous teacher, *Pippalada*, and asked him to accept them as his students. Pippalada was, apart from being very famous, also modest and simultaneously strict in discipline. He asked the boys to come and live in his *ashram* for a year at least, and live a pure and detached life. Only then he would answer their questions. After a year of disciplined life in the ashram each student asked their teacher a question to gain Supreme knowledge.

The first question deals with creation: how is it possible that consciousness could create from itself the duality of matter and life and, furthermore, how has this duality transformed itself into a multitude of phenomena.

The second and third question deal with *Prana*, the life force, and how it manifests itself in living beings.

The fourth question deals with the three states of human experience: sleeping, dreaming and waking.

The fifth question deals with pure consciousness, the foundation and motivator of the relative states of consciousness and all existence.

The sixth question, finally, deals with the Supreme Being, Purusha, and His sixteen aspects, *Sodasha Kala*.

Naturally, the sage Pippalada gave beautiful answers to these questions, which we have already discussed at length.

Especially fascinating are Pippalada's reflections on Prana, the life force. Prana corresponds to demigods like Agni, Surya and Indra.

Prana supports and nourishes everything in the universe. Prana can be compared to Prajapati, the Lord and creator of all beings. Prana moves like the seed of the father in the womb of the mother and is born then as a child, after the image of the parents. The entering of Prana into the body deals with what the mind at that moment wishes or desires for. Prana is, therefore, closely connected to the activity of the mind. It forms the bridge between the mind and body and for this reason the movements of Prana in the body can be controlled by the mind. At the end of life, it travels via the upward breath (*udana*) through the sushumna towards the crown of the head and leaves the body. Pippalada explains that the last thoughts we have at that moment have an influence on the next life. So, not only our deeds but also the thoughts and words we speak in this life influence the quality of our next life.

Scheme 8.2

Qualities and Functions of Prana

QUALITIES	COSMIC RELATIONSHIP	BODILY FUNCTIONING	BODY AREA
PRANA	Sun	In breath	Higher regions
APANA	Earth	Out breath	Lower regions
SAMANA	Space	Even breath	Middle regions
VYANA	Air	Spread breath	Whole body

(Source: Ten Upanishads of Four Vedas)

Scheme 8.2 Breath in living beings is a manifestation of Prana, the cosmic life force. Each of the five qualities of Prana in the human body is influenced by their cosmic counterpart. The Sun corresponds to prana, which is active in the eyes. The Earth corresponds to apana, which regulates excretion and generation. Space corresponds to samana, which regulates the digestion. Air corresponds to vyana, which provides the whole body with energy, and fire corresponds to udana, which supports life. Here again we see a direct relationship between the universe and man.

In the human being, Prana is the life breath. The teacher says about the relationship between Prana and the senses, that we can compare this with the queen bee and the bees that follow and serve her. Prana divides itself in the body into five qualities, of which each has their own function. We can compare this with a king, who assigns five villages, and asks his officers to take command over these under his guidance. The five qualities are: *prana, apana, samana, vyana* and *udana*. What their functions are and in which part of the body they are located, we can find in scheme 8.2.

The proper functioning of all five qualities of Prana is of fundamental importance for our health and the vitality of the body. Whenever one of the qualities does not function properly, it will have its drawback on the body. As mentioned earlier, the movements of Prana in the different parts of the body can be influenced by the mind. Quite some chronic diseases in certain parts of the body find their origin in the functioning of the mind. Their healing lies also in the mind by distributing the five movements of Prana evenly in the direction of the effected part. Meditation, pranayama (regulation of breath) and asanas (body postures) are in this case indispensable.

It is possible to invoke Prana as Father, in order to bless the mind and senses, and as Mother, in order to ask for protection, well-being and wisdom.

How is Prana related to Purusha, the cosmic Being? Purusha is the never-changing, infinite, homogeneous Divine, always holding His transcendental form. In the sixth question, posed by *Sukesha*, son of the holy Bharadvaja, sixteen qualities of Purusha are distinguished. In this case it is not about the qualities of Purusha, but about its manifestations. They are the instruments through which they, in a human lifespan, can be experienced. Prana is His first manifestation. The holy Pippalada states them as follows:

***

'From Prana He created faith, space, air, fire,
water, earth, senses, the mind and food.
From food came power, meditation (tapas), hymns,
work and the worlds.
Thereafter, in the worlds, he created names.'
– Prashna Upanishad 6.4

***

After Pippalada had answered all six questions, the students honoured him by offering flowers. They said: 'We consider you as our father, because you have given us a new life by your knowledge. You have helped us to cross the ocean of ignorance, which equals birth, old age, disease and worries. Gratitude to you and to all great seers, who possess the wisdom of Brahman and pass that on from one generation to the other.'

In summary: Atharvaveda and its Upanishads offer the divine basis for many techniques and practical applications, that are essential for the development of a high quality of life on earth. Its further elaborations in the Vedic literature are of a great support in clarifying ideal life patterns. In this context we can think of ideal behaviour, ideal living environment, and ideal life patterns connecting men, cultures and countries. He, who makes all these levels of existence his own, becomes the owner of creation and gains mastery over nature.

VIII.7 UPAVEDA OF ATHARVAVEDA

The Upaveda of Atharvaveda is Sthapatyaveda, the subordinate Veda, which deals, quite practically, with home-planning and the organisation of the environment. It forms an extremely important instrument to lead humanity to a higher level of happiness and well-being. It is also known as *Vastu Shastra*, derived from the Sanskrit root, where *vas* means to *dwell.* It is the science of structure and, therefore, it is closely connected to Atharvaveda. This shastra is the holistic approach to architecture, living and urban development, yielding junction points to astrology and astronomy, natural medicine, chemistry and yoga-philosophy. Its goal is to organise our living environment in such a way, that it contributes in the highest degree to the increase of happiness, health and well-being of its inhabitants. Only by taking Vastu Shastra very seriously, by building and working according to its universal principles, might we still be able to diminish further damage to our environment and prevent global disasters like floods, earthquakes, tsunamis and climate change.

Sthapatyaveda is based on universal principles. Earlier we saw that everything in the universe, including the Earth, is the expression of natural forces and energy fields. On a wide-open plane these forces and energy streams operate freely and a dynamic equilibrium arises. When we erect a building on this plane, the equilibrium of the energy field is disturbed and needs to be restored. When this takes place in the correct way, a harmonious energy stream will fill the whole building.

This energy stream will influence the well-being of people who live in the building. This is because their own and the building's energy fields are connected to each other by electromagnetic forces. If the construction of the building, according to the criteria of Vastu, is faulty, the energy stream will have a negative impact on the health, happiness and well-being of the inhabitants. That these effects take place can be easily determined through practical experiments and this has already happened many times in the past. The reverse is also true. Extensive experiments with pyramid structures have clearly indicated that a strikingly homogeneous energy field exists within the four walls of a pyramid. The word 'pyramid' means *fire in the centre* and fire, here again, means *energy*. This means that in the centre of a pyramid an enormous power field with healing qualities arises. The same is true for houses, domes or other buildings that are built according to the science of Vastu. Often we can feel, when entering such a building, that it breaths a refined and light atmosphere and that it is very pleasant to dwell in it.

Origin

Vishvakarma, the architect of the universe, has revealed the wisdom of Sthapatyaveda to humanity. He passed it on to *Maya*, who became a famous architect, and who in turn passed it on to the sage *Narada*. Later, Vedic seers have gained all knowledge through their long meditations, and kept it for their posterity. Nowadays, the human consciousness is limited and we often see that scientific discoveries become superseded by new discoveries. The old sages had direct access to the area of consciousness that is unlimited and contains eternal truth. Nevertheless, care is needed in the study of the Sthapatyaveda because later scriptures and comments can contradict each other, or interpret the real meaning of Sanskrit words wrongly. Vishvakarma 's goal was to give directions of architecture and organisation of the environment that would lead to a peaceful and harmonious life in this world. The basic principle is, that everything in the universe is in a dynamic equilibrium with everything else. Therefore, Sthapatyaveda deals with the integration of man into the universal blueprint. It may very well be that freemasonry, that developed much later, is a successor of this. The thinking and action of man can be influenced positively when the house (village, city, country, etc) in which he lives, is set up according to universal natural laws. In the Vedic epic Ramayana, we find detailed descriptions of the building, division and organisation of the palace of king Rama. All this was meant to provide him with an ideal basis for his own health and well-being, as well as for a righteous rulership of his people.

Next to old scriptures like the *Vishvakarma Vastu Shastra*, many of these guidelines can be found back in the *Puranas*. Of course, they were especially applied for the building of temples and palaces, but in

India complete cities, like the ancient *Jaipur*, have been built based on the principles of Sthapatyaveda. In our times, again, it was the spiritual master *Maharishi Mahesh Yogi* who, on a global level, has designed extensive plans to reconstruct the whole world according to the principles of Sthapatyaveda. The knowledge of Vastu is a mixture of science, philosophy and practical experience. The ancient texts about this subject give very clear indications about the natural forces and processes lying at the root of organisation, building and living. This is especially true about the natural principles of *orientation, proportions* and *correct division*. Most likely, this ancient Indian wisdom has been brought to other countries, like China, where it is known as *Feng Shui*, literally meaning *water and wind*. Nowadays the principles of Vastu and Feng Shui are not parallel anymore in a number of parts.

The five elements
Vedic architecture finds its origin in the way it made use of the five basic elements in nature, namely ether, air, fire, water and earth. During the time of Vedic civilization, one knew how to make use of these in a correct manner. As we have already seen in earlier chapters, these elements arise from a common intelligent source. We are made up of this source, we are born from it and again return into it. It is always around us, and continuously influences our body, mind and behaviour. In order to make use of it effectively, it is important to know the origin and the different qualities of the elements emerging from it. One knew in Vedic times that it was possible to invoke these forces in a certain way, for instance by rituals, and communicate with them. Certain yajnas were prescribed to propitiate the natural elements. Very well-known is the *Agnihotra*, in which the fire god Agni (creative intelligence) is asked for food, success, and a long life. Furthermore, in India certain rituals or actions are still performed when one buys a piece of land, which is being prepared for building upon, or when a house is entered for the first time. On the other

hand, Vastu in itself is not ritualistic, but it can be applied universally and systematically, and can be of great advantage, like yoga, for the whole humanity. All natural principles that are used by Vastu, can be found back in physics and are consistent in their effects.

VIII.8 RELATIONSHIP WITH OUR BODY

Atharvaveda is the Samhita of the known (the objective world) in the field of consciousness. Qualities of the Chhandas-value are also covered, hiding, extending and moving. Maybe that is why, because of the aspect of hiding, Atharvaveda has been more in the background. In the human body, it almost naturally represents the musculoskeletal system and the organs of action. As was said before, Atharvaveda originally consisted of nine Shakhas or parts, of which only two have survived in time. According to Dr. Nader the nine original Shakhas correspond to the nine parts of the musculoskeletal system, namely: (1) the head; (2) the neck; (3) the upper limbs; (4) the chest; (5) the back; (6) the belly; (7) the pelvis; (8) the cleavage and (9) the lower limbs. The whole body consists of 206 bones and about 515 muscles, together 721. They correspond exactly to the number of suktas in Atharvaveda.

In Sthapatyaveda, too, the Chhandas quality of consciousness dominates. It is the science of structure on the individual and on the cosmic level. It represents the anatomy of the body and establishes wholeness of life by connecting the parts with the whole. When we project the human body on a circle or a square, we see a beautiful correspondence with the cosmic patterns. Leonardo Da Vinci made drawings of this and also in the secret geometry these symbols play an important role. The functioning of the human body (cells, organs and limbs) establishes a wholeness that is more than the sum of its parts. And this is exactly what Sthapatyaveda as a science aims at: to organize the environment in such a way that every part falls into the right place and is in synchrony with the whole cosmic structure. The complete anatomy of the body, pertaining to its different components, can be traced back to the principles of orientation, proportions and division, that form the basis of Sthapatyaveda. The thirty-five segments of the spinal column, divided into a symmetrical left and right half, together making up seventy, correspond to the seventy chapters of Sthapatyaveda, according to Dr. Nader in his revealing book.

CHAPTER IX

VEDA AND QUANTUM PHYSICS

'Indra always wins the battle for the cows.'

- Rigveda IV.17.10

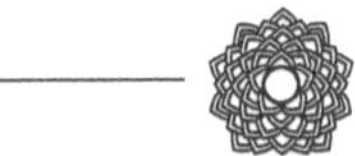

If we want to know more about the smaller than the smallest, seen from a Vedic viewpoint, we come across the interesting book: *Vedic Physics, Scientific Origin of Hinduism* of Raja Ram Mohan Roy, Ph.D. Throughout the ages, many different meanings have been attributed to the Vedic hymns. As we have noticed, the texts contain, seen superficially, many mysterious riddles and unusual metaphors. We come across winged horses, strength showering bulls devoted to the Devas and the Cosmic Being Himself, having thousand heads, thousand eyes and thousand feet. The seers used the language (sound) as instrument to give shape to their cognitions, but it is in a language and form that we cannot understand or explain from the ordinary waking state. Maharishi's explanation of the three-in-one structure of the Veda has opened our eyes in a unique way, by indicating that the Vedas contain all knowledge about the different levels and expressions of *consciousness*. Furthermore, Maharishi has shown, together with his scientists, that also the human body is an exact replica of the Veda. But how is this in the world of atoms? Mohan Roy claims that the Vedic gods are expressions of the micro world of particles and waves. In other words, do the Vedic hymns contain all knowledge of quantum physics? Probably not in the way quantum physics is practiced and described today. On the other hand, from texts of the *Samkhya* and *Vaisheshika* (Upangas) it can be derived that the Vedic sages were fully acquainted with the world of atoms as well.

IX.1 THE GOLDEN EGG

According to Roy, the ancient seers have encoded Vedic knowledge in a simple way, so that it could be understood by everyone in the times of the ancient Indus civilisation. Rigveda itself confirms in chapter IV.3.16 that its texts have a hidden meaning. In later times, one started thinking more and more that the Vedas describe and explain all kinds of natural phenomena, like knowledge about the Sun, the rain and the clouds. The deeper meaning, though, got lost. This was the reason why the texts were considered primitive by Western commentators and not relevant any more for this time. The real meaning of the Vedas differs considerably from what we nowadays think that it is written. Roy wonders what exactly happened at the moment of creation and what happened before, referring to a hymn of Rigveda.

***

'Before creation there existed a golden egg (womb); the only Lord of all created beings was born.
He supports the earth and this heaven.'
– Rigveda X.121.1

***

Creation is a manifestation of the Supreme Being, but where was this Supreme Being before creation started? According to the hymn above, this happened within a golden egg. The colour gold stands for energy in the Vedic literature and the egg for the cosmic womb. The metaphor of the golden egg occurs, by the way, also in a number of other cultures. The state of Being before creation has been described very precisely in the so-called Nasadiya hymn of the Rigveda.

***

Rigveda X.11.1

The Rishi is Prajapati Parameshthin; the Devata is Paramatma and the metre is Trishtubh

'Nothing was manifest nor non-manifest.
There was no earth, no firmament, nor something above it.
What was covered and where was whose hiding place?
Where was the deep, unfathomable water? (1)

There was no death nor immortality.
There was no distinction between day and night.
There was only That, by Its own will, without breath.
There was nothing else than That, wherever. (2)

Before, there was darkness, everything was covered in darkness.
All this was in an undifferentiated liquid state (salila).
Whatever was there was covered by emptiness.
That One was born through the performance of tapas. (3)

In the beginning there was a desire to create,
which was the first seed of His mind.
The sages discovered through meditation
that the manifest was connected to the non-manifest.' (4)

***

Immediately, we are struck by a close similarity to the beginning of the Bible (Genesis I.1-2 en I.6-7) and the Koran (XXI.30). The state that was before creation is incomprehensible for the ordinary human mind. There was emptiness. There was neither space nor time. There was no matter and no energy. The emergence of the universe started with the creation of matter, energy and time, which, according to the hymn, would have a heating effect. This does not fit with the current modern concept of physics according to Mohan Roy, that creation originated from extreme heat. And what is meant by *salila*, the undifferentiated liquidity? Salila, that is generally translated as water, is the primordial state of the still non-manifest universe, and is therefore not the same as *apah*, water. Before creation, there is complete equilibrium and complete homogeneity. When this equilibrium is broken (Maharishi speaks of the collapse of the *'A'* of Agnim, the first word of Rigveda) as a result of the action of the fundamental laws of nature, there arises a state of inhomogeneity which is indicated by the word *apah* (water).

Verse four of the Nasadiya hymn declares that the universe sprang forth from the *desire* of the Supreme Being to create. This is also in contradiction with modern physics, which assumes that the beginning and expansion of the universe are spontaneous phenomena. The Vedas indicate that there is no difference between the Supreme Being and the universe, or maybe the difference is in the internal and external energy of the Lord. The Vedas, as well as physics, assume the expansion of the universe, but there are great differences of opinion in the details of it. The main difference is in the level of observation of existence. In the above hymn, as well as in other places, Rigveda indicates that the Supreme Being, the Vedic hymns and Devatas, exist in the *'parame vyoman', the transcendental field of consciousness*. It is this field that lies beyond our everyday perception of time and space, in which the Vedic seers have made their cognitions and fathomed the truth of existence.

Purusha Sukta

In the previous chapters we have emphasized the great importance of the Purusha sukta, in which the core of the Vedic vision of existence is contained. The holy *Vedavyasa* has declared in the *Mahabharata* that the Purusha sukta is the most important hymn of the Vedas, while Western commentators still see it as an ancient myth. In the whole Vedic literature, Purusha stands for the ultimate God or the Supreme Being. In chapter III of *Vedic Physics*, Mohan Roy gives an extensive and especially interesting comment on the Purusha sukta, of which we give the essence here. The second verse of the Purusha sukta goes as follows:

***

'This all is Purusha, everything that has ever happened and is going to happen. He is the Lord of Immortality, who grows through food.'
- Rigveda X.7.6

***

In this verse lies the origin of Vedanta philosophy. Everything is Brahman. Brahman is the transcendental field which is an instrument of the Supreme Being to create the material world. If indeed, everything in the universe is the manifestation of Purusha, we ourselves are also permeated by and are little particles of that Supreme Being. And when we rise up to that same elevated level of consciousness, the difference (seen from the perspective of consciousness) between God and man is qualitatively annihilated. Of course, man never can become God in the sense of becoming the creator of heaven and earth. But man can have the experience of *Aham Brahmasmi*, an experience which more people undergo already nowadays, even if it is only for a short while. The universe is nothing else than a manifestation of the Supreme Being and at the end of the full cycle of creation (*Mahapralaya*), everything goes back to Purusha, as if nothing has ever been. The Supreme Being and His spiritual world is eternal, while the material universe is transitory, coming up and going down at His divine will.

The last part of this verse indicates that Purusha grows through food (*anna*). Purusha is a personal, living Soul, the word literally means: man, or soul. *Anna* can be seen as the transformation of energy into matter in the universe, in the same way as man can grow in spiritual well-being through his daily food.

IX.2 THE BATTLE BETWEEN INDRA AND VRITRA

According to Roy, the names of the demigods and seers mentioned in the Vedas, are not proper names like we know them, but they have a purely scientific meaning. This can be derived from their etymological meaning. Rigveda is not the history of historical beings or persons, but it explains the evolution of the universe through personification of scientific phenomena. This would pertain to the names of the demigods, as well as to the names of the seers. Our commentary is, that this is probably correct, but concerning the seers one could say that their proper names were adapted in correspondence with their cognition or another important action that they performed. It is well-known that many seers had several names, but also that different seers became well-known under one name. Also, the Vedic scriptures are clear that the demigods, independent from historical facts, have been created by the creator (Lord Brahma), to become the administrators of the material world.

But it is just as likely, that the cosmological character of the Veda and the proper names, when dissected etymologically, represent the fundamental laws of nature and their seeds from quantum physics. One could think here of gravity, matter and anti-matter, waves and particles, attraction and repulsion, bosons and fermions, quarks, et cetera. Roy illustrates his finding with the story of Indra and Vritra, who, at different places of the

Veda, are engaging into a fight. According to Roy, Indra is the basic law of expansion and Vritra the natural force of contraction, as would appear from different hymns of Rigveda.

***

Rigveda I.32

The Rishi is Hiranyastupa Angirasa,
the Devata is Indra and the metre is Trishtubh

'Now I will describe the glorious deeds of Indra, who kept Vajra.
He killed the snake and let the waters flow.
He broke the heart of the mountains. (1)

He killed the snake, who hid in the mountain.
Tvashtri made the Vajra for him.
Like the cows making noises,
the flowing waters reached the ocean. (2)

The mighty Indra choose the Soma, and drank from the three containers.
The charitable Indra held Vajra in his hand and killed the first-born
among the snakes.' (3)

***

Which fight takes place here? The waters were liberated after Indra had killed the snake (Vritra). In verse twelve of this hymn, it is mentioned that the seven rivers could flow freely after Vritra was killed. The idea in the Vedas that the waters are obstructed by a snake is found in many myths all over the world, in which the snake Veda often changed into a frog. Quantum physics speaks of four fundamental forces of nature, namely gravity, the electromagnetic force, and the strong and weak interactions. The electromagnetic force consists of the electric and the magnetic force. According to Roy, Indra would be the electric force. This explains that Indra is considered to be the god of the thunderbolt (!), which is confirmed in the Vedic scriptures more than once. So then, who and what is Vritra?

Vritra is the surface tension or counter pressure of the universe, that forces the universe to shrink. The electric force has to 'conquer and kill' this surface tension in order to allow the expansion of the universe. Vritra, therefore, is the surface tension. The reason that this fight between Indra and Vritra gets so much attention in the Vedic hymns lies in the fact that without the victory of Indra, the universe would not stand a single chance to survive. It is an eternal battle, in which neither ever give up battling against each other. It is no wonder that the snake, the enemy of Indra, king of the demigods, was considered throughout time a symbol of death. Everyone knows the story of Eve and the snake in the Bible (Genesis III.3-15) and we come across the same idea in the fight between Apollo and Python in Greek mythology. Anyway, more than two hundred fifty hymns of Rigveda are about Indra, whereby hymn II.12 occupies an important place, explaining extensively the role and position of Indra.

In this way, Roy analyses the hymns of Rigveda and explains many names and other symbols. He does this in an impressive way and his findings contain definitely some grain of truth. But even more important than the quantum mechanical coding enclosed in the Vedic texts is Rigveda as the Samhita of knower, process of knowing and known. The whole Vedic literature is concerned in the first place with the process of creation and how this is related to the evolution of man.

Scheme 9.1
The Meaning of Names and Symbols in the Veda

VEDIC NAME	APPARENT MEANING	PHYSICS CONCEPT	CONSCIOUSNESS CONCEPT
Salila	water	homogeneous primordial fluid	transcendence
Brihaspati	teacher of gods	universal expansion	wisdom, knowledge
Indra	king of the gods	electric force	Wholeness
Vritra	demon	surface tension	seduction, stress
Prithivi	earth	world of perception	material, stable
Antariksha	atmosphere	sky	gap
Dyau	heaven	world of light	transcendental field
Vishnu	god of maintenance	universe	maintenance principle
Vayu	god of wind	air	movement, prana
Agni	god of fire	energy	creative intelligence
Apah	water	matter, anti-matter	liquidity
Gau	cow	particle	sense organ
Pushan	god	set of particles	Sun
Varuna	god	electron	night, exhalation
Mitra	god	proton	day, inhalation
Aryaman	god	neutron	eyes
Soma	soma plant	electrical charge	Moon, mind
Indu	soma juice	electricity	thinking power
Madhu	honey	magnetic field	Attraction
Ashwins	twin gods	magnetic poles	health, well-being
Surya	Sun god	light	higher Self
Vasishtha	holy sage	nucleus (core)	seer, teacher
Chakra	wheel	rotation of the universe	energy centre

(Source: Vedic Physics, Scientific Origin of Hinduism)

*Scheme 9.1 This schema gives an overview of the most important names
and symbols in Vedic hymns together with their meaning in physics, as
indicated by Mohan Roy, as well as their meaning in the context of the
Samhita structure of consciousness.*

It is the story of our own consciousness and how it expresses itself on the
different levels of existence. Indra is then not only an electric force, but
especially the wholeness of consciousness which tries to get even with all
opposition of seductions in our lives (Vritra, the snake), and who wants
to gain mastery over all the senses (the cows). It may be quite obvious that
this concept of consciousness runs completely parallel with the structure
and set-up of the quantum mechanical field. The same fundamental
principles of evolution (stability, flexibility, integration, purification and
growth) we can find back at any level or at any point of creation.

IX.3 THE THREE LOKAS

We do not want to downplay the vision of Mohan Roy here, but rather to
make it even more clear what its real significance is in the Vedic scriptures,
by drawing parallels to it with Maharishi's technology of consciousness.
In chapter VI of *Vedic Physics*, he discusses the division of the universe
into three worlds (*lokas*), an important and frequent subject in the
Vedas. It deals with *prithivi* (earth), *antariksha* (sky) and *dhyau* (heaven),
together forming the *triloka* (three worlds).

* * *

*'These lokas were together in the beginning.
Then earth and heaven were separated from each other, and the space in
between became the sky (antariksha).'*
– Shatapata Brahmana VII.1.2.23

* * *

In fact, the universe was split up in two, or indeed in three? And where can we localize these worlds? The current opinion is that *prithivi* is the material universe, in which we live as human beings, and *dyau* stands for the spiritual world where the Supreme Being eternally lives with the free souls. Then, there is a space in between, which seems to bridge the gap between the spiritual and the material world. As is apparent at a few places in Rigveda, these are the three steps taken by Lord Vishnu in his fifth incarnation as a dwarf. It is clear from these verses that the third step *dyau* does not lie within the scope of ordinary human perception, but has been made completely invisible by the *antariksha* (gap).

Vamanadeva, avatara of lord Vishnu, who came to earth as a dwarf and who carries a begging bowl in one hand and an umbrella in the other. (Source: kamat.com)

Once the demon Bali performed a yajna, which would give him unlimited powers and make him the ruler of the universe. Everything seemed to indicate that the yajna would succeed. In panic the Devas fled to Lord Vishnu, as to the maintainer of creation. Vishnu decided (the first time in the shape of a human) to descend to Earth as the son of the holy saint Kashyapa and his wife Aditi. He did not grow fast and remained a dwarf. His name was Vamana and he always wore an umbrella in one hand and a water pot in the other. As a begging monk he went to Bali and asked him for a piece of land. Bali did not like the idea, but *Shukaracharya*, the spiritual preceptor of the demons, explained to Bali that he could not refuse such a request during the performance of a yajna. Therefore, Bali decided to give the dwarf a piece of land not bigger than three steps, which Vamana could make. With only three steps the dwarf, who in reality was Lord Vishnu Himself, covered the whole universe and thus the Devas remained rulers of the whole material world.

The question is at what level the seers have perceived the world. In Yajurveda we find the following hint:

***

'I place heaven and earth in you.
I place the vast space in between also in you.'
– Yajurveda VII.5

***

This indicates that we should locate the three worlds also inside ourselves. According to Roy, the three worlds are physical phenomena, namely the world of perception (observation space), the intermediate space, with a frequency we can only rarely perceive, and the world of light (light space), which we cannot perceive at all as human beings. Our commentary on this is that this does not have to be incorrect, but that the emphasis here also lies again on our inner world. In this connection we can consider the five levels of human observation mentioned in chapter VII: annamaya kosha, pranamaya kosha, manomaya kosha, vijanamaya kosha and anandamaya kosha.

First, we have our world of the senses. Then we have the switch (gap) between the subjective and objective worlds. It is this intermediate space where the process of growth in the spiritual seeker takes place. Inner growth leads to the world of anandamaya, the transcendental field of consciousness, which we, ordinarily speaking, cannot perceive, unless we strive for enlightenment with a strong focus.

The transcendental field of consciousness (parame vyoman) is the field where the Devas abide, and it is connected to heaven (dyau). All this is summarised concisely in the last verse of a beautiful hymn from the Rigveda, which is completely dedicated to heaven and earth.

***

Rigveda I.185

The Rishi is Agastya Maitrivaruni, the Devata is Dyavaprithivi and the metre is Trishtubh

'Mother Earth and Father Heaven,
what I ask you here, let that become a reality.
Become the protector of the gods.
May we receive food, strength and a long life.'

***

Mother Earth and Father Heaven refer to the material and the spiritual worlds. Their co-operation is needed in order to walk the spiritual path with success. They can bring us in harmony with the Devatas, the impulses of creative intelligence who, according to human standards, are immortal (Yajurveda XXXII.10). Our award is food (spiritual transformation), power (shakti), and a long life (health and well-being).

The spiritual meaning of heaven and earth, that the Vedic hymns aim at, has receded into the background through the long lapse of time, and has been substituted by the *apparent* meaning of heaven and earth. In almost all world religions and ancient cultures, the division of the universe into heaven and earth comes up. In the Bible, it is said that in the beginning God created heaven and earth (Genesis I.1). The Koran speaks of a division of the universe into heaven and earth (Koran XXI.30). In Greek mythology, it is said that in the beginning there was Chaos, a churning formless mass, from which *Gaia* – Mother Earth – emerged together with her spouse Uranus, the heaven. In Egypt, *Seb* (earth) and *Nut* (heaven) were a couple, that gave birth to many gods. In the Chinese tradition of wisdom, the complementary opposites yin and yang represent earth and heaven. Many other cultures know the same phenomenon (see also chapter XII).

IX.4 SARASVATI

Roy assigns a cosmological meaning to the gods, like Rudra, the Maruts, Vayu and Soma, mentioned in Rigveda. The goddess *Sarasvati* is, according to him, the flow of matter and energy in the universe, bearing magnetic properties. In Rigveda, two hymns (VII.95 and VII.96) are attributed to Sarasvati, the goddess of wisdom, education and speech. Sarasvati was one of the three famous rivers in the north of India, together with the Ganges and the Yamuna. The Sarasvati river, however, dried up after the Vedic civilisation and has been since an underground river. It is said that it will surface again at the start of a new era of wisdom. The three holy rivers meet at *Prayag* in one point. This is a very sacred spot in India, where every twelve years the big *Kumbha Mela* is held and where millions of pilgrims gather to take a ritual bath. Sarasvati is mentioned among others in Rigveda I.142.9 and IX.5.8 together with her divine sisters *Ila* and *Bharati*. Roy assumes that the three goddesses represent the three worlds. He further asks himself how Sarasvati repeatedly is associated with speech and with a river, two such different things in Rigveda. With respect to the etymological meaning, every word of Rigveda means exactly what it says. Speech (*Vach*) is a holy concept in India and is a different form of the Divine. Sarasvati became the goddess of education because of her association with speech. 'Speech is Sarasvati' as it is stated in several Brahmanas. In Vedic tradition, speech is connected to sound and vibration, the Rishi aspect in the Samhita of consciousness. Concerning Sarasvati as a river, together with the rivers Ganges and Yamuna, we again see here the number three surfacing. What we often see is, that a certain ancient wisdom can be located in the landscape of India, the land of Veda. From a spiritual point of view, it seems obvious that Sarasvati, together with Ila and Bharati, each represent one of the three important energy channels or nadis in the subtle body, *Ida, Pingala* and *Sushumna*. This is confirmed by a description in Yoga literature:

***

'Ida bhagirathi prokta
pingala yamunayacha
thayor madhye gatam nadi
sushumnakhyam sarasvati'

***

Ida is said to be the stream of Bhagirathi (the Ganges). Pingala is the Yamuna and the nadi that leads to the so-called third eye in the forehead (Sushumna) is the Sarasvati. As long as the chakras are not opened up, Kundalini cannot flow through Sushumna. This would also explain why the river Sarasvati in our time of ignorance cannot come to the surface.

In Rigveda VI.61.10, one speaks about seven sisters, while in other places one speaks about seven rivers. In Rigveda, it is indicated that the rivers find their origin in one source, they merge into each other, and return to the same place. The number seven occurs at several places in Rigveda, for instance wherever the seven Rishis, the seven metres, the seven covers, the seven dimensions, etc are mentioned. We have already seen that the three worlds (earth, heaven and sky) each consist of seven levels. In a number of places in the Vedas, therefore, one speaks about *thrice seven*. Sometimes it seems more obvious that the seven states of consciousness mean the: sleep state, dream state, waking state, transcendental consciousness, cosmic consciousness, god consciousness and Brahman consciousness. And in the case of the seven sisters or seven rivers, it seems logical to connect these with the seven energy centres or chakras in the body, that lie alongside the sushumna and through which the Kundalini energy is flowing (see also chapter XII).

IX.5 ANIMALS IN RIGVEDA

In the Vedic scriptures many animals are mentioned and it is interesting to investigate what their deeper meaning is, because this area is frequently misunderstood. Very often in Rigveda, one talks about the *strength showering bull* in connection with cows. Earlier we saw that cows represent our senses. This means that the strength showering bull probably indicates Indra, who invigorates the senses. In this connection the word *Vaja* also occurs, which can be translated as vital force. Here we deal with the vital force of the senses, whereby their ability to perceive the wholeness of existence increases.

In the Purusha sukta we come across this verse:

***

'From that universal sacrifice curds and butter were provided.

*It formed those aerial creatures (vayavya) and
animals (pashu) both wild (aranya) and tame (gramya).'*
– Rigveda X.90.8

***

Curds is the state of the universe when it loses its homogeneity. Before that state, the universe consisted of *salila*, comparable to liquid helium that is generated at an extremely low temperature. Liquid helium is a superconductor endowed with the property that it flows through anything, even a thick wall. From salila, mini-particles are formed, which are indicated by the name *pashu*. According to Mohan Roy, three particles are involved, namely bosons, fermions and field-particles. The original meaning of pashu is animal and that would have caused a lot of confusion for commentators. The gramya particles can be divided into four types, namely *aja*, meaning goat, avi meaning sheep, ashva meaning horse and *gau* meaning cow. In verse 10 we read:

***

*From it sprang horses, and all animals with two rows of teeth;
cows sprang from it; from it goats and sheep.*
- Rigveda X.90.10

***

These four domesticated animals keep recurring in the hymns of Rigveda, and they each have a specific task. Cows are hidden in the mountains, horses draw the chariots of the gods, sheep wool is used to filter the Soma juice and the goat is the vehicle of Pushan. The confusion that originated after the Vedic Civilisation in India surrounding the interpretation of the four domesticated animals, has caused great problems concerning the hierarchical varna system, the subdivision of the society into *brahmins, kshatriyas, vaishyas* and *shudras.*

The brahmins perform spiritual work, they live a simple life and are the custodians and propagators of the Vedic knowledge.

The kshatriyas are busy with administration and the army for the protection of the society and the maintenance of law and order.

The vaishyas are merchants and agriculturists, who trade and practice agriculture and are focussed on the acquisition of material wealth. They are supposed to support the brahmins and kshatriyas in their living.

The shudras have a serving function.

As it seems from another verse of the Purusha sukta, this division had already existed in the Vedic era as a natural social division, but it was certainly not based on birth. The Western philosopher *Plato* describes three similar classes of people for the Greek society. In the Vedic time, it was a completely natural division of living and working, more or less comparable to the guilds in the Middle Ages. This system respected the equality of all people and established class differences solely according to the nature of people and their chosen profession. In the epic *Mahabharata*, king *Yudhisthira*, the eldest of the Pandavas, confirms that the varna-system plays with the qualities of the head and the heart, not of someone's birth. Lord Krishna says in the *Bhagavad Gita* that varna is determined by someone's deeds (karma) and qualities (guna). Unfortunately, in our time it has turned into a rigid and often heartless system that is only based on the birth into a certain family, from which there is no deviation any more.

In the era after the Vedic civilisation, the four animals in the Purusha sukta were associated with the different castes: the cow (*gau*) represented the brahmin, the horse (*ashva*) represented the kshatriya, the sheep (*avi*) represented the vaishya and the goat (*aja*) represented the shudra. This division is confirmed in some Vedic scriptures. Because the Vedas forbid the slaughter of a cow, also the killing of a Brahmin is reckoned to be a serious crime. Furthermore, because *aja* means born once, a difference was made between a shudra, on the one hand, who was only born once, and the other three castes, on the other hand, which were twice-born. For the twice-born the performance of the so-called Upanayana ritual is required and the shudras were excluded from this. This means, among other things, that they were not entitled to study the Vedas. All this has led to an extremely painful situation within the Hindu society, which is very palpable even today.

It is clear that the four animals mentioned in the Purusha sukta carry another meaning than what they are associated with in the post-Vedic period. Wherever the Vedic literature talks about sacrificing gramya animals (cows, horses, sheep and goats), it definitely is not referring to the ritual slaughtering of these animals. In Rigveda, the performance of a yajna is called in a number of places *adhvara*, which implies: without violence. In the language of physics, it is about the transformation of particles in the quantum field and when we apply it to ourselves, it is about the processes meant to change our perception of the value and purpose of the external world.

Summing it up, we can conclude that, although Mohan Roy's research offers great perspectives for the unravelling of the Vedic secrets, it is not the only possible pathway to follow. His approach, though brilliant in itself, stays within the perspective of the modern, objective science, forcibly constrained by the limitations of intellectual thinking. Without the experience of pure consciousness, the intellect will never be completely able to gain insight into the all-embracing concept of the Vedic approach, because the field of pure consciousness is timeless and its range thereby is infinite.

The Vedic seers had access to an almost unlimited ability to perceive in a way that gives insight into the secrets of existence. Nevertheless, Mohan Roy has carried out a remarkable investigation and opened the door to the uncovering of a complete quantum theory, which without doubt lies hidden inside the Vedic hymns. Moreover, since the Veda is the domain of human consciousness, it also contains a practical side, which can lead mankind to its ultimate destination from darkness to light, from ignorance to wisdom and from death to immortality.

CHAPTER X

PATH AND GOAL OF THE VEDA

---

*'During samadhi (fourth state of consciousness), sushupti (deep sleep)
and moksha (fifth state of consciousness) the observer experiences
Unity with the Divine.'*

\- **Samkhya V.79**

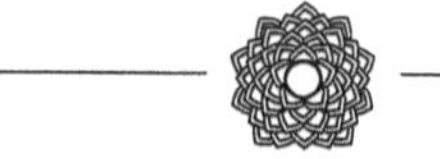

The investigation into the essence of the Vedas and the path leading towards that, is especially indicated by the Upangas or the Six Systems of Indian Philosophy. They are not divine revelations, like the four Vedas; they originate from the human intellect. However, they are closely connected to the Vedas and are universal in their range and approach. These six Upangas are: Nyaya, Vaisheshika, Samkhya, Yoga, Karma Mimamsa and Vedanta. They contain scientific knowledge about the inner and the outer world and on how they are connected. The Upangas are also called Darshanas, which means: 'visions about the truth.' They are discourses about the origin and logic of existence as well as about the goal of human evolution.[1]

---

1. For a description of all six systems of Indian philosophy, see Hinduism, Back to the Source, Saraswati Art Publishers, fourth edition, 2016

X.1 WHO ARE WE?

Already from the beginning of creation, we are deeply devoted to the mysteries of the universe in relation to ourselves. Who created this universe? Who am I? Where do I come from? Where do I go after this life? The Vedic seers turned within and found the answers in themselves. The Upangas are philosophical, scientific, religious in their origin, and are based on the totality of knowledge, which is already always present in the universe, as well as deep within man himself. They present a holistic explanation of the reality seen from different angles, including everything that can ever be known about the objective and subjective world, and what connects them with each other. They also, above all, give practical techniques and means to experience 'everything that can be known' by the human mind.

Samkhya deals with getting a complete insight into the knower or the subject. It does this by analysing all its twenty-five basic values in six books. It starts its investigation from the transcendental Self (Purusha) and then follows the path of the mind from the subtlest levels of creation towards the grosser levels. Kapila, the compiler of Samkhya, sees the individual as a wholeness of body, mind and Self. While body and mind are part of the manifest world, the Self (Atman) is non-manifest. Atman is the basis and core of the human being, with the body and the mind as its powerful instruments.

Kapila describes the mind as consisting of manas, buddhi and ahamkara:

Manas	= the mind as thinking entity and observer
Mahat or Buddhi	= the intellect, the discriminative instrument
Ahamkara	= the ego, our identity

Beyond the mental activity we can experience the Self. It is the silent, non-involved witness, immersed in the process of observation.

Its beautiful qualities are love, purity, peace, intelligence and truth – a truth that never changes. The soul or the Self (Atman) is a spark of the cosmic intelligence, the omnipresent and intelligent creative force of the world.

***

Sa hi sarvavit sarvakarta
He (God) is the omniscient and omnipotent cause of the world
– Samkhya 3.56

***

God is Ishvara, or Purusha, and enclosed in His nature lies the whole manifest creation, Prakriti. Purusha and Prakriti are inseparably connected to each other. Prakriti (= nature) is the material cause of the universe. Kapila explains that the only cause for human suffering lies in the fact that the functioning of our intellect has become separate from the Self. The limited intellect (buddhi) does not recognize its own origin. The intellect identifies itself with the movie playing all day, and not with the underlying white screen (the Purusha quality), that makes the projection possible. *Liberation* means that we are able to experience the Self, as the unprejudiced observer, under all circumstances in the midst of relative life. The state of consciousness in which wholeness of life is experienced, is accompanied by a continuous experience of happiness and inner fulfilment.

Direct experience
Next to the intellect, ego and mind, there are five senses of perception to gain knowledge of existence (jnanendriyas), namely hearing, feeling, seeing, smelling and tasting. The physical body has five corresponding sense organs at the physical level (ears, skin, eyes, nose and tongue). The whole subjective creation (man) can be explained from these eight

fundamental values. The senses of knowledge are connected with the mind (manas) and send all they perceive to it for further transmission. The information that the mind receives is then sent to mahat and from there to ahamkara. Ahamkara is the most subtle level of operation of the human mind.

Scheme 10.1
The Connection of the Senses with the Self

Senses for Knowledge	Hearing Feeling Seeing Smelling Tasting	Manas-Mahat-Ahamkara-Soul/Self

Scheme 10.1 The Soul or Self is in close connection with ahamkara and processes the knowledge that enters the senses.

The soul or the Self is in this scheme 'the knower' and 'enjoyer' of the experience concerned. The mind in a broader sense (manas, ahamkara and buddhi) is the processor and through the sense organs, a certain result is put forward into the field of action. But in the state of enlightenment, the soul itself becomes the doer when mind, intellect and ego are completely tuned in on it. Then it is the soul who sends the mind, senses and action spontaneously in a life supporting direction. The individual action is then in accordance with the cosmic action. In that state ahamkara or the ego (the individual identity) merges with the experience of the soul and becomes completely pure.

The initially false ego does not stand in itself, but is, in a limited way, the expression of the soul. In that state, it is ignorant about its real identity, until it starts searching and decides to transform itself into the direction of its higher goal. At the moment when it becomes humble and able to fully surrender itself to God, it experiences the reality of things and the pure Self can support its role completely.

X.2 STATES OF CONSCIOUSNESS

The five states of consciousness are:

- Deep sleep state (*sushupti avastha*) when body and mind are both resting but the mind is not aware of it;

- Dream state (*svapna avastha*), when the body is resting, but the mind is active;

- Waking state (*jagrat avastha*), when body and mind are both active;

- Transcendental consciousness (*turiya avastha*), when body and mind are in deep rest and the mind keeps registering this;

- Cosmic consciousness (*turiyatita*), when body and mind are active while the state of transcendental consciousness does not get lost.

In the ordinary waking state, we go through periods of happiness and pain. The experiences of this state are subjective in nature, from the perspective of our relations as well as in time. As we feel, so the world appears to us. Sometimes we like something and enjoy it, at other times we feel bored. Sometimes we like somebody, at another moment we do not. These are subjective experiences we all can recognise.

In the dream state, the senses are not involved, we create thoughts unconsciously and mostly based on earlier undigested experiences in the waking state. In this state, we also go through periods of pain and pleasure and the experiences are subjective. For the dreamer, however, these experiences are very real. His fantasies, fears or other experiences take him for a ride, although a dream can also be meaningful and explainable.

So, once upon a time king Janaka, who was a very wise and righteous ruler, dreamt that he was a beggar. The dream was very real, but when he woke up, in the light of the day he realised that he was a king. Confused by this experience, he wondered: 'Am I a beggar who dreams and thinks he is a king, or am I a king dreaming he is a beggar?' Because he could not answer this question, he took the advice of a holy saint who told him that he was neither this nor that. This confused him even more. But the wise man continued and said: 'When you are in the waking state you think you are a king, and when you are in the dream state you think you are a beggar. And when you are in deep sleep, you are neither of them. None of these experiences reveal your real identity. In reality you are Atman, pure consciousness.'

The waking state occurs concretely at a certain moment while the dream state is related to something that has happened before. Furthermore, the dream state is only a subjective experience of the dreamer and stands apart from a real environment. But an interesting question is: is not the waking state maybe also a kind of dream experience? Just as in the dream state, everything is changing in the waking state, it is subjective and reality often seems to be ambiguous. In other words: *Do we live in a dream? Are we dreaming something within our waking state inside a bigger whole? Are we the thoughts in the dream of a higher intelligence? Is the world of the waking state a mere illusion?* Surprisingly, the ancient sages confirm this vision and even modern science is steadily reaching the conclusion that *nothing is what it seems to be*. The sensory world of classical physics $(1+1=2)$ is therewith completely turned upside down.

It is the fullness of the Self that is always with us and is present within us. It is so subtle that many people cannot consciously experience it, but in the state of deep dreamless sleep we make contact with our innermost source. That is the reason why we experience deep sleep as so pleasant afterwards. In essence, the *fourth state of consciousness* is nothing else than the deep sleep state, except that we experience it *consciously*. In meditation we directly experience how pleasant it is to go beyond thinking and to be in a state of non-thinking. Here we can experience the three qualities *sat-chit-ananda* of the energy field lying at the source of our thinking. During the dreamless sleep, as well as in transcendental consciousness, we are 'free' from our mind, in particular from mahat, and then we experience real happiness or bliss.

While we experience the effect of bliss gained in dreamless sleep only afterwards, in the fourth state we experience it in the moment itself. The lasting experience of the fourth state is when the mind experiences full liberation and freedom (atyantapurushartha), the essence of all existence. Our limited mind only holds us back from who we really are: spiritual beings in a human experience. The states of consciousness of waking, dreaming and deep sleep seem to be sub-states, pulling an impenetrable veil before us. This insight can only be gained through the direct experience of samadhi. The reality and sense of life become only alive by the experience of the state of transcendental consciousness. It is here, that our spiritual journey back towards the spiritual world really starts. That is why Kapila gives so much attention to this experience (for instance in the practice of meditation), on which a great number of his aphorisms and those of Patanjali's sutras are based.

In Kapila's research, we see a logical explanation of the essence and goal of the Vedas, and about our own origin and purpose in life. We consist of different 'layers' or bodies, from material to refined-material, which we can use as instruments for our growth. The states of consciousness and the layers are connected to each other, or in other words: each state of consciousness has its own corresponding 'body'. It is not our purpose in the physical world to be the slaves of our mind, but to train our mind to focus and concentrate on that which really matters. The quality of the Self is reflected in our mind. If the mind is refined and silent, there is a pure reflection of the Self. If the mind is impure or clouded, the reflection of the Self is disturbed. It is because of the false ego that we experience life as separate from the Self. The different states of the mind determine how we deal with pleasure and pain.

It appears that through the direct experience of transcendental consciousness, we can free our mind and experience only the pure field of consciousness. This is the experience of inner happiness, purity and wisdom. This is human evolution.

In the Bhagavad Gita (BG VI.21) Lord Krishna explains to Arjuna:

* * *

'In that joyous state (samadhi), one is situated in boundless transcendental happiness and enjoys himself through transcendental senses. Established thus, one never departs from truth.'

* * *

X.3 THE YOGA SUTRAS

The word yoga comes from the root *yuj*, meaning 'to unite', implying unity or integration (of opposites). In its broader meaning, yoga is simultaneously the path and goal of spiritual liberation. This means that it is directed toward the ultimate expansion of the limited, individual consciousness into a cosmic dimension, which has its own, completely specific qualities. We can compare this to the fast developments in modern physics that makes progress into the direction of a quantum physical world view.

Yoga is a discipline, a way of life, through which the individual, by self-practice, transforms into a complete human being – complete in the sense of enjoying a fully and harmoniously attuned relationship between body, mind, behaviour and environment. This comes quite close to the definition of health by the World Health Organisation (W.H.O.).

Important in this vision is, that the individual, and thereafter the society, too, is reconnected to its spiritual base, the cosmic intelligence, of which everything and everyone is a part.

Also, in the healing of diseases, the holistic approach of yoga plays a significant role. In Western countries, yoga has become a big hit in the last few decades. Research has brought to light that efficient practise of *yoga* brings relief from diseases like high blood pressure, diabetes, bronchial asthma and hyperventilation; in short, intensely stress related symptoms of an overly hectic way of life.

Patanjali

Yoga in the sense of union, of merging with the source, can give a human complete insight into his true essence and can lead him to a state in which he thinks and acts spontaneously in harmony with the cosmic law. The fourth Upanga consists of four chapters (*padas*) with 195 sutras in total. The word *sutra* means cord or thread. A sutra is a concise aphorism, that was learned by heart by the students, and often daily recited. The guru or spiritual teacher transmitted the sutras to his students and taught them their explanations. Like this, the sutras were passed on orally and preserved this way. Ultimately, they were collected and edited by the sage Patanjali, who lived probably around 200 BC. We find the oldest sutras back in the chapters II.28 till III.55, in which the eight famous 'limbs' of yoga, the *Ashtangayoga*, are described. But also, the first chapter – *Samadhi Pada* –, that probably has been added at a later stage, immediately starts explaining what yoga actually is. It starts with the following three aphorisms:

***

1.1 Now starts the exposition on yoga.
1.2 Yoga is the transcending of mental activity.

1.3 Then the observer is established in his own nature.

***

So, yoga is first of all a mental process, because Patanjali describes the process of meditation here. When we are able to settle our mental activity completely, the observer experiences his own essence, the Self. That is the silent, unmoved observer in ourselves, who rises above thoughts and feelings. To experience this Self is like 'coming home', the experience of the core of the human-being.

Patanjali continues his exposition with the following sutra:

***

1.4 In the other case the mind identifies itself with its activity.

***

Yoga or meditation is the transcending of mental activity (Patanjali)

In moments when the mind is not identified with its own nature, which means moments when the mind is generally active, it identifies itself with the objects of perception. We identify ourselves with our thoughts and feelings, with love and hate, with fear and greed and so forth. Only by working hard on ourselves, we can finally free ourselves from that identification; we become free from the bondage of the turbulence of the mind. This is what is meant in Vedic literature by spiritual detachment or enlightenment. This is the permanent experience of cosmic consciousness, the fifth state of consciousness. In this state, the Self is not overshadowed by the thinking activity any more, but it stays present throughout all states of consciousness (sleeping, dreaming, waking). It is the silent witness, who perceives everything, but is itself not involved in any expression of that perception. It is the safe feeling that a child has when the mother is at home. This state of cosmic consciousness gives someone the feeling of being 'at home' with all he thinks and does. His life is no longer dominated by weakness, pain or suffering, but by a permanent state of inner fulfilment. In this state, personal suffering has fled away. Moreover, the Self has become the natural leader of the thoughts. This means the thoughts do not lead their own uncoordinated life any more, but are in complete service of the Self. Every thought is the pure expression of the Self and is therefore fully creative, orderly, loving and sharing.

X.4 RAJAYOGA: THE EIGHTFOLD PATH

Yoga is, apart from the goal, also *the path* that leads to enlightenment. In chapters II and III of the Yoga-sutras, Patanjali comes up with an integrated form of yoga, called Ashtangayoga or Raja-yoga. The eight parts or limbs are:

- *yama*　　　　　restraints
- *niyama*　　　　observances
- *asana*　　　　　physical postures
- *pranayama*　　　regulation of breath
- *pratyahara*　　　withdrawal of senses from their objects
- *dharana*　　　　concentration

- *dhyana*   meditation

- *samadhi*   transcendence

In fact, all forms of yoga can be traced back to these eight limbs. All are equally important; they form one wholeness and should be practiced next to each other. That is why we speak preferably about eight limbs (= ashtanga). In order to strive for enlightenment, we find here the path that leads to that goal. The only way to feel really free, to experience unity in the world of diversity, is to walk consequently the path of Raja-yoga, to be directed to the goal and take the instructions and suggestions of our teacher seriously.

Lifestyle

The yamas and niyamas, the rules of moral restraints and correct way of living, will gain in quality the more our spiritual growth advances. By restraining ourselves from useless things, by learning to do the right things, and by applying good habits and customs, we can cultivate our mind. But also, if we approach it from the other side, the cultivation of our mind through the means of yoga and meditation will develop our need for an ideal lifestyle. The knife cuts on both sides. this is what makes the path of Ashtangayoga so fascinating and integrated.

Patanjali says we should better obstain from certain things, because they confuse the mind, and instead we should engage in other things, because they refine the mind.

1. **The yamas are:**
- *Non-violence;* the thought behind non-violence is that we do not harm others (men, animals, plants) in no form what so ever (thought, word or action).

- *Speaking the truth*; this quality requires a developed mind and high morals, that can be attained through many years of spiritual discipline.

- *Non-stealing*; this can be taken both in a literal or figurative sense. The thought to possess someone else's wife is also considered to be a form of stealing.
- *Non-spilling of energy*; from Sathya Sai Baba is the saying that you should never waste energy, money, food and time. The sages find it very important that we control our vital energy, with special emphasis on our sexual energy.
- *Non covetousness*; do not live on someone else's pocket, do not accept any more from someone else than you really need. And always think, it is better to give than to receive.

When we, according to Patanjali, are more aware of the yamas, it will create a calming influence on the mind.

2. Patanjali's niyamas are:
- *Purity*; keeping the body pure and clean, however this niyama also implies mental purity and inner integrity in the field of action.
- *Contentment*; God gives us everything we need, trust in it and you will notice how everything comes to you.
- *Discipline*; orderliness, spiritual discipline and a regular lifestyle are important qualities that we can train ourselves to achieve.
- *Study of holy scriptures*; this provides us with insight into the eternal wisdom of life. In principle, all holy scriptures teach us the same, but each from a different angle depending on time and culture.
- *Devotion to God*; surrendering and serving the Ultimate Supreme Being and letting the higher Self be the guide of all your thinking and actions.

These are the spiritual tools Maharshi Patanjali hands down to us to apply in daily life. And as we see, the yamas are about our relationship with others, while the niyamas are about our own way of life.

Remaining limbs

Now we will explain, in short, the other parts of Ashtangayoga:

- *Asana.* For a good result of the meditation, a correct sitting posture (asana) is necessary. The back should be as straight as possible and we are sitting in a way to move as little as possible. Our sitting posture is also a reflection of the mind. The advice is: sit firmly, but comfortably. Forcing oneself, of course, does not make sense, there are only a small number of Western people who can sit easily in the lotus-position for a longer period of time. If this is difficult, we choose the cross-legged position or we sit on a suitable chair.

- *Pranayama.* Regulation of breath is called Pranayama. Our breathing is closely connected to our mind. The more we control our breathing, the quieter the mind will be. In practice, this means we are less easily disturbed by emotions, we are calmer and more relaxed, and tend to make better decisions. Moreover, the regulation of breath will have a favourable influence on our physical well-being, because it generates vitality and strength.

- *Pratyahara.* After having prepared ourselves with asana and pranayama before the practice of meditation, the moment has come to close the eyes and withdraw from the world of our senses. This is called pratyahara. We leave the surroundings for what it is and start exploring our inner world. Noises from outside are not important any more, thoughts no longer matter, all that is left is the unfathomable depth of our inner world.

- *Dharana.* Dharana means concentration on the goal of meditation. There needs to be a certain focus for the mind, otherwise it runs in all directions. The object of meditation may be a person (e.g. the spiritual teacher) or something else (e.g. the mantra). The idea is that the mind stays resolute in its focus.

- *Dhyana.* The word dhyana means meditation. In the beginning, the mind will be restless and losing its focus all the time. But the more the quality of the meditation improves, the more silent the mind will become, and it will experience deep rest. Meditation in this case does not mean a continuous mental effort, but the ability to allow the attention to flow in an unbroken stream towards the object of meditation and even transcend it.

- *Samadhi.* When we go beyond the object of meditation we speak of the transcending of our mental activity. The turbulence of the mind has completely settled down. In the state of samadhi subject, object, and the relation between them (the process), have completely merged into each other. The experience of this is the silent bliss of infinite Being, a state of inner joy that cannot be captured in words. It is the level of all possibilities, where the seer experiences his own divine nature. It is the final destination, the fulfilment of every seeker of truth, of the way back to God.

X.5 HIGHER STATES OF CONSCIOUSNESS

In the Yoga-sutras, Pure Being is described as a state of infinite silence. In Karma Mimamsa (the fifth Upanga), it is described as an infinite dynamics within the structure of this silence. Both approaches are completely authentic and real, in spite of the apparent contradiction. After all, it is Vedanta that solves this paradox and leads us to the ultimate experience of human existence.

As long as we dwell in a human body, we live in a world of duality, a world in which everything is relative. We are used to the opposites of light and dark, hate and love, good and bad, silence and activity. If we look around us, and also to ourselves carefully, we will see that nothing whatsoever remains the same, even for a second, and that we ourselves are also a bucket full of contradictions. Vedanta (literally: 'the end of the Veda') explains that our human mind and intellect make mistakes all the time and introduces thereby the word maya, which means illusion or non-existent. Through the senses, the limited human mind perceives the material world, but the ultimate reality behind that world of changes remains hidden to it. The absolute reality of life, called Brahman in the Vedic literature, is that the whole of life is united in the wholeness of consciousness with all its various aspects. This wholeness is unchanging, eternal and complete in itself. Under the influence of maya, Brahman appears as the manifested world. Knowing this does not mean that we should neglect the relative, changing life. Some groups cherish the thought that relative life does not matter so much because, after all, everything is absolute and predestined. But for the average man, the relative life is definitely a daily reality and something to be taken seriously. On the other hand, knowing that the transient life is not the ultimate reality, can ease our suffering on this earth considerably and put it in a different perspective.

It appears that next to the five above mentioned states of human consciousness, man can apparently evolve further, to an even higher state of consciousness. This is the deeper teaching of Vedanta and a fact from which only a few souls are aware. In cosmic consciousness, the fifth state of consciousness, there is still a difference of experience between our inner world and the outer world. Even though there is much more a 'we' feeling and the mind has in principle reached its evolutionary final goal, we still live in a dualistic world. What can the human mind experience more than Being, amidst a world of dynamic activity? The answer is: nothing more! Still, a further refinement of the senses is possible, whereby the mind little by little comes to experience the subject and object of perception as being fully identical with each other. This is the highest state of consciousness of man, called *Brahman consciousness* (Brahmi chetana), in which man is continuously aware that Being is the essence of all that has been created. All differences between knower, known and the process of knowing have dissolved, what remains is complete Union. This is the ultimate experience, that you and me are in essence the same, namely fluctuations of creative intelligence, which arise from the same source and are absorbed again therein. And, strangely enough, this apparently surrealistic experience is the most logical, most realistic and most practical completion and ultimate crowning achievement of man.

Relationship with the Vedas
In the Vedas, Indra represents this all-embracing wholeness of Brahman consciousness. Indra's abilities are the senses that have undergone a progressive refinement on the spiritual path. In the Vedic hymns, they are symbolised by the cows, while the milk stands for the fulfilment that the senses experience.

Now, how can we know if we walk the path of yoga correctly? In our first experience of growth to a higher state of consciousness, we feel more compassion with our fellow creatures, including also animals and plants, and we have a more favourable attitude towards the other. The next step is, that we perceive more synchronicity and unity in the things around us – in the world, in life, in our mind and in our soul. Furthermore, we start to see more and more, that life is a cosmic game, a drama in which we are a part of a much greater whole. And we appear to be very well able to deliver a positive contribution to that greater whole. Life-supporting properties that we develop are: love, creativity, happiness, simplicity, harmony, humility, joy and wisdom. At a still later stage, we are able to fully surrender to the Supreme Divine and see that everything springs forth from that one Brahman and everything is an expression of Brahman, which we can call the Kingdom of God.

This all is what is meant in the Vedas by the flow of pure soma: Indra drinks the soma, or the mind unites with Indra. Also, the cloths derived from the cows, i.e. the milk (satisfaction), is mixed with soma. The one, who undergoes this ultimate experience, becomes a Rikvan or an Atharvan (compare with Rigveda and Atharvaveda), called a knower of Brahman. The Rikvan or Atharvan possesses the integrated wisdom of life – Vedanta – the end of the Veda, and experiences in a natural way its most exalted goal of total Unity.

CHAPTER XI

STUDY OF THE VEDA

'All creatures follow their own nature,
even the enlightened man acts according to his own nature.'

- Lord Krishna in the Bhagavad Gita

The structure of the Veda is often compared to a human being, complete with nervous system, limbs, organs, and other functions. The book of Dr. Tony Nader about the correspondence between the Veda and the human body, indicates that this comparison is not strange at all. We, human beings, are a tiny drop in the ocean of the wholeness of life. As above, so below is true here again.

Just as the different limbs and organs of the human body form an integrated whole, so do the Vedic scriptures take their own position in the totality of Vedic literature, and so each part fulfils their specific function. This place and function of each part is associated with the distinction between knower, known and process of knowing. Earlier, we have already became acquainted with the divisions of shruti and smriti. This distinction is respectively about that what is heard and that what is remembered.

201

The shruti is concerned with texts from divine revelations (Vedas and Brahmanas), while the smritis comprise the commentaries; further elaboration and practical applications given by very enlightened sages.

The Vedangas belong to the smriti, but give an explanation of all aspects of the shruti. Their place in the whole of Vedic literature is of such a nature that they are intimately linked to the Vedas. Their profound wisdom is of an extraordinarily high level. Without the study of and insight into the Vedangas, no human being is able to grasp the real meaning of the Vedas. Next to the Vedangas, the Itihasas and Puranas fulfil a supporting role in the study of the Veda.

XI.1 VEDANGAS

The Vedangas, the angas or limbs of the Vedas, are a confirmation of the human character of the Vedas. They form the nose, the hands, the mouth, the ears, the feet, and the eyes of the Veda (see scheme 11.1)

Scheme 11.1

The Vedangas

VEDANGA	SUBJECT	SAMHITA	ORGAN
SHIKSHA	phonetics / pronunciation	Rishi	Nose
KALPA	rituals	Devata	Hands
VYAKARANA	grammar	Chhandas	Mouth
NIRUKTA	etymology	Chhandas	Ears
CHHANDAS	metre	Devata	Feet
JYOTISH	astrology	Rishi	Eyes

Scheme 11.1 Practically seen, the Vedangas indicate in an exact and systematic manner how to understand the Vedas in depth.

The Vedangas fulfil an essential role in the way we study and understand the Vedas. They give a commentary on the mechanics and structure of the Vedic hymns; which parts the Vedas consist of, how they are built up and how we can understand them in the light of the whole. As the above scheme shows clearly, there are six Vedangas.

Shiksha

Shiksha represents the nose of the Veda. Its composition and elaboration is attributed to *Panini*, but in total thirty-six authentic scriptures pertaining to Shiksha exist. It is the science of sound and deals with pronunciation (phonetics). It explains how sounds are formed and if their combinations have a life-supporting effect or not. A lot of effort has always been made to preserve the Vedas in their original composition and division. The correct pronunciation of the Sanskrit sounds plays an important role herewith. The Taittiriya Upanishad I.2 gives an enumeration of five phonetic principles in order to emphasize the importance of the correct pronunciation of the Sanskrit texts.

varna	pronunciation
svara	pitch
bala	the way of expression
sama	intonation
sanatana	continuity

These principles also apply to the chanting of *mantras* and *bhajans* during satsangs. Elementary education in the correct pronunciation of Sanskrit for visitors of these spiritual gatherings would be appropriate.

The Shiksha texts are the Pratishakhyas of Rigveda, Yajurveda and Atharvaveda. We see that in the different parts of the Vedic literature the same texts keep appearing, but often there is a difference in the way the words are pronounced. Furthermore, within the same texts, some words are replaced by other words which, however, have the same meaning.

The purpose of this is apparently to remove misunderstandings about the meaning of the hymn, or it might have been a help for students to discriminate between the texts of the different parts. In any case, we know that there has been careful thinking about every word and its placement in the whole of the texts, and that every word expresses exactly what it means. One of the reasons why many commentators in the past did interpret the Vedas wrongly, has to do with the fact that they had insufficient knowledge of Sanskrit. Therefore, they could not study the Vedangas, hence gave incorrect meanings to words. Only a few commentators are worth reading, one among which is Shri Aurobindo, who strongly emphasizes the consciousness aspect of the Vedas and the supporting role of the Vedangas.

Kalpa

Kalpa, the hands of the Veda, symbolises the field of action. There is one scripture known about Kalpa, which consists of eight chapters. This scripture is the study of the dynamic activity contained in the Veda. It comprises procedures about rituals and how they make use of the dynamics in *parame vyoman*, the transcendental field of consciousness. The rituals and ceremonies are meant to fulfil human desires and are an instrument to experience higher states of consciousness. Together with Jyotish, Kalpa provides the knowledge of how to use the Vedas. In chapter VII, we have dealt elaborately with the phenomenon of yajna. On the one hand they can play a very important role in the process of growth of the seeker of truth, on the other hand, we should also not overestimate their value in our present time. They can be an impediment on the spiritual path, in case the difference between means and goal is not clear in the mind.

For this reason, the followers of Arya Samaj consider the many rituals and honouring of *avatara's* (divine incarnations) and murtis (idols of divine qualities) to be a deviation from the original Vedic wisdom. According to the teaching of its founder, Shri Dayananda, man is, without exception, bound by the laws of karma and reincarnation, and this cannot be annihilated by any kind of ritual. His opinion is, that all religious and other knowledge is contained in the Veda. He had progressive ideas for his time. He did not judge the varna-system without a good reason, but he held that it should be based on individual differences in character and other qualities. He showed that he was a promoter of marriage based on free choice and wanted to put an end to child marriage. He recommended that men and women have the same right for education, especially with respect to Sanskrit grammar (vyakarana). For him, this formed the basis of gaining insight into the meaning of the Vedas. In his commentaries, Swami Dayananda claimed that all new discoveries of modern science have already been written in the Vedas, a statement that we cordially support.

Vyakarana

Vyakarana, the mouth of the Veda, is attributed (like Shiksha) to Panini. His scripture consists of eight chapters, each subdivided into four sections. Vyakarana is the discipline of speech; it expresses the grammar of language of nature. Panini's research is to this day the leading thread for Sanskrit students and is indispensable for understanding the meaning of the Vedas. Earlier, we have already eulogised Sanskrit – the language of the gods. It is a natural language that beautifully reflects the quality and perfection of the totality of Being and the development of existence. Because it is the language of nature, it directly refers to our brain functions. This implies that the study of Sanskrit is an instrument of personal growth, moreover, it induces a harmonizing effect. Because of its logical, mathematical structure it is not very difficult to learn, unlike people often think. Its structure is, like in the Veda, present in seed form at the simplest level of our awareness. At that fundamental level, sound, grammar and meaning form a complete unity.

Nirukta

Nirukta, the ears of the Veda, is like a dictionary dealing with etymology (derivation of words). Language has a direct relationship with our sense of hearing, which is the most subtle one among the senses and, therefore, can easily transcend sound vibrations. Our hearing ignores space and time. We 'hear' time, but also what goes beyond it, and what still has to come. We sometimes need only half a word to understand our fellow creatures. Interesting in this connection is the statement of a blind comedian, who said: 'With my ears I probably see the most. Sound contains a lot of information. Through my ears, for instance, I like to look at art and paintings.'

The arrangement of sounds in Sanskrit is essential. Every word in Sanskrit consists of one or more syllables that can tell a whole story like, for instance, the word *guru*, which means teacher or master. In the Guru Gita (see chapter XVII) the word guru is described as someone by whose light knowledge is revealed. Literally *gu* stands for darkness and *ru* for light. A guru is someone who brings light in the darkness of ignorance (GG vs. 23). The syllable gu stands also for maya (illusion), while ru stands for the highest knowledge, which can annihilate the illusion of maya (GG vs. 24). A little bit further on in the Guru Gita, the Guru is equalled with Brahma, Vishnu and Shiva:

***

Gururbrahma gururvishnur
gururdevomahesvarah
gurureva parabrahma
tasmai shrigurave Namah
- Guru Gita vs 32

***

The sadguru is Parabrahman, he supersedes even the trinity of Brahma, Vishnu and Shiva. This example shows that every word has been carefully thought about. Sanskrit was not derived from an earlier language; it has naturally developed itself as it is. It is directly connected to the vibrations of the energy centres in the subtle body. *Chakra* means wheel. The energy centres make turning movements like those of a wheel, which produce the Sanskrit sounds and their meaning. The Vedic seers were very much aware that the wisdom of the integration of life would get lost in time. That is why the Vedas have been composed carefully and by analysing the roots of every word it is possible to decode it and decipher its hidden wisdom.

Chhandas

Chhandas, the feet of the Veda, deals with the metre, the way to maintain the rhythm and the role this plays in the eternal preservation of the Veda. There exists one authentic scripture on Chhandas, subdivided into eight chapters. The function of our feet is to stand firmly on the ground. In music, a fixed metre is needed to give structure and harmonious continuity to the melody. Without a metre, it would quickly become chaotic. Within the structure of the metre the composer can improvise to his heart's content. In Indian music, it is not so much the composer but the musician, who can improvise freely within the structure of the raga.

In the Vedas every hymn is bound to a fixed metre (chhandas); sometimes several metres are used for only one hymn. There are seven prominent metres, of which Gayatri, Trishtubh, Anushtubh and Jagati, are the most well-known. Each metre consists of a number of padas, which in their turn are connected to a number of syllables. The most frequently used metre is Gayatri, consisting of three padas with eight syllables each. The Gayatri metre consists of 24 syllables in total. As an example, we repeat the first verse of the Rigveda here:

***

Agnimile purohitam
yagyasya devam ritvijam
hotaram ratna dhatamam.'

***

In his Vedic Science, Maharishi has explained that the twenty-four syllables of this first verse are not based on chance, but that they, together with the meaning of the words, give a purely scientific exposition of the process of creation. The recitation of the Vedic hymns on the basis of fixed metres is also, as mentioned above, an ideal way to preserve the hymns throughout the ages in their original form.

Jyotish

Jyotish, the eyes of the Veda, is the science of the influence of the cosmic transformations on the life of men. Its goal is to let the light of Atman, or pure consciousness, shine in the heart of every man. Practically speaking, it supports the fulfilling of the four goals of human existence, namely: *dharma* (allotted duty), *artha* (wealth), *kama* (desire) and *moksha* (spiritual liberation).

Everything in the universe moves and changes and is interwoven with the fabrics of time. The Sun and the stars are sources of light and energy, which they spread throughout space. Without the Sun, life on Earth is impossible. We are continuously influenced by the light and energy of the Sun and other celestial bodies. The science of Jyotish, nowadays usually called Vedic astrology, makes use of precise mathematical calculations in order to establish the positions and transformations of the celestial bodies. With this knowledge, it is able to explain the life (past, present and future) of every human being on earth.

According to the teaching of the three doshas in Ayurveda, every human has a unique physical constitution, called *Prakriti*. In the same way, everyone also has a unique planetary constitution, depending on the specific time and place at the moment of birth. The Vedic astrologer makes a Vedic birthchart (*kundali*) of this moment and can use this for many purposes. In this way, he can check the health, interests and someone's strong and weak points. He can see if there is a good matching with the (future) life partner and where the successes lie in other life areas. In this way, we can even determine the time of conception with the help of Jyotish, or the start of building a house in accordance with the most favourable planetary constellation. With its calculations, Jyotish can even exercise influence on the destiny of a society and that of the whole world. But above all, Jyotish is a spiritual instrument that can transform our life in the direction of inner Light.

In almost all holy scriptures, we come across the application of anatomy and astrology. Like, for instance, in the age-old Maya culture, the ancient seers rather observed the cosmos than they made use of their calculations, as we are nowadays used to in Vedic astrology. But, gradually, rational thinking replaced intuition as the main characteristic of human consciousness. Great saints like Parashara and Jaimini have further worked out their *Jyotir Vidya* (astrological knowledge) in their shastras (holy scriptures). They have used different methods to investigate and describe the ultimate reality. Maharshi Parashara, who is considered the father of Jyotish, mentions at the end of his scripture, the Brihat Parashara Hora Shastra, that Brahma himself has revealed this wisdom to humanity:

The branches of Jyotish that emerged, have been traditionally divided on the one side into *skandhas* (parts) and on the other side into *angas* (limbs). In scheme 11.2, the division into skandhas, which is dated earlier, is shown.

***

'The knowledge that I have passed on to you,
is the same Jyotish that Lord Brahma (the Creator)
has told Narada (the divine messenger)
and which Narada passed on to Shaunaka
and other saints, from whom I received it.
I have told it to you as I have learned it from them.'
- BPHS 97.1-2a

***

Scheme 11.2
The three Skandhas and their Meaning

GANITA SKANDHA	Astrological and astronomical calculations
SAMHITA SKANDHA	Different observations, including omens in the sky, the weather, economic cycles, earthquakes, successes of a country, house building, and research into water wells.
HORA SKANDHA	Interpretation based on the Vedic birthchart

Scheme 11.2 Jyotish enables man, with mathematical precision, to open
his eyes to the wholeness of the time phenomenon: past, present and future.
Simultaneously, it provides insight into the different qualities of time,
depending on the cosmic influences. Its areas of applications are still lively in
the culture of India today and enjoy an increasing popularity in the West.

Jyotish possesses six angas or limbs, just like there are six Vedangas for the Vedas. (see scheme 11.3)

In the beginning, astronomical observations were made mainly to establish auspicious days or times for the performance of yajnas. Throughout time, one gradually developed a mathematical system to perform precise calculations: the birth of the actual *astrology, based on a birthchart*, as we know it now. Here, just as in Western astrology, signs, planets and houses are being used, but there are also important differences to the Western system of astrology.

Scheme 11.3

The Six Limbs of Jyotish

GOLA	Astronomy and astronomical observations
GANITA	Astronomical and astrological calculations
JATAKA	Astrology based on a Vedic birthchart; prediction
NIMITTA	Interpretation of omens
PRASHNA	Astrology in response to a question, on the basis of a birth chart or otherwise
MUHURTA	The estimation of auspicious moments for important activities or events (first entry into a house, marriage, signing of a contract, selling and buying, and so forth).

Scheme 11.3 Jyotish makes use of the seven main planets, i.e. Sun, Moon, Mars, Mercury, Jupiter, Venus and Saturn. Next to these, the so-called moon nodes, Rahu and Ketu, also play an important role in the Vedic birthchart. They form the mathematical points in space where the eclipses of the Sun and Moon take place.

Prashna is a special branch based on a query. This can happen by making a horoscope, but also by looking at other indications at the moment the question is asked. In this context, we can think of the structure of the question (number of syllables, etc.), the body parts that the questioner touches, the direction that he faces at the moment of the query, or of a random number that he/she can choose. In the case of the use of omens, we can think of a flight of birds, certain sounds we hear, the falling of objects, the passing of meteors, the blinking of the eyes, or other physical sensations.

Muhurta is that part of Jyotish which estimates auspicious days or times, and this part is still often used in India. All holidays and festivals are, for example, based on the Moon calendar (*Panchanga*), which is the most important instrument for Muhurta in the estimation of auspicious times.

Summary

As regards the Vedangas, what use of his body a man has, if he cannot know and learn to use all of its parts? Without insight into the fundamental values of Vedangas and their profound knowledge, man is not able to comprehend the Vedas – the wisdom of existence. The study of Sanskrit is, therefore, a first requirement. Everyone can enjoy Sanskrit as the sound and energy dance that it is, just as children have learned it playfully throughout time. If we invested time in chanting, reciting and playing the Vedic mantras, we would quickly discover how sounds always unfold themselves in the same way from deep within and *create* words. This process gives energy to the whole system, just like atoms charge themselves up by connecting to their own original source. Next to this, the divisions of Jyotish and Kalpa give deep insight into our individual path and the way to walk it as comfortable as possible. By making the Vedangas our own, it becomes possible to gain mastery over time, space and activity, and this way we will be able to enjoy the fullness of life.

XI.2 ITIHASA

Itihasa, to which the epics *Ramayana* and *Mahabharata* belong is, regarding its content and meaning, related to the *Puranas*. Both scriptures contain mighty metaphors of Vedic wisdom, meant to make us familiar with the wisdom of the Veda. The difference is that Itihasa expresses the *chhandas-value* in the wholeness of consciousness while the Puranas express the *devata-value*. Another difference is, that Itihasa deals mainly with human beings and the Puranas with celestial beings.

Itihasa expresses the highest value of the Veda by means of stories and characters, familiar for everyone. Also here applies that we can interpret the content of the stories on all levels of creation, depending on our ability to use them as inspiration for the spiritual path. In Ramayana, our main figure, prince Rama, is the expression of the full value of the Veda, the higher Self. Mahabharata has, in contrast with Ramayana, many heroes, who together represent the total value of the Veda. Bhagavad Gita forms a small part (700 verses) of the total of original 74.000 verses of Mahabharata, but is a master piece of wisdom and can be considered to be the pocket edition of the Veda. Its practical aim is to restore and apply the fundamental life principles to everyone's life and lead the true devotee back to God.

Ramayana

King Dasharatha, the mighty king of the Kosala kingdom, had four sons with his three wives. When he became old, he decided to officially install *Rama*, the son of his first wife, as successor to the throne. Because Rama was beloved by everyone, all ministers and inhabitants of Ayodhya were very happy with this important event and rejoiced in the upcoming ceremony. But instead of becoming the crown prince, Shri Rama, through the intrigues of his step-mother, was sent into exile to the forest, for fourteen years. His beautiful wife, Sita, and his younger brother, Lakshman, accompanied him.

One day in the forest Sita was kidnapped by the demon king Ravana, after he had lured Rama and Lakshman away with a trick. Ravana took Sita away in his aerial chariot to Lanka, but because she stubbornly refused to become his wife, he imprisoned her under a tree in his garden. In the meantime, Rama and Lakshman did everything they could to find and liberate Sita. They thereby got instructions from the king of the birds, and a colony of monkeys and bears helped them, too. It was finally the monkey chief, Hanuman, Rama's most devoted disciple, who found Sita 's hiding place on the island of Lanka. Hanuman saw how desperate Sita was and under what difficult circumstances she remained loyal to her beloved Rama. Therefore, he quickly returned to his master, Shri Rama, and his allies to inform them of his discovery.

Shri Rama in exile in the forest, accompanied by Sita and Lakshmana
(painting: Rozalia Hummel)

Rama, Lakshmana and the whole army of monkeys and bears went immediately in search of Sita to save her from the hands of Ravana. Under the guidance of Shri Rama, they built a bridge between the Indian continent and Lanka. Upon arriving in Lanka, an intense fight followed, in which Rama offered several times to stop fighting in exchange for the liberation of his wife. But Ravana refused to give up and was ultimately killed by Rama. Having returned into their own country, Shri Rama and Sita were crowned king and queen of Kosala. Thereupon followed a long period of Shri Rama's rule, which was eulogised for ages by minstrels, as a golden age of peace and justice.

Shri Rama, symbol of leading a life attuned to the higher Self, was already in his youth well-known for being a wise and righteous prince. He intuitively felt that the play of the three *gunas* (symbolised by the three wives of the king) is the real motivating factor that stimulates people to think and act. Therefore, he could not become angry at his step-mother, and, to great confusion of his family, went in exile without any protest. Usually we think we have everything under control, but in fact we are completely absorbed in our desires and ideals. Rama's step-mother thought, quite wrongly, as it turned out afterwards, that she did her own son, Bharata, a big favour by granting him the throne. Such an erroneous calculation of the situation occurs, when the intellect is not in harmony with the Self, which is unprejudiced and accepts any event as it happens.

Mahabharata

Mahabharata is the Vedic epic, that shows us the consequences of what happens when people want or do not want something, when they can or cannot do something. It describes the dramatic battle between two related branches of a royal family, the *Pandavas* and the *Kauravas*. The Kauravas are sons of a blind king and they stand as symbols of passion and greed in man. Their cousins, the Pandavas stand for virtues and ideal behaviour. They have noble thoughts and strive to perform the correct deeds.

King Dhritarashtra, father of the evil Kauravas was blind. The deeper meaning of this is, that his vision on life is overshadowed by pride and attachment. He acted as an ignorant man, and was even aware of this, but was unable to change it. The five Pandavas, sons of his elder brother Pandu, had the oldest rights to the throne. But Dhritarashtra's own sons had only one goal in view, namely to destroy the Pandava's virtue, wisdom and harmony, and to ensure the throne for themselves herewith. Every time they needed the support of their father, he gave it to them, against all odds. Many times, Lord Krishna, who was a close friend of the Pandavas, tried to re-conciliate, but in vain. In this way, the blind king

Dhritarashtra was personally responsible that a war, between the good and bad forces in the world, became inevitable.

Bhagavad Gita
After a bloody battle, the Pandavas won the war on the battlefield of Kurukshetra with the help of Lord Krishna. Lord Krishna Himself did not participate in the battle, but was the charioteer and coach of his friend, Arjuna.

Bhagavad Gita, as mentioned before, is a masterpiece of wisdom and explains the essence of the human being as a spiritual soul, together with his attachment to the material world and the way he can finally return to the spiritual world or *Krishna loka*. Lord Krishna teaches Arjuna in a beautiful and perfect way about all aspects of life and existence. Arjuna, famous for his skill in archery, was one of the five Pandavas. The battle which the Pandavas had to fight, is the 'fight' that takes place in each of us and which is necessary to grow in wisdom and compassion. Every man has to follow his own path in order to discover who he is, and what he wants in and with his life. Arjuna is an example for us from whom we can learn a lot. By proving himself to be a devoted disciple, he learns from Lord Krishna, who in fact is the Supreme Being, all knowledge about truth, the principles of nature, life and death, evolution, time, the right action and detachment. After Lord Krishna had spoken to him lovingly, and revealed to him all secrets of life, Arjuna knew enough in the end, and acted accordingly, surrendering fully to the Divine.

XI.3 PURANAS
The Vedic wisdom is a science, because it is confirmed by objective research and direct (subjective) observation or experience. Next to that, it contains a number of religious and mythological characteristics, which, however, also possess a scientific core. In every tradition of wisdom, there is a distinction between true knowledge, philosophy and mythology.

True knowledge is *shruti,* that what is divinely revealed and heard by ancient seers. This shruti is much more complete than the modern branches of science, because the latter only investigate and explain the external world. *Philosophy* is an essential characteristic of a culture that holds wisdom in high esteem. The Greek word itself says it already: *sofia* means wisdom. Next to that, *mythology* explains and illustrates the religious and philosophical aspects of a culture by means of legendary, often very ancient stories of great souls or (demi)gods.

There are eighteen *Mahapuranas*:

Scheme 11.5
The eighteen Mahapuranas

Brahma Purana	Markandeya Purana	Skanda Purana
Padma Purana	Agni Purana	Vamana Purana
Vishnu Purana	Bhavisya Purana	Matsya Purana
Narada Purana	Linga Purana	Kurma Purana
Bhagavata Purana	Varaha Purana	Brahmanda Purana
Shiva Purana	Brahmavaivarta Purana	Garuda Purana

Scheme 11.5 Most of the Puranas are of very old date. Some of their stories about celestial beings, living on different planets, go back millions of years. They contain fascinating stories to keep alive the interest of the people in sanatana dharma, the eternal law.

The Puranas (Purana means: old, ancient) express the *Devata principle* within the wholeness of consciousness and show how the laws of nature function. The stories narrate the lives of gods and saints, the origin and process of creation, rules of honouring God, and many instructions for correct behaviour. Also, in the Puranas we find family trees of kings, saints and Devatas. Throughout the ages, they have been passed on orally by village priests, parents, grand-parents and the roaming minstrel. Many temple walls are covered with carvings of puranic stories and especially in the villages, they are told in songs, dance and drama. These are imaginative ways of educating people in the simple but profound truths of morality; in what the correct and incorrect behaviour is.

Traditionally, in case of death one reads from Garuda Purana and the *Guru Gita*, a song of praise to the Guru, which can be found at the end of the Skanda Purana. Many *Puranas* contain mythological stories that have occurred sometimes millions of years ago. Although most of the myths are assumed to have really taken place, they do not have a historical sequence to them. Through the long lapse of time stories get changed or are placed into a different context and the same happens to the main characters. What is true and what is not? This question is not that important, much more important is the deeper message that they want to transmit through writing, words or by depiction. Shakespeare's drama, *Hamlet* can be compared in that sense to a Purana.

The purpose of a Purana is mainly to indicate the processes along which life progresses. On this ground we can gain insight into the basic values and purposes of life to promote our personal growth. To learn geography, we need both the help of maps and the explanation of a teacher. On the map, not one real city or country is found, but it helps us gain important knowledge about the countries or cities. By means of the mythological stories we can explore the subtle questions of life and do something about them for our own well-being and that of the society.

Shrimad Bhagavata Purana
Shrimad-Bhagavata Purana occupies a very unique place in the extensive Vedic literature. After the holy saint Shrīla Vyasadeva had composed the four Vedas and wrote other Vedic scriptures, he wrote the Shrimad-Bhagavatam, which consists of twelve Cantos (volumes) with 18.000 verses altogether.

In Shrimad-Bhagavatam it is explained that, besides the material world, there is also a spiritual universe with countless planets, each under the supervision of Narayana, Lord Krishna. On these so-called *Vaikuntha* planets live the eternally liberated souls who have become fully detached from the material world and have completely surrendered to Lord Krishna, the Supreme Lord of all existence who is even in His manifestations both immanent and transcendental.

Vyasadeva's spiritual teacher Narada Muni advised him to write the Shrimad-Bhagavatam, which became the most complete and authoritative explanation of Vedic wisdom. (Painting: Dominique Amendola)

Lord Krishna is known as Brahman (Absolute Truth), Paramatma (Supersoul) and Bhagavan (Supreme Godhead). The Bhagavatam teaches how human beings can be detached from the material world by the practice of *bhakti-yoga*, devoted service to the Supreme. Intensive practice of bhakti-yoga, which can be considered the highest form of yoga, lifts the soul up to the spiritual planets, where life is eternally blissful and full of wisdom. It has been His Divine Grace A.C. Bhaktivedanta Swami Prabhupada (1896-1977), founder and spiritual master of the Hare Krishna movement, who wrote an extensive and bona fide commentary on the verses of Bhagavatam. When we look around in the world, we can easily ascertain that mankind is in crisis. All material achievements, developed through modern science and technology, have not made human beings happier, healthier and wiser. There is an urgent need of a holistic vision on how humanity can establish one common goal that leads to peace, friendship and prosperity among all countries and people in the world. Shrimad-Bhagavatam fulfils that need, because it offers a unique social and spiritual solution for all the problems in the world, based on the eternal wisdom of the Vedas.

XI.4 VIMANAS IN THE VEDIC LITERATURE

In many parts of the Vedic literature we come across fascinating information about flying spacecrafts, called *vimanas*. These historical airplanes were able to travel through interspace and from planet to planet. From the Vedic scriptures, we learn that on different planets the living beings use all kind of planes. All demigods, like the Devas, Asuras, Gandharvas and Siddhas, have their own flying vehicles with which they can travel easily throughout space. These airships are much more advanced than our modern planes powered by heavy engines. Moreover, they look very beautiful and are usually decorated with gold, pearls and gemstones. There are also aerial chariots of a completely transcendental built, sent by Lord Krishna to bring His true devotees to His eternal abode. Of course, these airships can't be seen by modern scientists, who also cannot imagine at all how these airships are able to move.

The very advanced spacecrafts described in the Vedic scriptures, are often powered solely by spiritual tools, like for example the use of *mantras*. Also, it seems that certain heavenly vehicles are just *living beings* who, by their own intelligence, are able to fly and cover immeasurable distances. From Lord Brahma we know that he uses a cosmic swan for travelling through interspace and Lord Vishnu is flying on a huge cosmic bird named Garuda. As we have seen above, there is even a Garuda Purana contain in all the knowledge about it. And other higher beings, especially from Siddhaloka, even if they don't need a flying chariot, can just travel from planet to planet all by themselves. Also, from Narada Muni we know, that he can travel wherever he wants, from the spiritual to the material universe, and vice versa, and that he travels with the speed of thought.

On our earth Sitadevi was kidnapped by the demonking Ravana and brought to Lanka in an airship, which he had stolen from his half-brother Kubera. (painting: Rozalia Hummel)

As already mentioned, many examples of space travel are given in Ramayana. Famous is the passage of Shri Hanuman, Rama's most devoted disciple, who had the ability to move through the air. He flew across the ocean and discovered Sitadevi's hidden place. Lord Rama then immediately proceeded to Lanka with an army of monkeys and bears to free Sita. After several days of fierce fighting, the chariots of Rama and Ravana finally faced each other. Both fought with so-called *astras* that we can compare to our own nuclear weapons. Suddenly, Ravana made use of his magical powers and sent his chariot into the sky to attack Rama from above. But at the same time, Rama's charioteer Matali also sent his chariot into the air, and the battle continued unabated. At one point, Matali deftly maneuvered his heavenly chariot, which actually was the vehicle of Indra, to Ravana's right. From the higher spheres the demigods watched the drama with fascination. Ravana had ten heads, which Rama shot one by one, but each time another head took their place. Nearly desperate, Lord Rama then used the *Brahmastra*, a hellish weapon that he had once received from Saint Agastya. This weapon had the destructive radiation of the sun and was deadly as fire.

Rama took the weapon in his mighty hands, summoned it according to the prescribed rules, and placed it on his bow. The whole earth shook when he released the missile. It flew straight towards its target, hitting Ravana right below his navel, where his weak spot was. Ravana fell dead to the ground and the Brahmastra, as a devoted servant returned to Rama's quiver after having performed its duties.

Only with the support of the transcendental chariots it is possible to reach the spiritual world where Narayana and his true devotees dwell eternally. From the four Kumaras, the wise sons of Lord Brahma, we know that when they arrived to the Vaikuntha planets, they transformed into transcendental beings and left the material world behind for ever. We can thus conclude, that our modern space vehicles are completely unsuitable for interspace travelling, but by the support of the perfect Vedic principles, the yogis can move from planet to planet and even reach the spiritual universe. Unfortunately, today's human consciousness no longer has the ability to observe or perceive all this, let alone making use of it.

CHAPTER XII

INFLUENCE OF THE VEDA

'In the Beginning was the Word, and the Word was with God, and the Word was God.'

- Saint John 1.1

Since the beginning of human civilisation, the wisdom of the Veda is spread all over the world. Although the origin and hidden meaning of this knowledge got lost long before in the past, many of its myths and symbols have been adopted by later cultures and religions. Also, without doubt, words in many languages find their origin in ancient Sanskrit. So, we could imagine that the word *Amen*, which means 'so be it' and which is considered to be derived from the Hebrew language, has an etymological connection with the mantra Aum, as well. Many ideas that we come across in Christianity, Tao or Islam, are clearly derived from the Vedic scriptures and very often without having any idea about their original, hidden meaning. It may be obvious, then, that we can only give a few examples of them in this chapter.

XII.1 THE STORY OF CREATION

Not one myth has captivated the minds of people so deeply as the story of creation, which can be found all over the world, in every religion and culture. A peculiar characteristic of this is, that all these different stories make use of the same descriptions and symbols which occur frequently in the Vedic scriptures dating back much longer.

In the creation story of Rigveda, the oldest records of mankind, we read:

***

'First there is Brahman, the Lord of all, together with the Word, and truly the Word is Brahman.'

***

In the beginning of the gospel of Saint John we find the following text:

***

'Through the Word everything has been created and without the Word nothing has become (.....). The Word has become flesh and has come to live among us.'
- Saint John I.1

***

Moreover, it looks like certain texts of the Old Testament – especially of the book of Genesis – are completely inspired by the Vedas. In western countries we may still remember from childhood that even before the beginning, God's spirit wandered above the waters. The Vedas explain that before creation, there was *salila*, a homogeneous and liquid substance. Salila is usually translated as *water* but it looks more like a kind of liquid helium. The concept that before the creation of heaven and earth everything consisted of a water-like substance, is spread all around the world and has been taken over by almost all religious scriptures.

We also come across variations of creation stories, which narrate that the universe sprang forth from a big, cosmic egg. These stories are all derived from Rigveda. In the Matsya Purana, we find the following version:

'After the *Mahapralaya*, the dissolution of the universe, darkness was everywhere. Everything was in a state of deep sleep. There was nothing, not even a single movement. Then *Svayambhu*, the Supreme Being, lying far beyond sensory perception manifested Himself. He first created water (salila) and deposited therein the seed of creation. That seed grew out into a golden egg. Then Svayambhu entered the egg, therefore He is called Lord Vishnu.'

In the Bible, the earth was desolate and empty in the beginning. In the Vedas, the still virgin earth crust is compared to the back of a tortoise:

***

'Before, the earth was without any hair,
like the back of a tortoise.'
- **Mahabharata Shantiparva 300.6**

***

The analogy between the barrenness of the earth and the back of a tortoise was long forgotten, but later another myth emerged, which assumes that the earth rests upon the back of a tortoise and that earthquakes come about as a consequence of the movements of the tortoise. By the way, the Vedic seers already knew that the earth is round and is turning around its axis, several thousands of years before the birth of Copernicus.

We come across the ancient image of God as Supreme Soul (Purusha), as a universal form of man Himself in the Bible, where we learn that man was created in the image of God (Genesis I.27) and for instance in the *Tao*: 'The nature of heaven belongs to man' (Yin Fu Ching I.3.4).

And God saw that it was good and rested on the seventh day (Genesis II.2). In one of the Vedic scriptures, of a much older date, we read:

***

'After He had created the universe and men,
Prajapati (the Creator) lied down and rested.'
– Taittiriya Brahmana I.2.6.1

***

In the astrological cycle of the seven days of the week, Saturday is the seventh day and is naturally a day of rest, the day of the Lord. In the Jewish tradition, the Sabbath is still honoured on Saturday, but in the West, it has been shifted to Sunday and nowadays many people do not even rest at all. Cosmically speaking, this is wrong and even unhealthy, because Saturday is the day of Saturn (the planet of disappointment, delay and separation), and from this point of view it would be much wiser to keep Saturday as a day of rest and meditation.

In the Bible, it is written that God created the man, Adam, and thereafter he created a woman from one of his ribs. Then follows the story of Eve and her meeting with the snake. The snake, in the Bible, represents evil or Satan, but this has not always been the case. In many cultures, the snake is and was a holy animal, and is considered to be a divine messenger. Lord Vishnu rests on the king of all snakes, called Shesha, possessing seven heads. The ancient inhabitants of the Ganges and Brahmaputra valley worshipped the Naga (cobra) and were called Nagas. Lord Shiva has snakes wrapped around his body, symbolising the conquest of the lower instincts. It is said that

Buddha, during a period of seven days, while he was in trance and before he became enlightened, had taken shelter under the head of a snake. The ancient Druids, who were the high priests of the Celts, called themselves snakes or Nagas and declared that they got their wisdom from the Eastern yogis. Via ancient Mesopotamia, where the snake was considered holy, it was later taken over by the Greek culture as a symbol of medicine. In the New Testament Jesus probably referred to the yogis from the East when he requested his apostles to be wise as snakes and non-violent as doves, before he sent them out to spread the word of God.

In many cases snakes represent the Kundalini energy. The kundalini is the divine energy that lies coiled up like a snake in a sleeping state at the basis of the spine. Whenever one talks about a five headed snake or there is an association with the number seven, there is probably a connection with the seven energy centres of the subtle body, through which the kundalini is flowing, once she is awakened.

***

'Who killed the snake and let the seven rivers flow,
who let the cows go that were hidden by Bali,
who created Agni between the two stones,
who kills the enemy in war?
Oh people, his name is Indra.'
- Rigveda II.12

***

In this hymn of Rigveda, all honour is granted to Indra, the king of the gods and the universal intelligence, who represents wholeness of consciousness. It sounds logical that the snake (kundalini energy) is enlivened, so as to flow upwards through the energy centres. But it is more likely that here the snake refers to maya (illusion) or ignorance. As a result, the senses can function without any obstruction and the Agni force can work freely. Indra is rightly called the destroyer of all ignorance. But the same snake, that is recognised in Vedic times as the bringer of happiness, was considered a bad omen later on, under different circumstances. Later religions did associate the snake with the arrival of disaster and divine curse. But above the entrance and on the pillars of almost all Hindu temples in India, the cobra is still depicted as a holy symbol.

XII.2 THE DELUGE

In the four Vedas, nothing is mentioned about a deluge covering the whole earth. This is strange, because the last flood must have happened around 12.000 years ago. Did the Vedic seers overlook something that important as a world disaster or has there never been a flood?

The oldest version of a flood we can find in the *Shatapatha Brahmana I.8.1.1.6*. On one day *Manu*, son of *Vivasvat*, held some little drops of water in the palm of his hand to clean his mouth. He saw that a little fish was swimming in that water. The fish promised Manu, that if he released him, he will protect Manu against the upcoming deluge. The fish asked Manu to keep him in a pot and to throw him back into the ocean afterwards. Manu wondered how the fish would protect him, but did what he was asked to. The fish told Manu to prepare a boat until the flood arrives. When the flood arrived and Manu was floating with his boat on the waters, the fish appeared out of the water, but now as a giant fish with a horn on its head. Manu tied a rope around the horn of the fish, who brought him to the top of a mountain. The fish asked Manu to stay on this spot until the flood subsided.

In the Puranas, we also come across this story. Here the fish seems to be an early incarnation of Lord Vishnu, who saves mankind from destruction. Also, in other cultures, we come across this story of the flood, like in an old Native American tribe. The natives believed that the whole human race was destroyed by a deluge. Only one god-fearing man escaped and landed with his big canoe on the top of a high mountain. All the people descend from this man. And in an old myth from Peru, a man and a woman escaped from a flood. They floated in a big box many hundreds of miles away from their original dwelling place. The Creator asked them to stay there until the water goes away. And of course everyone, who has read the Bible, will recognise the story of *Noah* and the Ark (Genesis VI-VIII). Noah survived the deluge together with his wife and three sons and with him many animals in pairs, which he had allowed to join them on the ark. Noah got stranded with his ark on the mountain Ararat, in today's Turkey. When one day the dove he had let loose returned with a twig, he knew that the water had receded and he could prepare to leave the ark. His three sons became the stem fathers of a new human race. This cosmological story of Noah and the ark may be directly derived from the Vedic scriptures.

The Ark of Noah (source: Wikipedia)

XII.3 THE WORSHIP OF THE LINGAM

Lord Shiva, who has his dwelling place on mount *Kailash*, is not only the god of destruction, but in the form of a *lingam* he also represents the Absolute. The lingam is an erect, pillar-like object representing the non-manifest aspect of existence. It has already been worshipped since prehistoric times in different religions and cultures, as the symbol for renewal and procreation (the phallus symbol). In Vedic tradition, one pours water, oil, honey, curd, milk or ghee (clarified butter) over it and places flowers on it. The lingam can be of any size, and is made of all kinds of material. It also occurs spontaneously in nature in the form of ice, rock or wood.

In the Genesis chapter of the Bible, Jacob places a pillar as a symbol of God's house, and pours oil over it. And Thera, the father of Abraham, was making pillar-like objects and idols meant for worship. Abraham, the grandfather of Jacob, worshipped a mountain god (!) together with His symbol in the form of a lingam (!). It looks as if Lord Shiva himself had descended there. In the Bible, it is said that Abraham consecrated a pillar in Beersheba in the honour of his God, before he left for Egypt. This God was addressed with the name *El Shaddai*, a name that very much resembles *Shaddayan*. Shaddayan is one of the names referring to Lord Shiva in the early Vedic period. The worship of El Shaddai by Abraham and his offspring continued till the time of Moses, who changed the name of El-Shaddai into 'YHWH' or Jehovah. One could also wonder if the name Abraham is etymologically related to Brahma, the Creator, or Brahman, the Absolute.

XII.4 THE TRINITY

The principle of the divine Trinity is a widespread belief and can be traced back in every religion or ancient culture. In old tales, legends, and other writings of humanity, there is an uninterrupted reference. The Egyptians had their Osiris, Isis and Horus, the Babylonians their Anu, Ea and Bel, the Norwegians Odin, Thor and Freya, and in the West, we have grown up with the Father, the Son and the Holy Spirit. They all symbolise in their own way the concept of the relationship between God (heaven) and man (Earth) and that what is in between (the intermediate space). The Vedas make clear that this principle of Trinity repeats itself on all levels of creation. It emerges and grows in the silence of our awareness when knower, process of knowing and known are uniting in wholeness.

In the previous chapters, we have become familiar with the three-in-one structure of the Veda, the wholeness of knower, process of knowing and the known. We have discussed the concept of the higher spheres, the lower spheres and the intermediate space. The three gunas *sattva*, *rajas* and *tamas* live and act in nature, which they enliven. In Vedic astrology, we work with signs, planets and houses, which represent intelligence, transformation and structure respectively. In the human body, we deal with vata, pitta and kapha. When the so-called doshas are in equilibrium, we speak of *samadosha*. In the body, we can localize the three fundamental energy channels, the ida, pingala and sushumna. In the state of enlightenment, they function as an integrated whole.

In the Vedic Tradition, Brahma, Vishnu and Shiva form the divine Trinity. They stand for creation, maintenance and destruction. In the four Vedas, only Brahma and Vishnu are mentioned next to the god Rudra, to which prayers are offered to save people from the effects of lightning. In later times, Shiva replaces Rudra. Shiva, Lord of Yoga, dwells on the mountain Kailash in the north of the Indus valley.

It is said that Shiva was worshipped in Arabia before the arrival of the Islam. Shiva's consort is Parvati, the divine Mother. She is the *Shakti*, the divine energy. Shiva and Parvati have two sons, *Shri Ganesha* and *Kartikeya*. Shri Ganesha was born without the interference of Shiva and Kartikeya is the creation of Shiva, in which Parvati did not take part.

The birth of Kartikeya was necessary to liberate the demigods from the domination of the demons.

In the New Testament, we come across the Trinity of Father, Son and Holy Spirit. Jesus says:

***

'But I say to you, be perfect, like my Father in heaven is perfect.'

***

Jesus speaks of a personal God who is perfect and lives in Heaven. He sees Himself as the mediator between heaven and earth, comparable to the Devata-principle (the mind), which plays a transforming role. In that sense, Jesus can be considered a divine incarnation, comparable to the avatara concept from the Vedic tradition. Like in other religions, His only goal is to lead people back to God. There may be differences according to country, time and circumstances, but all spiritual Masters from past and present agree, that there is a spiritual world beyond the material world to which we really belong.

By the way, there are striking resemblances in the stories surrounding the birth and growing up of Krishna and Jesus. First of all, both of them were born in very strange places, Lord Krishna in a prison and Jesus in a stable. Then, in both cases there is a cruel king who wants to kill them at any cost, and does not even shy away from mass child murder.

Finally, the Holy Spirit is the Life Breath, which manifests itself in the human body as the awakened kundalini energy. *'And they spoke with fiery tongues'*. Here, too, the influence of the Vedas reaches into the New Testament. One could even wonder if there was a relationship between the number four of Vedas and the four Gospels. Just as Rigveda is a great source of inspiration for the other three Vedas, so is the Gospel of Mark an important source for Matthew and Luke. But only further research could tell if a relationship between the origin and set-up of these scriptures could indeed be revealed.

The number *seven*, that we have mentioned a few times before, occurs in countless places in the Vedic scriptures. The seven heavens, the seven rishis, the seven intermediate spaces, the seven cognitions, the seven relations, the seven rivers, the seven metres, the seven coverings, and so forth. The sevenfold nature of the cosmos and in extension of man, has never been questioned by any religion or sage or philosopher. Pythagoras calls the number seven the chariot of man and cosmos.

And God spoke: '*Let there be Light*' (Genesis I.1). We know that the light spectrum falls apart into seven colours and that the Biblical creation took place in seven days. In *Proverbs 9.1* it is written: 'Wisdom has built its house; it has hewn out its seven pillars'. In other words, the number seven is a universal data and is on the human scale related to the seven subtle energy centres in the body and to the seven states of consciousness. Are we, humans, ultimately not a replica of the sevenfold Light, with which creation commenced?

It seems logical, that the ancient Vedic wisdom has found its way into later religions and cultures and became incorporated in them. Religions are not that much interested in history than in wanting to express their deepest feelings about man. The stories and myths express the forces of nature most clearly. They are meant to make us familiar with the universal intelligence and the cosmic laws, from which, as man, we have become estranged. But except for Hinduism, religions have throughout times been created by founders, by men. The Vedas, however, are not compilations of the human intellect. They are divine revelations coming from another world, the spiritual world. That is why we have to accept them as they are, as transcendental knowledge. At the beginning of the creation of the material world, Lord Brahma was the first living soul to receive the Vedas directly from Lord Krishna. He passed it on to Narada Muni and in this way, until today, the Vedic knowledge came down through a Holy Tradition of Masters.

XII.5 VEDA AND HINDUISM

Hinduism is the oldest religion in the world and is practiced today by more than one billion people. Buddhism, which is of a much later date, is related to it and many countries in South-East Asia are strongly influenced by its cultural ethics. Present day Hinduism springs forth from the high civilisation of the Indus valley, dating more than five-thousand years back. But when the Hindus refer to their own religion themselves, they speak of *Sanatana Dharma* which means 'eternal religion', meaning that their religion is universal and of all times.

The characteristics and fundamentals of Hinduism find their roots in the Vedas, and can only be understood from this universal concept of wisdom. This does not mean, at the same time, that both would agree very much on this matter, or that their approach would be exactly the same. Like any other religion, Hinduism, too, has fallen prey to the decay of values and principles characteristic of Kali-yuga. The many inimical attacks from outside, and the English domination did also clearly leave their mark. Nevertheless, nowadays, due also to the present economic development of India, there is a huge potential that the original Vedic wisdom can be re-enlivened and successfully shared with the rest of the world.

The essence of the Vedas is, that they are an expression of the pure knowledge of life, which is unchanging and eternal. The Hindus certainly believe that the Vedas contain all knowledge of the laws and principles of nature and man himself. But when in the post-Vedic period these laws are less and less observed, an increasing decay of norms and values occurs. Then other religions emerge, reflecting the quality of their own time, in order to lead man back to his original source. Hinduism has, as the first religion, developed itself from the Vedas and assumes total freedom of faith and beliefs. Simultaneously, it emphasises ideal behaviour and a correct way of life in harmony with one's personality.

The Vedas have revealed how to think and act in harmony with the cosmic law. They contain all universal codes of conduct that enable man to achieve spiritual liberation and find the way that leads back to God. Therefore, every Hindu accepts the Vedas as the highest authority of universal wisdom. Additions to the ancient scriptures or changes of codes of conduct take place from time to time. But the deeper values of the Veda based on the cosmic law, which is eternal and unchanging, is valid for all times and cannot be violated.

The scope of the Veda is responsible for its universal approach, which is no longer limited to Hinduism alone. Practical applications that have become popular in the past few decades all over the world are, among others, the different forms of Yoga, Ayurveda, Gandharvaveda and the study of Sanskrit. Vedic wisdom belongs to every human being and every society on Earth. Great scholars from all times and cultures that took notice of the Vedic principles of life have, after thorough research, often taken this knowledge as a starting point for their own lives and that of humanity. For instance:

* * *

"Accessibility to the Vedas is the greatest privilege this century can claim compared to all previous centuries."
- Robert. J. Oppenheimer, American physician (1904-1967)

* * *

Oppenheimer is often referred to as the 'father' of the invention of the nuclear bomb. So, it is not by accident that, especially in our times, this Vedic wisdom is cherished in the hearts, and put into practice by millions of people all over the world.

***

END OF PART I

THE VEDAS FOR EVERYONE

PART II

VEDA IN OUR DAILY LIFE

CHAPTER XIII

HOW TO PROCEED

'He who only sees diversity in the objects goes from death to death.'

- Upanishads

In Part I, we learned about the origin, true meaning and purpose of the Vedas. They are the blueprint of all principles and laws of existence and of our own life. Veda, being the source of pure knowledge, is indestructible and human beings are eternally connected to it. It is for each part and at every moment of the evolution a shining Light of creative intelligence that indicates how we can apply it for our own growth towards enlightenment.

In the Vedic era, Self-realisation was the basis of existence and an integrated part of education. The effort was focussed on refining the intellect, awakening the heart-chakra and developing the level of consciousness in the students. Next to yoga and meditation, the children in the *gurukula* (school and dwelling place of the spiritual teacher) were taught early on to respect nature and take care of the cattle with love. In our present-day educational system, there is hardly room for such an integrated development of intellect and consciousness, where emotional intelligence, too, is included. Later on, either in the professional field or in relationships this can work against us, and we might be easily thrown

238

out of balance in more difficult situations. Fortunately, nowadays some schools started to pay more attention to creativity, work from the heart and the development of the feeling faculties. Proper and complete education is the basis of success and wellbeing, both material and spiritual, in any society.

XIII.1 UNIVERSITY EDUCATION

The study and research of consciousness should be in the foreground of academic attention. Never in the history of mankind the knowledge taught in a university has been so fragmented and costly and has been primarily employed 1) in service of a good job, status and money and b) in service of solving social and political problems. The name 'university' literally means: wholeness in diversity. Therefore, a vision of the wholeness of knowledge should precede the division of her into different parts. Knowledge of the whole is knowledge of consciousness and of the development of consciousness, as well as of the basis upon which different manifestations of consciousness can be studied. The fragmented areas of knowledge, which nowadays are taught at the universities all over the world, lack every basis of life. This is the reason why the real motivation to study and acquire knowledge is missing in students. As Maharishi repeatedly said: *knowledge is structured in consciousness, and can only be developed in consciousness.* Therefore, research into the phenomena of consciousness should be the first step in the field of knowledge. Students become utterly frustrated if this foundation of knowledge is missing, and as a result the whole society and the whole world, as can be seen today, falls into a crisis.

Where can we locate this wholeness of knowledge and her different parts? *Agnim* is the first word of Rigveda and it literally means fire. In this most ancient scripture of humanity fire means: the fire of knowledge, the *creative intelligence* of nature. By nature, this cosmic intelligence is wise and life-supporting. In the great Vedic civilisation, which lies far behind us, society was characterised by wisdom and harmony. In those days the *varnasrama* system, which is part of the Veda, worked very well and there was peace and harmony in society. There was a continuous communication between the higher and lower worlds, between humans and God. Self-realisation was a natural part of life and the whole society was organized in such a way to be conducive to it. The practises of meditation, yoga and the performing of rituals were integrated in the Vedic culture. Holistic health care, natural diet and nutrition, developing a flexible mind and body were important. In the daily activities and in the care for nature, harmony and respect were the starting points. One lived with the idea that what you do to another, including animals, trees and plants, you do to yourself. The ideals of this time have had a profound influence on Indian history throughout the ages. With every holy saint gaining enlightenment, a part of this way of life and the knowledge connected to it, has been preserved or brought to life again. Nowadays, all this wisdom can be easily spread all over the globe. We can make use of it and can start to create a new world characterized by peace, love and harmony. But a first prerequisite to realise this on a global scale, is to start with a holistic approach of education and a Vedic upbringing of our children.

XIII.2 LIVING IN HARMONY WITH NATURE

What does it mean to live in harmony with nature? One thing, with which we are heading in the completely wrong direction nowadays, is our relationship with nature. This takes place on three fronts:

* We try to subdue nature

* We manipulate nature

* We violate nature

There are plenty of examples to clarify this. Think of the use of vaccinations, food manipulation, industrial pollution, bio-industry and so on. And what consequences does this all have for climate change:

advancing deserts, devastating forest fires, increasingly violent hurricanes and tsunamis are the order of the day. The destruction of rainforests, the widespread killing of animals and the disastrous conditions of our oceans and rivers are some other examples. Trying to control nature is a very senseless and naive approach, because nature will always, and in every way, outsmart us. We humans are an integral part of nature and can never be above it. Nature has its own universal intelligence that no human being (scientist, virologist, politician, pharmaceutical industry) can compete with. Every violence we do to nature comes back to us like a boomerang. Meanwhile, all basic elements that constitute nature, such as earth, water, air and space, have been polluted to the bone by humans. That also applies to ourselves. In the form of climate change, forest fires, tsunamis, viruses and all kinds of diseases, all of this is coming our way. At the moment, nature on earth is about to collapse, but it cannot be blamed for it. It is the asinine human who cause all this, and still does not understand and does not even want to understand how nature follows her own intelligence.

We think we are good at treating symptoms. If there is too much drought, we will come up with all kinds of ideas to combat the drought. When there is a virus, all attention is focused on developing vaccinations. When the oceans are heavily polluted, we try to clean it again. When we get sick from eating unhealthy, manipulated food, the doctors prescribe drugs that make us even sicker. Our political leaders invariably come up with "countermeasures" to combat the problems, without taking any interest in their causes.

XIII.3 BACK TO VEDIC WISDOM

To acquire a deep insight into the laws of nature, it is possible to make use of the Vedic wisdom, in the first place. For instance, let us make a deep study of the wisdom of the Upanishads, as some scholars also did in the past:

* * *

*'In all the world there is no study so wholesome and so lofty
as that of the Upanishads. It has been the blessing of my life -
and it will be the blessing of my death. '*
- **Arthur Schopenhauer, German philosopher (1788 - 1860)**

* * *

The Upanishads explain the deeper meaning of the Vedas with the help of metaphors and analogies. The two birds on the tree, one restless while the other watches innocently, shows so beautifully what the purpose in life is, namely the permanent experience of returning home, of the human mind connecting to the higher Self. The Upanishads describe the lack of experience of the wholeness of life as:

* * *

'He who only sees diversity in things goes from death to death.'

* * *

They contain many of these universal expressions of wisdom, that are always deeply cherished in the hearts of the people from India. When we do not experience the wholeness of existence, our intellect and ego will start living their own, separate lives. Just like the walking Jew, we will be constantly and restlessly looking for something that we can never find.

Bhagavad Gita describes what happens on the battlefield of life in an extraordinarily profound and illustrative way. When the more subtle levels of thinking and acting are not well developed or are obstructed, we perceive things differently than what they are in reality. This happened to the blind king Dhritarashtra. He was not able to surrender to the higher

Intelligence, which is pure and full of wisdom. Because he did not open himself to the good advice of Lord Krishna, he and his fellow men were conquered and killed in the battle. So, the result of the limitation of the intellect is a state of suffering, confusion and disaster.

***

'Unhappiness is that which depends on others.
Happiness is that which depends on oneself.'
- Manu Smriti

***

Happiness or a good health is not something we can just catch or buy. *Being happy* is a subjective state we possess or not, but which we can certainly develop from inside. To search for the inner Kingdom – the Holy Grail – is the main lesson of all sources of wisdom.

XIII.4 THE FOUR GOALS

This does not mean we should give up all other pursuits, unless we make it our ambition to become a monk. The monk chooses out of free will to live in solitude and surrender himself fully to God. We can also choose to remain a part of society. The Vedic scriptures mention four fundamental duties for a householder, which, when all four are pursued in the correct way, will give him the greatest possible fulfilment and wealth in life.

These are:

Dharma : Life destiny and moral

Artha   : Comfort and wellbeing

Kama   : Enjoying and fulfilling desires

Moksha : Union of mind, intellect and Self.

The Vedic concepts of wealth (artha) and pleasure (kama) do not correspond to the general Western notions about them. In the first place, they need to remain within the context of dharma, within the limitations of morality, integrity and our duty in life. It is part of the essence of a king that he administers his country, it is part of the Sun that it radiates light, heat and energy. When we do something that really belongs to us, we can enjoy it most.

Nevertheless, our dharma can place us sometimes in unexpected, embarrassing situations. In the epic Ramayana, Shri Rama is the perfect leader, who displays perfect behaviour in every situation. It makes him very beloved among his family and friends, and he enjoys the full confidence of the citizens of Ayodhya. But Rama's destiny also implies that in his life he suddenly gets separated from Sita in a cruel way.

In the forest Sita asks Rama to catch a beautiful, golden deer for her, which is the immediate reason for their separation. In a situation like this, the intellect can easily get confused, whereby we can suddenly feel uncertain. Only by staying very close to ourselves and by continuously consulting our inner source, can we learn to deal with difficult and unforeseen situations. Prince Rama understood the art of staying connected with his inner source and could therefore handle any situation.

According to the Veda, spiritual liberation, or *moksha* is what a human being can reach during his life here on earth. In that state, the higher Self is the administrator of all our thinking and actions. Then man is fully prepared to surrender completely to God, through which the cycle of birth and death (samsara) can be concluded, and the soul can dwell eternally in His spiritual world. To put it simply, it will not return into an earthly body again.

Sita asked Rama to catch a beautiful, golden deer for her
which was the immediate reason for their separation.
(painting: Rozalia Hummel)

XIII.5 KARMA AND FREE WILL

Depending on our actions in past lives, we carry our package with us into a new birth in another physical body. This package is our quality of consciousness, formed by the etheric body, that goes from one life to the other. As a new-born baby, the soul is very pure and fragile, but already very quickly after birth the quality of consciousness adapts itself to the level it had at the end of the previous life. The concept of reincarnation makes life extremely righteous, because in this way every human remains always responsible for his own thinking and actions. If someone has no insight into the law of cause and effect, he or she can experience life as senseless, unbearable and random. But the *law of karma*, which involves that every action calls forth an equal reaction, is of a sublime simplicity, on which the whole perfection of the universe is based.

The spiritual masters tell us, that we don't have to feel guilty about the consequences of the law of karma. A life that expresses itself through disease, shortage and poverty, and sometimes lasts only for a very short time, does not make less sense than a long and prosperous life. Everything fits into the cosmic purpose of birth, death and reincarnation until the cycle is completed. In Western society, we have been raised with the idea that passing away is something scary and you have to postpone it as long as possible. That is why so many people are afraid of dying. But in reality, there is no other difference between life and death, than that the gross physical body is born, and, after having done its duty, it disappears again. Only a sage knows that he is immortal.

Now, what is free will, and does it actually exist? This topic has been discussed for ages, and we are still not finished. In some scriptures, it is stated that the reason why a human being is unique is that he is endowed with *free* will. In other words, a man can do what he wants and at first sight that is what we see happening in the world. But, on the other hand, Vedic astrology teaches us that our life periods are already fixed right from the moment of birth. Indeed, we are in essence not much different from the Sun, Moon and planets – impulses of creative intelligence – circling around for thousands of years which can all be calculated in advance. Furthermore, we are part of a cosmic plan, a single thought of the Creator, a plan that is perfect and proceeds straight to its goal. Does it actually fit in into such an orderly plan, that people can just go ahead in their own way without any regard to the content of this plan? The thought behind creation is so much more beyond the human intellect and comprehension. Indeed, consciousness of our ordinary waking state does not leave room for the integration of the two opposite principles, freewill and predestination. Yet both exist at the same time and both are true.

Man, as the crown of creation, is endowed with free will, but he is only able to make a limited or no use of it at all. Often, we are victims of our own existence. We think we control our lives, but nothing is further away from the truth. Only those who have a fully developed consciousness, the enlightened souls among us, use their free will. The funny thing is, however, that their free will is exactly in line with the cosmic plan, so there is no friction at all between the micro- and macro-cosmos here. It is even more funny to see that the actions of a non-realised human being are also in complete alignment with the cosmic plan. Only he has little, or no influence at all on what is actually happening, nor on the consequences. He is drifting as a play-ball thrown by the influences of the three *gunas*. By learning to understand how we can reach a higher goal in this life, we gain more freedom step by step. So, free will has to do with the quality of our consciousness that knows how to deal with it. In a limited awareness, free will cannot thrive. In all cases, and here again we run into the paradox, it is a matter of karma which, again, means that everything is already fixed.

Making the wrong choices always hurts. But we can also see it as a game. The Creator of heaven and earth has placed us in a drama and has given us the possibility of making our own choices. At every moment of the day and in our life, we are confronted with it. The only intent of this is to lead us back to God, into the hands and guidance of the Divine Himself. We really cannot do it on our own. We are always inclined to think we know it better, we want to do it differently, thinking the other way is not for us. Being separate from the source is a painful experience. We may think that we have achieved great successes in this relative world, but one day we will realise that it all does not mean much. The well-known story of the Prodigal Son in the Bible is a beautiful metaphor that wants to make this clear to us. The lofty thought behind the creation is much more perfect than what we have ever held possible and teaches us, through trial and error, to be able to choose the good.

XIII.6 CONSCIOUSNESS AND ITS EXPRESSIONS

In chapter X, we have seen that our senses are nourished by the mind (*manas*), the intellect (*buddhi*) and the individual ego (*ahamkara*). Also, our body, our action and the way we deal with the environment, play an important role in our functioning. If we put everything to the place it is meant to be, we arrive to the following sequential aspects we have to deal wherewith: pure consciousness, ego, intellect, mind, senses, body, behaviour and environment.

Let us take a look at how we can refine, develop or improve these expressions of our consciousness and find out which Vedic tools belong to each aspect.

Pure consciousness

In the past decades, in many Western countries people have re-discovered that human consciousness is open to further unfoldment. Development of consciousness establishes a stable equilibrium in the body and the mind. It is not that our source changes, but we are more able to connect to it and thereby develop life-supporting qualities in ourselves. Many of us feel that we are restricted in our thinking and actions. This expresses itself in disappointment, sorrow, irritation, frustration, loneliness or fear. All these symptoms show that mentally and emotionally we are out of balance and unable to live a pure, happy and prosperous life. There are so many possibilities for a human being to grow toward a more refined and balanced consciousness; to understand who we really are, to experience our real nature. As soon as we notice that this works, our environment will spontaneously grow with us in love and harmony. The best contribution we can make for a better environment or a more ideal society, is to start with ourselves. *Transforming the world, by transforming ourselves.* Extensive scientific research has shown that we can develop and refine our consciousness through daily *meditation*, yoga and other spiritual tools.

Ego

When our individual ego is dusty and impure on account of past experiences and rigid convictions, our mind and intellect cannot function purely. There is too much noise in the line and no matter how hard we try, we cannot attune our inner radio properly. This has to do with our conditions and associations from the past. We are like Dhritarashtra, the blind king, who has to rule his country, but does not want to see the difference between good and evil. He keeps himself blind to reality, leading to bad consequences. When many people consider the unreal world in which they live as the real one, a confusion of tongues, like in Babel, quickly arises, where nobody can hear or understand each other. A similar situation can arise at any level: in the world, in the parliament, in the society, in any organisation, in our family and in ourselves. That is why we should purify our individual ego from all these false convictions that distort our perception. Only then can every thought impulse arise freely from the inner source and can our actions be strong, harmonious and effective. In chapter XVI, we will go deeper into the possibilities of purifying the false ego.

Intellect

Intelligence and intellect are two different values of consciousness. It is often thought that the intellect forms our consciousness, but it is just the other way around. The intellect is that part of our consciousness that enables us to discriminate. As long as consciousness is not fully developed, the discrimination faculty of the intellect is incomplete. Our individual reality does not coincide with the universal reality. In that case, we see the world through spectacles, that distort reality and make it seem different than what it is. By studying the *holy texts*, leading a *disciplined life* and through *sacred conversations*, we can refine and purify our intellect.

Usually, we have a tendency to over emphasize our intellectual abilities. In politics and other areas of society, knowledge of dossiers is greatly appreciated. It is not that the intellect would not be important, but feeling and intuition form part of the more subtle areas of life. They are the more profound levels of consciousness. Systematic development of the quality of our emotional intelligence fills the heart of any human with increasing contentment and happiness. Every human soul is naturally drawn towards happiness, because that is the essence of the Self. As soon as we allow head and heart to function together in unison, happiness gets the opportunity to express itself on every level of life – mind, body, behaviour and environment.

Mind

Our mind is the bridge between the Self, the silent awareness, and the external world by means of thoughts. A mind which is fully attuned to the Self is in every respect most harmonious and effective. Whoever wants to act with success in life, should not be afraid to look underneath the surface of the mind to learn how to discover his or her deeper sources. In the epic Ramayana, Prince Rama needed the help of the monkeys to win Sita back. The monkeys represent our thoughts. Just as a monkey jumps from branch to branch, so restless and uncontrollable our mind is. But when we become able to bundle our thoughts together and focus them at one-point, as Hanuman did, we can move mountains. It is the difference between the force of ordinary light and a laser beam. Under the guidance of Prince Rama, the avatara of God, the courageous monkey army was able to remove all obstacles it came across on the path. They built a bridge between the Indian continent and Lanka, and acted heroically in the liberation of Sita (intellect, wisdom and devotion). The lesson we can learn from this is, that we have to harmonize our mind and liberate it from all conditioning, which limits our choices enormously. An expanded and well-developed ability to perceive implies that we can assess a situation without prejudices. It goes together with the ability to accept the differences in each other.

Apart from yoga and meditation, we can work mentally on a positive attitude and pure lifestyle, too.

Senses

There are many methods to refine our sensory perception. They are related to developing our ability to hear, feel, see, taste and smell, but also, for instance, the art of speech. For the refinement of our senses of perception, we can think of listening to or making music, aroma- and colour therapy, eating wisely, et cetera.

Our perception of the world expresses itself in speech. It is the tone of our voice when and how we say something, the sequence of sounds and even the thoughts we think. The quality of our individual consciousness determines the depth of our perception and therewith the power and quality of our speech. Ideal speech is the unified expression of the heart and mind; it springs up from deep inside. Whenever heart and mind form a unity, speech will bear a high value and will cost the least amount of energy. One can often estimate someone's development through the way he expresses himself. Communication is effective when we are able to use words to describe what we feel. Before we have to speak in front of a group, we are often afraid to lose face, while everyone might be very understanding in case we make a mistake.

The more sensitive the situation is, the more difficult it is to translate our feelings into words (symbols) correctly. Prince Rama was not only a gifted speaker, but his choice of words was under all circumstances very delicate. He used his speech to inspire and encourage people. He spoke from the tenderness of the Self. His delicate way of speaking was meant to nourish, support and enrich the transcendental value of the Self – where all feelings come together in a common source.

Body

In the West, the practice of yoga has become very popular during the last decades. From experience, we know that physical postures (*asanas*) and breathing exercises (*pranayama*) promote the integration of body and mind in a pleasant way. Asanas exercise a soft, gentle pressure or stretching influence on certain vital points in the body. Those points are called marmas in Sanskrit, points that connect mind and body – consciousness and matter. Together, the countless marmas in the body form, as it were, a central control room, where energy channels (*nadis*) emerge from. A special Vedic exercise, which we can perform daily, is *Suryanamaskara*, also known as the Sun salutation. This exercise strengthens all important muscle groups in our body and improves the neuro-muscular and neuro-respiratory integration.

Breathing forms a subtle bridge between mind and body. The regulation of breath (pranayama) is meant to improve and balance the natural functions of mind and body. Just like the correct practice of the asanas, breathing exercises loosen up blockages and impurities, which then, through the practice of deep relaxing meditation, can be further released.

From time to time, it is necessary to eliminate accumulated toxins from the body. Ayurveda knows an effective, physiological purification therapy for the body, which is called *panchakarma*. This is a program for internal and external purification of the body. Panchakarma programmes are traditionally applied in India, but nowadays also successfully in many Western countries as well as on other continents.

Also, guidelines on how to use our daily food, which has been adapted to our body type is an important and very effective means for the improvement of our health. In chapter XX, we will see that it is possible to attune diet and nutrition to our individual constitution and to the season. Proper food habits can be effectively used both to prevent diseases and heal the body.

Behaviour
The effects of our actions are very complicated and have – cosmically

speaking – such a vast range that we ourselves are not able to judge what is good or bad for us. Seen from the perspective of the *law of karma* (action = reaction), the best advice is not to do anything that could possibly be wrong. A sage is someone who is only focussed on a higher goal. That has everything to do with devotion, humility, surrender and with an innocent *adjustment* to the environment. Ultimately, we are the creators of our own circumstances. Behavioural advice for an ideal daily routine related to the seasons, can have a beneficial effect on the synchronising of biorhythms in the body. It is possible to align our personal rhythm with the rhythms of nature. If things come to a head, ideal behaviour depends on the quality of our consciousness. That is why yoga and meditation fit in here to help attune our behaviour to the laws of nature. Next to that, the performance of *seva* – selfless service – to Guru and God can become the guideline for all our activities (see chapter XVII).

Environment
We can make use of our environment in a positive way and yet not become dependent on it, no matter what kind of environment or situation that is. Again, we refer here to the reanimation of the laws of nature through the performance of certain rituals, the so-called yajnas, on the level of the unified field of consciousness. In the context of *Vedic astrology*, yajnas are performed to prevent negative and unforeseen events. Both Vedic astrology and Ayurveda emphasize that we are not only responsible for ourselves but also for our environment. Our personal health influences the collective health and vice versa. If we ourselves grow in love and harmony, then naturally an eco-friendly, less noisy and crime-free environment will be promoted. Every man is part of the collective consciousness of his family, his village or city, his country and the whole world. Everyone is responsible for everyone else, because soulwise everyone is connected to everyone. By *group meditations*, which are also a kind of yajnas, we can inject positivity into the collective consciousness. The Vedas offer

us all kinds of means to optimize individual and collective health and harmony, and thereby strive for world peace.

254

CHAPTER XIV

VEDIC APPLICATIONS

'Avoid the danger that has not yet come.'

- Maharishi Patanjali

How can we now practically continue with this? Yoga, Ayurveda and Vedic astrology are like three sisters. As practical applications, they are directly derived from the Vedas and they are connected to the higher Self; the Self is their common parent. They are like rivers springing from the same source and envisioning the same goal. That goal is: *achieving wholeness of consciousness* by means of, respectively, a balanced mind-body coordination (Yoga and meditation), optimal health (Ayurveda) and the harmonizing of all our activities with the time factor (Vedic astrology).

Scheme 14.1 shows which instruments the three sisters are working with.

If we want to integrate the Vedas in a practical way, the three sisters offer a very effective package of possibilities. The whole package of fulfilment of life can easily be applied, it does not have to be expensive and is very comfortable. The goal of life is to grow in Self-consciousness and that is the essence of all three approaches. Moreover, they complement each other wonderfully.

Scheme 14.1
Relation between Yoga, Ayurveda and Vedic Astrology

THREE SISTERS	PRINCIPLE OF THREE	PRINCIPLE OF SEVEN
Yoga & Meditation	Body, Mind and Self	The Seven Chakras (energy centres)
Ayurveda	Vata, Pitta and Kapha	The Seven Dhatus (body tissues)
Vedic Astrology	Signs, Planets and Houses	The Seven Planets (together with Rahu and Ketu)

Scheme 14.1 All parts of Vedic literature are based on the same principles, are built up in the same way, and are connected to each other naturally.

Vedic astrology provides insight into the cosmic influences on our health and Ayurveda uses this knowledge to prevent and cure diseases. Vedic astrology can determine physical strengths and weaknesses based on the birth chart, such as the nature of a disease and the condition of the organs or other parts of the body. It can also play an additional role in determining mental and physical constitution. Vedic astrology can further indicate in which life periods the possibilities of becoming ill are more visible, already long before the first symptoms of the disease occur. By reading the pulse, the Ayurvedic doctor can do exactly the same, not only by examining the physical body, but above all by including (potential) imbalances present on more subtle levels in his research.

When analysing disease in the Vedic birthchart, the astrologer first of all determines whether the major planets Sun and Moon have been affected or not. If they are both strong, that is beneficial for health, both physical and mental. An affected Sun in the Vedic birthchart indicates long-term internal ailments, while an affected Moon reveals acute problems, often caused by external circumstances. The Sun works organically, the Moon works functionally. In case of illness, certain yoga exercises can be advised to initiate recovery. In the field of remedies, Vedic astrology and Ayurveda also complement each other, whereby both preventive and curative remedies can be used. Yoga, Ayurveda and Vedic astrology all have unique remedies to prevent or cure imbalances of the mind and body.

XIV.1 YOGA PRACTICE

In Chapter X of Part I, we discussed the Yoga-sutras of Patanjali in detail. The higher purpose of Yoga is to develop our consciousness. In the context of the Yoga-sutras, the practices are, in addition to a correct and honest way of life: meditation, postures and breathing exercises. Practicing correct body postures is a precious gift to our joints, muscles, connective tissue and tendons. Most of us are aware that we don't really have our physical body under control. We feel stiff, cannot bend or turn the body properly, our breathing is shallow, and we have little or no stamina. Just being able to sit in a good and comfortable posture is not always easy. Yoga exercises have a beneficial effect on the physical body, internal organs and the circulatory system. If we practice yoga with awareness, it is a blessing for the body as well as for our mental well-being. Besides that, yoga and breathing exercises are an excellent preparation for practicing meditation. In chapters XVI - XVIII, we will also examine the effects of kundalini-yoga, bhakti-yoga and other forms of Yoga.

XIV.2 THE SCOPE OF AYURVEDA

Ayurveda is that part of the Vedic wisdom which explains in a natural and practical way how to live a healthy, peaceful and long life. It indicates the perfect route for obtaining optimal mental, emotional and physical health. The primary cause of all diseases is the result of all the karma we carry from the past. When unfavorable karma comes to light at any given time, it manifests through illness, problems and obstacles. The Vedic birthchart provides us with insight into this and together with

Yoga and Ayurveda we can look for solutions from a holistic approach. As far as Ayurveda is concerned, its basic activities are the prevention and cure of diseases, together with maintaining and developing a healthy, comfortable and happy life.

As we explained in Chapter V, Ayurveda assumes that three bio-energetic principles or *dosha's* operate in all living organisms: vata, the principle of movement, pitta, the principle of transformation, and kapha, the principle of structure. This is the profound teaching of the tridosha. These three energetic principles guide the five basic elements of which we are built: earth, water, fire, air and ether.

Every person is born with its own unique combination of these five elements or its three bio-energetic principles, the doshas. Any illness begins with an imbalance of the three doshas and then manifests itself in one or more body tissues or *dhatus*. But as a science for developing a long and healthy life, Ayurveda is concerned with all aspects of life. As a holistic approach to medicine, Ayurveda includes the following eight parts:

General medicine. General investigation of causes, symptoms and cures of diseases; lifestyle, nutrition and cleansing; prevention and cure; herbal therapy.

Paediatrics. Conception and pregnancy; birth, breastfeeding and upbringing in the first years of life; causes, symptoms and cure of childhood diseases.

Psychiatry. Research, causes and symptoms of mental disorders and mental illnesses; spiritual and psychological therapies for healing.

Eye, throat, nose and ear medicine. Causes, Symptoms and cures of diseases of the head.

Surgery. Surgical treatments in any field of medicine when other treatments no longer work; use of instruments in operations.

Toxicology. Mind and body are constantly under pressure by pollution from within and from the environment (air, water, earth, etc.). Pollution of the earth itself and of animals and plants is also examined in this branch.

Regeneration and Rejuvenation. Ayurveda has many rejuvenation therapies based on prevention (yoga and meditation practices), herbal preparations and cell renewal methods; cures for the recovery of impaired memory, thinking or vital organs.

Sexual Medicine. Methods and means of promoting sexual vitality and potency.

Ayurveda looks at a person's living and food habits, emotional, mental and spiritual state, genetic influences and other external environmental influences when examining someone's unique body type. Its aim is to restore the balance between the three doshas. The treatments are therefore individual and can differ from person to person for the same disease, as described in Western terms. Furthermore, an appeal is made to the self-regulating and repairing capacity of man to regain and restore his health. The client is therefore actively involved in the treatment and, above all, is primarily responsible for his or her own health.

XIV.3 PULSE DIAGNOSIS

Of course, it is of first and foremost importance to gain insight into the quality of our health or the gravity of our illness. Relying merely on the symptoms that arise is a limited approach, which can cause many problems. The diagnosis may be incorrect and, as a result, a completely incorrect treatment could be prescribed. In medical practice, many people are sometimes put on misuse of medicines for years. A holistic approach to diagnosis is therefore not a luxury but an absolute necessity. The holistic way of 'reading' the pulse as used in Ayurveda is unique in the world and has been around for thousands of years.

An experienced Ayurvedic doctor can extract all possible information from reading the pulse, both in time (past, present and future) as well as on the levels of body, mind and consciousness. At the same time, the reading of our pulse by an Ayurvedic doctor is actually part of the treatment itself.

Ayurvedic students in the past had to first learn to play a stringed instrument so as to develop a special sensitivity in the fingers in order to learn this system of diagnosis. Only by feeling the pulse in a special way it is possible to check the natural and personal vata-pitta-kapha ratio (prakriti) in the body and then determine to what extent one or more doshas are out of balance. The doctor uses three fingers and under each finger he can detect seven (sub) levels of vata, pitta and kapha. In order to do his job properly, the Ayurvedic doctor himself must be healthy and alert. Moreover, he must have good qualities (moral, social and spiritual) to be able to make a good and complete diagnosis.

A well-known story in India is that of a *maharaja* (king) whose daughter was very ill. The maharaja sent for an Ayurvedic doctor with a particularly good reputation to examine the princess, but according to the laws of the country, the doctor was not allowed to see her. All he could do was feel her pulse as she put her arm through a hole of a curtain. The Ayurvedic doctor felt her pulse and was able to tell very precisely what problems the princess had and even what breakfast she had taken that morning. The maharaja was speechless. But the doctor also explained what the princess looked like, that she had some spots on her skin and that she felt depressed because she could not lead an ordinary social life. The doctor prescribed only some herbal preparations for the princess and before he left, he assured the king that she would feel a lot better the next day. The maharaja, of course, rewarded the physician generously for his tremendous wisdom and practical approach.

An ideal time to feel the pulse is when the stomach is still empty. An Ayurvedic doctor will usually feel the man's right pulse and the woman's left pulse to make his diagnosis. An experienced Ayurvedic doctor will also look at other parts of the body to complete his diagnosis. He can look at the face or eyes, at the hands or feet, or at the nails, and usually diagnoses the tongue as well; what does the tongue look like, wet or dry, the colour of the tongue and whether the tongue is cracked. He then informs the patient about his body type (prakriti), which dosha is most unbalanced, what the problems and causes are and which problems are latent. Meanwhile the doctor now knows everything about the patient's food habits and informs and advises him or her about this. Only then can the patient bring forward his complaints and the doctor compares these with his own observations. Usually, the doctor will then prescribe a special diet, supplemented with specific regimen if necessary, and he can also prescribe some herbal preparations or recommend a purification treatment. The treatment he prescribes and the advice he gives will relate to the body, the mind, lifestyle and behaviour of the client.

Ayurveda has a strong preventive character and it provides a very natural approach to heal the body without all kinds of chemical means. It is based on the principle that the body can heal itself best by eating natural food, additional herb preparations and a lifestyle in harmony with nature. Besides, a natural purification and rejuvenation treatment can take place based on *panchakarma*, which unique approach occupies a central place in the whole array of Ayurvedic treatments (see also chapters XX and XXI).

XIV.4 VEDIC ASTROLOGY

Vedic astrology, called Jyotish in Sanskrit, is one of the greatest gifts the Vedas have left to mankind; it is the mathematics of nature. Jyotish means inner light (the divine light that is present in every human being) and its purpose is to awaken the light in us as was the case with the Vedic seers to a great extent. The word astrology has a similar origin: astro refers to the stars and logos means science. The stars are embodiments of light and fill the space with their cosmic energy. The light that is diffused by the stars and planets is received by the earth and affects the earth itself together with all life on it. The Vedic birthchart or *kundali* is the blueprint of our karmic life. It shows who we are, our qualities, our challenges, our possibilities and our destiny. We can also use it for time planning – how to plan our life, what to do this year, what to do next year, or what better not to do. It is a very precise recording of the universe, seen from the earth, which shows the functioning of the laws of nature in a simplified way. It provides an all-encompassing insight into the intimate relationship and the never-ending dynamic process between man and the universe.

Jyotish therefore explains that man is inextricably interwoven with the universe. Ayurveda teaches that every person has a unique body type, called prakriti. Likewise, Jyotish teaches that every human has a unique planetary constitution as well. Planets operate in the magnetic and electric force fields and influence the life of every person on Earth constantly. The effect of the cosmic energy that they emit and with which they influence everything and everyone depends on time and place. To determine these influences for a particular person, the geographic location, the date and time of birth are of great importance. When it comes to the geographic location of the Earth's position, the calculations make use of the latitude and longitude coordinates.

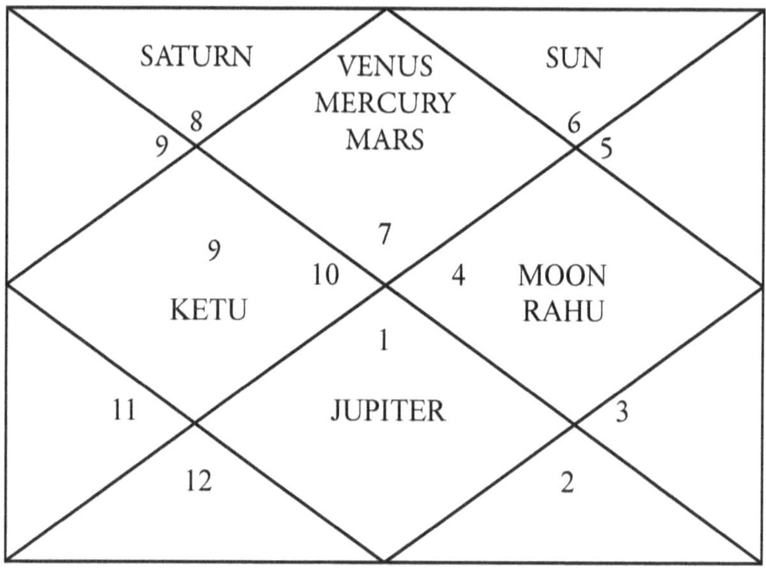

Kundali of Mahatma Gandhi, saint and liberator of India
Born on October 2, 1869 at 7.33 AM in Bangalore, India

The possibilities of Vedic astrology are almost inexhaustible and its methods can be applied in almost any area of life. The scientific value of Jyotish is not to be doubted. The whole structure of creation is based on the operation of natural laws, which are eternally unchanging. The cycles of the Sun, Moon and planets can be calculated with extreme precision. Man himself is part of the functioning of the laws of nature and all the transformations of the heavenly bodies are also taking place within ourselves. By knowing the universe and its dynamics we can get to know ourselves (and vice versa) and Vedic astrology is an instrument that was developed to do this long ago.

Besides interpreting the Vedic Birthchart, we can also make use of the Vedic Moon calendar, or *Panchanga*. This calendar is based on the cycle of the Moon, and shows the auspicious days and times. In this way, we can make optimal use of the time factor based on the influences of the Sun, Moon and planets. Sometimes, the influence of the celestial bodies supports us, other times it does not. Whatever happens in the universe, also happens within us. The Sun, for instance, is not only the Sun we can see, but it shines within ourselves as well. In ourselves, it represents our soul, just as the Moon represents our mind. As soon as we know which changes can be expected, we can anticipate them, and turn the situation into the most desirable direction. *'Avoid the danger that has not yet come'*, is an old saying, which lies at the foundation of the ancient science of Vedic astrology.

XIV.5 REMEDIES FOR PLANETARY INFLUENCES

Based on the Vedic birthchart, the Vedic astrologer makes a diagnosis of the auspicious and inauspicious periods that occur in our life. Furthermore, specific remedies are used to strengthen the auspicious and, respectively, to alleviate, deviate or neutralize the less auspicious indications. The effects of the remedies are to a certain extent bound to karma and this is different for every person. The remedies that Jyotish offers focus on the effects of the seven main planets plus Rahu and Ketu. The remedies mentioned in this book, have amply withstood the test of time and have been widely applied by millions of people in India and the world over.

The most important remedies are:
- The wearing of gemstones
- Honouring the planet of the day
- The use of planetary mantras and yantras
- The performance of Vedic rituals.

The experienced Vedic astrologer can also give advice concerning food, diet, herbal preparations, periods of fasting, philanthropy, clothing and the worship of certain demigods - although these remedies have a more general approach. The effects of the mentioned remedies depend on a number of things, like:
- The accuracy of the diagnosis
- The quality of the (objects used as) remedy
- The expertise of the one who prescribes the remedy
- The given moment in time (muhurta) in which the remedy was received, is given, or (as in the case of the gemstones) is worn for the first time.

The wearing of gemstones
The wearing of gemstones in order to neutralize inauspicious effects is as old as the world. In ancient times, kings and (high)priests often made use of it with the counsel of their astrologers. Nowadays, almost everyone in India is still wearing one or more gemstones prescribed by the local astrologer.

Scheme 14.2
The Planets with their Weekdays, Gemstones and Colours

PLANET	WEEKDAY	GEMSTONE	COLOUR
Sun	Sunday	Ruby	Light brown, orange
Moon	Monday	Pearl, Moonstone	White, silver
Mars	Tuesday	Red Coral	Dark red
Mercury	Wednesday	Emerald	Green
Jupiter	Thursday	Yellow Sapphire	Yellow, ochre, gold
Venus	Friday	Diamond	White, mixed
Saturn	Saturday	Blue Sapphire	Dark blue, black
Rahu	(Saturday)	Hessonite	Dark blue, black
Ketu	(Tuesday)	Cat's eye	Brownish

Scheme 14.2 The tradition of Vedic astrology specifies exact rules on how to apply, on which hand or finger a certain gemstone, how it should be worn and, for instance, on which day and at what moment it should be worn for the first time. Some gemstones can be worn together while others cannot, depending on whether the planets involved are in a friendly or unfriendly relationship with each other.

It cannot be explained in a few words why wearing gemstones can have such a profound effect on our wellbeing, just as it is difficult to understand why the position of the stars at the time of our birth can have such an all-embracing effect on our whole life. A gemstone contains profound *healing energy* at deeper levels, just like our body itself. Its primordial characteristics and vibrational energy stored in the stone in a very condensed form, correspond each to one of the planets that are, in turn, connected to the energy patterns of our body. By wearing carefully selected gemstones on the skin (in a ring or in a necklace), planetary energies or influences can be bent in a direction we desire. Scheme 14.2 shows which stones, days and colours belong by nature to the nine planets (*naugraha*).

The propitiation of the day-planet

Each of the seven main planets is related to a weekday and play with this creatively. Let us say that in our Vedic birthchart the planet Venus causes an inauspicious influence. Venus stands among others for beauty, luxury, art, romance and vehicles. In all these areas, we will have problems during a certain period (or periods) in our life. The weekday of Venus is Friday, which means that the energy of Venus is most powerful on this day. We can propitiate this by undertaking certain actions on this day. Concerning our clothing, we can dress in white or multi-coloured clothes (the colours of Venus), or buy a bunch of white flowers and place it in our meditation room, on our altar or at any other good place in the house. And, as part of our spiritual discipline, we can recite a mantra for Venus. We can do a lot on such a day to please and soften the energy of Venus. In early days, one thought it to be quite normal to communicate with the cosmic intelligentsia and in the present time we can return to developing this quality again.

The use of mantras and yantras

In order to neutralize the less auspicious effects of the planets, specific mantras are available for each planet. Mantras in general are a combination of Sanskrit sounds the usage of which is known to have a healing effect. What actually really matters when contemplating a mantra, is the sound value (vibration), much more so, than the literal meaning of the words. It is the sound value of the mantra that has a profound and certain effect on mind and body, thereby transforming the concerned planetary influence. The rule that we use the mantra pertaining to the given planet in our Vedic birthchart causing the inauspicious influence applies here, too. Traditionally the mantra is passed on by the Vedic astrologer or pundit (priest) during a small ritual. Often a mala (rosary) of 108 beads is used for the repetition of the mantra. The Vedic astrologer can indicate how to use the mala in the correct way when contemplating on the mantra. The best way to repeat the mantra is silently, in the morning before breakfast, in a comfortable sitting posture, in a quiet place, after our morning bath.

Yantras are mantras in visual form. They have the same energetical effect as when we place a picture of our spiritual teacher on our little home altar. Each planet has its own energy pattern, which can be visualized in a geometrical form. By concentrating on this form, or on its details, it is possible to soften or neutralize the inauspicious effects of a given planet. Besides this, each planet is also associated with a numerological yantra consisting of a specific combination of nine numbers, which also expresses the energetic quality of the planet. Traditionally, a numerological yantra is used as a talisman, and we can be carrying it with us during a certain period of the planet.

These are pictures of the geometrical (left) and the numerological yantra for the Moon. An experienced Vedic astrologer can indicate which yantra for a certain period is suitable to use.

The performance of rituals

We have elaborated extensively on the value of the performance of rituals in chapter VII. Applied to the astrological situation, the ritual sets in motion a process of purification from the unwanted planetary effects and yields auspicious results for the future. A well-known ritual in the Vedic tradition of wisdom is to honour all nine planets (naugraha) during the performing of a *pooja*.

The challenge of our time is, for us to learn to look at every personal or social problem from its deepest origin. The Vedic approach of how the deeper (mental or spiritual) cause acts on matter – and how we can make use of it – is not only useful for a small group of people interested in the inner values of life. Every human being and society can make use of this holistic Vedic knowledge, which is often very self-evident, logical and natural.

XIV.6 HOME AND ENVIRONMENT PLANNING

We have already discussed Vastu Shastra, the science of Vedic architecture and home design, the upaveda of Atharvaveda in chapter VIII. Vastu is an impressive brother of the three Vedic sisters and is based on the same universal principles. An optimal lifestyle requires a life-promoting design of the house in which we live and of the environment, too. It is important that every part falls in the right place and is in harmony with the whole. In our present time, the basic principles of living in harmony with nature are often completely neglected. The land on which we build is chosen randomly, the building materials are of inferior quality and a harmonious relationship with the environment is almost always missing. It is not without a reason, that people in cities and suburban areas, which have been randomly set up, often feel deeply unhappy, stressed and their houses are quickly put up for sale again. The science of Vastu is as old as creation and aims to put all aspects of architecture, the furnishing of the home and the lay-out of the environment at the service of a healthy, peaceful and harmonious life for its inhabitants.

When we project the human body onto a circle or a square, we see its beautiful resemblance to the cosmic patterns. The brilliant scholar and artist Leonardo da Vinci made drawings and sketches of this, and these symbols are also extensively discussed in the secret geometry. The functioning of the human body (cells, organs and limbs) establishes a wholeness that is more than the sum of its parts. All the principles of the anatomy of the body and its various parts can be found in the principles of orientation, proportion and division underlying the science of Vastu.

The principle of symmetry

While older mansions or inner cities still often have a certain pattern-based, consistent design, our modern urban design usually impresses us as chaotic sight lacking in harmony, beauty and identity altogether. The basic principle of symmetry, which was held in high esteem for centuries, has almost completely disappeared from the modern street scene. Symmetry has an orderly and harmonious influence on our brain functions. For that reason, the mansions of the past, with their beautifully ornamented gardens, were always designed symmetrically. A stately front door in the middle with preferably a staircase that leads to the door from either side. The layout of the windows on both sides of the main entrance and on higher floors used to be completely symmetrical. A feast for the eyes, very pleasant for our brain activity and a blessing for the residents of the house.

It is remarkable that today's physicists are diligently looking for the phenomenon of symmetry in the material universe. Such a finding would make their research on the origin of the universe much easier. But so far, they haven't been able to find that anywhere. Again, our modern scientists are reluctant to assume that the entire universe is a manifestation of an underlying, infinite and symmetrical field of pure consciousness, the Veda. The inner experience of this symmetry takes place only in the consciousness of the enlightened human beings.

The principle of symmetry in buildings is important in the science of Vastu, because it exerts an orderly and harmonious influence on our brain functions.

Orientation

Another important basic principle is, that our braincells respond to the (wind) direction in which our head is placed; For example, if we face east, the braincells will function differently than when we face west. Therefore, according to Vastu, the main entrance of the house must face east or north. This also applies if there is a gate that leads to the house. A main gate or door facing east brings spiritual growth, abundance and fulfillment to the residents, while a north-facing main gate or door leads to prosperity, happiness and good health. Also, the front door should be larger than all other doors in the house and should open inwards.

Just following the Vastu principles ensures that the prana (cosmic energy) flows in the right direction, which is beneficial for the happiness and good health of the inhabitants and the harmonious relationships among them.

Guidance

In the Vedic scriptures it is repeatedly stressed how important it is for us to be guided on the spiritual path by an experienced guide. For all the

Vedic applications mentioned above, we can consult an expert teacher or consultant who is specialized in one of these areas. But making use of these applications is quite useless if at the same time we do not grow spiritually through developing our consciousness. In that case it is wiser to let ourselves be inspired by a spiritual teacher or Guru. Although the choice is entirely up to us, we will further elaborate on the meaning and background of the Guru principle in the next chapter.

CHAPTER XV

THE GURU PRINCIPLE

'If Lord Vishnu is angry, the guru protects you;
but if the Guru is angry, no one can save you.
Therefore, make every effort to take refuge in the Guru.'

- Guru Gita, verse 79

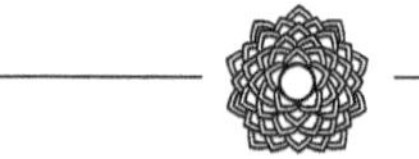

The enlightened souls of our times stand out through their inner wisdom, compassion, selfless service, simplicity and loving radiance. They are always connected to their inner Source. Their life does not necessarily have to run successfully, moreover, they do not even have to hold high positions in society. Often, they do not come into the lime light at all. The mayor's gardener can be the most enlightened person in the village and always ready to help or serve others. By working in the garden, he can enjoy fully enjoy his contact with the flowers, the plants, and the earth. The common characteristic of enlightened beings is that they mainly live *to serve others.*

XV.1 SPIRITUAL MASTERS

Then we have the noble Masters who come to Earth with a special task, to bring a message of inspiration to mankind. Some are already born enlightened, like the *avataras*, others become liberated at a later age.

All of them have their own authentic approach. But they all have one common goal: to serve humanity on the path to a better world, in which sharing together, working together and being together come in the first place. In the past, enlightened masters like Shri Rama, Shri Krishna, Adi Shankara, Buddha, Lord Jesus, Parahamsa Yogananda, Ramana Maharshi, Swami Vivekananda and many others have come to the Earth to inspire mankind and lead them back to their source. It is not by accident that lately a number of world teachers are present among man to give their life-supporting teachings and show us how to discover our spiritual origin. Everyone, who is unselfish, has no prejudices, and acts attuned to the Self, can of course be a good guide on our path. Also, our parents, friends or children can be an ideal teacher to us, from whom we can learn a lot. And what to think of the Sun, the Moon, the Earth, the dolphins in the ocean and so many other natural phenomena, can they not all be our teachers? Yet, when it is about the desire to gain enlightenment in this life, guidance of a true spiritual master, who is fully Self-realised and knowledgeable about the wisdom of life, is a must. Only those who are already there, can guide and support us to reach the final destination.

We can read all the beautiful books in the world, practice yoga & meditation techniques, follow inspiring programmes or courses, and still experience our spiritual journey as difficult. Following our inner path with its many pitfalls, is definitely not always that easy. We know that there is more between heaven and earth, but can we also experience it? That is what counts. We may know how to play the keys on the piano and may even be able to play some melodies, but does that grant us enough satisfaction? Wise people go search for an experienced music teacher, who knows how to support his students lovingly, so they can become good musicians. In the same way, if we are receptive and ready for it, we can grow spiritually in a most comfortable way, under the guidance of an enlightened Master. In his or her presence, our inner awakening can take place in a most natural and effortless way. All that we have read in books, and the various spiritual techniques we have learned, are then becoming a reality at a deeper level of our own experience.

Almost all great world teachers themselves have had a spiritual master, who served as an example for them and who initiated them. Lord Krishna's teacher was Sandipani, Shri Rama's guru was Vasishtha, Swami Muktananda's teacher was Bhagawan Nityananda and Maharishi's teacher was Guru Dev Swami Brahmananda Saraswati of Jyotirmath in the Himalayas. Jesus has probably spent a part of his youth with masters in India and was initiated by John the Baptist. Most of the great teachers or saints gained the state of enlightenment by the support of their own enlightened master. The sadguru knows that only by Divine Grace can the final transformation take place. 'Man cannot do it on his own,' the Indian Master Shri Ammabhagawan used to say. It is an initiation of the highest degree, which is transferred from a true teacher to his disciple. Only an *avatara* (divine incarnation) can be born enlightened.

The world teachers, among whom we also find female spiritual teachers, inspired millions of people all over the world, to follow the path of yoga (enlightenment). It is impossible to mention them all and describe their approach. The most important thing is that they all carry inestimable value and are compassionate to the well-being of mankind and the preservation and further development of the planet. On the path towards wisdom every human needs a guide. Feeling unhappy, experiencing restlessness, being egoistic, forcing conditions upon others, making the wrong choices; these are all indications that we have let ourselves be directed into a wrong direction. We really need a perfect example, that we can follow. If we had to do it all alone, we would need many more lives to reach the desired goal. A spiritual guide is someone who has the experience of the inner world and who wants to share this experience with the world and us. Of course, from time to time there might occur circumstances or periods, when there is no teacher available, or the Master is no more in a physical body. Then we can have faith in what we think is true and in what we believe. We can go by our own experience, our intuition, the words that come up intuitively and by the sources of wisdom that come to us from inside or outside. This can happen during a walk in nature or at the beach, during a conversation with a friend or at any moment in time. *But if it is possible, go and search for your spiritual teacher or divine Master, and you will definitely find him or her.* He or she always appears in the right moment. He is needed as the embodiment of the Self, who becomes a leading principle on our path. This is the path of the highest truth. It is a powerful and enjoyable path, because it protects us from the pains of the world.

The idea of a guru, a spiritual teacher, has often raised controversy in the West. People immediately think of submission, of depending on someone else, of not being allowed to be one's own self any more. It is surely true that there is a need to separate the wheat from the chaff and, therefore, we really need to be alert while selecting a guru. The Vedic scriptures express the following qualities of the guru:

- He has gained Self-realisation (enlightenment).

- He has knowledge of the holy scriptures.

- He is full of love and compassion.

Many people describe what they feel in the presence of the guru. And what the difference is when you experience the physical presence of the guru, through which your energy levels transform and you start experiencing your own source more and more. For instance:

- You feel lovingly surrounded by something you cannot adequately describe.

- You feel more freedom, no obligations, no manipulations.

- You are not forced to believe in something.

- Spontaneous changes occur in you, generating a feeling of joy.

Once we have found our true spiritual teacher, we are very fortunate. We feel that there is a perfect match, he is the mirror of our soul, our best friend. When we are with him or think of him, joy flows through our veins. Sometimes we can experience the guru as a shining Light in our hearts as well. The guru mantra is never far away, it dances up and down inside us, like a feather. We know what our guru is worth. His blessings are wonderful and extraordinary.

XV.2 DIFFERENT APPROACHES OF TEACHING

Each enlightened teacher has his own approach to lead somebody or a group of people to the spiritual goal. My first guru, the Indian master *Maharishi Mahesh Yogi*, was a great *jnana yogi* (teacher of knowledge). His focus was on developing the field of pure consciousness, guiding his followers in a very practical way. He considered the eightfold path of yoga as a total package that can be simultaneously developed through regular contact with the Source (samadhi). He taught in terms of transcendental consciousness, cosmic consciousness (turiya chetana), god consciousness (bhagavat chetana) and unity consciousness (brahmi chetana), in which unity consciousness is the highest possible state of human experience. By enlivening daily the field of pure consciousness with the help of transcendental meditation and advanced techniques, higher states of consciousness develop in the student spontaneously. By enabling students to meditate together in large groups, sometimes more than seven-thousand people together, Maharishi worked directly on the improvement and transformation of the world consciousness as well. As a real jnana yogi, he surrounded himself always with scholars from India and scientists from other parts of the world. He was verily a great sage who worked for more than fifty years tirelessly as a *jagadguru* for the well-being of humanity. I worked twenty years as a transcendental meditation teacher in his worldwide organisation, at the time that he, at older age, was living in Holland.

Next to this approach of consciousness, there are spiritual masters who practice and teach the way of *kundalini-yoga* or *siddha-yoga*. Kundalini-yoga works with the subtle energy bodies (mental, emotional and causal) and the most important energy centres (chakras) of the student. *Sri Vasudeva* from Trinidad & Tobago, from the tradition of Swami Muktananda and his teacher Baba Nityananda, is an example of a very qualified spiritual teacher (sadguru) who works with the awakening of kundalini. In a period of three years, after visiting Swami Muktananda's ashram in India two times, he gained full enlightenment at the age of twenty-four on May 5th 1978. Sri Vasudeva is a sadguru, who functions fully from the inner source and has the ability to give *shaktipat* to his students. This is the transmission of his higher energy level to the lower energy level of his students. Shakti is the divine energy and 'pat' means something like 'descending'. The giving of shaktipat can take place via the voice, the eyes, physical contact or just by mere intention of the teacher. This inner power of the teacher is present in every human being and is called the *guru principle* (guru tattva). The guru principle indicates that it is not as much about the physical guru, than about the qualities of the higher Self, that he has realised and wants to bring to life in his students, too. I met Sri Vasudeva for the first time in 1998 when I visited Trinidad & Tobago for a conference on Ramayana. While there, someone told me about him and about the Blue Star Ashram. Excited about what I heard, I decided, on an intuitive impulse, to visit him. That was the beginning of a lifelong disciple- and friendship with Sri Vasudeva.

The kundalini-yoga approach is very personal, which does not mean that the student needs to be in the physical presence of the guru all the time. Once a good connection between teacher and student has been established, they can communicate with each other from a distance and the teacher can keep on fulfilling his role as guide, mentor and coach. In this, the development and refinement of the chakras (see chapter XVI) plays an important role.

International Blue Star Ashram, Trinidad & Tobago

Next to the above approaches of teaching, there are also many masters who teach from *bhakti-* (devotion), *karma-* (good deeds) or *jnana-yoga* (knowledge), or a combination of these. Some teachers can probably not be put in any box, because they control all divisions of knowledge to the highest perfection and can put it into practice.

Besides Maharishi and Sri Vasudeva, other spiritual masters came into my life as well. It was as if they invited me from inside to connect to them and learn from them. One of these was *Shri Ammabhagawan*, a famous Indian couple, who established their Oneness University in the Chittoor district in Andhra Pradesh. I visited the Oneness University a couple of times, for the first time in 2012, and was very impressed with the Oneness teachings and learned how to give *Deeksha*. Since that time Shri Amma and Shri Bhagawan have always been a part of my life and spiritual practise, and I feel very grateful to them.

Shri Bhagawan introduced the *moola mantra* to hundreds of thousands of his students as a tool to connect with the Divine:

* * *

Om satchitananda parabrahma
Purushothama paramatma
Sri Bhagavati sametha
Sri Bhagavate namaha

* * *

Shri Bhagawan said that even without knowing the meaning of the words, this Sanskrit chant itself carries power. All the words together represent the complete range of the universe.

In 2016 I married a Hungarian lady, named Zsuzsanna or Zsuzsi. She is the treasure of my heart and life. Zsuzsi is affiliated with the Oneness University too, but also as a *vaishnavi* she is part of the Hare Krishna community in Hungary. Besides a beautiful temple and a Bhaktivedanta College in Budapest, there is a Hare Krishna community in the countryside, called *Krishna-valley*. With a beautiful site of about 300 hectare it is without doubt the largest and most perfectly organized eco-community in the whole of Europe. Krishna-valley was founded in 1993 by *Swami Sivarama Maharaj* who (in 2019) is still the very respected spiritual leader of the place. The few hundred devotees are self-supporting on all levels and live in beautiful cottages on the compound and in the village nearby. They live a life where life is meant for serving and worshipping Lord Krishna in full surrender, and always with a smile on the face. Their daily lives are marked by discipline, purity, mercy, gratitude and renunciation from the attachments of the material world. In an amazing natural environment, they are equipped with a beautiful temple, two schools, guesthouses, shrines, flower- and fruit gardens, ponds, land for agriculture and a cow stable.

In the company of family members, friends and Hare Krishna devotees, my Vedic marriage with Zsuzsi took place at Krishna-valley on September 9, 2016 (9-9-9) on a very auspicious Full Moon-day. Since Zsuzsi brought me to Krishna-valley for the first time, we go and stay there on a regular basis and participate joyfully in the perfect daily discipline. We even dream to live there one day ourselves, somewhere nearby, because for us this place is heaven on earth.

The Hare Krishna organisation, also known as the International Society for Krishna-consciousness, has many followers worldwide. Its roots go back thousands of years, but it became known in the Western world only after 1965, through the efforts of *His Divine Grace A.C. Bhaktivedanta Swami Prabhupada*. At that time, he began to spread the principles of Krishna-consciousness in the United States. In the years after, he travelled around the world fourteen times, lectured and founded temples, educational institutions and eco-farms everywhere. He wrote sixty books in English. His comments on the verses of Bhagavad Gita (As It Is) and Srimad Bhagavata Purana became famous all over the world. In those years Shri Shrimad Prabhupada taught his followers, including many hippies, the worship of Lord Krishna, the Supreme Personality of Godhead, with the purpose of developing complete devotion and love for God. As the perfect way of self-realisation, he emphasized the practice of *bhakti-yoga* as the highest form of yoga, remembering Lord Krishna's words in the last chapter of the Bhagavad Gita (XVIII.55):

* * *

'I can be known only by devotional service.'

* * *

An important part of the bhakti-yoga practice is the chanting of the *maha-mantra*, which is made up of sixteen words arranged in a special pattern, which makes it easy to learn:

* * *

Hare Krishna, Hare Krishna, Krishna Krishna, Hare Hare
Hare Rama, Hare Rama, Rama Rama, Hare Hare

* * *

These sixteen words are names of both the feminine and masculine aspects of God and by chanting them repeatedly, the devotee is humbly praying: 'O energy of the Lord, O Lord, please engage me in Your service.' In other words: *Hare* in this mantra is representing His energy part and *Krishna/ Rama* represents the Supreme Lord Himself. In the Vedic scriptures it is said that in our present time of Kali-yuga there is no other spiritual practice which is more effective than chanting the names of God. I feel deep gratitude that the profound Vedic teachings of Swami Prabhupada became a part of my life, also.

In 2014 Sri Vasudeva visited India with a group of his students and I was one of them. We also came by the ashram of *Sadhguru Jaggi Vasudev*, who is a spiritual teacher, very popular in India and known all over the world as a speaker and opinion-maker. Near to Coimbatore, in Tamil Nadu, he established a beautiful *Isha Yoga Center*, which has attracted many thousand students from all over the world. I was very impressed when visiting this serene place, where the students are trained into the deeper values of yoga. The eco-friendly environment, the sattvic food which was offered, the great discipline held by the students, and of course, the powerful Shiva-lingam with the whole set-up of the center is fabulous. Ever since, I follow Sadhguru-ji regularly on internet and enjoy his personality and teachings with great devotion and respect.

XV.3 QUALITIES OF THE GURU

Only a very capable, Self-realised teacher can take the student by the hand and accompany him on the path to liberation. One of the conditions thereby is, that the student is ready to surrender to the teacher (ultimately to his own inner teacher or the Divine Himself) and follows his instructions without hesitation. This makes it even more necessary that the teacher is a *true teacher* and there are only a few of them. *Sadgurus* (true teachers) and *jagadgurus* (world teachers) in this world are very rare. The fact that somebody calls himself that, or allows his followers to call him that, offers insufficient guarantee. As a new student, you have to be very alert if the desire for enlightenment intensifies. Certain characteristics can be attributed to the ideal teacher, although an *enlightened teacher* is very hard to recognize, for he can take up any role he thinks beneficial for the sake of the progress of his students. But usually, a qualified teacher can be singled out through his unselfishness, servitude, unconditional love, authenticity, compassion, correct behaviour, detachment and the ability to give without desiring anything in return. Such a teacher lives, thinks and acts permanently from the inner source and is a casebook example in following the *yamas* and *niyamas*, the Vedic rules of correct, moral and ideal lifestyle and behaviour.

A guru has the ability to drive away the dark side of our soul and enable the light, that we really are, to shine. The guru does not develop the Self in us, we already consist of and exist in the Self. What he does is clean up the pollution, that clutters our heart and mind. And is that not exactly what we need? The *Guru Gita*, a song from the *Skanda Purana*, that is completely devoted to the qualities of the guru (see chapter XVI), is very clear about it. The sadguru is a great blessing for our spiritual journey and for the well-being of the rest of the world. His qualities can hardly be comprehended, even by most of his followers. He sees who we are in the core of our being and transforms our ego. Only the guru is able to tackle our false ego and allow it to adopt to the quality of the Self. His mission is to help us further, and he does not need anything in return for his efforts, he himself has already got everything. His fulfilment lies in the principle of *giving*. Giving is his greatest joy, exactly as the Earth spontaneously gives all we need for food. Personally, he has no need in the least to ask for money in exchange for his teachings. He teaches and gives instructions in the same playful way the Sun lets its sunrays shine. He does not demand dependence nor submission from his disciples. He only wishes that we start to experience the same freedom as he does.

Jesus Christ, a perfect Spiritual Teacher

The true teacher is not only the embodiment of the Self, he is the Self. He is not in the Light; he is the Light. He thinks, speaks and acts as the Self. He lives in and moves in the Self. He is one with the Father. There is no moment that the Father and he are separate from each other. As Jesus said: '*Be ye perfect as your Father in heaven is perfect.*' The true teacher is the manifestation of the Divine and has control over all his senses, even in the midst of turbulent events. In a sadguru, we meet again the divine consciousness of unselfish love in and under all circumstances. Even when the sadguru seems angry or unreasonable, he is only taking up a role with the intention to teach a person or a group.

The Grace of the Guru

If we choose to perform good deeds, we are naturally supported by the intelligent energy field in which we all take part. The source of all life responds to our intentions, thoughts and actions. If our inner desire to meet a teacher is strong, one day he will stand before us. From that day on, the teacher will do everything that lies within his power to bring to the surface the love of God, truth and spiritual discipline in the disciple. It is God himself who puts the teacher on our path. And when the guru sees that we are ready for it, he blesses us and takes us by the hand. A true teacher does not really need rituals, therapies or other means to do his work, simply by his presence he does all that needs to be done. He walks softly through the audience and just through a word, a look or hand gesture, he is able to awaken the slumbering spiritual energy in a receptive person. This is the Grace (*kripa*) of the sadguru who represents the Divine.

Guru tattva means that the spiritual teacher is not just a human being, but he carries an *inner quality* which is invisible to the outside world. When we look at ourselves, we see only a very small part of who we really are. The sadguru sees so much more in us, he grasps the whole picture in one glance. He sees it in our eyes, he feels it when he shakes hands with us, he hears it in our voice, in short, he is aware of any part of where and who we are at a certain moment. And he uses that wisdom in order to take us lovingly by the hand and helps us to take a step further. Do not be afraid, his love knows no limits and is without conditions. He has no self-interest. It is only about you with the guru, about your well-being, your possibilities to make progress in wisdom and happiness. And you cannot make him happier than when he sees that you have grown further. As soon as he sees that you start to express the refinement of the guru-quality in your thinking and acting, he will let you go again with a content heart.

When we meet a teacher and become connected to him or her, a subtle change starts to take place within us. It resembles a rebirth. Only by connecting to such a Master and by following his teachings, we start experiencing a change. If we do not feel this, it simply means that we still have not met our true guru. When we meet *our* sadguru, a natural process of continuous change starts from that moment on, until one day we will have the feeling that we have adopted the same inner qualities as those of the guru and we will be able to express them in daily life.

XV.4 OUR OWN CONTRIBUTION

Swami Muktananda was a master in telling anecdotes and he liked to narrate about Nasrudin, a sheik from a Muslim tradition. Nasrudin had the peculiar habit of putting his ear to a wall and sit and listen for hours. His wife had studied him for several years and finally asked him: 'What do you hear behind that wall, my dear?' Nasrudin said: 'Why don't you try yourself?' He explained to her what she should do and his wife, too, sat down and started listening with her ear against the wall. She sat there for longer than a day and then said: 'Dear husband, I've been sitting here already for so long, and I still don't hear anything!' Nasrudin answered: 'You have only been here for eight hours, and already start complaining that you cannot hear anything. I myself have been sitting here for sixteen years without hearing anything, and you haven't heard me complain!'

Are we not doing the same by practising yoga and meditation for many years, without being able to mention astonishing results? Neither meditation, nor yoga, nor any other form of sadhana, how useful for our inner peace, can reveal the ultimate Truth to us. With our limited identity we are not able to lay hold on the Self, it is the Self that reveals itself to us, whereby we become able to see it. And the Self reveals itself most readily by the Grace of the Divine through the guru. Swami Muktananda, who lived in the previous century, roamed through India for forty years to discover the Truth of life. As he recounted about himself, he did not listen to anyone, he wanted to do it all by himself, and felt he always knew better than the sixty teachers whom he came across. Only when he finally met the guru from his younger years again, Baba Nityananda, did he start listening to him and felt that something started to transform him completely. By the Divine Grace of his guru, Muktananda's ego got completely transformed and he himself became a famous world teacher.

What can we do ourselves?

If we have not yet met a master in our life, it may mean that we are not yet ready. We have to prepare ourselves for it. Do not be disappointed, it will just happen to you unexpectedly. At that moment the universe tells us that we are ready for it! We are then ready to take a new, important step on the journey of our life. It is not wise to enter and follow the spiritual path on our own. As long as the fluctuations of our mind have not completely settled down and we are not completely connected to the Self, the message is: be alert. A little bit of knowledge is dangerous, the sages say. Going through the teaching process full of faith, under the inspiring guidance of your spiritual teacher, is the safe way. This does not mean that the teacher puts handcuffs on you and takes all your freedom away. Be selective in choosing your teacher. When you notice in all freedom that the loving guidance of the teacher produces good results, you know that you are on the right path. Good results mean that you notice that you look at things differently, you are more satisfied and happier inside and have a rock-solid faith in a meaningful future.

***

Sadguru jyota se jyota jagavo,
mera antara timira mitavo.

Sadguru, shine my light with your light,
dispel the darkness that covers my heart.

***

How do we really surrender to the guru? Once upon a day there came a nice, well-to-do businessman to Shri Vasudeva's ashram who decided to stay there for some time. He heard about Sri Vasudeva's plans to reconstruct the kitchen and the dining hall and offered spontaneously to pay for all the rebuilding costs. On the same day, he started to draw ambitious designs and presented them to Sri Vasudeva asking for his opinion. However, design after design was rejected, and after some days the businessman started to feel uncomfortable. What did Sri Vasudeva know at all about extending a kitchen and a dining hall and who is, ultimately, paying for it? This went through the mind of the businessman, who thought that he was the real expert for such a job. He decided to walk once more through the ashram to explain how everything could be set up most effectively and with style. When Sri Vasudeva dismissed everything for the umpteenth time, the businessman left the ashram, heavily disappointed, probably in search of a better teacher, who would at least understand him, and show him the respect he deserves.

The money of the disciple is not an issue for the teacher. The disciple also does not have to take the decision to leave his family and job in order to stay in his presence for years. Everything the guru does to us is in service of the transformation of the ego. He can only work on our ego if we follow his guidelines, however contradictory they may be, with love and without doubts. This is not always easy, because we are used to taking care of ourselves. The more success we have attained in the world, the more difficult it is to surrender ourselves. It does not mean we should adopt servile behaviour or feel small and weak in the presence of our teacher. The real teacher works through the power of universal

Love. He knows exactly what we need, and what is good for us. He will never give us an instruction which is in his own interest. Therefore, the secret of *sadhana* lies in the complete obedience to the teacher. Merely by serving the guru faithfully, honouring him with all our heart and soul and loving him intensely, our deepest wishes will be fulfilled. Only then it is possible for the teacher to take full responsibility for the disciple, and this he definitely will do. By surrendering unconditionally to the teacher and trusting him in everything, our false ego naturally dissolves and we merge into the universal energy and wisdom of the guru. Then, the disciple realises his own inner guru and grows to the status of the outer guru.

We all carry a different karma and if somebody is not fully focused on the highest purpose, he will, even in the presence of the guru, make little progress. In the first place, we can keep on faithfully practicing our spiritual discipline at home. Even more important is to have the insight that we cannot possibly be far away from the guru. The guru lives in our heart. The Self is always in us and the guru is the Self. His wisdom and his mantra live inside us. Therefore, a true teacher will always be with us and will at any desired time communicate with us. A sadguru is not just a human being. As we said before, his physical body is not the guru. The guru is the divine energy, the shakti, the Self and the expression of the Self. Nevertheless, we are able to find all those qualities also in his person.

***

Dhyana mulam guror murtih
puja mulam guroh padam
Mantra mulam guror vakhyam
moksha mulam guroh kripa

The root of meditation is the form of the guru
The root of worship is the feet of the guru
The source of mantra is the words of the guru
The source of liberation is the grace of the guru.
- Guru Gita verse 76

***

Because the guru represents the Divine, there is no greater blessing than meeting him and to accepting him with love into our life. Grace in our life can come from all sides, but it is by far the greatest if it comes from the sadguru. The sadguru creates the energy field that enables Grace to flow, annihilating thereby our false ego. He is a perfect instrument for giving Grace. The Vedas confirm again and again, that such pure souls have the power to bestow the Divine Grace on us. But we have to deserve it ourselves. The purer we become inside, the more we can receive from the guru, and the clearer we are able to see the Truth. Then we are open to shaktipat. If it overtakes you, you will experience it as a beautiful gift. If you earn it, you will unquestionably get it.

XV.5 THE TRUE TEACHER

But how do we recognise our true guru? That is a personal question. In India, it is not strange that husband and wife each have their own guru. Be very aware what happens when an enlightened master enters your life. That can be through a book, the media, a friend, a gathering or a personal encounter about which you only understand in retrospect that this was not as random as it may have looked at first sight. Sometimes there is a feeling of resistance, fear or threat at first. 'What does this person want from me? Does he or she thinks he can lure me, while I myself don't like that at all? Everyone can claim he is enlightened. I am a Christian and I will not give that up just for something as vague as a guru.' But in those who are ready for it, a feeling will surface from deep within:

* * *

*'This is what I always have been searching for. I recognize everything what
this person has to say. I have always felt like this, but I was never able to
put it into words so clearly. I feel my heart turning around with inner joy
and emotion!'.*

* * *

You will notice that whatever the teacher has to say, is useful for you,
that he touches something deep within, and now and then you may be
overcome by the feeling that you have already known the teacher for a
very long time.

This is the moment to embrace the situation. You learn to listen well
to the teacher and realise his words come to you from a pure source.
Because you cannot find the hidden treasure on your own, you surrender
to the teacher, who knows the hiding place and wants to guide you. Such
a step is quite a challenge, a fantastic opportunity, which we can take
wholeheartedly. Of course, we can also talk about it with the teacher,
until the idea of the search becomes clear. In the beginning, it is not
always easy to accept every gesture of guidance and support. But what
matters ultimately is an ideal heart connection between the teacher and
the disciple. In all things we do, we keep in mind the goal the teacher
has indicated. And by the Grace of the teacher we will grow and start
to experience what the teacher means. What could be more beautiful
than being a student of life, being able to really surrender to the deeper
meaning of existence?

Maharishi's teacher, Swami Brahmananda Saraswati (Guru Dev, †1953),
held the important position of Shankaracharya at Jyotirmath, in the
Himalayas. He was an eminent embodiment of the Vedic tradition of
wisdom. Maharishi spoke very devotionally about him:

* * *

*'I have experienced a life full of surrender at the feet of Guru Dev.
And then it is such a spontaneous thing, that you don't even have to think
about it. The whole thing is so spontaneous, without any second thoughts,
to live for him, because every breath is a wave of joy. It gives expansion to
the heart, expansion to the mind. Then there is no feeling of sacrifice.
There is only more fullness day after day, week after week, month after
month, year after year. In a very practical way, it grows in the always rising
tidal waves of life. If one lives for the other, one grows in the value of life, in
the structure of life for the other.'*

* * *

You can feel the bond between you and the teacher growing. You feel
comfortable in his presence although sometimes you will be very much
challenged as well. You have faith and are ready to be guided. And
when you notice that the relationship grows, and that you grow in this
relationship, then you know that this is the teacher who was meant to
enter your life. You feel it inside, your heart is telling you. Your intellect
might still be doubting, but do not trust it too much for the time being.
Although the intellect is also a very important instrument to walk the
spiritual path successfully, it can also be your enemy and can rather get in
your way. One of the pitfalls during the spiritual journey is that we start
judging the conduct of our fellow-travellers. There is a great danger in
this, because we have little or no insight into it. A criminal might change
into a saint in a very short time. Therefore, never think that somebody
else is less than you, or that they are less loved by the teacher, or that they
do not know how to use their intellect properly. Never compare, goes
the sage's advice. As long as we are not enlightened, we continue to live
in ignorance. The more we think we know, the less we actually know.
The real sage is always humble and modest and never boasts about his

knowledge. He knows that not the intellect is the measure of knowledge, but the infinity of the source, that contains all wisdom, all love and all possibilities.

If someone asks a guru: 'How do I know that you are my true teacher?', he will answer: 'You will know it, your heart will tell you. You will have the feeling that you have met your best friend. You will feel that you can trust the teacher completely and you will feel stronger the more the relationship grows, and you come more into your own power. Something inside will tell you; it is the deep connection with your teacher that you feel.'

The guru mantra

One day the teacher may give you a mantra, the guru mantra, that contains the shakti of the teacher. Repetition of the guru mantra is a very powerful technique to make a connection, inner and outer, with the guru. If we use the mantra, all qualities of the teacher surface in us naturally. The great advantage of this is that we do not necessarily have to be in the physical presence of the guru all the time. There can be many reasons why we cannot always be near him, for instance, because of our family, our job, our financial circumstances, or the country we live in. But by using the mantra, we invoke, as it were, the qualities of the teacher, such as his unconditional love, his peaceful and powerful radiation, his compassion and the loving words he speaks. All these qualities are the manifestation of the principle that lives in the teacher, the guru-principle, which goes far beyond the ordinary human being. When the teacher speaks, the Self speaks to us. Is that not already a divine thought, that we can directly communicate with the inner source, the Self? And does this not demand complete humbleness and modesty from our side? The teacher lives beyond the limitations of the ego; in him the Self and the ego work perfectly together and that makes him strong and altruistic. This is what we call unconditional love and we experience it as a deep peace within ourselves. By repeating the guru-mantra any moment of the day, we develop the same elevated consciousness in ourselves as that of the teacher. Moreover, after some time the guru energy makes us feel as if we have become the guru ourselves! The movement of our hands, our way of speaking and listening, our whole body feels as if it was the body of the guru. That is the essence of the repetition of the guru-mantra, by identifying ourselves with the guru, we ultimately enter the heavenly world of the guru.

The physical teacher becomes therewith the object of meditation. This is what, among others, is extensively described in the *Guru Gita* (see chapter XVII). We can make use of a picture, an object, a memory, a mantra or somebody who deeply inspires us. An object of perception is needed so that our mind can recognise it or identify with something or somebody. We need an example, that is exalted and perfect, and then we start to understand it ourselves and follow it. We do not even have to think per se of the physical guru, we awaken our *own light*, our own peace, our own inner joy! Do not small children also copy the behaviour of their parents automatically and often unconsciously? In the same innocent way, we allow the inner guru in ourselves to wake up with the help of the physical guru. Believe it or not, this is the simplest and, at the same time, the most effective way of inner awakening.

Being focussed on the goal
Once we have embarked on the journey towards our higher Self, it is an art to remain directed towards the goal. The teacher says: 'It is as if the destination comes to you at the same speed as you progress towards the destination.'

The relationship between the spiritual teacher and his disciple is a *love-story*. Again, your ego can be challenged a lot because it is the relation between the little self and the big Self. But the little self is melting more and more into the big Self and ultimately becomes the big Self. That is why we say that the relationship between teacher and disciple is a *soul relation*. Both teacher and disciple long for a complete merging of their souls. This takes place at the divine moment of the *paripurna diksha*, when the teacher gives the ultimate initiation, whereby the disciple gains Self-realisation. Then the relationship has arrived at the same point as Shiva, who, after having taken his most devoted disciple, Parvati, to be his consort, comes to a complete Union with her. Then Shakti becomes Shiva and together they are Parashiva, having risen beyond all duality. The connection is so profound and sacred that it transcends all other forms of relationships and can brave any storm. Very powerful.

***

Gurudeva hamara pyara
hai jivana ko adhara

We love our Gurudeva!
In this life he is our great support and refuge.

***

CHAPTER XVI

KUNDALINI YOGA

'*The path to go beyond the brow chakra is the one of complete surrender – complete surrender to the Divine with the awareness that we ourselves are nothing and that the higher Self is all there is. This is the union of the individual ego with the higher Self.*'

- Sri Vasudeva

The last decades have brought revolutionary insights into the human nature and, closely connected to this, into the possibilities of the development of a new awareness. At the same time, these modern days of hurry and competition exert their influence upon us and we have been overshadowed by stress and fatigue. As a result of this exhausting battle, all kinds of new, often psychic, disorders have appeared, to which regular modern medicine hardly has a solution for. No wonder one has started to look into and experiment with treatments from ancient traditions of health, which often bring surprising results. In the ancient traditions of healing in general, the emphasis lies on a holistic approach and one preferably starts with a prevention instead of waiting till the harm has already been done. As human beings we are used to give a lot of attention to our body. We feed it, we wash it and try to keep it young. If it falls ill or a limb is broken, we want to restore its healthy state as soon as possible. The attention for the body has to do clearly with our desire to survive. Often, we realise only partly, or not at all, that the body is a wrapping of subtler bodies that are at least as important. Although we cannot see them, due to their abstract nature, they play a fundamental role in the process of cause and cure of diseases.

XVI.1 DIFFERENT BODIES AND THEIR FUNCTIONS

The Vedic scriptures explain that a human being consists of six bodies or *koshas*, from gross to subtle, and their functions. In this chapter I like to mention the following ones:

- The physical body
- The emotional body
- The mental body
- The causal body

The physical body

In the Vedas, the body is compared to a royal chariot, that carries a very precious traveller, namely the soul. The body is part of the material world and is created as a vehicle for the soul, so it can experience the world of the senses. That is why our body deserves plenty of love and our special attention. In other places in the Vedas, the body is compared to a boat, which takes us to across the ocean of life. How important is this vehicle and how intelligently it operates! Each cell of the body is like an intelligent being, which has the ability to communicate with all other cells and connect to the rest of the universe. The body cells are a part of, and move in an intelligent field that is formed by the whole body. We can say, therefore, that the body has its *own intelligence*, because it needs food, wants to rest or just move sometimes. It knows how to coordinate all necessary processes, and the organs in their turn know how they should function. The endocrine gland knows exactly when certain substances have to be secreted, just like all other glands know what needs to be done. The body has a beautiful respiratory system, an immune system, a reproductive system, and a metabolic system. It is a very intelligent instrument that we have received from Mother Nature to undertake and fulfil our spiritual journey on earth with.

Closely connected to the physical body is the etheric body, which forms the aura that can be perceived by clairvoyant people and can nowadays be recorded photographically, too. This aura is a kind of protective layer of the physical body, which tries to keep pathogens and harmful substances at a distance. Somebody's health is highly dependent on a healthy aura, without holes or fractures through which life energy can easily flow away. The etheric body is an important link between the physical body and the subtler bodies and fosters the exchanges of information between them.

The emotional body
The emotional body is connected to the heart. Our feelings and emotions take part in it. The emotional body becomes more balanced with our progress on the path of Yoga. The aura of the emotional body has a greater range and can extend to a couple of metres around the body. Every mood expresses itself in this aura, therefore it moves all the time. The emotional aura stores all undigested emotions, fears and pains, which express themselves in the world around us. Depending on the state of the emotional body, particular situations and persons are attracted, that are often not really welcome, since they only confirm our painful shortcomings. If the undigested impressions are not solved during this life, they are taken to a next life, where they attach themselves to the new physical body. On the other hand, the more we become emotionally balanced and radiate love and joy, the clearer and more refined the aura colours will be and the more harmoniously our surroundings will behave towards us. We can balance the emotional intelligence of the body by working with the subtler bodies (mental, causal) and by connecting

to the higher Self. Obviously, the heart chakra plays an important role hereby. There are many ways to break through our human limitations, but one of the most powerful ways is through the heart – the awakening of the heart centre. The path of love, surrender and devotion. The journey of love means that we start cherishing it inside more and more and start transcending our limitations. If there is one thing that can lead us to the goal, then it is the realisation of unconditional Love.

The mental body

The mental body is the seat of our mind. This body is called, together with the emotional body, the *astral body*. The thoughts we experience, our intellectual qualities, and intuitive insights are connected to the mental body. The aura of this body, which has a higher vibration than the etheric and emotional bodies, can extend even further around the physical body. The power of the intellect distinguishes us from other life forms and is a powerful instrument that can support us on the way towards freedom. It can bring us closer to the experience of who we really are. It brings us to the gate of heaven. The intellect has the ability to distinguish between good and evil. By using our common sense, we are able to develop the kind of knowledge and insight which forms the basis of putting the acquired knowledge into practice. In the metaphor of the chariot the intellect is the charioteer, who holds the reins (mind) to guide the horses (senses) into the right direction.

The intellect formulates our goals clearly. Life is continuously challenging us, and exposes us to all kinds of temptations leading us astray and putting up thresholds in order to test us. We people are inclined to identify ourselves with our body, our emotions and our thoughts. Often, we know our weaknesses all too well. We get stuck quickly in all kinds of undesirable situations and moods. We cannot see ourselves apart from these, nor even want to see ourselves disconnected from it. In the Vedic scriptures, this is called ignorance about our own nature. Our intellect can take wise decisions and can loosen our attachment to all this unneeded ballast that we sometimes carry with us for years. Our discriminative faculty offers us the possibility to detach from all the things we essentially are not; to be aware that we are *not* our body; we are *not* our emotions; we are *not* our thoughts.

Whether we have a lot of fun or are in a sad mood, the wise teacher advises us to say: 'I am not this and I am not that, it is the emotions that come up in the body, but it is not me.' In this way we learn to come closer to our essence, which is pure consciousness and which is without pain, sorrow or old age.

In the day to day world, the functions of our mental body play a very significant role, we could not do a minute without them. Nevertheless, it would be good to allow the mind some rest from time to time. During periods of contemplation or meditation, the fluctuations of the mind can settle down and can merge into the level of Being. This is not only a pleasant experience, but it is also a highly useful way tof refreshing and purifying the intellect. We live in an era where we have become used to recharging all kinds of instruments, like our computer, mobile phone, tablet, et cetera. Do we not often overlook the needs of our own instruments? The mind needs to take a well-deserved rest from time to time and just be silent. This is a kind of meditation on the path of practical wisdom: being silent and in this silence, creating new possibilities to make the right choices and to allow our intellect to function more clearly.

The causal body
The causal body is connected to our memory. It is the storehouse of all our past experiences. Actually, we *are* our memory, the result of all he experiences we have ever had and which are stored in the causal body. It makes us very conditioned, because everything that we do or think first passes through the polluted filter of the causal body. That is the result

of the karma we have built up during many lifetimes. The causal body, therefore, needs to be purified again like the dishes and cutlery after a well-deserved meal. The spiritual teacher is the right person who makes us aware of the patterns in our life that keep repeating themselves and block our growth.

The causal body expresses itself through the false *ego*, the identity we have created for ourselves. Our thinking and acting consist of a sequential process, in which all levels from fine to gross feed each other. Our thoughts spring forth from the Self, and from the Self our individual ego, containing all our 'I's', is formed. Our acting, thinking and feeling are fed and coloured continuously by the ego. We can meditate, chant or practice yoga as much as we want, but with respect to our ego, it does not seem to be of much use. Because of the persistence of the ego, it is almost impossible to open our eyes to the truth of life. We constantly turn around in circles and hardly realise it. Our environment, on the contrary, does realise it all the more. The problem is that we identify ourselves with something we are not. We think that we are a man or a woman, poor or rich, young or old, good or bad, intelligent or dumb, beautiful or ugly. We identify with our personality, with the small and limited *I*. And all the while we are *a divine Being*, pure consciousness, pure love.

Swami Muktananda once told the following story about the holy Augustine. Augustine was restlessly searching for the Divine internally for years, but could not find Him anywhere. One day he walked along the ocean and saw a boy at the seashore, holding a cup in his hands. The boy seemed very sad. Augustine went up to him and asked him what happened.

The boy said: 'I try to catch the ocean in my cup, but for some reason I never succeed. The ocean is so big, and my cup is so small.'

Augustine thought for a moment and said: 'Why don't you just throw your cup into the ocean?'

At that very moment saint Augustine himself had a fabulous insight. He realised that he actually was trying to do the same thing. All the time he tried to catch the infinite bliss of God into the small cup of his limited ego, which never worked. Immediately, he threw away the cup of his ego and discovered that his individuality merged into the ocean of *bliss* or *ananda shakti* and so he realised full *Unity* with God. The drop became the ocean.

Do we not all stand, like the boy, along the seashore with a small cup in order to enjoy spiritual liberation? We look to the one next to us, how he does it, we compare ourselves to our fellow students, we think we are much more advanced than the other, who does not meditate every day. Moreover, we are very proud to have the best teacher in the world on our side. Is that not all ego?

The ego is an instrument of our existence, just like the mind, the intellect and the senses. We cannot do without it as long as we live in a form or body. But we can purify it so that it ultimately takes on the same qualities as the higher Self. The ego is often our greatest enemy, but we can mould it to be our best friend. This is a matter of *transforming* the ego. But how is this possible and how can we be liberated from all the suffering in the world? The truth is that we are totally helpless. We cannot do it on our own. But the sadguru sees and feels immediately how helpless we are, we cannot fool him. From that level, he takes us by the hand to show us the way. For that a loving and devoted surrender to the teacher is needed. Surrendering to our teacher is surrendering to the Divine, there is no difference at all.

Be honest, are you prepared to throw your cup into the ocean?

XVI.2 THE KUNDALINI ENERGY

The kundalini energy is located, in a concealed state, at the bottom of the spine. As long as she is sleeping, it is impossible to experience real love, peace, compassion or friendliness. In that state, our consciousness is limited and often caught up in survival matters, like eating, sleeping, procreating and quarrelling. We are continuously overtaken by experiences of pleasure and pain and feel victim of the circumstances. But when the kundalini awakens and moves upwards along the spine, our spiritual evolution switches on. She is like a closed lotus flower that opens up and, after that, is opening all energy centres (chakras) along her way. The opening of the energy centres expands our mind, which becomes more aware and loving under this influence. It is, therefore, of great importance that the kundalini energy is awakened in every human being. She is like the Sleeping Beauty, who is kissed awake after so many years by the prince on the white horse. Fortunately, in the last decades a lot of research was done on this hidden stored energy and on how to awaken it in an intelligent and secure way.

And not only recently, because just as the Holy Bible says:

***

'Wake up from your sleep and rise from death.
Then Christ will shine on you.'
– Ephesians 5:14

***

It could not have been said more beautifully and precisely, could it? Without the awakened kundalini we are still asleep and behave as if we were dead. Only after awakening completely we are alive and have started a second – a spiritual - birth. The kundalini energy is also called *Shakti*. She finds her ultimate destiny when she unites with *Shiva*, who is seated in the crown centre. Shiva is the silent aspect of consciousness (male) and Shakti is the energy (female) moving within the consciousness. Together they are timeless and inseparable. This is the basic teaching of Kashmir Shaivism and of the Siddha Yoga tradition, too. As a coiled snake, kundalini lies waiting in the root chakra for her journey along the energy centres to start, till she arrives back home into the crown where Shiva is waiting for her. She can move up and down along the spine and if she really becomes alive, she flows through the sushumna. She is very intelligent and in her awakened state, she is able to guide any movement, like walking, singing and dancing. The awakening of the kundalini has a great influence on the breathing, also, it restores its balance and thus breathing is experienced as more and more pleasant and healing.

The energy channels, called *ida*, *pingala* and *sushumna* come together in the brow chakra. The breath flowing through the left nostril, called *chandra nadi*, has a cooling effect, because of its association with the Moon (Chandra). It is connected to the right-brain hemisphere where we can locate our feelings and emotions. The right nostril, *surya nadi*, is connected to the left-brain hemisphere and the intellect. It creates a more heating effect, like that of the Sun (Surya). When chandra nadi and surya nadi are in balance (this happens when we breathe through both nostrils simultaneously), our mind becomes naturally peaceful and calm. The awakening of the kundalini brings a huge transformation in the subtle energy body and thereby on every level of human existence.

The kundalini experience is something very special and as soon as she starts her journey upwards along the spine, the one who experiences it knows immediately that something special is happening. The Shakti or kundalini energy herself decides the moment of her awakening and can occur unannounced at any time. She does not lose control at any moment during her journey. She is pure intelligence and at the same time the subtle energy that *leads* someone to a higher level of awareness and ultimately to enlightenment. No wonder that the enlightened ones among us never cease to eulogize her in every possible way. In the Bible, we come across her as the Holy Spirit, who radiates to all sides and lets those who are intensely touched by it speak with fiery tongues.

Kriyas

Sometimes, we observe that people make strange movements with the head, arms or other body parts during their spiritual practice. Sometimes all kinds of strange noises are produced or intense emotions are expressed. These are called *kriyas*. The movements are often uncontrolled and are for the most part side-effects of the release of obstacles in certain parts of the body. Kriyas can occur on a physical level (movements, headaches), emotional level (releases like weeping or laughing aloud), mental level (having all kinds of strange insights), and intellectual level (e.g. disagreeing with everything, resisting everything). It is not recommended to stimulate kriyas, rather, it is better to think that they are absolutely unnecessary for a proper development of the Kundalini energy.

XVI.3 THE CHAKRAS

There are seven energy centres or *chakras* located in the subtle body, that lie along the spinal column. We cannot see them with our ordinary vision. Each chakra is connected to a certain aspect of consciousness and has specific characteristics and functions (see scheme 16.1). We can consider them as control chambers, transformers and dividers of prana (life force) to and from the different bodies. They are closely connected and are continuously exchanging energy with each other by circular motions. Hence the name chakra (= wheel). In the subtle body of a man, these rotations take place to the right, in a female body to the left. They are energy centres at the interface of consciousness.

The subtle form and movement of these energy centres reminds us of a lotus flower that can open and close, each with a different number of petals. A chakra can be 'locked ', for instance, our throat chakra gets locked when we feel pinched in the throat area. On the other hand, it can 'open up' completely if we suddenly communicate with someone openly and freely. In this way we can easily determine in which state any of our chakras is, in a general sense or at a certain moment. The next step then is how we can develop these refined energy centres further and open them up completely.

Scheme 16.1

The Chakras and their Properties

AREA	SANSKRIT	QUALITY	GLAND	ELEMENT
Tail bone	Muladhara	Physical body	Adrenal glands	Earth (smell)
Sacral region	Svadhisthana	Sexual energy	Ovaries, prostate	Water (taste)
Navel	Manipura	Vitality	Pancreas	Fire (sight)
Heart	Anahata	Feelings, emotions	Thymus	Air (touch)
Throat	Vishuddha	Communication	Thyroid	Ether (hearing)
Brow	Ajna	Mind, Intellect	Pituitary gland	Mind in a broad sense (intelligence)
Crown	Sahasrara	Freedom, ecstasy	Pineal gland	Consciousness (light)

Scheme 16.1 The chakras are not part of the physical body, but they come to expression on this level through the functioning of the glands, organs and senses. Through the chakras a man is connected to the energy fields at different levels of existence and – whether they are aware of it or not – to the cosmic intelligence.

Root centre

The root chakra is most closely connected to the physical qualities of the body and the world around us. The awakening of the kundalini force can happen from this lowest chakra. We experience this as a feeling of heat at the base of the spine. Our desire to participate in the physical world becomes stronger and we will stand firm with both feet on the ground. From the root chakra the kundalini, the divine energy, starts working itself upwards and begins to feed the higher chakras. This can result in our giving less attention to the base centre and ultimately start neglecting it. A tendency might develop to lose contact with the physical reality and instead of standing with both feet on the ground, start living in the clouds.

A strong connection between the spiritual energy and the physical existence is necessary. The Self is then rooted into the material plane and brings balance, as with someone who might have his head in the clouds, but whose feet are nevertheless firmly on the earth. Then there is no fear any more that we could get lost in or become a prisoner of the physical dimension, instead we will add well-being and balance to it. This achievement will definitely benefit our health.

During meditation we can lead the prana to the root chakra by certain breathing exercises. We can, for instance, visualise a tree that is firmly rooted in the earth and that will give us the feeling of a strong connection to the earth.

Sacral centre

This is the chakra that is connected to our lower emotions. When it is activated, that feelings of lust, anger or strong negative emotions might come to the surface. Therefore, we should learn how to control our feelings of lust in the first place. It is actually possible to apply the sexual energy not for only physical, but also for spiritual purposes. In that case, the energy is pushed upwards in the direction of the third eye, where it is transformed into an even more refined energy. The sexual energy is very powerful, if it is fully under control. It is an important part of the Tantric tradition, which teaches us that we can control this subtle energy completely. A number of breathing exercises exist that can strongly promote the upward movement of the sexual energy. The more we start to understand the use of the energy of the second chakra, the more we start using it in the service of our spiritual journey. Kundalini shakti will fully support this wish.

Navel centre

The development of the third chakra, the *vitality centre* just above the navel, is of utmost importance for the spiritual path. *Manipura* means: *city of jewels*. The centre of gravity of the body is located in this area, and if we treat it well it gives us a lot of stability and energy. In fact, we find a treasure of the highest order here. This centre is the gate to the higher chakras and on the physical plane, it can develop the potential power of a sun. Not only in the ancient Indian tradition of yoga, but also for instance in the Japanese and Chinese martial arts one concentrates mainly on the navel. The Japanese speak of the *hara centre*. The navel chakra is reflected in their posture; the way they sit or stand. The Chinese give this area the same importance. In the Tai Chi lessons, the exercises are especially directed to open the chakras in the belly area. The use of (lower) belly breathing instead of breathing with the chest, makes us physically stronger and will, at a certain moment, eliminate fears and symptoms connected to it. Well-known and often applied breathing exercises in this connection are kapalabhati, bhastrika and mulabhanda.

The navel centre is also the area where we can create a whole reservoir of prana. The result of opening the navel chakra is a revitalising of the whole immune system, the digestion and other areas of the human body. At the same time a pleasant feeling of trust and optimism is developed. Runners, who concentrate on the navel centre during their workout, declare that their power increases enormously. In short, here we have a great treasure indeed, which we can draw upon daily.

So far we have discussed, the three lower chakras, which are sometimes neglected by the student of life, but they certainly do not deserve that. They lead to balance and stability on the emotional, mental and spiritual levels. Making use of their power is extremely beneficial.

The energy centers (chakras) are located in the subtle body

Heart centre

The heart chakra is the centre of feeling, emotions and love. The heart overflows with love when this chakra is open, creating a feeling of peaceful balance and inner well-being. It serves as a bridge between the lower and higher centres, dealing with the more subtle qualities than those of the lower chakras, and it is the promising passage to the higher centres connected to our mind, intellect and higher consciousness. Our emotional life connects in a beautiful way the lower centres with the higher ones. While in meditation, we feel a warm energy in the area of the heart when this chakra is touched by the kundalini.

Another characteristic of this chakra is that it can strongly influence our relationship with the environment. When we give love, we will receive love. But also: if we are blocked emotionally, it has a great influence on keeping our relationships alive. Whenever people enter the spiritual path, it is often the heart chakra that opens up first. It is the pure feeling of having discovered something beautiful, which offers a totally new vision on our life. At once we feel connected much more with everything and everyone around us and our heart overflows with joy and gratitude. We open up more to the other and suddenly understand the purpose of devotion and surrender – *bhakti-yoga*. You talk, think, work and sing from love. Your life has changed and you cherish this beautiful feeling of love as a golden treasure.

By means of our spiritual discipline, we grow into the direction of unconditional love, the final goal of the awakening of our heart chakra. Unconditional love means that we are there for the other in the first place and support the other in his or her desires and needs. If this was possible for us, every marriage or other kind of relationship would be a great success. The story of Shay, a handicapped boy, illustrates this beautifully. One day Shay walked with his father along a field, where some boys, whom Shay knew from school, were playing baseball.

Shay asked his father: 'Do you think I can join them?'. His father knew that most of the boys did not like to have Shay in their team, but he also understood how important the sense of belonging was for Shay. So, he approached one of the boys and asked if Shay could play with them.

The boy looked a little bit confused, but because nobody reacted, he took the decision himself and answered: 'We are six points behind and we are already playing in the eighth inning. But if you ask me, Shay can join in and we will see if we can get him hitting in the ninth.'

At the end of the eighth inning, Shay's team scored a few points, but it still remained three points behind. At the pinnacle of the ninth inning, Shay got a baseball glove and a place in the field. In spite of no ball coming in his direction, Shay was clearly excited that he was positioned in the field. He was grinning from ear to ear when his father waved to him from the side-line. Almost at the end of the ninth inning Shay's team scored again. With two points to go and all bases occupied, the moment had come to make the winning hit and it was precisely Shay's turn. Would the boys of his team let Shay play at such a crucial moment in the game and run the risk of losing the game? Surprisingly enough, Shay got the bat, although everyone knew that a sure hit was virtually impossible. Shay placed himself on the home base and the pitcher made a few steps forward to throw the ball gently so that there would be at least a chance for Shay to hit it.

The first throw approached him. Shay of course did his best, but missed the ball completely. After this the pitcher made another few steps forward to throw the ball a little bit even softer. The ball came and Shay hit the ball half, so that it rolled on the ground in the direction of the pitcher. The pitcher took up the weak ball and had all the time to throw it to the first base. Shay would then be out, and the whole game would be lost and finished. Instead, the pitcher took up the ball, turned around and threw the ball in a high arch to the right, completely out of the reach of the first baseman. At once, everyone started to shout: 'Shay, run to the first base!' Shay had never in his life reached the first base. Perplexed and with wide-open eyes he hobbled to the first base along the ground line, while everybody started shouting: 'To the second, run to the second!' By the time Shay was hopping passed the first base, the player at the right field had caught the ball. He could have thrown the ball to the second base, but then Shay would have fallen out, so he threw the ball high over the second base, while the runners before him started running like crazy, passing the bases on the way to the home base. When Shay reached the second base, one of the boys of the opposing team helped him to run in the right direction towards the next base, while he shouted: 'Run to the third!'

By the time he reached the third base the boys of both teams shouted: 'Shay, run to the home base, to the home base!' Shay limped further and, totally exhausted, but with an extremely satisfied feeling, reached the last base. Everyone went crazy and was cheering him, because he had hit a home run and won the game for his team.

Shay's father would always remember this day. 'On that day', his father often thought, while tears of emotion rolled down on his cheeks, 'On that day, the boys of both teams brought unconditional love into their game...'.

This is the miracle of the heart. The principle of giving and serving the other makes the heart receive everything it needs and from there, love can grow into pure love. The heart is an ocean of pure love, attainable for all seekers of truth, once we open this centre in all that we do. In our work, in a conversation or while chanting mantras, we can express our love and it will give us a feeling of connectedness, lightness and joy. How nice it would be, if this centre opened itself in all its beauty in everyone in the world.

Throat centre
When our spiritual energy awakens more and more, our throat chakra will at a certain moment open by itself. As a result, the power, sound and intonation of our voice will certainly change. Our ability to communicate and express ourselves will become much more effective. More love and compassion will resound in our voice and people will spontaneously be

attracted to what we have to say.

The throat chakra is not only the centre of sound and speech, it is also the centre of being silent, of the experience of pure silence deep within ourselves on the level where even the inner speech has subsided. This is a very pleasant experience, as if you yourself *were* silence.

This experience of silence is related to the *ether*, or space element with which this chakra is connected. Ether is an invisible element and is the medium through which our thoughts and feelings travel and through which our subtle energy flows.

***

'There is an awareness of something in your throat during this blissful silence. That happens when the throat chakra contacts the field of pure ether or akasha. There you will feel that your silence is not only individual, but seems to have extended into listening to the silence of the universe. You get the feeling as if you were in a big ocean of silence and that is fantastic. We know that from the ocean of silence intuitive ideas and feelings of inspiration can pop up. Also, images come up in this silence, we are able to receive images. If we embrace this silence, our intuitive power increases. We receive images from outside, but also from deep within our heart.'
- Sri Vasudeva

***

Our thoughts, feelings and words start moving freely through the field of ether and a time will come when we will be overcome by the feeling that the universe speaks through us. At that moment, we have become an instrument of the Divine, which expresses itself through our words.

The throat chakra is the channel through which refined arts like making music, reading poetry or writing a story can be expressed. Obviously, the quality of *chanting* is strongly influenced by this centre. The more open this centre is, the more it feels as if the singing was happening by itself and the more it feels powerful. The love of the heart and the purity of our intentions increases its power even more. If our ability to communicate increases and it is accompanied by a warm and open heart, this will improve the relationship with our fellow people tremendously. Especially, by chanting daily and putting our skills of speech in the service of a higher goal, we can add huge strength to this centre.

Brow centre

The sixth and seventh chakras lead us to the experience of the higher levels of consciousness. At the level of the lower chakras, we honour God as something that exists outside of us; on these higher levels we experience the Divine within ourselves. In our meditations we start to feel: *I am Divine. I am Pure. I am the Universe.* The brow centre, that is situated in the middle between our eyebrows, is also called the *third eye* and herewith nothing we say can be too much. It is the centre of an *inner vision*, and of an expanded vision. It is related to leadership, control over the senses, a strong ability to focus and it can connect us in a very powerful way with the spiritual teacher. It is the heavenly gate to the crown chakra. One could imagine that with a fully awakened brow centre, the quality of the meditation improves considerably, and one can enjoy every moment in life while the daily spiritual discipline comes with great blessings and intense experiences.

However, as long as this chakra has not yet opened, we cannot control our thoughts and keep experiencing some restlessness during meditation. The awakening of this centre can be accompanied by intense pulsating movements or a sensation of pressure or tingling between the eyebrows. Teachers in the tradition of Kundalini-yoga advise us to start to feel this chakra consciously. Focus your attention during the meditation gently to the forehead and do not force anything. As soon as the energy starts moving, the moment has come to stay concentrated more on this feeling. From a certain moment of awakening, the kundalini shakti allows us to play with her movements. During chanting or during deep meditation we can feel her moving to one of the other chakras, the heart, the throat, or navel centre and back. If our intentions are pure, Shakti will support us lovingly.

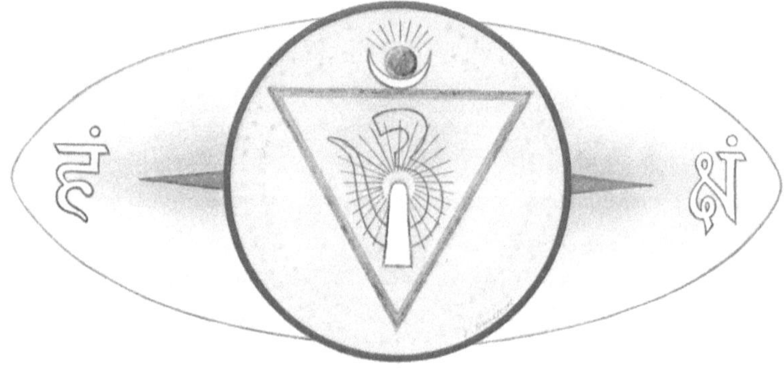

Ajna Chakra

The awakening of this centre prepares us for the final destination of our journey. It is said that when the divine energy comes into our brow and stabilises itself there, it will always stay with us and from here the journey continues automatically. This is the centre of the intellect and the mind. We will be able to control our mind fully, but the ego can still play a parts. When the mind and intellect become stronger, our ego will also grow in strength. At this level, we could develop misplaced and egoistic feelings of superiority and this could be a serious pitfall on our spiritual path. This takes place if we think *to be better or stronger than the other, or to be the leader, even the Guru.* As long as we remain stuck in that feeling, we will not be able to reach the final destination.

Here, at the level of the intellect and mind, we definitely have to let go of the ego and die a thousand deaths. This can only be done with full surrender in love and devotion to God and the Guru, from the heart centre. As soon as the brow and heart centre are ready to come together and co-operate, miracles are possible and the Divine Grace takes care of the rest.

***

'During my process of internalization, I started to feel a beautiful connection between my brow, my throat and my heart. It was a beautiful experience to feel during chanting that my brow centre produced an enormous concentration in my voice and words. My throat gave me a beautiful energy to give expression to mantras and sound, while my heart felt so much love during this process. This did not only happen while chanting, it also happened during speaking. If I started speaking, I felt the same amount of concentration as during my devotion and discipline. It just felt fantastic that my spirituality found a place in my ordinary life.'
– Sri Vasudeva

***

This centre, when opened, can awaken in us certain supernormal powers, the so-called *siddhis*. These are described in the Yoga-sutras of Patanjali, together with the way in which they can be developed. Furthermore, we are able to exert a strong influence on the mental space of someone else by the power of our thought. Great leaders often possess a well-developed brow chakra, but if their heart is not equally developed, this can still lead to problems. In any case, someone with an opened brow chakra will spontaneously put himself forward as a leader. It is the centre of the Guru-principle (guru tattva), meaning that we, once the centre opens up, will experience the qualities and energy of the Guru in ourselves. This naturally leads to taking up more responsibility and wanting to be a leader. However, those, in whom heart and head are balanced, consider themselves first of all an instrument of the universe. They feel connected to and in the service of the Divine and act accordingly. Such leaders do not have the need to be in the limelight and sometimes are even invisible, nevertheless they are able to influence the world around them in a very positive way.

The invisible leaders are the ones who have the real influence. When we meet a real leader in our life, we will feel that our strength, within his or her energy field, is restored. In his presence, we will feel that we come into our own strength and that there is never any form of intimidation, manipulation or any position of dependence. The greatest gift in life is to feel the power and energy of the brow centre and to experience that we are the instrument, God is the Doer and we are united with the supreme Lord.

Crown centre

After the permanent awakening of the third eye and the complete transformation of the ego, it is possible to enter the world of the *sahasrara* and stay in the fathomless depth of its inner Being. Full surrender to the kundalini is a prerequisite. The crown is not a chakra in the sense of the previous six energy centres which together form the path of development of the kundalini energy. This centre is an all-embracing, condensed consciousness, light and peace. It has the subtle form and movement of a thousand-petalled lotus flower, in which all Sanskrit primordial sounds come together in wholeness. It is the dwelling place of Parashiva, who can only be experienced by a fully awakened soul. When the siddhas reach this place, they experience the complete union of Shiva with Shakti. It is the area of unlimited freedom and complete ecstasy. Only the fully enlightened souls can describe its beauty and glory.

***

'When this last chakra is awakened, you feel complete satisfaction and no desires left. The whole universe is yours because you can get everything. You only need to desire and the universe reacts. This is how the enlightened soul works. He is so much in harmony with the universe that all his wishes are fulfilled. Even if he has nothing on the material plane, he is connected to the spiritual power that can give him anything. That is the path of the enlightened – the road of complete satisfaction.'
- Sri Vasudeva

***

This experience of the *sahasrara* is described as the divine expression of the thousand suns. Here the subtle dwelling place of the Self, *the blue pearl*, a radiating and very concentrated bluish light, is located. Even if it is not greater than the tip of a needle, it contains the whole universe. By the *shaktipat* of the Guru, even those who do not permanently stay here, can sometimes see and experience the blue pearl in their meditations. This centre of pure light administers our total being and is the meeting place of all nadis. The state of complete ecstasy that the siddhas experience here is beyond pain or death. Having come home in the centre of the universe, the enlightened soul says: *'I am perfect, everything is perfect'*. He considers the whole world as the expression of his own Self. He is not only in the world; the world is in him. He is the world expressing itself as pure light. He is not in the light; he is the light. He is all-embracing love. He is pure bliss. He is infinite wisdom. He is the full expression of the Veda.

XVI.4 WE ARE MULTI-DIMENSIONAL

We are so much more than human beings with just a physical body, we are multi-dimensional beings. We are able to transfer our thoughts over a great distance through the field that we call ether. Others are able to receive those thoughts and let them emerge in their own mind. Almost everyone has once thought of somebody, after which that person almost immediately called on the telephone. Ideas that come up in people can be received spontaneously by other people. Often the same invention is done at about the same moment in different parts of the world. Even thoughts that we experience at an unconscious level, can be received. Déjà vu experiences have to do with the past. All dimensions exist and play their role. The subtle energy field will continuously influence the physical body. Therefore, it is important to clean our subtle energy centres and to open them, it will benefit our health and well-being. We become more balanced and healthier. We can experience so much inner peace, that thinking thoughts seems to become superfluous. We desire to be silent and only want to experience the fullness of pure consciousness. Just *to be*, that is what it is all about (Shakespeare). If we are able to allow the activity of the mind to settle down, like Patanjali describes in his Yoga-sutras, we can experience a new and beautiful world, our real world. That is the world of love, harmony and permanent peace. In that state, which is the world of the Veda, we feel connected to everything and everyone.

* * *

Sadgurunath Maharaj Ki Jai
All glory to the true Guru.

CHAPTER XVII

SPIRITUAL DISCIPLINE

'Sadhana is the means to make your heart pure and strong enough to preserve the knowledge of Truth. The purer you are inside, the clearer you are able to perceive the Self.'

- Swami Muktananda Paramahamsa

We can come up with all kinds of things and pursue interesting goals in life, but the real goal is to discover what is going on in our inner world. All famous teachers in the past – Lord Krishna, Sri Rama, Jesus, Buddha and others – have brought this up. Objectively speaking, they spoke from the same source, which modern science calls the unified field of all the laws of nature. A field means that we can localize it everywhere in the universe. The sages say that we can experience this field within ourselves as well. This takes place when the objective and subjective worlds meet, that is, when the activity of the mind settles down completely. So, in a subjective sense, it is a field of consciousness or creative intelligence. After a long wandering through matter, we come to the discovery that matter is an expression of energy and that energy is creative intelligence. This creative intelligence manifests in the human being as consciousness expressing itself in thoughts, feelings, memories and activities. Those who really know, say that we are much more than we think we are. For instance, when we attend a funeral, we see how fearful people can be about death and express so much sadness for the one who has passed away. But if we know that the human existence has a much broader meaning and serves a much greater purpose than just dying, we can, even on a funeral, suddenly experience a lot of happiness and gratefulness out of pure love.

XVII.1 SADHANA

The creative intelligence in ourselves makes us creators of our own experiences. That means, we do not have to watch patiently how the creation evolves but, since we are part of it, we can co-create with the universe and contribute to human evolution. That can only be done from within. Spiritual discipline (*sadhana*) is a core concept to create balance and progress in our inner world. Practicing it will bring more light and wisdom in us and dispels the darkness of ignorance. The opening of the chakras plays a central role in sadhana. Each *chakra* is a centre of light and energy that is connected with a certain part of our being. Especially the root, sacral, and navel chakras vitalize our physical system. The heart, throat and brow chakras strengthen our mental, emotional and intellectual being. Spiritual discipline leads to the awakening of all subtle energy centres, by which more power, love and energy is channelled into our activities. This is the beginning of the spiritual journey that starts with the root chakra, where the kundalini energy lies coiled up as a snake. When she wakes up, she moves upward in a spiral through the other centres, to the crown chakra. The ultimate awakening of the crown chakra brings finally complete union between the chakras and the higher Self. Here lies the exalted final destination of the kundalini energy, where light and peace come together in supreme Bliss.

Prakritis

A more subjective approach is the work on prakritis. There are eight prakritis moving around in human consciousness. Scheme 17.1 gives a number of possibilities of how we can connect the different prakritis with spiritual practice or sadhana, in relation to the different forms of yoga.

Scheme 17.1
Sadhana and Yoga

PRAKRITI	SADHANA	YOGA
EGO	Surrender, transformation, causal body	Kundalini Yoga
INTELLECT	Study of holy scriptures, debating	Gyana Yoga
MIND	Attention, intention, positive attitude	Raja Yoga
HEARING	Sound therapy, chanting, meditation	Mantra Yoga
TOUCH	Love & devotion, satsang, prayer	Bhakti-yoga
SIGHT	Colour therapy, decoration, seva	Karma Yoga
TASTE	Diet and food, herbs, sexual control	Tantra Yoga
SMELL	Aroma therapy, nature, physical exercises	Hatha Yoga

Scheme 17.1 In essence, we are pure consciousness that expresses itself in the manifest world subsequently (from subtle to gross) as ego, intellect, mind, and the five senses. The latter ones are hearing, touch, sight, taste and smell. The prakritis are again closely connected to the different chakras and e.g. to the nine planets (eight plus one) of Vedic astrology as well.

When we start to become aware, that we are spiritual beings in a human condition, the need grows to emphasize a good spiritual discipline. Chanting, meditation, yoga, breathing exercises, prayer and service to God and our fellow people are powerful means to awaken the spiritual light in us.

***

'The story of man is the story of inner self-development, of Self-realisation, of enlightenment. If you try your whole life to achieve all kinds of goals that go beyond that, you behave like a child who builds sand castles on the

beach. If the flood comes, everything is washed away and nothing is left. The only things left are your ignorant, lonely and unfulfilled desires. But if you walk the spiritual path giving attention to inner growth and more love for yourself, you give attention to a very important journey and to the most important activity in your life.'
– Sri Vasudeva

***

Sri Vasudeva, Founder and Head of the International Blue Star Ashram in Trinidad & Tobago

XVII.2 SATSANG

Coming together with people who are striving for and want to serve the same goal, is another inspiring activity. We call this *satsang*, a gathering of people who undertake the same spiritual journey. Ideally, these gatherings are inspired by a spiritual teacher, but the enlightened master does not have to be physically present, as such. He or she possesses qualities that go beyond the physical, abilities that we can also find in ourselves. By coming together in satsang, we can receive guidance or inspiration of the teacher, which can help us further. Sometimes we can make a great leap at once; nothing is impossible. Anyway, in the company of spiritual souls we grow much faster and become stronger in our inner experience of the source. We learn to deal better with relations, disappointments, fears and loneliness and we become stronger and more self-reliant.

Sometimes it is said that life does not guarantee a silver-spoon welcome. A well-to-do person can suddenly lose all his money. If we think we are very healthy, suddenly we can become very ill. If we think we have friends all over the world, we can easily lose them. As we grow older, the body and mind can be very much challenged. Change is in the nature of life, there is nothing new under the sun and nothing is what it seems to be.

In a satsang, one speaks or meditates, but there is especially a lot of chanting together. The singing is called chanting, because it is not just singing. It is not a kind of entertainment or something that arises from a social need, because we have nothing better to do. The guru says: *'I do not sing for God but God sings through me'.* If we can have a glimpse of that, as an average spiritual soul, then we have already come a long way. The mantras and bhajans that are sung, bring the inner source to life, in the group and in everyone who is present. The mantra chanted is often repeated many times. Thereby the energy field is enlivened and can be experienced as shaktipat. Shaktipat is the power and inspiration of the spiritual teacher, that enters us. Our mind settles down and we leave all suffering and worries for a moment for what they are. The chanting brings us right *into the present moment.* We experience more freedom and suddenly we feel transformed to heavenly spheres, only by opening ourselves to singing. That is what satsang is doing for us. That is being touched by the real treasure.

In practice, we find that we forget our experiences easily and then we are not able to make some free time anymore and come together. When we have gathered, that is the moment when we remember the divinity within us, we experience the source and enter another dimension. It elevates us into higher spheres. Those who have really touched the source during a satsang – and those are many –, describe it as a feeling of ecstasy, a joy that cannot be expressed in words.

XVII.3 THE MANTRA

We know that the mind has the tendency to change and shift continuously, driven by a mental habit. If we allow our mind to be restless, it will surely be that. If we allow all kinds of thoughts to enter our mind, then the mind will follow them. So, we ourselves are the ones that encourage or stimulate the mind to become restless, by allowing it to do whatever it wants. Therefore, it is our own responsibility to control the mind by regulating our thoughts.

Because we are often caught within the boundaries of our thoughts, it is very useful to take up a certain sound, a powerful thought, which stimulates and inspires us. A mantra can be such a special word, with so much meaning for us, that every time we remember it, we recharge ourselves. Chanting the name of God, for instance, has become a mantra for many, because God has a divine meaning for people who are on their spiritual journey. So, every time we remember this mantra, we remind ourselves of the Supreme Being of the universe. Remembering God all the time can become a habit. Every name and every word that reminds us of something so infinitely great as God can be used as a mantra. For instance, repeating the *maha-mantra* is for many devotees a powerful tool to keep the focus on the Supreme Lord, and protect the mind against any form of negativity from outside.

The mantra that we get from a spiritual teacher, or on behalf of a holy tradition, possesses a special power. A mantra, blessed in this way, has the Shakti of the spiritual teacher and is very precious. This is because there is a strong association with the powerful energy of the teacher. Every time we repeat what he has initiated us in, or remind ourselves of it, we recall the power of and the connection with his enlightened soul. The guru and the mantra are in fact one, they express the same energy, and the guru is always nearby in the form of the mantra. By means of the mantra, his Shakti energy penetrates every cell of our body. Thus, the mantra becomes an important tool in our effort to overcome restless thinking. It becomes a special word and if we keep repeating it, we gradually begin to feel a change in ourselves. The more we pay attention to it, the more we repeat it, the more strength it will give us. It seems to penetrate deeper and deeper into our own source. The mantra appears to be a simple instrument, but it can be extremely powerful. To receive a guru mantra from an enlightened master is a great blessing.

We can use the mantra as a means for meditation. The purpose of meditation is to cease the activity of the mind, to have it rest. At the same time, stress accumulated in the body can be dissolved during this process. The only thing needed is a disciplined life. By leading a regular life, we can maintain and increase the accumulated energy in our body. But also, besides the meditations, even while working or at any other moment of the day, we can use a mantra. As soon as we begin to repeat the mantra, the mind will start to resist, but if we keep it up, nevertheless, it will support us in the end. If the mind is quiet and silent, the mantra pops up almost automatically, because it knows that we have the intention to start remembering it. And if we continue to repeat the mantra, we start to develop a loving relationship with it, because it reminds us of the light, of the goal we have in mind. The moment we pronounce it, waves of happiness and love rise up in us, we feel it. And the time comes, when we will experience an indescribable power the moment the mantra emerges in us. Apart from love and happiness, it also gives strength. An affirmation can create the same effect. Good affirmations for instance are: *I am very healthy. I love myself or May all people be happy.* An affirmation or mantra can lead us to our own power, when it is firmly rooted in the mind. Thoughts have the tendency to draw us into the past or the future, to unrest or towards depression. A mantra can keep us focussed on one single point. We can repeat it, while busy at work or meditating, with every breath. It is a very special spiritual tool.

XVII.4 LIFE IN THE ASHRAM

An ashram is a place dedicated to God, where the spiritual teacher lives with his devoted disciples. Often, one can visit an ashram as a guest and stay there for a shorter or longer period of time. It is a community with its own particular rules and daily discipline. The ashram has a special energy field that we can immediately notice upon entering. It is the energy field of the guru who stays there and who has built this energy up. It is a field of light in which the student can submerge. Already by staying in an ashram, a process of inner growth is set in motion. Moreover, the spiritual teacher guards his students and guides them as if they were his own children. Depending on the tradition from which he or she comes, the teacher will prescribe a certain daily discipline in which everyone who lives in the ashram, or stays for a certain period, should participate. To give an example, in the international Blue Star ashram of Sri Vasudeva in Trinidad & Tobago the fixed daily schedule applies as we can see in scheme 17.2.

Except for special days, in certain periods or during special events, the daily schedule in the Blue Star ashram is always the same. On Saturday evening, there is satsang and many people from outside the ashram are joining. Everyone is aware of the beautiful spiritual energy which is created when a big group of people come together in harmony. It feels like a celebration. The experience of the special atmosphere in the ashram is very inspiring, but this we can, to a certain extent, also create at home or at our work place.

Scheme 17.2
Daily Routine in the Blue Star Ashram

04.30	Get up, shower	12.30	Lunch
05.00	Guru Gita chanting	13.30	Rest
05.45	Meditation	14.30	Seva
06.00	Darshan	16.00	Sacred conversation
07.00	Yoga	17.00	Seva
08.00	Seva	18.00	Meditation
08.30	Breakfast	18.30	Dinner
09.30	Seva	20.00	Shiva Mahimnah chanting
11.30	Refresh	21.00	Tea or warm milk
12.00	Meditation	21.30	Lights off and sleep

Scheme 17.2 The Vedic scriptures say that a fixed daily routine might be uneasy in the beginning, but after some time, it is experienced as very joyful and ideal. The spiritual student (sadhaka), who has already lived in the ashram for some time, would not want to miss any part of this routine.

Guru Gita

We chant to enhance the glory of the Divine in us. While chanting, we often experience that we enter into another dimension, another field of power. It is as if the words spring up from deep within. In the ashrams of the Siddha Yoga tradition, one chants the *Guru Gita*, an homage to the sadguru representing the Divine early in the morning. The Guru Gita describes the nature and qualities of the sadguru, the guru-disciple relationship and the way to focus on the guru energy. It consists of 182 *stanzas* (Sanskrit verses) and is derived from the *Skanda Purana*. Chanting of a holy text is called *svadhyaya* and this practice of the

Siddha Yoga tradition goes back a long, long time. The representatives of the tradition say that the chanting of the holy text should take place every day at set times and with a deep feeling of reverence and devotion. *Svadhyaya* enhances inner brilliance, gives mental power and flexibility. It is a form of *japa yoga*, and it generates the same profound effects. We sit, thereby, in a clean spot, in a good posture and focus fully on the text. The chanting nourishes the love of the heart, offers joy to the mind and feels like nectar to the soul. It is directly devoted to God Himself, which is clear from the introductory mantra, sung at the very beginning:

***

Namo'stvanantaya sahasra murtaye
sahasra pada'kshi shiroru bahave
sahasra namne purushaya shashvate
sahasra koti yuga dharine namah

Salutations to the infinite Lord who has a thousand forms,
a thousand feet, eyes, heads, thighs and arms.
Salutations to the eternal Purusha with a thousand names,
who endures through ten billion ages.

***

Herein the praises of both the personal and the impersonal God (the Absolute) in all his qualities are sung. He, who is immeasurable, infinite and all-embracing. The earth, the sky and cosmic space are not more than the feet of the Lord, who we try to comprehend through the eye of a higher intelligence. The next verse, in which the sadguru is praised, goes like this:

***

Om namah shivaya gurave
sad-chit-ananda murtaye
nishprapanchaya shantaya
naralambaya tejase

Salutations to the sadguru, who is Shiva,
whose form is Being-Consciousness-Bliss,
who is transcendent calm; and who
does not lean on any support, and is pure Light.

***

The sadguru is the embodiment of *sat-chit-ananda* – existence, consciousness and bliss. Throughout the ages the exalted qualities of the enlightened master have been praised with songs, because he represents the Source, he is pure consciousness, the origin of the universe. Only by the Grace (*kripa*) of the guru, can the student grow in and transform toward perfection. The introductory verses are then followed by the chanting of the Guru Gita, songs of the highest devotion to the guru.

***

'It (Guru Gita) is pure ambrosia, a sublime song that leads to the peace of ultimate liberation. It is a song of praise to the Lord, living in our own heart. It makes disease disappear and provides a robust health, enhances knowledge, strength and fame and leads one to Self-realisation.'
- Swami Muktananda

***

Guru Gita is the exposition of the meaning and purpose of life by *Shiva* to his consort, *Parvati*. When Parvati asks Shiva about *the secret* of the devotion to the sadguru, Shiva answers that the chanting of this song, dedicated to the sadguru, leads to the fulfilment of all worldly desires and ultimately to spiritual liberation. Those who sing the praise of the inner guru in full surrender, acquire the same qualities as their master. The Guru Gita is their means and goal. After the chanting of the Guru Gita, several songs are sung in which the many names of God are repeated. The chanting of the names of God allows the heart to overflow with love and brings peace to the mind. The different chants are accompanied by several musical instruments, like the Indian harmonium, tabla (drums) and tambourines.

A special song that is sung early in the morning after the Guru Gita is the *arati*, which in India is a very popular tradition, performed at home or in the temple. By the singing of *arati*, the inner Lord and the guru are honoured, the Self that is present in everything. The performance of arati is a refined way to express love and devotion, a very recommendable practice that leads the student to the highest regions of human consciousness, to the union with God.

Darshan

After the morning session, there is opportunity for darshan and the students who are devoted to the guru make use of this possibility eagerly. Darshan happens when the sadguru pays personal attention to you and gives you his blessing. The guru looks at you, talks to you or touches you for a moment. When you are busy with a project in the ashram, he discusses it with you and gives instructions for the rest of the day. Again, the holy scriptures declare that the guru is not of flesh and blood; the guru is not a man or a woman; the guru is not an individual – he is the representative of the Divine. In that condition, he can transfer the Shakti, the divine energy, to his students so that they can develop their own inner strength. The guru is the divine instrument that dissolves ignorance and purifies the ego of the student. The Vedas are very clear about it, that it is impossible to reach the state of enlightenment without the sadguru. As

Jesus once said, the blind cannot lead the blind. It is essential to receive the Grace of the guru, the representative of God. When we are devoted students, this Grace is always there, but at the moment of darshan we become fully aware of this.

Only when there is a real guru-disciple relationship, can we receive the Grace of the guru completely. This means that we accept him lovingly into our heart, as our guide and inspiration for life. Even by thinking of him, we can transform ourselves and make his pure qualities our own. We have to allow the spiritual teacher to work on us, we have to give up our ego and pride. We have to surrender unconditionally to the sadguru and trust him completely, this is what it means to be his student.

The *inner guru* slumbers in everyone of us. It is not easy to localize and enliven this inner guru in ourselves. But the true guru, the sadguru, is able to lead us to this place, because he himself dwells there all the time. At the moment we touch our inner guru, we feel a deep connection to the external guru and will immediately understand every word he speaks.

Seva

Seva is selfless service that we dedicate with love to God or the guru. Wherever we are in the world, we can at any moment perform seva. Seva is like a yajna, we offer our activity with heart and soul to the Divine. In an ashram, there are always different routine jobs to do – like working in the garden, taking care of the cattle, reconstruction, helping in the kitchen or cleaning the toilets. When you perform this with love and devotion, it does not matter what you do. Next to that, there are the many special projects that take place in consultation with the spiritual teacher. Also, in seva, discipline plays an important role. When everyone in the ashram follows a strict discipline, the atmosphere will become charged with a lot of power, harmony and energy. People entering from outside will immediately sense this. On the other hand, the energy that is present in the ashram gives a lot of support in following this discipline. It is said that such sacred energy even attracts celestial beings from other dimensions.

Before Sri Vasudeva reached Self-realisation in a process that lasted forty days in 1978, he travelled twice to India to finally meet his guru Swami Muktananda. After his first visit, as a boy of twenty-one years old, he described his first experience with the ashram as follows:

***

'When I went to India the first time, I did not meet the guru physically. But I came in a beautiful atmosphere. Immediately when I walked in, I felt so different! I had visited different ashrams in India, but this ashram had a special effect on me. What made it so nice was the great discipline that was kept. You could not waste time, because you were always busy with one or the other beautiful activity – in the garden or library, in seva or meditation. The little spare time you had to rest was well spent in that peaceful atmosphere.'

***

Many people from different countries have visited the ashram of Sri Vasudeva in the past years and have worked and meditated there. After a longer or shorter stay, they go back as a different person, with the feeling that they have reached or even surpassed their goal. The ashram, as described here, is an example of the Vedic life in practice. Simply said, Vedic science is all about the principles of existence, life and growth, which keep their value throughout time and can be applied in daily life. A true seeker knows that the great happiness is difficult to find in the external world, so he is not really interested in power or worldly possessions. The true seeker is mentally detached, like the famous archer Arjuna, and focuses solely on the spiritual goal.

One day, the Pandavas were training in archery with their nephews. Drona, the teacher-acharya, asked Duryodhana to direct his arrow to the eye of a great, stuffed heron, which was placed high in a tree.

'What do you see?' asked Drona.

'I see a tree, Sir' answered Duryodhana, 'and the heron and the arrow that I direct now on the eye of the heron.'

'Enough!' said Drona sternly, 'let the others come forward and tell me what they see.' And one by one the Kauravas and the Pandavas came forward to say what they saw. But Drona was not pleased with their observations.

Finally, Drona asked Arjuna, his beloved disciple, to come forward and direct his arrow on the eye of the heron.

'What do you see, Arjuna?' asked Drona.

'I see the eye of the heron, Sir,' answered Arjuna.

'And further?'

'Further nothing, Sir,' answered Arjuna calmly.

Only now was Drona satisfied and gave Arjuna permission to shoot.

The epic Mahabharata is a mighty metaphor of Vedic knowledge. Arjuna was considered to be the best archer of his time. From his master, Drona, he learned all branches of the 'martial arts' of life. Arjuna represents the human mind, who, through innocent devotion, heads straight to his target. That is why Arjuna was so effective in fulfilling his life mission as a warrior, the destruction of everything that obstructed his path towards inner growth and fulfilment. Seva is a form of Karma-yoga and – if performed with devotion and love – a beautiful means to grow swiftly.

Shiva Mahimnah Stotram

In the evening hours, the Shiva Mahimnah Stotram is chanted in Sri Vasudeva's ashram, a song of praise to honour the greatness of Shiva, composed by a saint, named Pushpadanta. It is said that this is one of the most beautiful poems written in Sanskrit. According to the legend about the origin of this hymn, each day Pushpadanta worshipped his beloved Lord Shiva with flowers. He tried to get hold of the most beautiful flowers, but the most beautiful ones could only be found in the royal gardens. Therefore, Pushpadanta made it a habit to steal flowers from the garden of the king during the night, so he could offer them the next morning in the temple of Shiva. The guardians of the king were furious, because as soon as the flowers started blooming, they were stolen. They did everything they could to find out who the mysterious thief was. But they were not successful because Pushpadanta possessed a unique ability, namely, he could fly. He stole the flowers and flew away with them. That was the reason the guards could not find any trails or footsteps. But one day, one of the guards got a brilliant idea. He discovered that each time the flowers were stolen, they could be found back in the temple, on the altar of Shiva. He took a bunch of the flowers offered in the temple, and strew them out in the garden. Everyone who would pass now, would draw the anger of Shiva upon him, since the flowers had already been used once for the sacrifice. And so it happened, that Pushpadanta committed a great sin by stepping on the flowers and lost his power to fly. This ability he had once received from Shiva Himself, who now had punished him severely. When Pushpadanta understood what happened, he was very sad to have fallen out of the Grace of Shiva in such a cruel way. In his grief, he composed a hymn of forty verses with magnificent and devout praises addressed to Shiva. He took it to the temple and dedicated it wholeheartedly to Shiva, who was very moved by the beautiful chanting and decided thereon to give back Pushpadanta's ability to fly.

Lord Shiva

One of the hymns in which Pushpadanta expresses all his devotion to Shiva, goes as follows:

***

Trayi samkhyam yogah
pashupatimatam vaishnavamiti
prabhinne prasthane
paramidamadah pathyamiti ca,

rucinam vaicitryad
rijukutilananapathajusham
nrinameko gamyas
tvamasi payasamarnava iva.

Different paths (to realisation) are described by the three Vedas,
by Samkhya, Yoga, Shaiva doctrine and Vaishnava shastras.
People follow different paths, straight or crooked,
according to their temperament and depending on which
they consider best, or most appropriate – all leading to You alone,
like different rivers flowing to the ocean.
– Shiva Mahimnah Stotram, vs. 7

***

By reciting this hymn daily with a pure heart, learning it by heart or meditating upon it, the devotee of Shiva will gain wealth, fame, a long life and many children. After death he will go to Shiva's heavenly abode and become one with Shiva.

XVII.5 FOCUSSING ON THE GOAL

All holy scriptures lay emphasis, unanimously, on the importance of staying always focussed on the goal. In the Koran, it is written: 'Remember Me and I will always be there for you'. Of course, He remembers us also, even when we have forgotten Him. If that happens, He will knock constantly on our door and will do everything to support us and help us further. Often, we do not see that, because we are distracted by the temptations of the material world. But when we give Him our full devotion and service, we will receive anything He has to give us.

In Bhagavad Gita, the divine revelation, Lord Krishna says:

* * *

'Think of Me, one pointedly, intensely and I will fulfil all your needs'.

* * *

In the Bible, it is said: 'Love God with whole your heart, with whole your mind, with whole your soul, and you will surely enter the Kingdom of God'. And in the Yoga-sutras, Patanjali says: 'Those who are intensely focussed on it, will easily realise the Self'.

Step by step, the idea grows that we are all connected to the universal network (field) of Light and Power. We live in that energy field which is the Kingdom of God. Therefore, we are never alone. As long as we remain focussed on the pursuits of the world, all our attention goes there. Growing to enlightenment means, that we recognise the Divine within us and leave the attention to worldly desires step by step behind.

Jesus said:

* * *

'There where your treasures lie, lies also your heart'.

* * *

Where is our treasure? The answer to this question determines our life at this moment. Are we ready for the difficulties that life brings or do we fight a continuous battle in order to survive? That makes the difference between being engaged with the external world and giving sincere attention to our internal world. If we are able to stay focussed on the spiritual goal, while searching for the spiritual light that shines within us, and mirrors our true selves in the face of the Beloved, who is always looking for us, then that is where our real treasure is.

CHAPTER XVIII

BHAKTI-YOGA

'After being born and dead many times, the one who really has knowledge surrenders to Me, knowing that I am the cause of all causes and that I am all that exists. Such a great soul is very rare.'

- Lord Krishna in Bhagavad Gita

So far, we have discussed a number of approaches to yoga, but the question may arise: what is the highest form of yoga? It has taken me over forty years, to come to the conclusion myself that *bhakti-yoga* can lead us to the supreme goal. Yoga means: Unity. We can explain that in many ways. Unity with who or what? The answer to that depends on the question and on the answer as to why we were born on this planet in the first place. It is certainly not my intention to put aside all the yoga practices discussed earlier. Every person is completely free to practice the sadhana which he or she is most attracted to and should certainly continue to do so. But having said that, in this chapter I want to explore the importance and real meaning of bhakti-yoga.

Most people who practice meditation or yoga strive to become healthier, happier and to experience more energy and balance in their lives. This, of course, is not wrong in itself. Yet bhakti-yoga is not primarily about ourselves, but about our relationship with God. Bhakti means: devotion, surrender. In Bhagavad Gita our devotion and surrender to God is considered the highest form of yoga practice.

In the collective consciousness of many western countries, God has completely disappeared from view. We have replaced it by surrendering to the desire to pursue happiness and success in the material world. This applies not only to the purely materialistic people, but in fact even to most of the yoga and meditation practitioners. This is the age of Kali-yuga, the time of ignorance. We have completely written off existence and relationship with God, often without even realizing or understanding it. God has disappeared from our consciousness. In the West, the focus on the material world, with all its so-called pleasures, has been elevated to the status of the supreme goal and is supported and recommended by everyone, including the spheres of politics, technology, health care, et cetera. However, true yoga means that we detach ourselves from the material world, the world of our senses and turn our lives to the service of God or the Supreme Lord. In the Vedic era, that was the sole purpose of being born on this planet.

XVIII.1 PERSONAL OR IMPERSONAL

The question whether the nature of the highest God is personal or impersonal has always been a fervently discussed point in Indian history. Regarding this disputed question Maharishi said: God is both personal and impersonal and this view is confirmed in the Bhagavad Gita. In other words, God expresses Himself on the one hand as a universal transcendent field - Brahman or the Kingdom of God - which is the unified field underlying the material world. In the Srimad-Bhagavatam this impersonal manifestation is called the radiance (Brahma-jyoti) of His transcendental form. On the other hand, He is the Supreme Lord, our ultimate origin and creator, who, like us, has a personality. He differs from us in being the Supreme Personality - absolute, transcendental and eternal - while we are relative but integrated particles of Him. So, the Supreme Being, the cause of all causes, is both an all-encompassing Personality and a universal field, and in essence there is no difference between the two. God and the Kingdom of God form an absolutely equal and inseparable Unity. We human beings are individuals created in His image and therefore can be regarded as minuscule parts of the Supreme Lord.

The Supreme Lord is far beyond the imagination of worldly scholars, philosophers and scientists. His pure devotees, however, can easily understand him. Only when we transcend the limitations of empirical knowledge and put ourselves fully in His service, is it possible to comprehend His true Being.

In the Vedic scriptures, the oldest records of mankind, the Supreme is known as Lord Krishna, "the all-attractive." Also, Lord Brahma, the creator of the material world, declares that Lord Krishna is the Supreme Being, the highest of all gods and none can surpass Him. He is the Supreme Personality of Godhead; His form is eternal and filled with true knowledge and bliss. Both Lord Brahma and Lord Shiva are mighty gods, who govern cosmic affairs, just as ministers conduct their monarch's policies. They are indeed divine beings, but the Supreme Lord is the creator and supervisor of His administrators. Although He sometimes pretends to be a human being, the Supreme Lord is in no way human. He contains all variety, and He is present in all variety, even though He is different from everything and everyone. That is the unfathomable mystery of God's ability. He is the absolute God and only when we know how great He is, can we fully surrender to Him.

When we look around in the world, we can easily see that humanity is in crisis. All the material achievements developed through modern science and technology, have not made us happier, healthier, and more sensible. Hence, there is an urgent need for a holistic vision of how humanity can serve one common purpose that leads to peace, friendship and prosperity among all nations and people in the world. The Vedic scriptures, including the Shrimad-Bhagavatam, fulfil that need because they provide a unique social and spiritual solution to all the problems in the world.

XVIII.2 THE SUPREME LORD

It is often said that there is only one God, known by different names. But what are the qualities of this Supreme Lord? The Bhagavad Gita and many other sacred writings explain that the Supreme God has a personal identity and that He, along with His devoted associates, resides eternally in the spiritual universe. This makes it clear that there are two worlds: the material world and the spiritual world. Both worlds consist of countless universes with numerous planets. The main difference between these worlds is, that the material world is physical and impermanent, whereas the heavenly abode of Lord Krishna, or whichever name you choose to give to the Supreme, is transcendental and eternal.

Everything in the material world comes from the Supreme Lord. Although He resides in the spiritual world, He creates the material worlds again and again. Although their lifespan is often extremely long, the demigods, too, are bound to the cycle of birth and death, while the Supreme God was never born and will always exist. He lives beyond physical existence, is transcendental in nature, and is all bliss. It is this Supreme Being who has given Lord Brahma the responsibility to create the material world. Lord Krishna is known as Brahman (Absolute Truth), Paramatma (Supersoul) and Bhagavan (Supreme Lord). As Paramatma, He can be found in every particle and in the hearts of every living being in the material world, although He Himself never becomes part of the material world. Also, in

His avatara appearances, He always keeps His transcendental nature, and stays untouched by the three gunas, which exert their influence on the material world unceasingly. In the Bhagavad Gita, Lord Krishna says to his friend and disciple:

* * *

"I, Arjuna, am the highest principle of transcendence, and there is nothing greater than Myself. Everything that exists emanates from My energies in the same way that pearls are woven on a thread. '

* * *

His Divine Grace A.C. Bhaktivedanta Swami Prabhupada (1896-1977), founder and spiritual teacher of the Hare Krishna movement, commented uniquely on both the Shrimad-Bhagavatam and the Bhagavad Gita.

His Divine Grace A.C. Bhaktivedanta Swami Prabhupada, explains in his commentary on the Bhagavad Gita, that Lord Krishna's eternal abode (dhama) is a revelation of His inner energy, while the material world is a manifestation of His external energy. And he says that Lord Krishna is the supreme enjoyer, the supreme owner of every planet and the greatest friend of all living beings. According to the Vedic scriptures, there are 8,400,000 different kinds of living beings in the material universe. Since the living beings on all different planets are part of His external energy, all beings (demigods, humans, animals, trees and plants) are the children of one Father.

Lord Krishna is also our spiritual Teacher. We can fully trust what He teaches us in the Bhagavad Gita, for these teachings come directly from Himself. This Vedic wisdom is given by Himself to Lord Brahma at the beginning of every creation. It is not necessary, nor even desirable, to give our own interpretation to it. Since every intellectual interpretation is limited, we can only surrender and follow. That is called bhakti-yoga. Since Arjuna was a true devotee, he could understand and act on the teachings of the Lord. This makes it clear, that only true devotees are willing to accept the existence of God and are able to carry this beautiful wisdom forever in their hearts.

XVIII.3 MATERIAL AND SPIRITUAL WORLDS

If we have a strong desire to follow the spiritual path in our life, we need to know and understand everything about the material and spiritual world. Why are people born in the material world? We need to find an explanation and a deep understanding of this. Our daily experience is that this world causes us much suffering and misfortune. Of course, many material achievements have been made over the past few hundred years that have made our lives more comfortable. But our common experience is, that after being born, our childhood is by no means always a happy experience. And when we get older, all kinds of dramas and illnesses come along and after a certain time we leave the physical world again. All this seems so useless and unjust. Of course, we try our best to live a happy life, but now and again we get disappointed or frustrated by all kinds of circumstances. All the time we are in an unfortunate struggle for survival and there is no clear vision of how to do it differently.

The Vedic scriptures teach us that our inner Self is pure and naturally full of love, happiness and wisdom. Our inner field of Love is not contaminated by anything. However, we do not identify ourselves with the inner Self, but with our body and mind and with the material world. As Maharishi Patanjali teaches us, the inner Self is our true nature and its qualities are *sat-chit-ananda* (eternal existence, intelligence and bliss). But as we identify ourselves with the material world, our focus is mainly on how we look, what kind of job we have, who else can make us happy, how much money we make, when we can buy or sell a house, and so on. All of this we do under the assumption that it can make us happier. Even our government and educational institutions emphasize these material achievements as well, and want us to believe that this is the only way of living a happy life. We come across the same tendencies in society: everything is focussed on economic growth and on a more than extreme consumption pattern. Politics, modern science, education as well as cultural and social institutions, are all based on ignorance about the meaning and purpose of our existence. Of the rulers of the world, Jesus said in His day:

* * *

'Forgive them, O Lord, for they do not know what they are doing.'

* * *

Today it is nearly impossible to be detached from our material desires and attachments. But as long as the spiritual world has no place in our lives, we will never be really satisfied, despite all our efforts. The spiritual world underlies and transcends our body, mind, and senses and is of a much higher, transcendental order. In the age of ignorance, the body, mind and intellect are only limited instruments of the inner field of consciousness. Our body is nothing more than the home or shell of the soul:

* * *

"Just by cleaning his cage one cannot satisfy the bird."
- **Swami Bhaktivedanta Prabhupada**

* * *

XVIII.4 FALSE EGO

But where does this material world come from and what is the meaning and purpose of this existence full of suffering and pain? The Vedic scriptures answer this question very clearly and in detail. A long time ago, the Supreme Lord created this material world for the souls who had lost connection with Him. Using His external energy, He created the twenty-four elements making up the material world. As soon as we talk about a material world, the time factor immediately comes in, as the twenty-fifth element. There is no time in the spiritual world, but the material universe has its own laws of nature. The time factor and the sensation of the past, present and future play a major role in our world.

As soon as a soul enters the physical world through birth, an identity or false ego is created and the soul becomes entangled in all kinds of activities. The false ego has no connection with God and takes to a life of its own, unaware that the external world is a world of illusion (maya). Although a human being has a higher potential of consciousness than an animal, he behaves in the very same way purely out of ignorance, in order to achieve happiness and success in the external world. Like an animal, he is mainly concerned with eating, sleeping, working and reproduction and thus he does not function any better than an animal. Meanwhile, he is so entangled in, and overshadowed by material desires and attachments that his connection to the Divine has been completely lost. Our current religions are based mainly on a belief-as-concept and, because of their confusing dogmas, often no longer play a significant inspiring role. Many church buildings have since been converted into exhibition spaces, conference centres or even supermarkets. The Vedas, on the other hand, represent the eternal religion of the universe. They are divine revelations for the sole purpose of bringing us back to God. The *Srimad Bhagavata Purana* and the *Bhagavad Gita, As It Is* show us the way to liberate ourselves from the material illusion. Study of these sacred scriptures is necessary to make an end to all our insolvable problems in every area of life. Once we begin to ask ourselves quietly what the purpose of life is, where we come from, and where we go again, from here, these sacred writings will open themselves to us.

XVIII.5 SOUL TRANSITION

Many people struggle with the concept of reincarnation and reject it from the start. But all the ancient sacred writings report on this, since it is impossible to explain the meaning and purpose of life otherwise. Every human soul remains always responsible for its own thinking and actions and that makes the principle of reincarnation extremely righteous. Closely related to this is the law of karma, or action = reaction, as modern scientists call it. If we do not understand this law of cause and effect, we can experience our lives as utterly meaningless, arbitrary and often unbearable. But the law of karma, which implies that every action evokes an equal reaction, is of a sublime simplicity and the whole perfection of the material universe is based upon it.

How does the transition of the soul take place? And how is it possible, that in a next life and in a new body, we experience the consequences of activities we have performed during this life? Even the greatest of scientists cannot explain how our karma is transferred from one body to another. But in the Shrimad-Bhagavatam (Canto IV, 29, texts 58 et cetera), Narada Muni explains this to King Barhismana. First of all, we must understand that as a living being, we have two bodies, the gross and the subtle. The gross body is our physical body, while the subtle body consists of the mind, intelligence, and false ego. At death the gross body comes to an end, but not the subtle body. It is the subtle body that carries the individual soul to the next body. The soul is connected to our subtle body until it is released from its captivity in matter. In text 60 the great sage Narada says:

* * *

"During this life the living being acts in a gross physical body. This gross body is forced to act according to the subtle body, consisting of the mind, intelligence and false ego. When the gross body comes to an end, the subtle body still continues to exist, to suffer or enjoy. So, nothing changes."

* * *

This shows that the gross body is no more than an outer shell, which is controlled by the subtle body. The same subtle body, with all its experiences, continues to exist, while the physical body changes with each new birth. The continuous change of the gross body is not nearly as important as the development of consciousness through the subtle body. By purifying the mind, the intelligence and the false ego, all active senses of the living entity become spiritual and it then naturally re-experiences its true nature of sat-chit-ananda.

XVIII.6 BHAKTI YOGA

Shrimad-Bhagavatam teaches us how we can leave the addictions to the material world behind us through the practice of bhakti-yoga, devotional service to the Supreme. Intense practice of bhakti yoga, which can be considered the highest form of yoga, lifts the soul to the spiritual planets, where life is eternally blissful and full of wisdom. The first activities on the path of bhakti-yoga involve a proper sitting posture, meditation, regulating the air currents in the body and focusing attention on the Supreme Lord. A regular daily routine, such as taking a bath a few times a day, and regular fasting are also included. Drinking pure water is allowed at all times during a fast. As a result of these exercises, we learn to control our senses - eyes, tongue, nose, ears, and the sense of touch. This is a prerequisite for attaining self-realization and becoming a pure devotee of the Lord.

As mentioned before, bhakti-yoga can be practiced simply and by anyone. It can turn us outwards as well as inwards. It does not matter whether we are very advanced or just a beginner on the spiritual path. It is possible for everyone to surrender to the Supreme Lord, because everyone and everything is part of Krishna's cosmic play (leela). The natural consequence of practicing bhakti-yoga is that we leave behind all attachments to the material world. Only then can we begin to focus on the spiritual world. Detachment from the material world does not mean that we have to permanently withdraw into the forest and live as a solitary hermit. Detachment is a mental process. We keep dealing with the material world, but in essence we do not belong to it. Bhakti-yoga can change our lives in a profound way. Slowly we consider material matters as less important and we feel more connected to the Supreme Lord. True devotees have less or no need for trivial things (TV, newspaper, car, politics, possessions, etc.) and find more and more satisfaction in loving surrender to the Supreme Lord. They consider-bhakti yoga as the most sublime activity they can practice and are not concerned about what others think of it.

Thus, we can chant the Name of the Lord and visit His temples that we can find all over the world. The so-called *bhaktis* chant the Hare Krishna mahamantra which has the power to protect and liberate our minds. It is said that repeating the Name of God is the best and most effective spiritual practice in Kali-yuga. By chanting the *mahamantra* daily, it can bring us lasting happiness because it connects us to the Divine. This mantra consists of sixteen words which are easy to learn:

* * *

Hare Krishna, Hare Krishna, Krishna Krishna, Hare Hare
Hare Rama, Hare Rama, Rama Rama, Hare Hare

* * *

Lord Krishna is fully present in His names. The mantra can be repeated in two ways: gently, supported by a chain of beads (mala) - this is called *japa*. When done properly, it can become a powerful part of our daily spiritual discipline. In the Hare Krishna Temple in the Krishna Valley, Hungary, and in many other spiritual places around the world, the mantra is chanted in groups and this practice is called *kirtana*. Traditionally this is done both in the way of listening to and chanting the mantra. Both ways, individually or in a group, can bring about a huge transformation of our lives. Our hearts will lighten up, our minds will experience more peace and happiness, and we will gradually come closer to God and eventually will want to devote ourselves fully to His service.

The Hare Krishna community in Somogyvámos, Hungary (about 160 km southwest of Budapest) is a perfect example of how the bhaktas living there, have arranged their lives in full service to Lord Krishna. Founded in 1993 by His Holiness Sivaram Swami (Guru Maharaj), this community resides and lives on a beautiful estate of approximately 350 hectares. The natural flora and fauna of the Krishna valley consists of a mixture of exotic and indigenous species and is a feast for the eyes. The whole place exudes an atmosphere of peace and serenity. As the largest eco-friendly community in Europe, it is completely self-sufficient. In addition to the beautifully designed Krishna temple, you will find a cowshed, two schools, guest houses and an extensive vegetable, flower and fruit garden. The simple but beautifully built houses of the residents are nicely spread in the rolling landscape. The bhaktas get all their food from the crops that they cultivate and which grow organically on their land. They have their own cow stable for the dairy products and keep bees for the production of honey.

Scheme 18.1

The nine practices of Bhakti-yoga

SANSKRIT NAMES	NINE PRACTICES
SRAVANA	Listen to His stories
SMARANA	Always remembering His Name
PADHASEVA	Sitting at His feet
ARCHANA	Communication by performing rituals
KIRTANA	To praise Him by chanting
VANDANA	To bow down to Him
DASYA	To be His faithful servant
SAKHYA	To be connected to Him as a friend
ATMA-NEVEDANA	To serve Him with heart and Soul

Scheme 18.1 Of the nine ways of practicing bhakti-yoga, the listening to and the explanation of the teachings given by the bona fide Vedic teacher, about the plays and activities of the Supreme Lord (Sravana), is perhaps the most important in making our spiritual journey a real success.
(Source: Shrimad-Bhagavatam)

How do we know that God listens to us in our pursuit of devoting ourselves fully to Him? That is not difficult to experience, because we feel more supported in everything we do in our daily life. The next step is that we learn to communicate with Him through our heart. At some point, although we did not ask for anything at all, we just get everything we need to live a life in His service. It is a wonderful process and it will make us humble and give us great satisfaction.

Hare Krishna Temple in Krishna-valley, Somogyvamos, Hungary

In our original state we are already a perfect and integrated part of the Supreme; we have only forgotten this. This is called maya, and so our stay in the material world can never yield complete satisfaction. Those who work sincerely and devotedly for their spiritual progress can become a devoted servant of the Lord. That will naturally lead us to the state of Krishna consciousness and liberate us from the attachments of the material world. The attainment of Krishna consciousness is the ultimate goal of our spiritual journey on Earth and can lead us to Krishnaloka, the eternal abode of Lord Krishna.

CHAPTER XIX

FAMILY AFFAIRS

'Jaya patye madhumatim vacham vadatu shantivani'

*May the son follow in the footsteps of the father,
may he and his mother have unity of mind,
may the woman speak to the man in words sweet as honey*

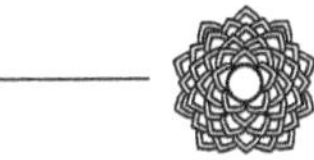

The Vedic tradition devotes a great deal of attention to purity and harmony in marriage and family life. This is because it is considered to be the basis of all happiness and harmony in our personal life and in the society. It is a symptom of our time that in Western society the value of marriage, the quality of family life and the role of women in it has been almost totally degenerated and destroyed. Western marriage consists of a contract which can be terminated any time. Moreover, the children are taking matters into their own hands in the family at an increasingly young age and women try to rival men in career planning. Often this happens at the expense of the marriage itself and, by extension, of the education and well-being of the children. All this is quite the reverse of what the Vedic scriptures say about marriage and family.

Often, we find a remarkable bond of deep affection between father and son (daughter), mother and son (daughter), husband and wife and brother and sister in the Indian society. The basis of harmony in family life is above all the relationship between husband and wife. The Vedic thought of *'Ardha narishwar'* - God is half man, half woman - carries a deep meaning in the traditional Indian community. It pertains specifically to a sense of genuine and lasting connection between man and woman.

XIX.1 FAMILY AND SOCIETY

Just like any individual, the heart and soul of a country grows by virtue of the ideals it sets for itself: well-being for all, justice and security, good education, ethical administration, and so on. In the high civilization of the ancient Vedic culture, spiritual freedom and non-attachment were embraced as the highest ideal for both men and women. The disciplines, rules and customs that were considered necessary to attain moksha (spiritual liberation) were therefore the same for both. The pursuit of such qualities as purity, self-control, devotion, and following the path of yoga applied to both men and women. But the Veda also deals with the differences between them, both biologically, mentally and with regard to their character; they are equivalent but not equal. Therefore, their activities are defined on the basis of their specific characteristics and path of life and for that reason they are prescribed different lifestyles and disciplines.

The resilience and quality of a society is supported by family life and it is the woman who plays a central role in this. She is the central person at home. The Vedas have wonderful stories about ideal women. Sitadevi, Savitri, Draupadi and even the wife of the demonking, Ravana, are still very inspiring examples for more than a billion people. In Vedic civilization, women enjoyed a lot of freedom. We need to realize that at that time spirituality was the most important thing people cherished, what connected them and what they lived for. Women were allowed to administer certain sacraments, study and teach the Vedas, or choose an ascetic life if they wanted to. It is due to the decline of the wisdom of life that in later periods all kinds of restrictions were imposed on Indian women, child marriages were arranged and various other abuses arose.

It did not go much better in the West, either, but it took a different direction. Because women started to feel dissatisfied with life at home and raising the children, they started looking for activities outside the home. Emancipation and the economic aspect play an important role in this. The cost of living has increased dramatically so that a lot of money is needed every month just to cover the fixed costs. In some households, the household money has run out already halfway through the month. This and all sorts of other social changes have brought little good to home life. When both men and women are working, the home has turned into a kind of hotel - it is hectic, family members scroll through the diaries for appointments and there is always a shortage of time and attention for family life itself. How many women, both in the West and in the East, have not found themselves in conflict with their inner nature? They could no longer be the resting point at home and the hope and comfort for all, a role they have fulfilled for thousands of years. The well-known writer Isabel Allende formulated the female values in an interview in a Dutch newspaper (2015) as follows:

* * *

"Women are more democratic when decisions have to be made, they are much more social than men, they are less ambitious and narcissistic than men. Women do more for others and find it less important to make a lot of money. For Michelle Bachelet, who was a paediatrician before she became president (of Chile), children's well-being was the main thing, she considered it more important than productivity.

* * *

One can hardly think of a more accurate expression of the qualities that make a real woman in her innermost being. Of course, there is nothing wrong with women pursuing a career outside the home. Margaret Tatcher, Angela Merkel and Indhira Gandhi are examples of great leaders in society. But to encourage women to work, as in the Netherlands, because it is important for the growth of the consumption pattern, is simply an insane political motive. The purpose of life is not material gain but spiritual liberation.

XIX.2 ARE MAN AND WOMAN EQUAL?

Today, a new trend is emerging in the modern West, called gender neutrality, which means that no distinction should be made between the behaviour of men and women. For example, it is possible to be gender neutral in terms of clothing, language, toys, professional practice, salary, and the education of children. But the question is whether this does justice to both men and women, who usually have different activities and responsibilities. In his book *Man the Unknown*, the renowned scientist, Dr. Alexis Carrel describes it like this:

* * *

"The differences between a man and a woman are very fundamental. The denial of this has led advocates of feminism and similar movements to believe that both have the same responsibilities and the same activities. But in reality, women are profoundly different from men. Every cell of their body speaks a different language. Physiologically but also mentally and emotionally they are governed by other laws. And these facts cannot simply be replaced by social measures or desires. "

* * *

XIX.3 GOAL OF MARRIAGE

Marriage is as old as the world; it is a natural state of living together. It is a contract of the heart and of the mind. It is an excellent exercise to gain more wisdom in life and also to make spiritual progress. Maharishi

Mahesh Yogi said about this:

* * *

"When one lives for the other, one grows in the value of life, in the structure of life for the other. This is the ideal of married life. And then this love expresses itself in the children, in nothing but happiness, in growing, tender waves of love. And this is the purpose of creation; what appears to be bonding, actually turns out to be the path to liberation. "

* * *

The purpose of Vedic marriage is to help each other grow together and promote each other's evolution. Man and woman are inseparable, one lives for the other. The woman takes care that the man grows to a higher consciousness and the man is completely devoted to his wife. In this way, both attain the most, and married life becomes a powerful opportunity for spiritual growth. The solution is to restore marriage to the place it deserves in society, and this lies in the domain of the development of human consciousness. The unfolding of a higher consciousness could represent another step forward in the field of harmonious relationships and could also assist the good of the whole family of nations. Maharishi also said:

* * *

"The love between a man and a woman is a path to yoga, or unity. Married life provides security and stability for the heart. Security is very necessary for both men and women. "

* * *

In summary, we can say that men and women are equal, but they differ from each other biologically, mentally and emotionally as well as in their character. In a harmonious society these differences should be recognized, nurtured and supported.

Nowadays, there will undoubtedly be expectant parents who think consciously and discuss in advance how they can optimally promote the quality of their offspring. The Vedic scriptures, especially Ayurveda, provide detailed guidelines on this. It almost goes without saying that the quality of the desired child depends largely on the health, nutritional habits and lifestyle of the parents. Before one consciously proceeds to conception, it is quite possible to devote earnest attention to it. The phases listed below are crucial to conscious birth planning and the quality of life of a soul incarnating in a body.

XIX.4 PRECONCEPTION

Bringing a child - which, in fact, consists of pure consciousness - into the world creates a great responsibility for the parents-to-be. Therefore, even before conception, parents should make sure that they are in an optimal mental and physical condition, which will benefit the quality of the offspring. As far as the monthly cycle is concerned, we can look at it from an Ayurvedic perspective. We can divide this into the qualities of the three dosha's: vata, pitta and kapha. We then get the following schedule:

Scheme 19.1
The Influence of the dosha's on the monthly cycle

MONTHLY CYCLE	PREDOMINANT DOSHA	EFFECTS
DAY 1 - 10	Vata Period	Restless, restless sleep, cold hands and feet
DAY 11 - 20	Pitta Period	Irritation, skin problems
DAY 21 – 30	Kapha Period	Restraint, introverted

Scheme 19.1 Both the woman and the man can consider and be aware of the effects that can occur during these periods of the monthly cycle.

During a pregnancy, external influences, such as the way the parents interact with each other during that period, have a major impact on the unborn child and influence it to a great extent. And in the later course of the child's life this will somehow play out. If we are always in financial trouble, or looking for security all the time, or arguing with colleagues constantly, or we are being very jealous, or feel a strong urge to break the laws of the country, these are all patterns which often have their root in what happened to us during the time of pregnancy, birth and the period shortly after we were born. In girls this can lead to chronic problems with menstruation.

The Upanishads describe the importance of the quality of food for reproduction as follows:

* * *

All beings on Earth come forth from food, survive through food, and return to food. So, our body was created through the intake of food of our parents. The food they take is converted from the coarser to the more subtle body tissues (dhatus). The last and most subtle of those body tissues is sperm in the man and the egg cell in the woman. By merging these two body tissues and the intelligence of nature, this can grow into a body. This body is continuously maintained in the mother's womb by the mother's intake of food. After birth, we take in food ourselves to develop and maintain the body. And when we die in time, our physical body will be cremated (sacrificed to the fire element, or agni) in order to renounce on it.

* * *

Ayurveda offers natural possibilities to promote pregnancy, such as administering certain massages, a suitable diet, internal cleansing and possibly the use of natural herbs as supplements.

XIX.5 CONCEPTION

In order to obtain progeny, we usually leave the moment of conception to chance and see what it yields. This is a bit strange, when we consider that a farmer chooses the season and the time to plant his seeds carefully. In the Vedic era of yore, celibacy before marriage was the norm, and having intercourse afterwards was mainly aimed at starting a family. The fact that we now live in a different era, with its own standards and values, does not change the value of that.

According to Ayurveda, the health quality and dosha constitution of the child depends on the parents' proportion of the doshas and their disturbances at the time of conception. It is for this reason, that Ayurveda pays so much attention to *paediatrics* as to distinguish it as one of its eight basic areas. This branch of medicine is concerned with the quality of the conception, the care of and attention to the child during pregnancy, birth and the first years of life thereafter. The health, food consumption and lifestyle of the mother, in line with that of the father, also, appear to bear great impact on the psychological, emotional and physical health of the child, not only during pregnancy but in fact for the rest of his or her life!

We may wonder whether the Ayurvedic vision and its applications still hold their value in our modern age. Besides the moral and spiritual reasons we can give, we should not lose sight of the fact that men and women are vast bundles of energy. If these bundles do not harmonize with each other at the time of conception, this can have adverse consequences for the offspring. That is why, especially when we are dealing with conception (for the purpose of reproduction) for the first time, it is of huge importance to keep it in the right direction and not leave everything to chance. Furthermore, we can also look at the process of reproduction from a cosmic perspective. When the seed of the man is introduced into the womb of the woman, a child comes forth that is nothing less than their own essence. Or, as the Vedic scriptures describe it:

* * *

The Self (the man) offers the Self (the seed) to the Self (the woman).

* * *

Giving birth to a child together is a natural thing and is often experienced by the parents as the greatest miracle of creation. The mother experiences the development of the foetus as a very intimate part of her body; therefore, she cherishes it like a gem. The father can feel deep gratitude to the expectant mother for the phenomenon developing in her womb and usually regards the newborn as his own soul and bliss. The concept of marriage is based on this whole event, and it is logical that it is seen in the Vedic scriptures as a holy sacrament. What in our age of superficial values is little more than a bourgeois contract, which can be dissolved at any time, was the most important pillar of society in the times of a highly developed civilization.

The ancient seers were not only spiritually gifted souls, but were also very advanced in almost every branch of science and were very well aware of the consequences of their investigations. An interesting question in this context is how we can optimally prepare for conception and determine which moment is most suitable for it. The Vedic scriptures, especially the Vedic Moon calendar (panchanga), give clear guidelines on this. When two people get married and want to start a family, it is advisable to understand the functioning of the human body and its reproductive system. It goes without saying that man and woman should be in optimal health before conception, which means that they should be physically, mentally and emotionally well balanced. For example, Ayurveda recommends that the woman has at least five to seven regular monthly periods prior to conception. Especially in the thirty-six hours before conception, one should pay close attention to the quality of the food that one consumes; only sattvic, vegetarian food is allowed, and even that in mode proportion, besides drinking water and herbal tea. In the few hours before conception, man and woman should bathe, nourish each-other and massage each other with warm oil.

It is also recommended to drink fresh, warm milk with certain herbs, such as nutmeg, turmeric, almond and other herbs with a mild aphrodisiac effect. When all these rules are observed, the chances are greatest that a healthy and well-developed child is born.

It is recommended that the parents-to-be prepare for that special moment spiritually as well. Before they engage in the love game, they could discuss with each other what kind of child they would like. It is important for them to be aware of the tremendous responsibility they bear in bringing a new human child into the world, in raising it and leading a happy life. Raising and guiding a child may be the most beautiful experience parents can have together, but it is not always easy or without complications.

Again, the quality of conception has a major impact not only on the development of the foetus, but also on the future health, strength and quality of the unborn child. The natural dosha proportion (prakriti) of the unborn child is also fully determined by, and dependent on the egg cell and sperm of the parents during conception. As we mentioned earlier, the doshas are derived from the five elements. The egg cell consists mainly of the earth element while the sperm consists of the fire and air elements. The uterine wall that nourishes it contains the water element and the uterine cavity is composed of ether or space. Thus, all five elements play an important role and are present in the creation of the foetus. It is mainly the blood that is formed by the water, fire and earth elements, and which initially nourishes and develops the foetus.

The conscious use of the guidelines for optimal conception is intended to guide the conception and the development of the embryo in the mother's womb in proper directions in order to give birth to the happiest and healthiest child possible. With the help of these guidelines from an ancient tradition of wisdom, we can take responsibility for it ourselves. Excessive sexual intercourse leads to damage to the dhatus (body tissues such as bone marrow, bone and blood), which weakens the body and makes it susceptible to disease.

XIX.6 PREGNANCY

It is recommended that during the first three months of pregnancy, the expectant mother maintains good health, proper nutrition and plenty of rest. Because our world is often characterized by haste and superficiality, we often fall short of these guidelines. It is well known that in the fourth month the expectant mother may have a need for food with a sour or pungent taste, but these flavours are not very beneficial because they stir up the fire element (pitta) too much. Soft foods with a sweet taste are best, such as fresh milk, ghi, ripe fruits, paneer, green leafy vegetables, carrot juice, rice, and grains. A few glasses of fresh, warm milk a day - in addition to bananas - is great for maintaining calcium levels, but this is not the case with the unsustainable factory milk which has all kinds of adverse side effects and should therefore be avoided. Sufficient natural calcium in the expectant mother's body ensures that the child will have healthy teeth and good bone development. The absorption of calcium is regulated by the thyroid and parathyroid glands and therefore the proper functioning of these glands during pregnancy is of great importance. Only natural salts, such as unrefined sea salt, are highly recommended and a tablespoon of *chyawanaprash*, a special ayurvedic *rasayana*, every day is very beneficial for a good pregnancy. Another suggestion is to take from time to time a spinach and watercress soup with fresh coriander or parsley.

For a pregnant woman it is good to supplement her diet with vitamins B12 and D. She also has a greater need for vitamin A, not only for herself but also for the development of the foetus. Drinking certain fruit juices daily, such as freshly squeezed carrot juice or orange juice (vitamin C), can help in keeping the intestinal walls strong and flexible.

In response to a question from one of his students, Sri Bhagawan, the Indian saint, emphasized the importance of the expectant father's attitude during pregnancy. His main job is to make sure his wife feels happy. An optimal loving relationship between husband and wife during pregnancy is highly desirable. The father must take the time every day to sit with his wife to communicate (together) with the unborn child. He should do everything to make the child feel very welcome. All these things have a major influence on how the child feels and behaves in his later life.

The foetus is a small but living creature that is very susceptible to external impressions during pregnancy. Shouting, arguing, all kinds of electronics and other negative impulses from the environment have a huge impact on the unborn child. Remember that the love for a child can never be more than the love for yourself.

A very interesting question is whether it is possible to impart knowledge to an unborn child. The Vedic scriptures confirm it and report several examples on this. Modern science is now also examining this phenomenon and a number of studies have already been published about it. As mentioned before, modern science is making "discoveries", step by step, that were known and applied thousands of years ago. For example, in the epic Mahabharata, the famous archer Arjuna informed his pregnant wife about this possible transmission of knowledge to the foetus. And he taught the later child, *Abhimanyu*, the secret art of managing army formations. Unfortunately, the expectant mother fell asleep during this teaching, so Abhimanyu's knowledge of this was not complete. Later, during the great war fought on the battlefield of Kurukshetra, Arjuna's son proved to be a great hero and used the knowledge of army formations, which he acquired in the mother's womb, with great success. But because it was incomplete, at one point he was trapped by the enemy and since he was unable to escape the enemy formation, he was finally killed in a valiant fight.

The process of new life starts with the use of food, which we extract from nature. Our food is eventually converted into sperm (in men) and ovum (in women) via the so-called body tissues (dhatus). *The quality of this, therefore, depends mainly on the food consumption and lifestyle of the parents.* In general, from conception, the development of the foetus takes place as follows: already in the third month, the foetus begins to manifest some human form, and from the fourth month onwards, the nerves and blood vessels develop. This is the period in which the mouth, tongue and nose start to develop and soon afterwards the eyes and ears as well. In the fifth month the motor and sensory organs begin to develop and from the sixth month the fingers, toes and nails on the arms and legs can be more clearly discerned. From the seventh month, the foetus starts to move more and in the eighth month it becomes increasingly viable. In the ninth month, hair growth takes place and the foetus prepares (changes position) to be able to leave the mother's womb at the end of this month. The cerebellum of the unborn child is active up to birth and after birth all processes and tasks are taken over by the cerebrum.

During pregnancy, the foetus develops through the nutrition of the mother and after the birth breastfeeding takes place, which should contain all the ingredients for the further development of the newborn child. How wonderful is the life cycle of man, which is based entirely on the perfect intelligence of nature but whose quality depends on how consciously we, as parents, deal with it!

A proper, healthy and preferably vegetarian diet during pregnancy is therefore of crucial importance. With regard to stimulants, like the use of caffeinated coffee, smoking, alcoholic drinks, cola and the use of (heavy) medicines should be strongly discouraged. The foregoing shows that all substances that the mother takes in, end up with the unborn child also, and these substances have a major influence on the quality of breastfeeding after delivery. The same applies to hormone-disrupting products, and for both foods with chemicals (parabens) and the use of many household products such as shampoos, cleaning products, et cetera. In Denmark, products containing such substances are not allowed for pregnant women because there is a serious suspicion that they may affect the health of the mother and foetus. Because the modern food industry itself has no self-regulating capacity to make healthy products, legislation has been passed in Denmark on this point, regarding also up to three-year-old children. Unfortunately, many governments and legislation are far behind in this respect. Why? The economic interests of the industrial producers prevail over the health and well-being of a pregnant woman and her (unborn) child.

Scheme 19.2

Vedic guidelines for an optimal pregnancy

* Do not argue or shout (disrupts fire and air element)
* Do not just walk outside alone at night to avoid negative influences
* Avoid strong emotions such as fear, worry or anger
* Refrain from sexual activity
* Don't sleep during the day or as little as possible
* Avoid allopathic medicines as much as possible
* Take plenty of rest, little or no climbing stairs after the sixth month
* Do not sit in a chair (behind the computer) all day long
* Pray or meditate for the smooth running of the pregnancy
* Being at home as much as possible with your loved ones
* Have positive thoughts and hold great ideals

With regard to food and nutrition, the following should be observed:

* Preferably take fresh food every day
* Refrain from narcotics and stimulants
* Refrain from foods that contain chemicals (parabens!).

The influence of the planets also asserts itself in the reproduction of humans. Mars exerts a great influence on the quality of our blood and the quality of Venus contributes greatly to reproduction. Venus in turn affects the quality of Mars. Without these planetary influences, the natural reproduction of humans and animals would be lost. Venus, the planet of love, is also responsible for an optimal relationship between a man and a woman. Their mutual love is the binding factor in the universal process of procreation and maintenance of the human race.

XIX.7 BIRTH

According to the Vedas, from a cosmic point of view, the birth of a human being on our planet is a completely unique event. A greater transformation - the incarnating of a spiritual soul into a physical body - is hardly conceivable. Very understandably, though, the actual birth is often experienced as dramatic, or even traumatic. The embryo, which until then has developed relatively safely in the amniotic fluid, goes with great force through a narrow and dark channel and suddenly ends up in a world to which it cannot immediately relate. This goes often hand in hand with a tremendous emotional shock and an urge to return to the safe harbour as soon as possible. Just the actual, often painful birth can give a traumatic effect and can haunt the child for the rest of its life. We all know people in our environment who still not have accepted to live in the physical world and feel very unhappy here. And we can imagine that a complicated delivery, for example with the help of a Caesarean section, or in the hospital, will be experienced as even more painful.

Research has found that children, who were mainly breastfed, were generally healthier and developed better. The use of antibiotics by mother or child appears to have an unfavourable influence on the intestinal flora. Differences have been noted in the health and growth of children born in hospital or at home. Children, who receive predominantly organic food and have more physical activity from birth, have less obesity between the ages of five and eight. In general, research indicates the direction which can be taken for the parents to live a healthy lifestyle, by which obesity and other problems in young children can be prevented.

The intestines of an unborn baby are sterile. But from birth, a baby receives the first bacteria from the mother and the intestinal flora grows into a complete household of micro-organisms that can normally keep themselves in balance. From birth, the immune system also forms and continues to communicate with the intestinal flora for the rest of life. But during and shortly after birth, all kinds of things can happen that affect the composition of the intestinal flora. Other important factors include the method of delivery and whether or not to breastfeed. In case of complications both the growth of the bacteria and the quality of the immune system can lag behind. Treatment with antibiotics, if used, hampers development even more, because it eliminates many beneficial intestinal bacteria. All of this weakens the healthy, balanced system of the intestinal flora with a greater risk of serious disease in later life. The conclusion is, that children born in a normal, natural way and breastfed for a longer period of time, develop the most favourable intestinal flora.

XIX.8 THE PERIOD AFTER BIRTH

Immediately removing the newborn from the mother can cause life trauma such as separation anxiety. The only place where the baby can feel safe at that time is with the mother, by feeling, smelling and hearing her voice. Only the father is allowed to take the baby tenderly in his arms at a quiet moment after birth and to whisper sweet words in its ear. Traditionally, in the Vedic tradition, he then gently touches the senses (nose, mouth, eyes, ears) of the child with his fingers and wishes him a healthy and long life, intelligence and comfort. He can do this silently or with the help of a mantra.

Breastfeeding

The mother can give the child a taste of some honey with a tip of her finger to prepare it for suckling at the breast. Only after the baby has produced its first dark faeces, can she start breastfeeding. In the first days, the mother's milk is a fairly thick substance with a high protein content. This milk is essential for the baby as it activates its body to develop its own body tissues (dhatus). The breast milk promotes the growth of the baby every way. But it is true that the quality of the breastmilk depends on the diet and the health or strength of the mother. By means of a simple test, the quality of the breast milk can be measured and it can be determined whether the milk is suitable for use. If possible, the baby should be breastfed for 12-18 months. However, much longer than 18 months is not recommended. Breastmilk should only be given during the day and no more than four times a day. While feeding, the mother should be in a good mood and not angry, excited, overtired, or nervous. According to Ayurveda, feeding should always start with the right breast.

The food industry suggests that bottled milk is an excellent substitute for breastfeeding. But don't be fooled by commercial institutes. Withholding breastmilk is one of the reasons why children are emotionally unbalanced or have more illnesses at a young age or later in life. The ingredients contained in breastmilk cannot be replaced in any other way and the way of giving breastmilk also plays an important role. The air element (vata) in a baby can easily be disrupted, which can cause fear or pain. Sucking on the mother's breast and swallowing the milk prevents that fear and gives the baby a feeling of comfort and security.

But what to do if breastmilk is not available? There are a number of possibilities: the best solution is to find a nurse, a woman who can take over the mother's job. If no nurse is available, goat's milk is best if cooked properly. Milk from a cow is too heavy and too fat and factory milk is certainly not recommended; most children and babies are allergic to this. If only (fresh, organic) cow's milk is available, it is recommended, but always only diluted and boiled in water; this makes the milk easier to digest.

Period up to six months after birth
Soon after birth, the baby can be given a daily healing massage with warm oil.

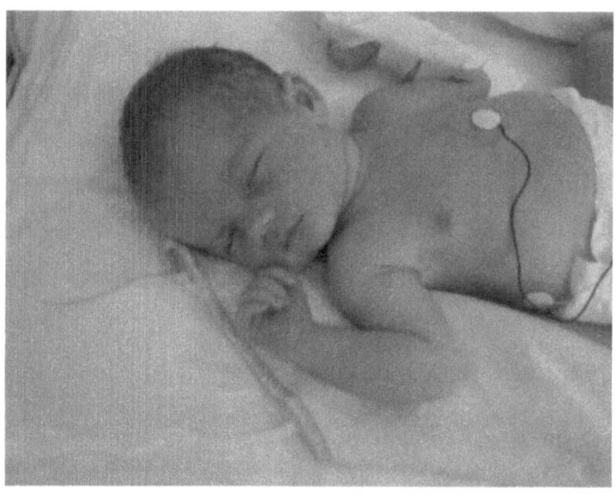

An Ayurvedic massage with warm oil promotes the health,
well-being and growth of the child to a great extent.

As far as food is concerned, the mother's milk can be supplemented after a few months with fruit juice, juice of light vegetables and honey water. Water should always be boiled in advance and then cooled; this makes the water "lighter". Liquid drinks are given in a gold or silver cup according to ancient Vedic tradition. The mixing of the drink with the metal is very useful for the development of the child. When the first tooth comes, one can start giving solid food, this will usually be between the sixth and ninth month after birth. A mash of mungdahl or rice, with a little honey or ghi and a little bit of sea salt, is the first solid food given to the baby according to Vedic tradition. The amount of food is then increased step by step. Unnatural, unfresh or manipulated foods should be strictly avoided.

Scheme 19.3

Some general guidelines for the wellbeing of the child

* Handle the body with the utmost care
* Do not wake up the child too suddenly
* Always speak softly and lovingly
* Never leave it alone
* Protect it from too bright sunlight, cold, wind etc.
* Only use silk or cotton sheets (not synthetic)
* Keep the newborn baby at home for at least four weeks
* Never try to tempt a crying child with sweets (it will only cry louder)

Scheme 19.3 The above guidelines almost speak for themselves, but by applying them consciously we can manage the well-being of the newborn child even better.

XIX.9 FIVE DAILY ACTIVITIS

In all phases of the marriage, the head of the family should take full responsibility for his wife and children. In Vedic times he was expected to observe five daily actions, the pancha mahayajnas, which are dedicated to all who support or assist him in this universe. They are mentioned in diagram 19.4.

Scheme 19.4
Five Daily Actions

DAILY ACTIONS	DEDICATED TO
Veda yajna	Vedas and the holy saints
Deva yajna	The heavenly Beings
Pitri yajna	The Ancestors
Bhuta yajna	All Creatures
Manushya yajna	All human Beings

Scheme 19.4 The daily performance of these rituals makes the family head realize that he is part of a much larger whole with which he is closely associated.

Why this fivefold obligation to nature? First, the head of the family has gained knowledge by studying the holy scriptures. Furthermore, he received a body from his parents and he has been supported by his friends and relatives. His body is nourished by the milk of cows, cereals, vegetables and fruits; the five elements support him and he cannot live without oxygen and water. The Devas and Pitris (ancestors) are blessing him.

* * *

"Let a person always engage in the study of the Vedas and in performing the rituals for the Devas; by engaging in this he supports the movable and the immovable worlds. "
- Manu Smritis

* * *

To give some examples, studying or teaching the sacred scriptures is a Veda yajna. The offering of water (tarpana) to the ancestors is a pitri yajna. Offering fire (homa) is a Deva yajna. Offering food to all kinds of beings is a Bhuta yajna, and hospitality to guests is a Manushya yajna. The latter also includes providing food, clothing or alms and sheltering the poor.

Any form of service to humanity is a Manushya yajna. By performing these acts of kindness and compassion daily, man receives divine Grace. Hatred disappears, the heart is expanded and softened, and universal love grows. The man who lives this way learns that he can only become happy by making others happy, by helping others, relieving their pain, and sharing what he has with them.

CHAPTER XX

HEALTH, PURIFICATION AND FOOD

'With the help of a balanced diet, a disease can be cured, even without the use of medicines. On the other hand, even the most effective medicines will not cure a disease without a balanced diet.'

- Vaidya Jivanam

We live in a modern society in which healthy living is an emerging trend. The cause of our search for more well-being lies probably in the fact, that we have not been feeling so good about ourselves for a long time. On a relational level, things often go wrong - the children go their own way at an increasingly younger age, the economic situation is completely unpredictable and viruses are lurking everywhere. Moreover, we have more free time and holidays, and we want something different than the hustle and bustle at home, on the road or at work. And what about the electronic age that we are in the midst of, and which is still expanding rapidly? Day in, day out, we sit at the computer, in front of the TV, talk for hours on a mobile phone and use the microwave increasingly. Nobody knows how harmful all this is for our health. No wonder we want to run away from time to time and lock ourselves up in a spa or sauna.

Ayurveda is the oldest approach to healthcare known to us. The difference between Ayurveda and modern trends of searching for more wellbeing is that it considers our health and the way we live as a natural and logical consequence of a spiritual view of life. The physical body is the shell of the soul and therefore requires our special attention and care. Sweat baths, massage with warm oil and other ways of purification are common in Ayurveda, but they serve a higher purpose. That goal is to bring balance to life by ensuring optimal functioning of body, mind and environment. Ayurveda considers man to be a spiritual being and from that point of view she wants to re-establish harmony between all parts. Its array of means to pursue this goal and prevent or control diseases is completely natural and almost inexhaustible.

XX.1 HOLISTIC APPROACH TO HEALTH

From a Vedic point of view, the holistic approach of Ayurveda is very important because it originates in Rigveda. According to the ancient ayurvedic teachings, health is not only the absence of disease, but is a state of optimal mental, physical and emotional functioning. Ayurveda is not only concerned with the curing of diseases, but above all with how to prevent diseases and how to maintain good health well into old age. Ayurveda may not lead to physical immortality, but in a spiritual sense it makes a fundamental contribution to the growth towards higher states of consciousness.

* * *

"Ayurveda Amritanam" - Ayurveda leads to Immortality
- Charaka Samhita 25:40

* * *

The famous ayurvedic physician Charaka (ca. 800 BC) pays a lot of attention to the spiritual aspect of man in his classical works. He describes man as a part of the universe. While Rigveda describes the state of full consciousness, Ayurveda aims to balance or bring the physiological state of man into balance. Its purpose is for the body to be refined and healthy enough to acquire and maintain the experience of pure consciousness.

Ayurveda mentions four causes for mental and physical illness:

1. The effect of wrong thoughts, feelings and activities in this life and in past lives (karma). This also includes breaking a leg and causing or having an accident.

2. The influence of the three gunas. In the material world we are under the constant influence of the three gunas (sattva, rajas and tamas), qualities that also express themselves in our mind. In order to maintain good health, the sattva quality (goodness, purity, wisdom) should predominate in life, work, and thought. We can strengthen this quality through meditation, appropriate dietary habits and a healthy lifestyle.

3. Imbalance in the three doshas, vata, pitta and kapha, which manifests itself at the biological level. Every person has his own prakriti or natural proportion of vata-pitta-kapha. When using food products and herbs, this can be taken into account and the natural proportion can be balanced.

4. Accumulation of toxins (ama) in the stomach and digestive tracts. *Ama* blocks the assimilation of absorption of necessary substances into the blood. Chemical medicines are causative agents of ama and therefore pathogens. Periodically, an external and/or internal cleansing regimen is required to remove the ama from the stomach and intestines. Fasting one day a week or twice a month is also very helpful.

According to Charaka, man's pursuit of a higher level of life takes place embedded in constant interaction with other systems including family, environment, society, planet and the universe. So, we humans are not only victims of accidental factors, such as germs, but depend on a complexity of fundamental elements that can become unbalanced. The doctor's task is then to prescribe appropriate treatments that not only relieve the patient of his complaints, but that at the same time have a supportive effect on a lasting state of balance in mind, body, behaviour and environment. Bacteria and viruses, to which allopathy attributes most of the diseases, then automatically keep their distance. These germs are mainly a signal that the damage has already been done. Good and natural medicine takes into account the above-mentioned causes, provides preventive guidelines and, if necessary, comes up with a solution for recovery. Moreover, this holistic approach can contribute to a new inspiration for people and society in their relationship to nature, Mother Earth and ultimately the entire universe.

In Vedic times Ayurveda was an important part of the education that the students received. In the epic Ramayana, Prince Rama and his brothers were initiated into all its parts by their teacher Vasistha. Like all students at the time, they learned how to maintain their health, including how to take care of good eating and living habits, proper behaviour, working in the fields and developing a good character. They were also initiated into the workings of the subtle bodies and the development of the chakras. Ayurveda sets rules for daily life, the different constitution types of people and the seasons in detail. It contains comprehensive dietary guidelines, regulating the balance of rest and activity, and everything that has to do with our daily routine. These rules are to be applied in accordance with the individual characteristics and the specific constitution, which is different for each person.

XX.2 DOSHAS AND DHATUS

Ayurveda assumes that the physical universe, including the human body, consists of five basic elements. In Sanskrit these elements are called the *mahabhutas.* These elements are: space, air, fire, water and earth. The fact that man and universe consist and are made up of exactly the same components, implies that all laws of growth, maintenance, and dissolution apply to both. Ayurveda makes optimal use of the close relationship between man and the construction, composition and development of the universe. The wise Ayurvedic scholar Charaka described this relationship at the time as follows:

* * *

"Man is a faithful copy of the universe. The universe is made up of what man consists of in all its parts. Man, in turn, consists of that from which the universe has developed. "

* * *

The five basic elements are only recognizable by their specific qualities. They can never be found in their pure state in nature. What we can perceive are always only certain compositions of the elements containing them in different proportions. Generally speaking, we can say that the ether or space element goes together with the property of the lack of resistance, fire with heat and energy, air with expansion or movement, water with fluidity and cohesion and earth with solidity.

Subjectively, the five elements correspond to our five sensory organs of hearing, touch, sight, taste and smell. The ayurvedic tradition has simplified the existence of the five elements by applying as its starting point the three doshas, which explains the (non-) functioning of all organisms (see diagram 20.1). Its central premise is based on the doctrine of the three doshas, three basic principles in the nervous system (and in the cosmic systems), which mutually control each other and balance the forces in the human body and in nature.

Scheme 20.1
Basic elements and Doshas

ELEMENTS	SENSE ORGANS	MANIFESTATION	DOSHAS
Space	Ears	Sound	VATA
Air	Skin	Touch	
Fire	Eyes	Light	PITTA
Water	Tongue	Taste	KAPHA
Earth	Nose	Smell	

Scheme. 20.1 We can find the five basic elements or mahabhutas in every atom of the universe. They are also the building blocks of our body, i.e. of the body cells, tissues and organs. The three doshas arise from the five elements: vata (movement) is created from space and air, pitta (transformation) arises from fire and kapha (structure) arises from water and earth.

The doshas can also be classified on the basis of another property. This classification is based on movement:

Vata stands for movement, the movement of something in space, such as the flow of blood or our breathing.

Pitta represents transforming or changing movements, such as the transformation of the food in the process of digestion.

Kapha stands for standing still or not moving, like a rock.

In Ayurveda, the teaching of the three doshas is an important tool in diagnosing and preventing or treating diseases. We can only speak of good health when the three doshas - vata, pitta and kapha - are present in the right proportion (this is different for every person) and work in harmony with each other in our body. Our health suffers when improper eating and living habits or other causes disturb and change the balance of the three doshas. In that case, illness, physical or mental, is inevitable. Ayurveda has several methods to determine which doshas are out of balance in someone. The best known of these is the pulse diagnosis (nadi vijnana), which can be extremely precise and detailed. This pulse reading technique has been around for thousands of years and, in case it is performed by an experienced Ayurvedic physician, it provides a great deal of information about the state of both mind and body, including the subtler bodies of the patient, in the split of a second.

The common view in modern medical science is, that many illnesses are caused by contamination from external bacteria or viruses that attack the body and thereby induce illness. Ayurveda does not deny that this happens, but teaches that it only happens when one or more doshas are out of balance. In that case, the immune system and other body systems no longer function optimally. Broadly speaking, we can say that the three doshas work together in all parts of the body and are present in every body cell. The word dosha means impurity. If one or two doshas are out of balance, we are ill and if all three doshas are out of balance, we are seriously ill.

The doshas are immaterial and therefore invisible, but they are visible through the effects they produce in the body. In sickness the doshas are disturbed and this disturbance manifests itself through (one of) the seven dhatus, the physiological core tissues of which the body is built. It is the dhatus or body tissues that evolve from the material aspect of the five elements (see Scheme 20.2).

Ayurveda considers the quality of the seven dhatus to be fundamental for our health. The second dhatu arises from the first, the third from the first and second, and so on. This implies that when, for example the lymph tissue is affected, all other tissues will also be affected. The last dhatu, shukra, therefore, first passes through all the other dhatus before it can arise. It is a very refined substance that the body produces from food.

Scheme 20.2
The seven dhatus and their predominating basic elements

DHATUS	BODY TISSUES	DOMINATING ELEMENT
RASA	Lymph, plasma	Water
RAKTA	Blood	Fire
MAMSA	Muscle tissue	Earth
MEDHA	Fat tissue	Earth
ASTHI	Bone tissue	Air
MADHYA	Bone marrow	Air
SHUKRA ARTAV	Semen Ovum	Water (man) Fire (woman)

Scheme 20.2 Shukra, the vital essence, is not only located in the reproductive organs, but is present throughout the body, creating a light that spreads a certain radiance even around the body: our aura.

XX.3 REGENERATIVE ABILITY

In addition to our mental well-being and lifestyle, the body plays an essential role in maintaining optimal health. In spiritual sense, our body is compared to a boat that takes us across the ocean of life. Birth and death are then presented as the two shores; life is the span of the sea or ocean covered in between. The body is like a boat that takes us from one coast to another. Without this important vehicle it is impossible to complete our spiritual journey. If we have a seaworthy boat with a powerful engine that can take us anywhere, then we can really enjoy the journey. In order to keep the body seaworthy, we must be aware that it possesses a great natural ability to keep itself healthy and recover if necessary. When we are aware of the intelligence inherent in the human body, we can make the most of its remarkable abilities.

Meditation can take us inward and help us appreciate the wonder and magnificence of our bodily functioning - the vital organs within us and their functions. The body experiences a lot of stress during the day due to the fluctuations of our moods and stressful thoughts, which is harmful to health. Moreover, in our modern society much more attention is given to activity than to necessary rest. The hectic life we live wears us down. If we want to keep our body in good shape throughout the journey, we must be astutely attuned to its well-being. Rest is the basis of our activity. Our feelings and the loving attention we give our body during meditation have a healing influence on it.

We can develop the awareness of when our body is overcome by stress and start immediately doing things that restore its balance. All the efforts we take to keep the body healthy are investments into our own future. During the day we can pay attention to how much we eat, how much we exercise, how much rest we take and how grateful we are for everything that comes to us. When the body is sick, it is a signal that we have taken a wrong turn. A clear understanding of how the three doshas - vata, pitta and kapha - work is a prerequisite of self-care, for example of adjusting our diet or lifestyle. A skilled Ayurvedic doctor (*vaidya*) can use the pulse diagnosis to easily determine which doshas have fallen out of balance and how the balance can be restored.

XX.4 PANCHAKARMA

One of the most effective means that Ayurveda offers is a complete cleansing of the body, which traditionally consists of five parts. Besides many other ayurvedic approaches such as herbal and aromatherapy, yoga and pranayama, the *panchakarma treatment* (literally: five actions) occupies a central place. The pressures and tensions of our modern, hectic way of life do much damage to our physiology. The natural repair and renewal cycles are disrupted and all kinds of impurities and blockages enter the body. Due to bad food habits, the skin, lungs, stomach and especially the intestines have a hard time. With the help of the panchakarma treatment, disturbances of the physiological balance are cancelled out and cellular impurities are removed. Every person has a body system which ensures that food calories are burned and converted into energy. But as the body ages, the whole system becomes more and more polluted. By systematically removing the waste products, which have often accumulated in the body over the course of years, the purification treatment of panchakarma restores the balance of the doshas effectively. Thus, the self-healing capacity of the body is restored and it can maintain its inner balance on its own. We can only speak of good health when the three doshas operate in our body in their natural proportion (prakriti) and in harmony with each other.

Panchakarma treatments take place in ayurvedic health centers that can be found almost everywhere today. Some treatments last for several days and can be repeated regularly, for example twice a year. First of all, there is an extensive consultation with the Ayurvedic doctor in which the constitution type (the natural proportion between the three doshas pertaining to the individual) and the possible disturbances in the balance of the doshas are determined. Furthermore, the predisposition to certain diseases can also be determined and a suitable treatment for the individual can be devised. Panchakarma itself consists traditionally of a pre-, a main- and a post treatment. The three parts of the main treatment are the oil massage (abhyanga), the steam bath (swedana) and the internal cleansing (basti).

Abhyanga

Abhyanga is an oil massage that is preferably performed by two technicians, using warm, spiced oil. This oil massage is one of the oldest forms of therapy in Ayurveda. It is a refined technique that was already used on the ancient battlefields. By applying this massage, the ayurvedic doctors got the fighting warriors swiftly back on their feet. Depending on the individual constitution type and particular complaints, different types of herbal oils and massages can be applied. Abhyanga has the ability to release the impurities even from the cell structure. The various body tissues (dhatus) making up the body (see scheme 20.2) are nourished and the massage has a rejuvenating effect on the whole organism. The oil acts in a special way on the skin so that it becomes more resistant, supple and clean. Even for only a few-week-old babies, this massage is ideal and has been used in India since time immemorial.

With a little practice we can apply abhyanga also on ourselves. When we practice this for example once a week, the quality of sleep will certainly improve. This is because using warm oil reduces vata and softens kapha. In general, the effect of an oil massage is very beneficial and revitalizing for both body and mind. Afterwards we feel relaxed, internally fresh and clean and this feeling can last for several days.

Swedana
Swedana is a steam bath with spiced steam to open all body channels - the *srotas* – loosening the waste and allowing it to be discharged through these channels. It stimulates the entire body in its metabolic functions in various ways and is a perfect preparation for the internal cleansing that follows. Besides, it also proves to be a good support for the body through its vitalizing effect, especially regarding vata disturbances. The best season for swedana therapy is early spring, but autumn and early winter are also suitable. Most effective is to combine swedana with a special, easily digestible diet, oil massage and internal cleansing. Ayurveda advises explicitly not to expose the head to the heat during the sweat cure. When we use a sauna, it is therefore recommended to wrap a towel around the head or to keep refreshing the head with a cool cloth.

Basti

Basti, an enema therapy, is the crowning glory of this special treatment, and has a strong vata-balancing effect. The waste products are removed from the body by means of an effective intestinal cleansing. This treatment cleans the colon up to the cecum and prevents chronic obstruction. Due to "plaque formation" (snails), the colon becomes contaminated over the years, so that the optimal function of the intestinal walls gradually declines. Basti removes stagnant intestinal content, bacteria and their toxins, as well as gases, mucus, fungi and other waste products from the cells. It thus enables the colon to fulfil its natural tasks of absorbing water, salt and vitamins and its assimilation function optimally. The basti treatment not only cleanses, but also nourishes the intestinal mucous membranes. According to ayurvedic teaching, colon cleansing is responsible for 50% of the cure of many complaints. A healthy gut is essential for a healthy body.

These three methods together form the core of a panchakarma treatment aimed for prevention and optimalization of the body functions. Nonetheless, there are a few more treatments worth mentioning here:

Vamana

Vamana is a vomiting therapy in which the waste products leave the body through the mouth. It is an effective method of releasing of excess kapha from the body. In this therapy the patient is asked to take a certain amount of plant extracts, after which the patient is helped to vomit several times. This method is mainly used for kapha disorders, such as asthma, chronic cold, forehead inflammation, bronchitis and diabetes.

Virechana

Virechana is a laxative therapy that is mainly used for pitta dosha imbalances. Laxation is induced by giving the patient a decoction of carefully selected herbs. This therapy removes pitta and kapha disturbances, such as fever, cough, skin diseases, headaches, epilepsy, digestive problems and worms in the intestines very effectively through the anus.

Shirodhara

This treatment, in which a trickle of warm oil is poured onto the forehead for about twenty minutes, has a harmonizing and soothing effect. It is used as a therapy to combat insomnia or nervousness.

Shirodhara

Netra Tarpana

Netra tarpana, a soothing eye treatment, is often given in between the main treatments to cleanse and heal tired, dry or irritated eyes.

Waste products that remain in the digestive system for too long cause fermentation and putrefaction and subsequently build up an excess of gases and bacteria. When the toxins pass through the intestinal wall, they enter the blood and this can cause all kinds of complaints, such as bad breath, headaches, liver stress and fungal diseases. In that case we poison our blood with the food we eat.

Both before and after the panchakarma treatment it is usually advised to take certain herbs and *ghee* (clarified butter). These promote the build-up of the intestinal mucosa and flora, and also improve digestion.

A good question is whether preventive action can be taken at an earlier stage. This is indeed the case. First of all, by improving our food and living habits, we can prevent our internal system from being constantly polluted. It is not even so much the food itself, as the result or end product of the it - ojas - that sustains our lives. *Ojas* is a very refined material, at the interface of body and mind. It supports and promotes health in every way, and counteracts the aging process. The amount of ojas that we "create" is visible on the outside through a radiance of youth, glowing skin and vitality. It is mainly produced by shukra, the last dhatu, but each dhatu by itself is capable of producing ojas. The quality and quantity of ojas is essentially determined by the quality and effectiveness of digestion, indicating its crucial role in the whole. The Sanskrit word for the digestive fire is *agni*, the first word of Rigveda! As above, so below, or: what applies for consciousness, evidently also applies for the body. Due to wrong food, overeating or other reasons, digestion might not work properly and so the food is not converted properly either. In this case, undigested residues remain in the body, which accumulate in the stomach and the intestines. The constant accumulation of these in the *srotas* causes chronic diseases, which sometimes come to light only ten or twenty years later. By undergoing a panchakarma treatment and following the guidelines on our eating habits, we can defeat our arch enemies - all the impurities in the body – even before they appear on the horizon. The effect is that we stay young and have no need to resort to other rejuvenation products so often, or maybe not at all.

XX.5 OUR HOLY FOOD

The sages call food holy, and the consumption of food is a sacred act of gratitude for what we have received from nature. Before the food is on our plate, it has already done a long journey. For instance, the grain is sown, grows up, and harvested, it is made into bread, and reaches finally into the shop where we buy it. Often without thinking about it, we rush to finish our sandwich. The Bhagavad Gita says that without control over the tongue - the organ of action with which we eat - it is impossible to follow the spiritual path and enter the house of yoga that leads to God. The basis of all forms of yoga is the eating of sattvic (pure, natural) food. A major cause of today's world disorder and various diseases is the eating of foods of mainly rajas (sharp, pungent) and tamas (spoiled, unnatural) qualities. Eating unhealthy food and chemical seasonings unbalance not only our body but also our mind, which can thus become captivated by cruelty, lust, depression and restlessness. The physical condition often declines already at a young age. ADHD and other illnesses are the result. Ayurvedic food and dietetics is very extensive, but among the many, we would like to mention a few themes here in particular.

Animal proteins

According to Ayurveda, animal proteins are toxic to humans. These proteins must first be turned harmless, which requires a lot of energy from the body. Animal proteins, especially also those from fish, reduce the functioning of the digestive juices. This results in an accumulation of *ama*. The more animal protein we eat, the more the intestinal content stagnates and the more toxins are absorbed into the bloodstream. The relationship between the consumption of animal proteins and fats and the development of colon cancer has already scientifically proven a long time ago.

Chewing well

The digestion of food already starts in the mouth, where the salivary enzymes fulfil an important and powerful function. How many mothers teach their children to chew properly? Due to our hectic and impatient way of life, we see that bad chewing habits form in many children at a very young age. This often leads to processing insufficient saliva being into the mash, hence the food is difficult to process during the actual digestion in the stomach and the intestines. Our liver is our largest detoxification organ, whose job is to separate all useful nutrients from the waste. The blood that enters the liver via the portal vein leaves the liver in a purified form, taking with it and delivering them to the body cells. Normally, the liver can easily cope with the detoxification process, but in today's society it is being put to the test. This manifests itself in hasty people who are under stress and quickly get tired, but often not even really notice it. In addition to guidelines for handling food in a healthy way (see schedule 20.3), Ayurveda also uses herbal preparations to help the optimal functioning of the liver and the intestines.

Scheme 20.3
Ten golden rules for proper food habits

1)	Eat in a relaxed and calm environment; working, reading or watching TV while eating should be avoided.
2)	Always eat seated and at about the same times of the day.
3)	Don't eat too slowly or too quickly; the stomach should be filled to three quarters.
4)	Avoid eating before a previous meal has been digested; snacks impede optimal digestion.
5)	Avoid animal proteins and fats.
6)	Avoid yogurt, quark and cheese in the evening; these nutrients are difficult to digest and hinder the digestive process.
7)	Preferably use herbs such as cumin, ginger, turmeric, cardamom, cloves, mustard seeds, asafoetida and black pepper.
8)	Avoid ice-cold drinks or foods as these interfere with digestion badly.
9)	Rest for ten minutes after lunch and take a walk after dinner.

> 10) Drink about two liter of water/fluid per day, but not immediately before or after a meal.

Scheme 20.3 Food arises from intelligence and is transformed back into intelligence by digestion (agni). When we become aware of this unique transformation process, we come to understand why the quality of food and the function of digestion is so important to us. All the golden rules mentioned here are directly related to optimal functioning of the digestive system.

XX.6 SATTVIC FOOD

Western physicians and specialists often have little or no knowledge at all of the influence of sattvic, rajasic or tamasic food on our mind, body and behaviour (see Diagram 20.4). This means that the medical world in the West can hardly contribute to better health by means of regulations on the quality and use of food.

Scheme 20.4
Overview of food with sattva-, rajas- and tamas qualities

SATTVA	RAJAS	TAMAS
Rice	Onions	Reheated food
Milk (fresh)	Peppers	Spoiled food
Mung beans	Garlic	Manipulated food
Honey, ghee	Leeks	Fungi
Sweet fruits	Sour fruits	Canned food
Pure water	Beets	Meat and eggs
Almonds	Strawberries	Microwave foods
Green vegetables	Radish, Tomato	Alcohol, drugs, cigarettes

Schedule 20.4 While sattvic nutrition is by far the best, we must use common sense when purchasing and preparing food. After all, many (supermarket) products of our time often no longer meet certain quality standards.

As for the quality and value of milk (which is often discussed), Ayurveda considers milk as a nectar, but then it means milk that comes straight from a cow and is less than twenty-four hours old. Many processed products can sometimes be completely unbalanced in terms of their original composition and quality.

The influence of food on our mind and senses should not be underestimated: food affects directly the quality of our mind. When we eat only with the intention of satisfying hunger, our minds will not benefit much from it. The quality of the food depends on many factors, such as what it is composed of, how and from whom it is received, as well as how it is prepared. In general, tamasic food is bad for the mind and ego while pungent rajasic food leads to strong physical desires. Sattvic food contributes to clear thinking, joy of living and optimal health. Sometimes, however, it can be helpful to use certain herbs or products with a rajasic quality, such as onions, garlic, peppers and red vegetables, but always in moderation and only for the cure of an ailment. An attitude of gratitude, not criticizing what is on our plate and regarding the food as a gift from nature is the best condition for proper digestion of the food.

Prasadam is food that is first offered to Lord Krishna before it is eaten.

As stated before, high quality food leads to refinement of the mind and control over the senses. Patanjali, the author of the Yoga-sutras, said that we can count ourselves lucky if we are able to control our tongue. Shri Sadguru Jaggi Vasudeva and many other saints have given many guidelines on the use of food and said that it is a great impediment to our spiritual discipline if our tongue is master over us. Respect for food is a great virtue; we don't waste it, we don't criticize it, we cook it with a positive feeling and we give it away to any creature who needs it. Anything we give to another living being with a sense of compassion and without asking for anything in return, will come back to us in the same quality, either in this life or the next.

XX.7 HEALTHY AGEING

From an Ayurvedic point of view, the best advice is keeping the doshas in balance, that's all we need to do. Once we have crossed our limits, it is advisable to rebalance it as soon as possible. When we consider that we have a body to express the soul's ability to evolve further, we will treat it with love. Most important in our human experience are the experiences that help the soul to express itself fully in everyday life.

When we surround our physical vehicle with love and the moment has come for it to go, our soul will depart from it with joy. If we are more spiritually awakened, this moment will no doubt be a joyous experience - one of peace, happiness and gratitude. We will be able to take a loving farewell to this life and our peaceful passage will be felt by all who are present at that event. Wherever we leave the body then, the place will be filled with great vibrations of peace and love. Can we view this wonderful gift God has given us as something very special? If we can internalize that vision, we will develop a lasting appreciation and awe for this wonderful gift of nature. Knowing that the body does not live forever, every day we spend on earth is a day that is memorable and one that we can cherish with all our heart and soul. And that is precisely the goal of Ayurveda, the full expression of the soul in the world of matter.

CHAPTER XXI

LIFESTYLE AND DAILY ROUTINE

'A simple lifestyle is the best medicine for good health'

- Shri Sathya Sai Baba

Itihasa (Ramayana and Mahabharata) expresses the timeless values of ideal behaviour and a righteous way of life with countless examples taken from everyday life. The Vedic stories and legends are events that inspire people of all times to become proficient in a refined perception and a broad vision of life. In the epics Ramayana and Mahabharata actions are highlighted from different points of view. We can consider the characters as the impulses and qualities of the Self. Prince Rama always does the right thing, even in the most extreme situations, and thus represents perfect behaviour. However, the Mahabharata describes the life of a blind king who, overshadowed by pride and attachment, keeps making wrong decisions. In both cases the plot turns into a war: a war between the good and evil forces of life. All of this takes place in the domain of human consciousness. It is our own choice, the free will of every human being, to develop inner wisdom and realize the highest ideal of happiness and wisdom. This highest ideal is to surrender to God and put us in His service. The Vedas and other sacred scriptures guide us to this ideal and to pursuing a way of life in accordance with Dharma, the law of evolution.

XXI.1 FUNDAMENTAL VALUES

Throughout the ages, spiritual masters have come to the world to guide people on their life journey. They all emphasize that they are very careful when it comes to action in life and that they try not to do anything that may possibly go wrong. Only do the right things and do the them well, is the advice. The Indian saint Shri Sathya Sai Baba recommended to behave according to the six basic human values (see Diagram 21.1). If we are able to make these values our own, we will undoubtedly be on the right track.

Scheme 21.1

Fundamental human values

SATYA	Truth
DHARMA	Justice, Correct behaviour
PREMA	Love
SHANTI	Equanimity, Peace
AHIMSA	Nonviolence
ANANDA	Bliss

Scheme 21.1 In the Vedic scriptures spirituality and principles of morals and ethics go hand in hand. This concerns norms and values that are universal and therefore apply to every person, regardless of religion or beliefs.

We find these values in the precepts of morality and proper behaviour as formulated by Patanjali in his Yoga-sutras. Remarkably, the teachings of Raja-yoga, the eightfold path, begin with guidelines about what we should or should not do in order to take control of our mind. There are things that lead to the confusion of the mind, such as speaking untruth, harming people, or wanting to take advantage of other living beings. In addition, there are certain things that actually purify and refine the mind and these include purity, contentment, spiritual discipline, and the study of and devotion to God. The purpose of living the yamas and niyamas, according to Patanjali, is to enable us to calm the whirls of the mind, allowing it to experience its own true essence. This is what is meant by controlling the mind. In that state, the mind remains untouched by everything we do while it stays immersed in experiencing the underlying unity. Then we will live fully in the present and will have realized the purpose of Raja-yoga - the royal path.

The Upanishads are by their nature reticent about giving rules of life, but they do imply that good behaviour is a prerequisite for spiritual life. In the Taittiriya Upanishad, the teacher gives his departing students a set of rules for life, which correspond in part to the values set by Shri Satya Sai Baba. The teacher of this Upanishad further emphasizes that we can continue to learn and study throughout our lives: knowledge gained today can be transformed into wisdom tomorrow. And we should treat our parents, our spiritual teacher, and guests who come to visit us as God. The application of *Atithi Devo Bhava* is deeply rooted in the Indian culture. When receiving guests, it is customary to offer food first to the guests, before taking for themselves. Finally, the teacher's students are advised to behave like the wise and the virtuous, not so much by imitating their behaviour, but by becoming like them and walking always on the path of Dharma.

The concept of Dharma, which we have discussed before, has many different meanings. Dharma comes from the root *dhri*, which means: to support or sustain. On a universal level, Dharma is the law of evolution; the entire universe is sustained by Dharma. On an individual level, Dharma means morality, ethics, proper conduct and destiny. Dharma is the expression of a person's, or of a group of persons' (society's, country's, world's) true, evolutionary nature. This can be different for each person or for each country, depending partly on their level of development. Properly walking the path of Dharma is one of the paths leading to *moksha*, spiritual liberation. Dharma expressly implies that we support our fellow human beings partly wherever is necessary. That is why it is repeated over and over in the Vedas:

* * *

'Paropakaro hi paramo dharmah'
Taking care of the welfare of others is the highest duty

* * *

Lord Krishna shows Arjuna His true cosmic form
(Source: Wikipedia)

This approach does not only benefits others but ourselves, too. Slowly but surely, (Western) man realizes that we are part of a larger whole on all fronts. It is striking to see, that when our consciousness first undergoes a change, then the environment adapts to it accordingly. Therefore, it is wise to start with the development of the *rishi* aspect of the Veda Samhita. Rishi is: the observer, the knower, which refers to ourselves. By transforming our inner experience of the world, that is, by enlivening the Self, the qualities of *devata* (process of knowing) and *chanddas* (the known) are spontaneously co-developed. This is what Lord Krishna means when he tells Arjuna on the battlefield of life: *Yogastah kuru karmani* - established in Being, perform your actions. By understanding this holistic process and its practical applications, we can experience and act from the fullness of life within ourselves.

XXI.2 THE NATURAL CYCLES

When we think of the development of our planet and its inhabitants, we cannot help but divide the millions of years since humanity has existed into smaller units. We ourselves are familiar with the natural cycles of days, weeks, months or a century, but the Veda sees creation as a recurring cyclic event, without a beginning or an end. In all phases of each cycle, both the knowledge of good and the knowledge of evil arise: the tree of the knowledge of good and evil. The good is everything that supports evolution and the bad is everything that is contrary to the path of evolution. The Vedas emphasize the mutual and ongoing influence between the cycles in the universe and the biological rhythms in man. We will feel rested and cheerful if we respect the inner rhythms of our biological system. The reverse is also true: we will discover that getting enough rest is the key to normalizing our inner rhythms.

Nature functions according to a fixed pattern, in which the cycle of rest and activity plays a prominent and recurring role: day and night, summer and winter, life and death.

As is the case with animals and plants, man is biologically programmed by his genes to partake in the natural rhythms of rest and activity. Dynamic activity is fine as long as we take enough time every day to relax. In our hectic society, more people are turning to practice yoga or meditation on a daily basis only to be more resistant to the daily pressures. But we can also bring more peace during the activity by living and working in a quiet environment, surrounded with pleasant people and by not taking our mobile phone everywhere. Ayurveda emphasizes not to eat in a hurry and to walk or rest after each meal:

* * *

After lunch rest a while,
After dinner walk a mile

* * *

Other good intentions may include not eating immediately before going to sleep and not turning on the radio or TV, or consulting the mobile phone immediately upon waking up. And let's enjoy all the elements in nature: the sun, the sea, the air and the scent of a real forest. There is so much beauty to see, smell and taste. Enjoy and achieve more!

XXI.3 NATURE AND HUMAN BEING

As indicated earlier, the biggest problem of our present time is that we try to master nature, while as humans we are an integral part of nature. The world-famous social anthropologist and film-maker David Attenborough, at the age of 93, after shooting many other documentaries on the topic, explained it all in detail in his recent documentary, *A Life on our Planet*, offered by Netflix. He tells about the evolutionary history of life on our earth and the dramatic loss of biodiversity in nature. All eco-systems are so interconnected that they sustain all life on Earth in a natural and intelligent way. But it is just humanity who disrupts biodiversity completely and pushes for the complete destruction of our planet. Life on Earth will be made impossible within a few decades due to ignorance, bad policies, wrong choices and human failure. Not only wildlife, but also the polar caps, our oceans with its coral reefs, the rainforests and the growing of sufficient food are seriously threatened. A clear signal is given by the unpredictability of the weather, which is becoming increasingly grim. Global warming by four degrees Celsius will make large parts of our planet uninhabitable, causing millions of people to lose their living environment. Within the span of a single human life, our Garden of Eden, our beautiful planet Earth, is in danger of being lost and we humans just let it happen. But the paradox is that no human with a common sense really wants this to happen. The question then is: how is man going to solve this global crisis that it has caused itself? Attenborough not only analyses the disastrous situation, but also offers an integrated vision of how we can still turn the tide. To give some examples of necessary changes:

* Let wildlife run their course

* Restoring Earth's biodiversity

* Restore healthy functioning oceans

* Restoring sufficient healthy forests (example: Costa Rica!)

* Stabilizing the world population

* Using of natural energy resources (sun, wind, water, etc.)

In the latter case, our big cities will become much cleaner and much more pleasant and natural to live in. David Attenborough says in his documentary:

* * *

"Nature is our greatest ally and our greatest inspiration. When we take care of nature, she will take care of us. "

* * *

XXI.4 INFLUENCE OF THE DOSHAS

In the context of the Vedas, it is the holistic approach to Ayurveda that shows in detail how we as human beings can create and enjoy a sustainable existence. Instead of disconnecting from nature, we need to become aware again that we ourselves are part of nature and that we move together with its natural rhythms. The alternation of day and night and of the seasons, for example, influence us to a great extent. The most important rhythms for our daily existence are: day and night (twenty-four-hour-cycle) and the cycles of the Moon and the Sun. Under the influence of this, the three doshas - vata, pitta and kapha - vary in our physiology. Sometimes we may need to take corrective action to maintain or restore the balance of the doshas. We can divide the day and night into a vata, pitta and kapha time. Waking up early promotes alertness, liveliness and lightness because vata dominates in the morning hours. If we lie down for too long, kapha is strengthened and that causes a feeling of dullness and heaviness. Pitta dosha is strongest around noon. Because pitta is connected with digestion, it is therefore preferable to take the main meal during lunchtime instead of the evening.

A similar division applies to the seasons. Ayurveda divides the year into three periods: spring, summer and winter. Generally, the kapha element predominates in the last part of the winter and spring, pitta in the summer and early fall, and vata in the late fall and first part of the winter. In the spring season it is advisable to exercise more, to eat lightly and not to sleep during the day. In the summer the sun is high in the sky; it is getting warmer and the body has to take measures to cool down. In severe heat it is better not to exercise too much and not to eat heavily. In wintertime we can take a bit heavier food again.

Also, Ayurveda works with the different stages of a person's life. In the first years kapha (growth, structure) is predominant. Babies sleep longer and are often a little chubby. In childhood, the mind and body are still developing and body weight increases. This is the build-up phase.

After puberty the pitta period begins in which responsibility is taken for establishing family and a role in society. We are normally entrepreneurial and dynamic during this period. This is the transformation phase.

The vata period begins in older age, in which our mental and physical functions slowly but surely decline in quality: the memory weakens, we are less flexible, the skin becomes drier and thinner. The weight decreases and the quality of sleep often deteriorates. This is the phase-out period.

Thus, we see that our course of life is influenced by the universal law of development, maintenance and reduction. If we really want to be or become healthy and happy, then a good understanding of the natural cycles of life is inevitable. The laws of physics in the universe are like a compass on which we can sail blindly. With this insight, which has always been known to all ancient traditions of wisdom, we can work in a natural way on optimal health and a youthful vitality.

XXI.5 IDEAL DAILY ROUTINE

Scheme 21.2 provides an overview of the ideal daily routine according to Ayurveda. We start by getting up early. The kapha period starts from six in the morning and for that reason the Indian yogis prefer to go to the river at four in the morning (or even before) to take a holy bath and then begin their sadhana. *Brahmamuhurta* is put between four and six in the morning, the time of Brahma and the moment when the creative principle (vata) is active in nature. The great benefits of getting up early should not be underestimated. It promotes alertness, liveliness and lightness. It is therefore wise to get up at 6:00 am at the latest. If we lie down too long, the qualities of kapha, such as slowness, lethargy and heaviness are enhanced and it takes more effort to get out of bed and the whole day will take a slow and heavy start.

Based on the science of Vastu (Vedic architecture), Indian people were used to build their houses facing east. When they leave their home early in the morning, they immediately benefit from the energy of the rising sun, which is most beneficial at this time of the day. The morning hour has gold in its mouth, it is said. At sunrise the positive energies are very strong and there is a lot of Prana in the air.

Scheme 21.2
Ideal Daily Routine according to Ayurveda

MORNING	
1.	Get up before sunrise
2.	Drink one or two glasses of lukewarm water
3.	Bowel movement (if possible)
4.	Brushing teeth and tongue
5.	Scraping tongue
6.	Cleaning face, eyes and nose
7.	Gargle with sesame oil if necessary
8.	Massage with warm oil
9.	Shower/Bath
10.	Spiritual discipline (yoga, breathing exercises, meditation, chanting)
11.	Light breakfast
12.	Work, study or play
AFTERNOON	
13.	Warm lunch (main meal)
14.	Rest (10 minutes)
15.	Work, study or play
16.	Yoga, breathing exercises and meditation

EVENING
17. Light evening meal
18. Evening walk
19. Recreation, enjoyment, chanting, praying
20. To bed, at the latest at 10 pm

Scheme 21.2 Ayurveda provides specific guidelines for the daily routine that apply to everyone. Its purpose is to balance the mind and the body and provide a strong foundation for personal growth. The ayurvedic art of living, aimed at maintaining good health and enjoying a long life is called swasta vritta.

Cleaning teeth and tongue

After getting up, we begin the daily cleansing of body and mind. We can start by brushing our teeth and cleaning the tongue. Cleaning the tongue is an ancient ayurvedic practice that has now become more widespread in the West, too. We can buy a tongue scraper in the health store or at the pharmacy. By cleaning the tongue, we remove the *ama* that has attached itself to the tongue. Gently scraping the tongue is also a good massage for the whole body, because the trigger points for all the organs can be found on the tongue. Tongue cleaning is a necessary part of our oral hygiene and provides fresh breath. After brushing and cleaning, we can gargle with warm sesame oil for a few minutes, so that we keep all parts in the mouth bacteria-free and soft. Gargling has a refreshing and positive effect on the quality of our voice.

Drinking water

Once the mouth is clean and fresh, it is time to drink one or two glasses of lukewarm water. This has a cleansing effect on the whole body and stimulates digestion. Drinking enough water after getting up is crucial for maintaining good health. In addition, it can help activate our defecation system.

Bowel movements

If we lead a regular life and maintain a regular diet (for example, by avoiding snacks or eating after seven p.m.), there is a good chance that the call of nature will present itself early in the morning every day. Defecation at this time of the day, before exercising and breakfast, is a boon for the functioning of the body and for maintaining good digestion.

Cleaning of face, eyes and nose

After the toilet visit, the science of Ayurveda advises us to wash hands and face well (again). Separate cleansing of the eyes in the early morning is desirable, either with water or by sprinkling them with a few drops of rose water. You can also put some rose water on a cotton ball and dab the eyes with it.

Ayurvedic massage with warm oil

After this, we can begin our oil massage, or maybe a few times during the week, which should take no more than about ten minutes. The oil massage keeps our doshas in perfect balance or, if necessary, restores the balance. We warm the oil up, start at the crown and end at the feet. Do not forget to cover the ear cups, too. After this we can take a shower or a bath. If we want to let the oil soak in the skin a little longer, we can do our yoga exercises and take a shower afterwards.

Neti therapy

We can also do a nose wash called *neti* a few times a week. This purification therapy is definitely recommended. There are several methods, of which rinsing lukewarm water with a spout cup in one nostril, going out from the other and vice versa is the most practical. Special pitchers are available at an ayurvedic shop or health centre. It is customary to add a spoonful of salt to the warm water. Neti not only cleans the inside of the nose (mucus) but also the frontal sinus. The neti method leads to a more refined breathing and to a better resistance to illnesses, such as colds and flu.

Copper neti pot

Taking a bath or shower

About twenty minutes after the massage with warm oil we can take a shower or a bath and we will notice that a very delicate layer of oil remains on the skin. Rinsing the oil has a cleansing effect, so do not use soap or shampoo. Taking a shower or a bath has a refreshing effect on the mind and body. As for the temperature of the water when showering or taking a bath, it is good to start with lukewarm water and finish with colder water. The cold water should be as cold as the body likes and not so cold that it starts shivering. With regard to warm water, we must take special care that we never rinse the head with hot water, as this will disturb the life energy, which is mainly located in the head. If the mirror in the bathroom is fogging, it is a sign that the water we are using is too hot. Vata people can use slightly warmer water while for pitta people water with a slightly colder temperature is recommended. In case of fever, showering or taking a bath is not recommended.

Sadhana

After the shower and before our yoga and meditation practice, we can begin our spiritual discipline or sadhana with alternate nasal breathing or nadi shodhana. It is a simple yet powerful exercise to cleanse the subtle channels of the mind-body organism while balancing the masculine and feminine aspects. This exercise improves lung function and breathing endurance, too. It helps sharpen our concentration, brings mental clarity, and it supplies equal amounts of oxygen to both sides of our brain. Usually it is practiced for about five to ten minutes while sitting in the meditation position.

Nadi Shodhana

Spiritual discipline or *sadhana* is a core concept for creating balance and progress in our inner world. Practicing it will bring more light and wisdom into ourselves and contribute to dispelling the darkness of ignorance in society. American research has shown that daily meditation practice can lead to structural changes in the brain within eight weeks.

More grey brain mass is found in the *hippocampus* (little sea horse), an area associated with our memory and learning ability. At the same time, research showed that anxiety and stress decreased. Thus, meditation not only creates a sense of calm and physical relaxation, but it leads to the fascinating conclusion that it also yields cognitive and psychological benefits. This is something that people who practice meditation on a daily basis have been able to ascertain through their own experience for years. It is recommended to learn a useful and effective meditation technique from an experienced teacher.

Light breakfast

After the spiritual practice, it is time for a light breakfast. The discussion whether or not having breakfast is good, often flares up. In Ayurveda this depends, among other things, on the individual dosha constitution. For people with a vata constitution, a nutritious breakfast is definitely recommended, they can use some extra energy at the start of the day. Pitta people can eat a light breakfast if it calms their hunger and kapha people can basically skip breakfast. It goes without saying that a fruit breakfast, whether or not in the form of a fruit juice, is very good because fruits digest very easily. Due to their specific digestion process, we should not take fruit and milk in combination with other foods.

XXI.6 DAILY ACTIVITY

In daily life we often experience a dilemma between the necessity of work or study and the fulfilment of our deeper life mission, of that which we really want to do or achieve in this life. Through spiritual practice it is possible to gain more insight into this and achieve an optimal balance between the two. We can only be truly happy when every action is experienced as a fulfilling activity that allows us to feel freer from all the limiting influences of relative life.

Who or what is the doer of our activity? Is it our ego (the little I) or is the inner Self leading all our actions? In the latter case, the art of living is to allow the Self to co-operate with us, for it is, after all, the source of our being. The inner Self has already got everything we can think of as potential, including any activity that can lead us to the goal of life. We can observe how the Self works in us and how it wants to manifest itself in our actions. *Not my will, but Thy will be done.* It is not easy to allow the Self into our existence (after all, we are much too busy for that in general), but it is essential to grow further internally and give priority to our own, unique evolution.

All knowledge of right and unselfish action can be found in the Bhagavad Gita, both about the cause and effect, and the source of actions, the field of pure consciousness. At some point, a situation may arise where every action is a life-promoting act. Since every action is followed by an equivalent response to it, we automatically acquire the blessings of the cosmic Intelligence. In this way we grow into a state of higher consciousness, in which we become completely free from limitations and we no longer perform harmful actions. Only when more people start to experience this from a higher consciousness, will it become possible that all nature reacts to it in a harmonious way, as was the case in the time of the Vedic civilization: the sun shone in time, the rain fell in time, the harvest and the seasons were timely, and both the administrators of society and its subjects lived in peace and optimal well-being.

Lunch

Pitta dosha is dominant around noon, from 10 a.m. to 2 p.m. This is the time of transformation and so the most appropriate time to have our main meal of the day is around noon, as was the case almost everywhere in the time of our grandparents. After all, the pitta fire promotes digestion. For good digestion it is useful to rest for a short time after lunch, but not to sleep.

Do less, achieve more

Ayurveda recommends taking a little rest after lunch and the universal advice on work is: do less, accomplish more. From a calm mind we can achieve much more and also experience much more pleasure in our work. This has everything to do with healthy ageing as well. So also, at other times of the day it is beneficial to slow down and build in intervals of rest. Nothing is more restful than taking a walk in nature, enjoying the little things around us and especially, focusing on activities that we enjoy.

From an ayurvedic point of view, the best advice for the period of work is: keep the body in balance, that's all it needs. Once we have gone beyond our limits, it is advisable to rebalance our system, as soon as possible. Do not keep the body under stress for extended periods of time; it needs our constant attention and care. We know that the body is impermanent. The more we allow our soul to express itself fully in all areas of life, the more we will enjoy life's journey. As the body ages, its functions weaken, its efficiency decreases. If we are not consciously concerned with the deeper values of life, such effects can be very unpleasant and frustrating. But if we are able to cope with ageing well, we can continue to enjoy the experiences of the body. We can take care of her age and enjoy observing her spiritual journey even in the later years of our lives.

XXI.7 EVENING AND NIGHT

By evening, after taking some rest or practice a meditation, it is wise to have an easily digestible meal such as kicharie, and preferably before 7 pm.

Scheme 21.3
Receipt for dinner

> KICHARIE (mungdal and rice)
>
> Boil the mungdal (small yellow lentils) for 20-30 minutes in plenty of water to which you can add a little garlic, turmeric, tulsi (basil) and a teaspoon of ghee. You can also add a little sea salt and black pepper.
>
> This creates a soup-like substance that is very easy to digest and is a natural and effective antibiotic for tumours and similar conditions. Mungdal is the perfect sattvic detox food in Ayurveda and very easy to digest. A mixture of equal parts mung beans and white rice is called kicharie in India and is also considered as a perfect evening meal.

A heavy meal in the evening does not give our body the rest it needs for regeneration. This regeneration takes place during sleep, when the day's food is digested and new tissue is developed. For that reason too, it is recommended to lie in bed no later than 10 p.m.

* * *

Early to bed and early to rise
makes a man healthy, happy and wise!

* * *

Preparation for sleep

Before going to sleep, we can clean our mouth and teeth and wash our head, hands and feet with water that is neither too cold nor too hot. Taking a shower or a bath is of course also good. It is particularly beneficial to massage our feet lovingly with sesame or mustard oil for a few minutes before going to sleep, especially if we have difficulty with falling asleep. The Vedic scriptures further recommend asking for forgiveness before going to sleep for what you may not have done right that day or for possible sins you may have committed. You can also express your gratitude for all the precious people who surround you and for all the good things that came your way during the day. By being grateful, we can eliminate the negative aspects of our blueprint of life. Sri Bhagawan said about this that a prerequisite for spiritual growth is that we are full of gratitude for everything and everyone, starting with our parents.

Regular, uninterrupted sleep maximizes the production of *soma*, the most subtle element in the body that creates intelligence and gives the body its radiance. We cannot live without sleep, but there are people who are conscious of their sleep or of their dreams. They just know they are sleeping and they are able to direct their dreams. Dolphins seem to have the same experience: they turn off one hemisphere of the brain while the other remains vigilant. By living a good life and spiritual practice, we can develop this experience within ourselves.

The state of dreaming consciousness is important, even indispensable, and its contents can have two meanings:

* It removes tension, stress and excessive experiences
* It gives us insights or directions for a healthy existence

When our mind is overactive, it will be more difficult to fall asleep. In this case our dreams will be restless or fierce and as a result we will not be well rested the next day. This phenomenon mainly occurs in people who have become exhausted (burnout), have anxiety attacks or are depressed. In the Netherlands about 15% of the population suffers from this. More rest in the workplace, daily yoga & meditation practice and sufficient sleep are the natural solutions to counteract this and after some time make it disappear completely. And when our consciousness expands, our dreams can take on a more spiritual quality. We can dream that we can fly, or our spiritual teacher appears in our dream.

CHAPTER XXII

WORLD PEACE (RAM RAJ)

*'Know that we all strive for a common goal and that we are destined
to live together in perfect harmony, to enjoy together,
and to experience fulfillment together.'*

- Rigveda X.12.40

The original meaning and value of Vedic science and culture has been forgotten for thousands of years, but it has not disappeared and cannot be destroyed. Its universal wisdom is forever anchored in human consciousness and can be revived at any time. It is based on a life in unity consciousness, a life and existence in full accordance with the universal law of evolution. Like no other tradition of wisdom, the Veda has the invincible ability and means to lead the world back to peace and harmony. It is an all-encompassing and unique gift that has always been handed back to humanity at crucial moments of its existence.

The Veda offers the opportunity to realize peace in the heart of every human being through the development of a higher consciousness. We are free to choose any other path, but a positive transformation of human consciousness is the only practical path that can lead to a sustainable world peace. We must be willing to overcome the fundamental limitation of the human intellect - *pragyaparadha*. Instead, wisdom is required. All expressions of illness, conflict and suffering have their ultimate cause in pragyaparadha, in a distorted perception of reality. Our limited minds do not see things as they are, but there is a latent desire in every human being to go beyond these limitations. Through the study and practical applications of the Vedas it is possible to understand the course, meaning and purpose of existence and experience its essence in our own consciousness.

XXII.1 UNION

Political and economic forces in the world adhere scrupulously to the laws of matter, money and self-interest. This implies that the principles of being together, sharing and cooperating, which are essential for the wellbeing of this planet, cannot be sufficiently addressed. The old thinking continues to be entrenched in the one-sided view that only economic growth can help humanity further; the new way of thinking believes that care and love for each other form the basis of a better life on earth. Fortunately, although often invisible, many people believe in this and want to work for it. Our solar system is currently in a phase transition in which it is shifting into a different vibration level. Just like the earth, our sun functions on the basis of electromagnetic processes, too. In recent years, an unusual increase in solar activity has been observed which has a major impact on the development of the planets of our solar system, including our Earth. With time it will come to light that humanity is actually evolving into a higher dimension that lays much more emphasis on spiritual union with each other, peace and harmony between countries than ever before.

It is already evident, that in all areas of science and technology, philosophy and religion, the basic patterns and values of existence are being re-evaluated. We live in a time when we will put all the pieces of the great, universal puzzle together. As a result, people around the world may begin to express more unity and show less division. Despite or perhaps just because of the major problems that now hold the world in their grip, it will become possible to take a completely different approach to life on earth. Many people view this time of transformation as a time of spiritual cooperation, for making a higher quality of life a living reality. The real powers to transform the world operate from an invisible, spiritual level. The unifying principle that unites all people will undoubtedly become stronger, ending the violence, terror and fear that still dominate life on Earth today.

The noble thoughts, embodied in the Upanishads and in the other Vedic scriptures, have inspired great souls like Swami Vivekananda, Mahatma Gandhi, Pt. Nehru and many others to stand up tirelessly for tolerance between different religions, nonviolence and world peace. Gandhiji could only maintain his strategy of non-violence for the independence of India because the people of India understood so deeply what he meant by the principle of *Ahimsa* (non-violence). India's path from nonviolence to independence has greatly influenced other countries to achieve their freedom peacefully, without bloodshed.

Nevertheless, India has subsequently also fallen prey to all kinds of Western influences and can only disentangle from it if it embraces the traditional values of the Veda again, in all its purity, as the basis and starting point for its society. If there is one country able to inspire the world towards tolerance and nonviolence, it is India.

XXII.2 THE BOW OF SHIVA

In the Vedic era there were kings who were renowned for their wisdom and justice in governing their land. In the epic Ramayana, King Janaka was one of those wise kings. King Janaka was a philosopher-king, known not only as a perfect ruler, but also as a great seer. In administering his kingdom, he adhered strictly to the rules and guidelines set forth in the Vedic writings for *kshatriyas*, the order of kings and rulers in Vedic society.

One day he organized a tournament for all noble princes in the world. The winner of the tournament was allowed to marry his daughter, Sitadevi. Many princes who had heard of Sita's divine beauty came to the city of Mithila to participate in the tournament. The achievement to be delivered consisted of lifting and stretching an immense bow, a tour de force that was actually considered impossible. Originally, the bow came from the great god Shiva, the dissolving principle of the world. Once upon a time, this bow came into the possession of King Janaka. During the tournament it turned out that no prince was able to lift and string the bow. When it was finally Prince Rama's turn, the other princes began to laugh aloud. How could a prince of barely sixteen years of age be capable of such a superhuman achievement? After respectfully requesting the blessing of his teacher, Vishwamitra, Prince Rama approached the eight-wheeled chariot on which Shiva's bow laid with deep compassion. With visible ease, Rama lifted the bow and stretched it with such force that it broke into two. King Janaka was very relieved, and Sita hung a garland of flowers around Rama's neck to show that she accepted him as her husband.

What is the deeper meaning of Shiva's bow? This bow represents the individual ego that must be stretched and broken in order to reconnect with the Self (Rama) and the intellect (Sita) harmoniously. The eight-wheeled chariot, on which the bow was located, symbolizes the eightfold nature or *Prakriti*. All other princes were unable to draw the bow because they acted primarily on the basis of external power and arrogance. Realizing that he could only bend the bow with the help of universal love, Rama is the embodiment of that harmony and love. Real power in life comes from within. Being able to perceive the world in the light of unconditional love, which can only come from within, is to live without fear and with full confidence. Then we can see the other as part of ourselves, and there is no room for suspicion and anger anymore. Rama's mind is pure and stable because he acts from the inner Self and then there is nothing he cannot realize. The invincible Self is in charge of his own thoughts and actions. The resulting loving manner of functioning gives Sitadevi complete confidence in accepting Rama as her husband.

(Picture: Wikipedia)
Prince Rama, who was, in reality, God Himself who had descended to Earth, breaks the Bow of Shiva and by this He achieves union with Sitadevi

It is fascinating that the vast field of knowledge that the Veda - or in narrative form, the epic Ramayana - covers, is in fact nothing but the basic structure of our own consciousness, the Self. The Self is the basis of all knowledge: all knowledge proceeds from it and all knowledge returns to it, just as our universe is only one of a long series of worlds that arise and disappear again into the lap of the Supreme Being. But the laws of nature responsible for this are always the same, unchangeable impulses, and these are structured just as the Veda in human consciousness and in human physiology.

In essence we are the Self, we are the Veda, minuscule particles of the Supreme Lord. We have come to the material world, just to return one day back to our home, to Lord Krishna's eternal abode.

XXII.3 IDEAL RULERSHIP

Rulership is the way in which administrators deal with themselves, with others and with the wishes of the society. Ruling a country well does not mean that we are primarily concerned with solving all the problems that arise, but that we rule in such an efficient way, that hardly any problems can arise. When the rulers of the world could make the decision to focus on people's wellbeing and spiritual progress, instead of giving priority to self-interest-based political or other selfish strategies, true rulership would develop:

FROM:	TO:
Being dependent	To being autonomous
Power as the highest goal	Service as the highest goal
Problem-oriented approach	Looking for new possibilities
Selfish political approach	Put the interests of all people first
Focus on material gain	Focus on developing consciousness
The desire to fight opponents	The desire to make allies
Economic interests come first	Focus on wellbeing for everyone
Predominantly intellectual approach	Emphasis on wisdom in action
Draw up rules and procedures	Promote the creativity of people
Conflict resolution	Making win-win agreements
Hard work	Relaxation

Harmony and wellbeing in a country are determined by the quality of the collective consciousness of its citizens. In fact, the government is nothing else, but an innocent mirror reflecting exactly what is going on in a society. In this sense, it is wrong to blame a government for everything when things are not going well in a country. When there is discontent among the citizens of a country, this will be reflected in the quality of the administration. When citizens are harmonious and creative, this will also show itself in the government of the country. No government or administration of a country can escape from this *natural principle of government*, as formulated in the last century by Maharishi Mahesh Yogi. Every decision the administration makes is an expression of the quality of the collective consciousness of the people of that country.

Ram Raj, the ideal rulership of Shri Rama
(Painting: Rozalia Hummel)

The Vedic wisdom, the knowledge of how the law of evolution governs and supports all creation, is an important means for a government and a society to protect them from errors, mistakes and problems. Nature teaches us that the supreme Lord of the universe directs creation from the level of the field of pure consciousness. This is a field of minimal activity: apparently, like the universe, we are able to accomplish much more by doing less. In Ramayana this is illustrated by the rulership of Rama, who in the process of governing does nothing but stays in touch with the higher Self. This is the formula for perfect administration: maintaining an optimal balance between rest and activity, because this spontaneously promotes the evolution of everything and everyone.

The righteous government of Shri Rama, called RAMRAJ, is described in the *Ramcharitmanas*, composed by the saint and poet Tulsidas. In Uttara Kanda XX.1, at the end of the epic, we read:

* * *

"In all of Rama's realm there was no one who suffered physical pain, was unhappy, or in bad circumstances. Everyone loved their neighbour and was satisfied with their situation in life as determined by birth, and in accordance with the teachings of the scriptures and the highest morals. The four foundations of life - Dharma, Artha, Kama, and Moksha - were established all over the world; no one even thought of sin. Both men and women were devoted to Rama and enjoyed all the blessings. There was no premature death and everyone was healthy in body and soul. Nobody suffered poverty, was worried or stressed; no one was ignorant or unhappy. All people, without exception, were good and pious, capable and intelligent. Everyone praised his neighbour's achievements and was educated and wise himself. All were grateful for the unsuspecting and unselfish policy of King Rama."

* * *

XXII.4 CONCLUSION

The universal law of evolution, which sustains everything, calls us to live in harmony with each other and to realize that we all belong to one world-family. Peace and harmony arise when every person and every country follow their dharma, their true destiny, and fully respect that of the others. This happens naturally when the inner Self is guiding us. After all, everything in the world is part of a divine plan and therein lies the possible salvation of humanity as well as of our life on earth. No doubt this divine plan has been in place for some time and contains a practical and effective program to end the selfish political, commercial, and religious powers that have ruled the world for centuries. The trials we must face first have already started coming in many forms by now, but we certainly do not need to lay our heads despondently in our lap. On a personal level, in particular, we can contribute a lot to creating more peace and harmony in our environment and the world. Especially, we must place our hope in the hands of a younger, wiser generation to take leadership in these times of necessary transformation of the global climate change, inequality, terror and corruption. Moreover, by continuing to work individually and in groups on inner development, we can keep the turmoil in check and offer real help. Through our spiritual approach, we can nourish the collective forces in society with harmony and love and enrich it with positive energy. Or, when we join others in the form of group meditations or satsangs, the spiritual energy generated and focused can radiate outward. The Vedic applications of wisdom are the designated channels for carrying out the divine plan and for heaven to descend to earth.

OM Shanti, Shanti, Shanti

May we experience peace, may all living beings experience peace, may the whole world experience peace

***

END OF PART II

GLOSSARY

A

Abhyanga	Ayurvedic massage with warm herbal oil; part of panchakarma treatment.
Adhvaryu	One of the four Vedic priests. The other three are Udgatri, Brahma and Hotri.
Adi Shankara	Famous saint who wrote commentaries on, among others things, the Brahmasutra, an explanation of Vedanta.
Aditi	Wife of the holy Kashyapa and mother of the twelve Adityas, who symbolise the twelve months of the year.
Advaita	The insight that the ultimate reality is One, without a second (non-dual).
Agni	Lit. Fire god; receives sacrifices and transfers them to higher regions; one of the five elements (fire); impulse of creative intelligence; digestive fire.
Agnim	Lit. fire; first word of Rigveda, with which creation starts.
Agnihotra	Ritual of offering sacrifices into the holy fire.
Aham brahmasmi	I am Brahman, I am the totality; one of the four mahavakyas (great sayings).
Ahamkara	Individual ego; identity.
Akasha	Space, ether; one of the five basic elements.
Akshara	Imperishable; the transcendental field of

	consciousness where all impulses of creative intelligence abide.
Ama	Residues or plaque formation in the body due to poor digestion.
Amrita	Immortality; nectar of immortality; legendary beverage associated with Soma.
Ananda	Bliss; quality of the field of pure consciousness (sat-chit-ananda).
Ananda Shakti	The power of absolute bliss.
Angiras	Teacher in the Mundaka Upanishad.
Anna	Food; matter; is also used in connection with spiritual transformation.
Antarjyotis	Inner light; refers to God inside and the light of wisdom.
Apa(s)	Primordial water, stems from ap, meaning: to pervade; one of the five basic elements.
Apana	One of the five aspects of prana in the human body; out breath.
Apaurusheya	The Vedic hymns of divine origin commenting themselves by their sequence of sounds, verses, hymns and mandalas.
Aranyakas	Lit. forest books; part of the Brahmanas and part of the shruti.
Arati	Thanksgiving after sacrificial ceremony or to the spiritual teacher. (from Skt. aratrika)
Arjuna	Famous archer from the Bhagavad Gita, who was Krishna's most beloved disciple; one of the five Pandavas.
Artha	Wealth; one of the four goals of life, of which the other three are: dharma, kama and moksha.

Aryaman	Vedic deity, one of the Adityas.
Arya Samaj	Movement within Hinduism, founded by Swami Dayananda Saraswati, who wants to give again Vedic knowledge its central place.
Asana	Body posture; part of Patanjali's Ashtanga Yoga.
Asat	Non-existent; it is said of Brahman that it is both sat and asat, existent and non-existent.
Ashrama	A place devoted to God; the dwelling place of a spiritual teacher and his/her students.
Asura	demon; opponent of the gods.
Ashwins	Twin gods specialised in medicine.
Atharvaveda	One of the four Vedas; represents the Chhandas aspect in the Samhita of the Veda – see Vedas.
Atma(n)	The higher Self, which is present in man and that lies at the basis of all his functions; the Upanishads declare that Atman and Brahman, the universal Self, are in essence the same.
Aum	Also: OM. The primordial mantra which symbolises both non-manifest and manifest Brahman. All manifestations in the universe spring forth from this primordial sound.
Avatara	(Lit. He who descends) An incarnation of the Supreme Lord, or of one of His representatives, descending to the Earth, to restore the religious principles.
Avidya	Ignorance about the ultimate reality.
Ayurveda	Upaveda of the Rigveda, about health and longevity.

B

Basti (Skt. vasti)	Enema; part of the panchakarma treatment.
Bhagavad Gita	(Lit. Song of the Lord) Famous part of the Mahabharata; Lord Krishna's divine teaching to His devoted friend Arjuna.
Bhagawan	God; Supreme Lord; someone with divine qualities.
Bhakta	Disciple, fully devoted to the Lord.
Bhakti-yoga	Practise of pure love, devotion and surrender to God or Guru.
Bhuma	Earth.
Bhur(loka)	Material world.
Bhuvah	Intermediate space; gap.
Bindu	Lit. dot; point, spot; mark; drop; Strong concentration of Shakti in one point from which the whole universe emerges; one point of light called the Blue Pearl; material cause and substance of the universe.
Blue Pearl	The subtle dwelling place of the inner Self; a radiant point of blue light that can be perceived in meditation at the brow centre.
Bow of Shiva	Invincible bow, symbolic for the individual ego.
Brahma	The Creator, first being of the universe; part of the divine trinity Brahma, Vishnu and Shiva.
Brahmin	Somebody belonging to the priesthood.
Brahmacharya	Someone who takes the vow of celibacy; first order of spiritual life.
Brahmaloka	(or Satyaloka) Abode of Lord Brahma.
Brahman	(or Brahmajyoti) The Absolute; the transcendental Reality, the One without form,

	the impersonal aspect of the Supreme Lord.
Brahmana	Scripture belonging to the shruti and deals with the use of mantras and the correct way of performing rituals.
Brahmanas	Vedic scholars or saints who are responsible for protecting the Vedic wisdom.
Brahmananda	The Bliss that emerges from Brahman-realisation.
Brahmastra	Weapon which was used in Vedic times with the power of nowadays nuclear weapons.
Brhigu	Saint; seer of Rigveda (see also Taittiriya Upanishad, chapter 3).
Brihaspati	Seer of Rigveda; Guru of the gods; another name for Jupiter.
Buddha	Avatara from the time of Kali-yuga, to teach humanity non-violence.
Buddhi	Intellect; logic; one says that the relative mind consists of three parts: manas (ability to perceive), buddhi (intellect), and ahamkara (false ego).

C

Chakra	Lit. wheel. Energy centre in the subtle body. When the kundalini energy wakes up, she rises up and purifies and opens these centres.
Chhandas	Metre; the known; one of the six Vedangas.
Charaka Samhita	Sanskrit text about Ayurveda of Charaka (8th B.C.).
Chit(ta)	Consciousness, the power of perception; see also buddhi.

D

Darshan	Blessing from the Guru or saint.
Dayananda Swami	Swami Dayananda Saraswati is the founder of the Arya Samaj (1824-1883), who wanted to put the meaning of the Veda in the centre of the Indian society.
Deva(ta)	Demigod; lit. 'the shining one'; the demigods represent different qualities of creative intelligence.
Devata	Process of knowing; relationship between subject and object of knowledge.
Devayana	The path of light followed by the soul after death, when we have followed successfully the spiritual path on earth.
Dhanurveda	Upaveda; gives knowledge to restore and maintain purity in the field of action.
Dharana	Steadfastness of the mind; part of Ashtanga Yoga.
Dharma	Religion; the universal law of nature, which supports everything; our allotted duty in life; justice; see also Sanatana Dharma.
Dhatus	The subsequent elementary core tissues in the physiology: rasa, rakta, mamsa, meda, asthi, majja and shukra.
Dhyana	Meditation; one of the eight limbs of Ashtanga Yoga.
Dhritarashtra	The blind king from the Mahabharata.
Divya	Divine.
Doshas	The three basic principles of our physiology: vata, pitta and kapha.

| *Duryodhana* | Eldest son of the blind king Dhritarashtra who wanted to destroy the Pandavas. |
| *Dvapara-yuga* | Third era of the cycle of four yugas; Copper Age. |

G

Gandharvas	Heavenly beings (angels) excelling in dance and music.
Gandharvaveda	Upaveda that deals with classical singing and music.
Ganesha	Lord of all creatures; deity with head of an elephant; son of Shiva and Parvati; god of wisdom and of the removal of obstacles.
Ganeshpuri	Village north of Mumbai in the state Maharashtra, where ashrams have been founded of Bhagawan Nityananda and Swami Muktananda.
Gaudapada	Teacher of Shri Adi Shankara's teacher, who wrote an authoritative commentary on the Mandukya Upanishad.
Gautama	Author of Nyaya (Upaveda).
Gayatri	Most frequently used metre in the Vedas.
Gayatri-mantra	Famous mantra from Rigveda, dedicated to the Sun.
Ghee (ghi)	Clarified butter used for sacrifices.
Goloka	(Krishnaloka) Abode where Lord Krishna and his devotees eternally live; the spiritual world.
Gosvami	Someone who is competent to explain the Vedic scriptures.
Grihastha	Second order of spiritual life; period of housekeeping and social life.

Guna-avatara	Avatara who is the ruler of one of the three gunas; Brahma rules rajas, Vishnu rules sattva and Shiva rules tamas.
Gunas	Three qualities in nature, in food and in our own functioning; see sattva, rajas and tamas.
Guru	Spiritual teacher established in the Self, who guides his disciples on their spiritual journey towards surrendering to God.
Guru Gita	Lit. 'Song of the Guru.' An ancient Sanskrit text, describing the qualities of the guru, the relationship teacher-disciple and the way to meditate on the (inner) guru.
Gyana indriyas	Sense organs of perception, namely hearing, touch, sight, taste and smell; in the Upanishads they are considered as Devas.
Gyana shakti	Power of wisdom; see shakti.
Gyana yoga	The yoga of knowledge; see yoga.

H

Hatha-yoga	Physical exercises for the relaxation of mind and body.
Hotri	One of the four Vedic priests; see Adhvaryu.
Homa (havana)	Fire sacrifice.
Hora	Part of the Vedic Astrology which deals with the analysis and prediction on the basis of the Vedic birthchart.

I

Idam	(Lit. this) With this is meant the universe.
Indra	King of the gods; principle of wholeness of consciousness; god of thunder.

Indriyas	Senses of perception.
Ishta devata	Personally chosen deity; deity one preferably invokes or worships.
Ishvara	Universal God; Supreme Lord.
Itihasa	(Lit. History) Part of Vedic literature that expresses and explains the Vedic principles in the form of stories (Ramayana and Mahabharata).

J

Jaimini	Author of Karma Mimamsa (Upaveda).
Janaka	King of Mithila; Sita's father, who was considered an ideal and very wise king.
Japa	The repetition of a mantra or the name of God.
Jiva, Jivatman	The individual Self in man, that returns after death into another body.
Jnana	(Lit. knowledge) Spiritual knowledge to discriminate between the physical and spiritual world.
Jyotish	One of the six Vedangas; deals with astrology and astronomy.

K

Kala (purusha)	Time; the essence of time.
Kali	Tamas form of goddess Parvati, the divine mother.
Kali-yuga	Era of ignorance; Iron Age; era of decay of norms and values.
Kalpa	Part of the six Vedangas; study and explanation of Vedic rituals; period of a day of Brahma (4.320.000.000 year).

Kama	Pleasure, desire; one of the four goals of life, see artha.
Kamadhenu	Wish fulfilling cow who lives in Goloka Vrindavana.
Karma	(Lit. activity) The consequences of someone's actions; the accumulation of the actions one has performed in the past.
Kanada	Author of Vaisheshika (Upanga).
Kapha	One of the three doshas; stands for: structure, building-up.
Kapila	Author of Samkhya (Upanga).
Karma	Activity; principle of cause and effect.
Karma indriyas	The five sense organs of action: tongue, hands, feet, reproduction and excretion.
Kauravas	(or Kurus) The hundred sons of king Dhritarashtra (symbol for vice and deception)
Karma Kanda	Part of the Veda dealing with regulations for proper use of the Vedic rituals.
Kirtana	Chanting of the Name of God in a group; one of the nine devoted activities.
Krishna, Lord	The Supreme Lord and cause of all causes; divine teacher of Arjuna in Bhagavad Gita.
Kriya	Physical, mental or emotional purification often accompanied by movements or sounds caused by awakening kundalini.
Kshatriya	Somebody belonging to the warrior (rulers) caste.
Kundalini	Pure energy or shakti, coiled up at the basis of the spine in the subtle body, that can be enlivened by the guru. When the kundalini

enters the sahasrara, the spiritual centre located in the crown, the unity with the higher Self is reached (Self-realisation).

L

Lanka	Kingdom of demon Ravana (Ramayana).
Linga(m)	Pillar formed object, symbol for the non-manifest aspect of Shiva; the male principle in nature.
Loka	World. There are different worlds or spheres, like Brahma Loka, Pitri Loka and Siddha loka.

M

Maha	Great.
Mahabharata	Vedic epic about Krishna and the Pandavas entering into the battle against the evil forces in life. Bhagavad Gita is an important part of it.
Maha-mantra	(Lit. great mantra) Mantra which is used by the Hare Krishna's to free themselves from the bondage of the material world and to generate love and devotion for God.
Maharishi	(Lit. great seer) A spiritual master who has the ability to understand the wisdom of the Vedas; Maharishi Mahesh Yogi was a world teacher who again brought to light the profound meaning of the Vedas.
Mahat-tattva	The twenty-four elements of the material world.
Mahavakyas	The four great aphorisms (essential truths) in the Vedas: Thou art that, I am Brahman, I am Veda, Atman is Brahman.
Maha-yuga	The four yugas together: Sat-, Treta-, Dvapara-

	and Kali-yuga.
Manas	Mind.
Mandala	(Lit. circle) chapter in the Vedas.
Mantra	Subtle Sanskrit sound or name of God which is repeated; the Vedic mantras or verses; the knowledge-aspect of the Veda.
Manu	The first lawgiver; also considered the founding father of humanity (compare: Adam).
Maruts	Vedic gods; the wind; organs of perception; sons of Rudra.
Maya	That which is not; illusion; the rope that is mistaken for a snake.
Mian Tansen	Famous musician from the Gandharvaveda tradition.
Mitra	Vedic god; one of the twelve Adityas; the day; inhalation.
Moksha (mukti)	Spiritual liberation, Unity with Brahman; enlightenment.
Muhurta	Part of Jyotish that deals with the determining of auspicious days or times for important events.
Muladhara	Energy centre at the bottom of the spine where the kundalini resides in a hidden state.
Muni	Wise soul or saint.

N

Nachiketa	Boy who takes up a dialogue with Yama, the god of death in Katha Upanishad.
Nadi	Channel in the subtle body through which vital energy flows; the subtle body seems to contain 72000 of this energy channels (big and small).

Naga	Snake.
Nama rupa	Name-form (compare mind and body).
Narada Muni	A famous saint and one of the ten sons of Brahma; a great devotee and servant of Lord Vishnu; he appears in many Vedic scriptures as the messenger of the gods and can travel everywhere in the spiritual and material world.
Narayana	Full Krishna-expansion with four hands who rules the Vaikuntha-planets.
Neti (nasya)	Ayurvedic method for purification of the nasal cavity and sinuses.
Nimitta	Part of Jyotish that deals with prediction based on omens and gestures.
Nirukta	One of the six Vedangas; explains the etymology (derivation of words) of Vedic hymns.
Niyamas	Rules for living; part of Patanjali's Ashtanga Yoga.
Nyaya	The first of the six Upanga which explains the logic of existence.

O

Ojas	The most refined product of digestion.
Om	See Aum.

P

Panchakarma	Ayurvedic purification treatment consisting of five parts.
Pancha kosha	Five layers of the human being: physical, vital, mental, spiritual and bliss.
Panchanga	Vedic Calendar and Almanac.

Pandavas	Five brothers from the Mahabharata who were noble and virtuous.
Pundit	Vedic priest.
Para	Transcendent; beyond.
Paramatma	Supersoul; full expansion of Lord Krishna who lives in the heart of all living beings and in every atom of the material world.
Parabrahman	The Absolute that is endless and formless; Lord Krishna.
Parvati	Consort of Shiva.
Patanjali	Author of the Yoga-sutras (Upanga).
Pippalada	Teacher in the Prashna Upanishad.
Pitri loka	The world of the ancestors; see loka.
Pitta	One of the three doshas; stands for transformation, or for the fire element.
Prabhupada	Title that is assigned to a great devotee or pure representative of Lord Krishna.
Pragyaparadha	(Lit. mistake of the intellect) ignorance about our real nature, first cause of suffering and disease.
Prajapati	Lord of all living creatures; the Creator.
Prakriti	(Lit. nature) That of which the material world is made; corresponds to shakti; the individual constitution.
Prana	Life principle; cosmic energy or power; refined breath; in the human body prana expresses itself in five aspects.
Pranam	Bowing down; greeting with reverence.
Pranava	Name of the mantra Om.

Pranayama	Regulation of breath; one of the eight limbs of Ashtanga Yoga.
Prasada	The offered food one gets in return with the blessing of the deity.
Prashna	Part of Jyotish that deals with prediction in response on asking a question.
Pratyahara	Withdrawal of the senses from their objects, a limb of Ashtanga Yoga.
Prithivi	The earth-element; one of the five basic elements.
Puranas	Part of Vedic literature; brings to light, in the form of stories and legends, the deeper meaning of the Vedas and codes of conduct.
Purna	Full; fullness; wholeness.
Purusha	Supreme Lord; the Cosmic Being, the Absolute.
Pus(h)an	Other name for the Sungod.

R

Raga	Structure of music within the Gandharvaveda musician improvises.
Rajas, rajasic	One of the three gunas; the quality of passion; activating, egocentric, provocative.
Raja Yoga	The royal path towards spiritual liberation.
Rama (Shri)	Supreme Lord; main character in Ramayana. Shri Rama conquers the demonking Ravana and afterwards establishes an ideal society.
Ramayana	Vedic epic about Shri Rama, a divine incarnation, who was an example of ideal behaviour and a perfect ruler.
Ram-Raj	Ideal Vedic kingdom and society.
Ravana	Demonking in Ramayana who kidnapped

	Rama's wife Sita and was killed by Shri Rama.
Richas	Verses of Vedic hymns.
Rigveda	The most ancient and important of the four Vedas which, by virtue of the structure and construction of the sequential mantras, provides a systematic explanation of existence, creation and the development of consciousness; it represents the Samhita (wholeness) aspect of knowledge.
Rishi	Seer; saint who cognized the Vedic mantras.
Rik (Rk)	Verses of the Rigveda.
Rudra	Earlier name or quality of Shiva.
Rupa	Form; body.

S

Sadhana	Spiritual discipline and exercises leading to higher consciousness; spiritual journey.
Samaveda	One of the four Vedas, representing the Rishi-aspect (knower).
Sahasrara	Spiritual centre in the crown of the head in the form of a thousand-petalled lotus flower; in this centre one experiences the highest form of human consciousness.
Samadhi	State of transcendence of the mind during meditation; the experience of union with the Absolute.
Samadosha	Balance of the three doshas.
Saman	Verses of Samaveda.
Samana	One of the six aspects of prana in the human body; the even breath.

Samaveda	One of the four Vedas; representing the Rishi aspect (the knower) of the Samhita of the Veda.
Samhita	Wholeness; Rigveda is the Samhita of the three-in-one structure of the Veda, the totality of knower, process of knowing and the known.
Samsara	The world of phenomena; the cycle of birth, death and rebirth.
Samskara	Collected impressions of events of life that are carried on to the next life; the sixteen Vedic purification rites which a human has to go through in his life.
Sanatana dharma	The eternal law (religion) sustaining the universe in its life-supporting principles.
Samkhya	One of the six systems of Indian philosophy; it investigates the different qualities of human consciousness, the subject.
Sankīrtana	Chanting of the holy names of God, especially recommended in Kali-yuga.
Sannyasi	One who is initiated into the lifestyle of a celibate; an ascetic; devotee of Lord Krishna.
Sat	The Absolute Truth.
Satsang	Coming together in chanting the names of God.
Sat-yuga	The Golden Age; period in which everyone lives in accordance with dharma.
Sattva, sattvic	One of the three gunas; quality of purity, harmony and orderliness.
Shaunaka	Disciple of sage Angiras (Mundaka Upanishad).
Seva	Unselfish service; the performance of activities in e.g. an ashram as part of sadhana; work done with loving devotion.

Shakti	Divine energy, creating, maintaining and dissolving everything in creation.
Shaktipat	Spiritual awakening by the grace of the teacher; the transmission of spiritual power (shakti) from guru to disciple.
Shanti	Peace.
Shiksha	One of the six Vedangas; science of phonetics and pronunciation.
Shiva	Supreme god or Mahadeva; part of the trinity: Brahma, Vishnu and Shiva; symbolising the Absolute but also the dissolving aspect of creation.
Shraddha	Faith.
Shrimad Bhagavatam	Vedic scripture that contains the stories, legends and teachings of Lord Krishna; one of the Mahapuranas, composed by the great sage Vyasadeva.
Shri Sathya Sai Baba	Indian saint and world teacher (1926-2011).
Shruti	(Lit. revelation) Divine revelations; Vedic hymns cognized by seers.
Shudra	Somebody belonging to the serving caste.
Siddha	(Lit. a perfected one) One who has realised the union with God.
Siddha Yoga	State of spiritual perfection experienced by the seeker of truth, when kundalini is fully awakened.
Sita (Seeta)	Devoted spouse of Shri Rama, who was kidnapped by the demonking Ravana.
Smriti	(Lit. memory) Vedic scriptures that were enlivened by the saints in their consciousness and were passed on.

Smritis	Codes of behaviour; there are eighteen smritis of which Manu Smriti is the most well-known.
Soma	Mind, the Moon; subtle substance that is produced by the body from food as the result of refined digestion; substance responsible for the experience of bliss.
Soma yajna	Famous fire sacrifice.
Sri Vasudeva	Spiritual teacher from Trinidad & Tobago, who started his Blue Star mission in 1993 to guide his students in their spiritual journey and to contribute to world peace.
Sthapatyaveda	Upaveda; Vedic science of architecture and urban planning.
Surya (devata)	Sun; Sun god; symbol of source of life.
Suryanamaskara	Vedic exercise with powerful effect for mind and body, dedicated to the Sungod.
Sushumna nadi	Most important channel in the subtle body, connecting the heart centre with the crown of the head; in the state of enlightenment, the shakti (kundalini energy) can freely flow through this channel.
Sutras	(Lit. thread) verses in compact shape with a profound content; see Yoga-sutras.
Svaha	Invocation during sacrifice; consort of Agni.
Svarga loka	Heaven.
Swami	Manner of addressing a sannyasin; member of monk order; saint.
Swedana	Steam bath; part of panchakarma.

T

Tamas, tamasic	One of the three gunas; quality of inertia; lazy, untidy; bored.
Tapas, tapasya	Austerity; detachment; practice of spiritual techniques.
Tat tvam asi	Thou art That; one of the four great aphorisms (mahavakyas) in the Vedas (Chhandogya Upanishad).
Treta-yuga	Second period or yuga; Silver Age.
Tridosha	Ayurvedic teaching of the three doshas.
Tulsidas (1532-1623)	North Indian poet and saint; author of Ramcharitmanas, containing the life story of Shri Rama in Hindi.
Turiya	(Lit. four) The fourth state of consciousness, called transcendental consciousness; the experience of pure consciousness or samadhi going beyond the states of sleeping, dreaming and waking; the experience of the higher Self during meditation.

U

Udana	One of the five aspects of prana in the human body; the upward moving breath.
Udgatri	One of the four Vedic priests; see Adhvaryu.
Udgitha	Important, melodious verses in Samaveda.
Uma	Daughter of the god of the Himalaya and consort of Shiva.
Upangas	Also called Darshanas; six systems of Indian philosophy; scientific treatises of the objective and subjective creation.

Upanishads	Collection of philosophical texts containing great wisdom and considered to be part of the shruti, the divine revelations.
Upavedas	(Lit. subordinate Vedas) practical applications of the knowledge of the Vedas.

V

Vach	Speech.
Vaidya	Ayurvedic physician.
Vaikuntha	The spiritual world, eternal and full of bliss. A transcendental world where Lord Krishna eternally resides with His devotees.
Vaishya	Somebody belonging to the caste of farmers and undertakers.
Vaisheshika	Second of the six Upangas; explanation of the theory that everything in creation consists of atoms.
Vaishnava	Devotee of Lord Krishna.
Vamanadeva	Avatara who came as a dwarf to the earth.
Varna (system)	Original name for the present caste system. The four varnas are: Brahmins, Kshatriyas, Vaishyas and Shudras.
Vastu	Popular name for Sthapatyaveda, the teaching of architecture and urban planning in harmony with the cosmos.
Varuna	Vedic god of the night and exhalation.
Vata	One of the three doshas; stands for movement.
Vayu	Vedic god of the wind and prana (life principle); one of the five basic elements.
Veda	(Lit. knowledge, wisdom) The divinely revealed

	wisdom of the Samhita (wholeness) of knower, known and process of knowing.
Vedangas	Six parts that in a scientific way explain the meaning and value of the Vedic hymns.
Vedanta	(Lit. end of the Veda) The last part of the Vedas, dealing with the Absolute and that builds on the philosophy of the Upanishads.
Vedas	The four divinely revealed scriptures Rig-, Sama-, Yajur- and Atharvaveda.
Vedic (demi)gods	Impulses of creative intelligence in the universe that are manifestations of the One Supreme God.
Vedic metres	The Vedic hymns are recited in certain rhythms or metres, of which the most well-known are: Gayatri (24 syllables), Trishtubh (44 syllables) and Jagati (48 syllables).
Vedoham	I am the Veda; one of the great aphorisms.
Vyana	One of the five aspects of prana in the human body; the diffused breath.
Vyasadeva	Avatara of Lord Vishnu who compiled the Vedas, composed the Shrimad Bhagavatam and is the author of many puranas; also known as Vedavyasa.
Vidya	Knowledge, wisdom.
Vishnu	Vedic god, part of the trinity Brahma, Vishnu and Shiva; the principle of maintenance in the universe.
Vishvadevas	The gods of the world.
Vyakarana	One of the six Vedangas; explains the grammar of the Vedas.

(Veda) Vyasa	See Vyasa.

Y

Yagya (yajna)	Vedic ritual in which the gods are invoked to ask for their blessings; sacrifice, life supporting action.
Yajnavalkya	Famous Vedic teacher (Brihadaranyaka Upanishad).
Yajurveda	One of the four Vedas; represents the Devata-aspect in the Samhita of the Veda; Veda in which sacrifices have a central place.
Yamaraja (Yama)	God of death.
Yamas	Great moral duties; part of Ashtanga Yoga.
Yoga	(Lit. union) the state of union with the Self or finally with God; the practice leading to that state.
Yoga-sutras	Upanga; yoga teaching composed by Patanjali.
Yogi (m) / yogini (f)	(Lit. one who practices yoga) one who has realised the state of union (yoga).
Yugas	Eras of humanity, i.e. Sat-, Treta-, Dvapara- and Kaliyuga.

LITERATURE

His Divine Grace A.C. BHAKTIVEDANTA SWAMI PRABHUPADA, Bhagavad Gita As It Is; The Bhaktivedanta Book Trust International, 2003.

His Divine Grace A.C. BHAKTIVEDANTA SWAMI PRABHUPADA, Srimad Bhagavatam, Cantos I-IV; The Bhaktivedanta Book Trust International.

His Divine Grace A.C. BHAKTIVEDANTA SWAMI PRABHUPADA, In Essence -Evolve Your Vision – Change Your World; The Bhaktivedanta Book Trust, 2019.

His Holiness MAHARISHI MAHESH YOGI, Bhagavad Gita, Chapters I-VI with His comments; MIU Press, The Hague, 1979.

His Holiness MAHARISHI MAHESH YOGI, Maharishi about marriage; December 8, 1969, Rishikesh, India.

SRI VASUDEVA, Messages from the 40 Days Observances; Blue Star Trinidad & Tobago, 2003 - 2006.

SRI VASUDEVA, Seek God Within; Blue Star Trinidad & Tobago, 1998.

A HINDU MONK, What every Hindu ought to know; Rashtrotthana Mudranalaya, Bangalore, 1968.

ANANDSHANKAR PANDAY, Hindu Thought and World Harmony; Ramayana Magazine, 2002.

COOS VISSER, Hinduism, Back to the Source; Saraswati Art Publishers, Amsterdam, fourth edition 2016.

ED VERHOEFF & COOS VISSER, Maharishi Ayurveda, To be and to remain healthy; Mirananda, The Hague, 1989.

ED VERHOEFF & COOS VISSER, Do Less, Accomplish More; Mirananda, The Hague, 1994.

ED VERHOEFF & COOS VISSER, The Self as the Leader; Mirananda, The Hague, 1998.

GERARD T. SATVIC, Know Yourself, the Gate to mental and physical health, Shri Sathya Sai Baba's in His own words; Sai Towers, India, 1995.

GURUMAYI CHIDVILASANANDA, Ashes at My Guru's Feet; Syda Foundation, USA, 1990.

Pt. HARISH JOHARI, Tools for Tantra; Destiny Books Vermont, 1986.

Dr. B.R. KISHORE, Rig Veda/Sama Veda/Yajur Veda/Atharva Veda; Diamond Pocket Books Ltd., New Delhi, 2001.

JOGCHUM DIJKSTRA & SALVATORE CANTORE, Seen Through Yoga; De Toorts, Haarlem, 2006.

NARADA KUSH, Vedic Astrology, Analysis and Practical Application; SA Publishers, Netherlands, 3rd edition, 2018.

NARADA KUSH, Hindu Marriage; SA Publishers, Amsterdam, Netherlands, 2011.

NARADA KUSH, The Epic Ramayana, and her deeper meaning for our time; SA Publishers, Amsterdam, Netherlands, 2nd edition 2012.

NARADA KUSH, Vedic Life/Lifestyle, Prevention and Selfhealing; Gopher BV, Harderwijk, Netherlands, 2nd edition 2018.

RAJA RAM MOHAN ROY, PhD, Vedic Physics/Scientific Origin of Hinduism; Golden Egg Publishing, Toronto, 2003.

RAM K. PIPARAIYA, Ten Upanishads of Four Vedas; Bharatiya Vidya Bhavan & Indus Vista Publications, Mumbai, 2003.

RANKORATH KARUNAKARAN, The Riddle of Ganesha; Book Quest, Mumbai, 1992.

SIR JOHN WOODROFFE, The Serpent Power; Ganesh & Company, Madras-17, 1995.

SUBODH KAPOOR, Vedas for Beginners; Indigo Book, Cosmo Publications, New Delhi, 2003.

SWAMI MUKTANANDA PARAMAHAMSA, I Have Become Alive; UBS Publishers Distributors Ltd / Syda Foundation, USA, 1985.

SWAMI MUKTANANDA PARAMAHAMSA, Secret of the Siddhas; Syda Foundation, USA, 1980.

TONY NADER MD, PhD, Human Physiology / Expression of Veda and the Vedic Literature; Maharishi Vedic University, Vlodrop, Netherlands,1995.

YOGI RAMACHARAKA, Advanced Course in Yogi Philosophy and Oriental Occultism; L.N. Fowler & Co. Ltd., London, 1905.

www.ingramcontent.com/pod-product-compliance
Lightning Source LLC
Chambersburg PA
CBHW061418150726
47987CB00001B/15